D0934329

# Industrial and trade policy reform
# in developing countries

CONTEMPORARY ISSUES IN DEVELOPMENT STUDIES

*general editors* F. I. Nixson and C. H. Kirkpatrick

# Industrial and trade policy reform in developing countries

edited by
*R. Adhikari, C. Kirkpatrick* and *J. Weiss*

Manchester University Press
Manchester and New York

*Distributed exclusively in the USA and Canada by St. Martin's Press*

Copyright © Manchester University Press 1992

Whilst copyright in the volume as a whole is vested in
Manchester University Press, copyright in individual chapters
belongs to their respective authors, and no chapter may be
reproduced wholly or in part without the express permission in
writing of both author and publisher.

*Published by* Manchester University Press
Oxford Road, Manchester M13 9PL, UK
*and* Room 400, 175 Fifth Avenue,
New York, NY 10010, USA

*Distributed exclusively in the USA and Canada*
*by* St. Martin's Press, Inc.,
175 Fifth Avenue, New York, NY 10010, USA

*British Library Cataloguing-in-Publication Data*

A catalogue record for this book is available from the British
Library

*Library of Congress Cataloging-in-Publication Data*
Industrial and trade policy reform in developing countries / edited by
   R. Adhikari, C. Kirkpatrick, and J. Weiss.
      p. cm. — (Contemporary issues in development studies)
      ISBN 0-7190-3553-8
      1. Industry and state—Developing countries—Case studies.
   2. Developing countries—Commercial policy—Case studies.
   I. Adhikari, Ranesh, 1951— , II. Kirkpatrick, C. III. Weiss
John. IV. Series.
   HD3616.D45153 1992
   338.9′009172′4—dc20                                   91-44102

ISBN 0 7190 3553 8 *hardback*

Typesetting by STM Typesetting Ltd, Amesbury, Wilts.
Printed in Great Britain by Redwood Press Ltd, Melksham

# Contents

INTRODUCTION

I: INTERNATIONAL PERSPECTIVES

# Tables

# Figures

# Preface

The 1980s was a decade in which many developing countries adopted major programmes of economic policy reform, often as part of a structural adjustment effort. This volume examines the performance outcomes that have followed from the implementation of policy changes by countries in the developing world, focusing particularly on the trade and industry sectors.

Trade policy is generally recognised as having a major influence on the pattern and pace of industrial development, and has been a key component of the economic adjustment programmes adopted by many Third World countries in recent years. Both trade and industrial policy reform have featured prominently in the conditionality attached to World Bank lending for structural adjustment.

The effects of policy reform continue to be disputed, however, on both theoretical and empirical grounds. Critics argue that there are no firm grounds for believing that trade liberalisation will increase the growth rate of the industrial sector; to the contrary, they argue that protection of infant industries can raise economic growth. Again, it is suggested that in designing reform programmes the advocates of trade liberalisation have typically given insufficient attention to the unique economic characteristics of the reforming economy. Finally, the empirical evidence that has accumulated over the past ten years of policy reform has been interpreted in very different ways. For some, it confirms the benefits of policy reform, for other observers the gains are less obvious.

These issues are examined in this volume. The chapters in Part One offer a cross-country, overview perspective on the effects of trade and industrial policy reform. The remaining sections provide detailed country studies: Part Two focuses on sub-Saharan Africa, and Part Three considers the policy reform experience in Asia.

The chapters in this volume were originally presented and discussed at a conference on 'the impact of policy reform on trade and industrial performance in developing countries', held at the Development and Project Planning Centre, University of Bradford, and organised by the Development Studies Association's Industry and Trade Study Group. Financial support for this conference was received from the

UK Overseas Development Administration (ODA), The British Council, The Nuffield Foundation, the University of Bradford Research Fund, the Development and Project Planning Centre, and the Development Studies Association.

The volume is in turn part of a larger research programme on Trade Liberalisation and Industrial Performance in Developing Countries. This research has been supported by a grant (to C Kirkpatrick, P Cook and J Weiss) from the UK Overseas Development Administration's Fund for Economic and Social Research (ESCOR). We are grateful to the ODA for making this work possible.

The manuscript has been prepared at the Development and Project Planning Centre, and has been typed by Pearl Golden who, with her usual efficiency and tolerance, wrestled with the vagaries of multiple authors and three editors. We thank her for her tireless efforts. We would also like to thank Maureen Yaffey, Jean Hill and Sue Mackrill, all of whom helped at different stages in the production process.

# Contributors

*Dr Ramesh Adhikari* is Senior Economist with Maxwell Stamp plc, Economics and Business Consultants, London

*Gerard Chambas* is Chargé de Recherche CNRS, CERDI, at the Université d'Auvergne, France

*Esther Chau* is Lecturer in Economics at Hong Kong Baptist College

*Roland Clarke* is Lecturer in the Development and Project Planning Centre, University of Bradford

*Paul Cook* is Senior Lecturer in Economics in the Institute for Development Policy and Management, University of Manchester

*Dr Basil Edward Cracknell* is an Evaluation Consultant in Kingston-near-Lewes, Sussex

*Dr Chris Edwards* is Senior Lecturer at the University of East Anglia, Norwich

*Jean-Marc Fontaine* is Director of the Centre de Recherche Economique, Institut d'Etude du Développement Economique et Social, Université Panthéon-Sorbonne, Paris

*Anne-Marie Geourjon* is Maître de Conférences, CERDI, at the Université d'Auvergne, France

*Professor Helen Hughes* is Executive Director of the National Centre for Development Studies, Australian National University

*Dr J. Keith Johnson* is Senior Development Policy Officer in the Development Policy Office of the Asian Development Bank, Manila, Philippines

*Colin Kirkpatrick* is Professor of Development Economics at the Development and Project Planning Centre, University of Bradford

*Dr H. M. Leung* is Senior Lecturer in Business Policy at the National University of Singapore

*Martin Minogue* is Director of the International Development Centre, University of Manchester

*John Nash* is Senior Economist in the Trade Policy Division of the World Bank

*Dr Frederick Nixson* is Reader in Economics at the University of Manchester

*Dr S. M. Shafaeddin* is with UNCTAD in Geneva

*Professor H. W. Singer* is at the Institute of Development Studies, University of Sussex

*Dr Colin Stoneman* is at the Centre for Southern African Studies, York University

*Dr S. H. Tang* is Principal Lecturer in Economics at Hong Kong Baptist College

*Dr John T. Thoburn* is Senior Lecturer in Economics at the University of East Anglia, Norwich

*Vinod Thomas* is Chief Economist for the World Bank

*David Wall* is Reader in Economics at the University of Sussex

*Dr John Weiss* is Senior Lecturer in the Development and Project Planning Centre, University of Bradford

# Introduction

# Background and overview

Industrial policy reform has been high on the policy agenda of many developing countries for at least the last decade. Macro imbalances and micro inefficiencies have combined to force reconsideration of policy towards industry. Much of the policy advice offered to governments, or imposed upon them as part of structural adjustment loan packages, has been informed by the 'market paradigm'. Emerging from the neo-classical tradition of development economics (Little 1982), this paradigm sees market liberalisation and moves towards freer trade as critical to improvement in the efficiency of industry. Consequently industrial reform programmes have concentrated on measures that include

- removal of price and other controls on enterprises;
- removal of quantitative barriers to trade and the rationalisation and reduction of taxes on imports;
- exchange rate devaluation;
- privatisation of state-owned enterprises;
- encouragement of new industrial private foreign investment.

Trade reform is central to the process of industrial reform, since industry generally produces tradable goods and exposure to foreign competition is viewed as essential to stimulate efficiency gains. The literature on the relative merits of inward-looking import-substituting policy versus outward-looking export-promotion provides much of the empirical evidence to support the case for moves to a more liberalised trading position. For example, the summary volume from the OECD country-studies on industrial performance in the 1960s (Little, Scitovsky and Scott 1970) gave a lucid and apparently devastating critique of import substitution and interventionist policies that ignored market signals. However, around the time that study was being prepared events were unfolding in some of the East Asian economies which give grounds for questioning the wisdom of blanket generalisations on the merits of alternative strategies.

The South Korean case, in particular, demonstrates that the distinction between import substitution and export promotion is over-simplified, and that selective interventions by a government bureaucracy using a combination of direct and price instruments almost certainly produced an industrial structure more geared to the long-run needs of economic development than would the market functioning in an unrestrained fashion (Weiss 1988).

The ambiguity in interpreting the evidence on past industrialisation in developing countries allows considerable scope for disagreement on the appropriate way forward in the 1990s. Does South Korean success with policies that appear to have combined features of import substitution and export promotion, and price and non-price interventions, simply demonstrate an exception to the general rule, or is it clear evidence of what potentially can be achieved elsewhere with an active interventionist industrial policy?

Currently, probably few authors writing on issues of industrial policy for developing countries would argue strongly in favour of 'old style' import substitution. There is ample evidence that in many countries this encouraged high-cost, inefficient activities that registered little productivity gains over time, partly due to their sheltered position in the domestic market. Further, in social terms such policies were often associated with regressive shifts in the distribution of income and a disappointing performance in terms of employment generation (Cody, Kitchen and Weiss 1990).

The main alternative positions on industrial policy are related directly to the confidence authors place in market-based solutions. The current orthodox position (as exemplified forcefully by Hughes in this volume) argues that market liberalisation, including major trade reform, will create stronger industrial sectors in developing countries. Short-run transitional problems are noted, as resources shift in response to new market signals, but the confident expectation is that successful new industries will emerge that can compete internationally in the medium to longer-term.

Critics of the current orthodoxy are less confident, however, of this outcome. They stress the potentially serious effects in the short run if weak local industry is exposed to foreign competition. Further, they continue to believe in the long-run arguments that have been used conventionally to qualify the case for free trade, particularly relating to learning and dynamic economies of scale, achieved in a protected but growing domestic market (Weiss 1984). In addition, the political economy dimension is introduced. Policies justified in terms of 'market rationality' can have important implications in terms of changes in ownership and class relations. After a major market reform programme economies can emerge with quite different ownership structures, with a much reduced public sector and a greater role for foreign investors. The changes in Chile in the 1970s, and Mexico in the 1980s illustrate this clearly. Such changes have an economic as well as a social dimension, since they impinge directly on the functioning of the economy in a way which critics argue will be negative, rather than positive.

Differences in perception on the consequences of introducing market-based reform packages, and in particular the shift towards trade liberalisation, can be represented diagramatically using the standard production possibility frontier in a 2-good model. In Figure 1.1 two goods, say rice and cloth, are produced under competitive conditions,

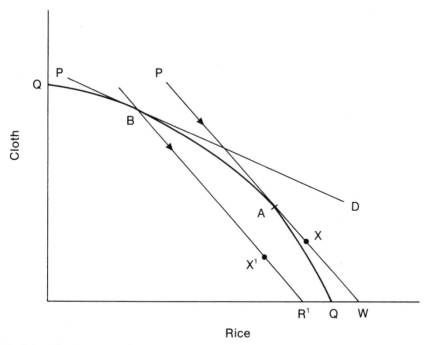

Fig 1.1 Allocative costs of protection

and resource and technological constraints allow maximum production on the frontier QQ. PW is the international price line that prevails under free trade, whilst PD is the domestic price line with some form of trade barrier. Under free trade A is the efficient production point on the frontier, whilst trade along PW allows a combination of goods X to be attained. Under protection B is the production point, and trade under these restricted conditions along PW will allow a lower combination of goods $X^1$ to be obtained. The loss in terms of rice is given by $R^1W$ on the horizontal axis. $R^1W$ is an allocative efficiency loss in that production under protection is still on the production frontier, but at the sub-optimal point.

However, frequently the more significant cost of protection is seen as the loss of potential output due either to rent-seeking behaviour (lobbying, bribery etc.) to receive preferential treatment from a control system, or to the negative incentive effectives of protection, which induce X-inefficiency and raise unit costs (Bhagwati 1989). Either effect can be illustrated as an inward shift in the production possibility frontier to $Q^1Q^1$ (Figure 1.2). Now production under protection is at point C and trading along PW allows the combination of goods $X^2$. The total loss of goods in terms of rice, as compared with the free trade position, is now $R^2W$ on the horizontal axis.

All this assumes that protection and controls create costs, not benefits. The counter-argument is that under free trade one will operate on a different but lower production possibility curve than under protection. This may be because with an

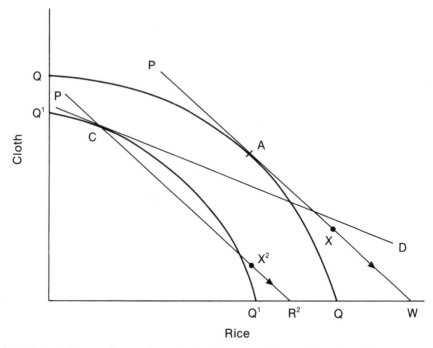

Fig 1.2   Total costs of protection: allowing for rent-seeking and incentive effects

open trading policy, but internal resource immobility, liberalisation policies lead to the closure of some industries, but the failure of resources to shift successfully into others. It is liberalisation, therefore, that causes an inward shift in the production possibility frontier. Alternatively, if there are genuine dynamic benefits associated with protection they can create an outward shift in the frontier relative to the free trade position (Figure 1.3). Here specialisation under protection is illustrated with a new frontier $Q^2Q^2$, which as a result of protection is skewed towards greater cloth production in comparison with the original frontier QQ. In Figure 1.3 production under protection is at point E, and trading along PW allows a combination of goods $X^3$, which is above the original free trade combination of X. The gain in terms of rice is $R^3W$. However, in this view the exact production point reached on the frontier is less relevant than the fact that a higher frontier has been achieved. The merits of these alternative perceptions still remain to be demonstrated conclusively. The chapters in this volume, which examine the evidence on the effects of adopting trade and industrial policy reforms in developing countries during the past decade, are a contribution to this on-going debate.

The chapters in Part One offer differing international, cross-country perspectives on the experience of developing countries with industrial and trade policy. The contribution by Hughes seeks to explain the contrasting economic growth performance of the East Asian and Latin American countries during the 1980s, in terms of the strategies pursued. Adopting an orthodox, neo-classical stance, she argues that the

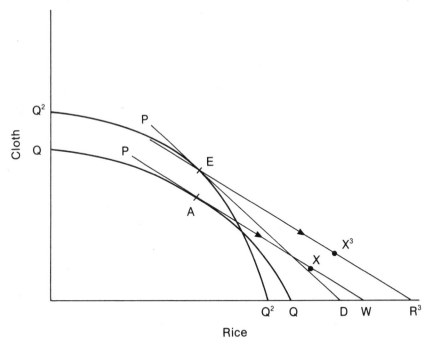

Fig 1.3   Gains from protection

failure of the Latin American economies to achieve reasonable growth rates can be ascribed to excessive government intervention in the economy, a neglect of macro-economic management, a lack of concern with micro efficiency issues, and a failure to exploit the opportunities of expanding manufactured exports. The Latin American economies' adherence to these growth-inhibiting policies is contrasted with the choices made in the Asian countries, where the adoption of outward and private-enterprise-oriented trade and industrial strategies enabled them to achieve rapid and equity-oriented growth.

The chapters by Thomas and Nash, and Clarke and Kirkpatrick are both concerned with the impact on economic performance of trade policy reforms. The aim of the Thomas and Nash study is to bring together statistical evidence from cross-country samples as well as case studies of individual countries, on the experience of trade policy reforms carried out under World Bank structural adjustment conditionality. The chapter considers four major issues. First, it reviews the literature relating to the expected gains from trade reform. It then considers the experience of developing countries that have undertaken reforms to determine how much reform actually took place and how effective it was in promoting the desired outcomes. The third and fourth issues discussed relate to the sequencing of separate trade policy changes, and the links between trade liberalisation and macro-economic stabilisation. The authors find that progress in reform has been slower than anticipated in many countries, but where significant reforms have been implemented the results in the external sector, and economy-wide, have been positive, although often falling short of expectations. The chapter by Clarke and Kirkpatrick also deals with the effects of trade policy reform programmes on economic performance. Following a review of earlier empirical investigations, the authors report on the results obtained from applying a generalised estimator procedure to a group of eighty low and middle income developing countries, many of which adopted trade adjustment programmes during the 1980s. Seven alternative performance variables are tested for the effect of trade liberalisation programmes, using dummy variables. In contrast to the results reported by Thomas and Nash, the Clarke and Kirkpatrick study finds no statistically significant evidence of trade reform programmes having a positive impact on economic performance.

The pursuit of trade policy reform during the 1980s was conducted in the context of the international debt crisis. The chapter by Singer stresses the additional burden of adjustment that this imposes on many developing countries. The pursuit of additional export earnings 'at any price' can lead to 'inefficient' export expansion and ultimately can be self-defeating if many debtor countries are required simultaneously to implement virtually identical trade adjustment measures involving devaluation and tariff liberalisation.

The effectiveness of devaluation as an instrument of trade reform is examined in the chapter by Shafaeddin. The author estimates empirically the extent to which nominal devaluation has been eroded by induced domestic price increases. It is found that devaluation has had a significant inflationary impact in most developing countries during the 1980-87 period, thereby limiting the degree of real exchange rate realignment achieved.

In the final chapter in Part One, Cracknell concentrates on the effect of industrial policy reform on industry project performance in developing countries. By the end of the 1970s it was evident that industrial projects in many smaller developing countries were performing poorly. The response of the aid agencies was to redirect their assistance towards small and medium-sized enterprises, while at the same time promoting policy changes aimed at encouraging the development of the private sector. The main part of Cracknell's contribution is to summarise the lessons that have been learned from the results of adopting these new policies towards the industrial sector. Drawing on an extensive body of evaluation reports, the author concludes that where the new policies have been adopted and implemented, the achievements so far are encouraging. At the same time it is argued that both macro-policies and government policy towards the development of the private sector need to change in order to create the environment within which the industrial sector policy reforms can succeed.

For most sub-Saharan countries, the 1980s was the 'lost decade' of development, with negative growth of real per capita GDP, falling investment levels, and declining terms of trade. Against this background of deteriorating economic conditions, many African economies embarked on programmes of structural adjustment, involving significant changes in their industrial and trade policies. The chapters in Part Two provide four detailed country case studies of the impact of policy reforms introduced during the past decade.

In Chapter 8, Stoneman examines the experience of Zimbabwe, which recorded one of the highest growth rates in Africa in the 1980s, achieved a significant increase in manufacturing output, and expanded the volume of manufactured exports. These achievements were made despite the retention of tight trade controls and high levels of manufacturing protection. At the same time certain other components of the standard structural adjustment package were part of Zimbabwean economic policy. These included the maintenance of an appropriate real exchange rate, and the provision of an effective structure of supply incentives for agricultural producers. Stoneman suggests, therefore, that the standard policy reform package needs 'depackaging', to allow for the differing effectiveness and relevance of the separate components. In particular, it is argued that in the Zimbabwean context, the wholesale abandonment of trade controls and protection would damage seriously the prospects for further industrial growth and development.

The chapter by Weiss discusses the key industrial policy reforms adopted in the war-torn economy of Mozambique since the mid-1980s, and comments on the limited policy options open to the government. Economic policy reform followed Mozambique's membership of the IMF and World Bank in 1984, with a package of reforms similar to the structural adjustment programmes elsewhere in the region. For industry, the key reform measures were greater enterprise autonomy, the encouragement of private investment through fiscal incentives and exports through export earnings retention, and exchange rate devaluation. The policy changes were accompanied by a major increase in aid financing much of it directed at plant rehabilitation. While accepting the need for some market reform and liberalisation, Weiss maintains that given the general backwardness of skills and infrastructure, continued protection is necessary for industrial recovery. It is argued that manufactured exports are unlikely to become a major element in Mozambique's industrialisation, and efforts should be concentrated therefore on developing relatively efficient products that serve the local low income market. Wholesale trade liberalisation leading to increased import competition would undermine the possibilities of industrial sector recovery and growth.

The contribution of Fontaine analyses the impact on the manufacturing sector in Ghana of removing anti-export bias through devaluation and foreign trade liberalisation policies. Drawing on Ghana's experience under structural adjustment during the 1980s, it is argued that the adoption of these measures has modified incentives in such a way as to discourage private investment. The conclusion drawn is that even if one accepts the view that restoration of efficiency in the manufacturing sector implies the reduction of protection through devaluation and trade liberalisation, the private sector cannot be relied upon to invest in manufacturing while these rationalisation policies are being pursued, so that the expected efficiency gains will not materialise unless the state enters as a direct investor, or by engaging in an active industrial policy.

The final contribution on sub-Saharan Africa examines the impact of industrial policy reform in Senegal. The new industrial policy was introduced in 1986 with the support of the World Bank, and provided for a set of reform measures aimed at liberalising trade and restructuring the industrial sector. The measures proposed increased rationalisation of the tariff structure and elimination of quantitative restrictions, removal of price controls, and changes in labour market regulations. In their assessment of the effects of the reform programme, Chambas and Geourjon draw attention to the problems of phasing and implementation where tariff reform has proceeded more rapidly than the other measures. This has distorted the adjustment process in the industrial sector, and has induced the government to adopt some measures to reverse the initial tariff reductions.

Part Three contains seven country case studies for the Asia region. The diversity in the economies of this region is reflected in the country chapters: two relate to South-East Asia (Malaysia and the Philippines), one deals with South Asia (Sri Lanka), two deal with 'socialist' transitional economies (Myanmar and Vietnam) and the final two are based on the People's Republic of China. All are concerned with the impact of trade and industrial policy reform undertaken during the 1980s.

In Chapter 12, Edwards assesses the new industry policy in Malaysia, which emphasises the development of capital goods and heavy industrial projects by public sector investment. Launched in the early 1980s, the heavy industrialisation programme failed to perform according to expectations and contributed to the economic crisis of the mid-1980s. Edwards argues that the heavy industrialisation strategy attempted to reproduce the South Korean model, but failed to appreciate the different social-political environment in Malaysia, which limited the possibility of replicating the Korean experience. In particular, the bureaucratic weaknesses, combined with a strong rentier class based in the dominant Malay political group, prevented the emergence of an efficient industrial strategy administered on South Korean lines.

The contribution by Johnson assesses the forces that have impeded the progress and impact of exchange rate, trade and industrial policy reforms in the Philippines. The author argues that to understand the constraints on the implementation of policy reform, it is necessary to recognise the policy legacy that was inherited by the Aquino government in the mid-1980s. Drawing on a historical review of the earlier period of inward-looking policies, Johnson shows how the recent attempts at reform in the areas of exchange rate policy, industrial policy and trade liberalisation have been compromised by short-term responses to macro economic exigencies, the persistence of rent-seeking by special interest groups, and a lack of harmony in the initiation, scaling and phasing of the various programme elements.

The chapter by Adhikari examines the process of trade policy reform in Sri Lanka, and in particular the growth of manufactured exports from the export-processing zone. The evidence suggests that the non-traditional export sector, especially textiles and garments, has emerged as an important source of foreign exchange earnings, but the linkages with the domestic economy and the transfer of technology have been limited. Trade liberalisation was partial, and the bias against traditional exports was not removed. There was also some reversal of the initial liberalisation measures in later years. The author concludes, therefore, that a less than complete government commitment to the reforms, administrative and institutional constraints in implementing policy changes, and vested interests in both government and the private sector, combined to form a major impediment to the full implementation of trade policy liberalisation in Sri Lanka.

The attraction of foreign investment was a key element in the open policy adopted by China under the post-1978 reforms. The chapters by Wall and by Thoburn,

Leung, Chan and Tang both deal with the impact of the special economic zones (SEZs). Wall stresses how the SEZs developed on a more or less *ad hoc* basis, with an absence of any clearly identified objectives or well defined rules and regulations. The author assesses the achievements of the zones, in the areas of management techniques, employment growth, and growth pole effects. The limitations of the SEZs in each of these areas are also discussed in some detail. Wall concludes that the economic achievements are much less impressive that the available gross data suggest, and that such net output growth as there has been was bought with a net outflow of foreign exchange. The major limitation on the success of the zones has been their failure to develop the market style economy, with a continued reliance on the favoured connections, or *guanxi* system, for the distribution and allocation of resources. The chapter by Thoburn, Leung, Chan and Tang provides a detailed study of the economic impact of investment by Hong Kong companies in Guangdong Province, adjacent to Hong Kong. Drawing on material from interviews, it is argued that the inflow of foreign investment, in response to the incentives offered, has brought substantial benefits to the region in the areas of market access, technology transfer, and employment.

The chapter by Cook and Minogue examines the use of conditionality in the area of political change, as a precondition to economic reform, using the case study of Myanmar where the international agencies suspended their operations pending political reform and cessation of human rights abuses. The authors maintain that to make economic reform a hostage to political reform is a simplification of the development policy options available to the decision makers in Myanmar. A 'survival strategy' appears to be sustainable, at least in the medium term, based on the acquisition of technology through joint venture arrangements, and exploitation of natural resources. In addition, the authors suggest that it is highly questionable that all external agencies will put political change before economic self- interest, except in the short term.

The final chapter by Nixson argues that the contemporary development of, and the problems faced by, Vietnam, can only be fully understood within the appropriate historical context, in particular the lengthy period of armed conflict which preceded reunification in 1975, and the post-1978 period of international isolation. The Vietnamese adopted the Soviet model of rapid industrialisation and the creation of a heavy industry sector. Although initially generating high rates of growth of industrial output, problems emerged very quickly – lack of access to modern technology, excess capacity, foreign exchange shortages. The Second Five Year Plan (1976-80) was not fulfilled – the years 1979-80 were years of crises (especially with respect to food supply), and since the early 1980s there have been a number of increasingly radical reform and liberalisation measures. By 1989 a significant transformation of the economy had occurred, although Vietnam is not yet a market economy. With respect to the industrial sector, growth of output has been fairly rapid, with a shift towards the consumer goods sector. Unemployment, however, has become a major problem, in part because of liberalisation. The chapter concludes with a discussion of the problems that still face the economy in the post-liberalisation period.

There is little dissent among the contributors to this volume from the view that the economic policy framework which existed in many developing countries at the beginning of the 1980s was in need of fundamental reform. The nature of trade and industrial policies typically represented a major constraint on economic recovery and sustained economic growth. The evidence presented in the separate chapters shows clearly, however, that the experience of trade and industrial policy reform is unique to each country, and that both the formulation of the reform measures, and the impact which they have on economic performance, are conditioned by the economic and political circumstances of the reforming economy.

We began this introductory chapter by reviewing the alternative perceptions on the consequences of introducing marked-based economic reform packages in developing countries. By moving beyond ideological statements of certainty regarding these alternative approaches to an assessment of the empirical consequences of reform programmes under particular circumstances, it is hoped that this volume will contribute to a increased understanding of the trade and industrial policy reform process in developing countries.

## References

Bhagwati, J. (1989), 'Is free trade passé after all?', *Weltwirtschaftliches Archiv*, Band 125, Heft 1.

Cody, J., Kitchen, R. and Weiss, J. (1990), *Policy Design and Price Reform in Developing Countries*, Wheatsheaf, Brighton.

Little, I. (1982), *Economic Development*, Basic Books, New York.

Little, I., Scitovsky T. and Scott, M. (1970), *Industry and Trade in Some Developing Countries*, Oxford University Press, Oxford.

Weiss, J. (1984), 'Manufacturing as an engine of growth: revisited', *Industry and Development*, no. 13, pp. 39-62.

Weiss, J. (1988), *Industry in Developing Countries*, Croom Helm, London.

# I: International perspectives

# Explaining the differences between the growth of developing countries in Asia and Latin America in the 1980s

### Introductory hypothesis

Asian and Latin American developing countries have performed differently since World War II. Several Asian countries have grown faster, more steadily and achieved greater social equality than Latin American countries throughout the period. The difference between the growth of the Asian and Latin American countries widened in the 1980s. While the Asian countries took advantage of the rapid recovery of the industrial countries from the recession of 1981-82, the Latin American countries stagnated, missing out on the long prosperity of the 1980s.

Table 2.1 *Average annual real growth of GDP, 1960-88 (% in 1980 $US)*

|  | 1960-70 | 1970-80 | 1980-88 | 1960-88 |
|---|---|---|---|---|
| Latin America | 4.1 | 4.6 | 1.6 | 3.1 |
| (Brazil) | (6.1) | (8.0) | (3.0) | (6.5) |
| South Asia | 3.3 | 3.8 | 5.6 | 4.2 |
| (India) | (2.8) | (3.6) | (5.7) | (4.0) |
| South-east and East Asia (excluding China) | 6.7 | 8.2 | 5.6 | 7.2 |
| China, People's Republic of[a] | 6.1 | 5.1 | 10.3 | 7.3 |

*Note*
[a]China's growth figures must be treated with extreme caution.
*Source*: International Economic Data Bank, Australian National University.

The economic performance of the four most rapidly developing economies (Hong Kong, the Republic of Korea, Singapore and Taiwan) and of Thailand has been particularly impressive in equity as well as growth terms. Indonesia and Malaysia have also developed strongly, utilizing their rich resource endowment better than most other countries with ' booming sectors'. India, Pakistan and Sri Lanka, though growing weakly by East and South-east Asian country standards, experienced stronger growth in the 1980s than in the 1970s. In per capita income growth the differences between East Asia and Latin America are even greater because East Asian population has been declining as a result of strong GDP growth and effective family planning policies. China's 'basis needs' standard of living for much of its population of one billion people stands out as a major achievement, although China's growth indicators must be treated with extreme caution because it lacks the statistical infrastructure necessary for even modestly accurate GDP and population data. Only the Philippines appears to be a geographically displaced 'Latin American' country.

The Latin American countries, despite having the highest per capita income and human and physical capital endowment among developing countries at the end of World War II, and despite favourable natural resource endowments, only doubled their per capita incomes between 1950 and 1980 and stagnated in the 1980s. The high performing East Asian countries, in marked contrast, doubled their per capita income in every decade since the 1950s. The per capita income of the Republic of Korea, in 1951 devastated by war and one of the poorest developing countries in the world, is now higher than that of Argentina, one of the highest income developing countries 40 years ago. In 1900, moreover, together with Australia, Argentina had the highest per capita income in the world (Maddison 1982).

Table 2.2   *Average annual real growth of per capita GDP, 1960–88 (% in 1980 $US)*

|  | 1960–70 | 1970–80 | 1980–99 | 1960–88 |
|---|---|---|---|---|
| Latin America and Caribbean | 2.4 | 2.5 | −2.5 | −5.5 |
| (Brazil) | (3.2) | (5.5) | (0.7) | (8.9) |
| South Asia | 1.9 | 1.4 | 3.3 | 1.8 |
| (India) | (1.6) | (1.0) | (3.3) | (1.7) |
| South-east and East Asia (excluding China) | 4.0 | 5.5 | 3.6 | 4.7 |
| China, People's Republic of[a] | 3.8 | 3.2 | 9.0 | 5.3 |

*Note*
[a] China's growth figures must be treated with extreme caution.
*Source:* International Economic Data Bank, Australian National University.

The voluminous development literature suggests that natural resource endowment, country size, geography, location and capital inflows (notably of aid) are not the principal causes of differentials in national growth rates. On the contrary, difficulties of appropriate policy formulation and implementation make resource-rich countries the most likely candidates for 'booming sector' crises. When countries are grouped by natural endowments (Chenery and Syrquin 1975 and Syrquin 1988), the rapidly growing outliers turn out to be countries with poor natural resource endowments.

Differences in economic performance also do not appear to have cultural origins. The work of Weber (1922) and Tawney (1926) and their recent followers of the Confucian school (Chen 1989) has demonstrated that various cultures contain the seeds both of growth and economic decline. Protestant, Roman Catholic, Greek Orthodox, Confucian, Buddhist, Hindu, Shiite and Suni Muslim cultures have seen rapid economic development and no development at all, depending on the economic policy environment that has encouraged the various traits within each culture to develop. Several East Asian countries have shown – at various times – that the Confucian ethic is as conducive to stagnation as to rapid development.

Degrees of democracy, autocracy and political cohesion vary within and between the South Asian, East Asian and Latin American regions. Focused and careful analyses (Haggard 1988 and Mackie 1988) have not been able to elicit general causal relationships between political systems and economic performance. Rapid economic growth has been an important factor in political stability in South-east and North-east Asian countries. The lack of growth has led to perhaps the greatest political upheavals of modern times in Eastern Europe as well as in many other countries. Some political regimes, however, have been able to survive despite very poor economic performances. The only constant that seems to emerge from past experience is that political stability is essential to growth. And political stability requires some degree of consensus and popular support for governments, even if they are not elected democratically.

The assertions that poverty in developing countries is increasing and that growth does not lead to poverty alleviation, have been highly damaging to development. The evidence that growth is essential to poverty alleviation and improved income distribution is clear (Fields 1989). The Kuznets hypothesis that as development proceeds, income distribution first deteriorates but then improves at higher levels of income, does not hold universally. The Kuznets pattern has occurred in many developing countries that have taken an 'import substitution at all costs' development path, but it can be avoided by outward-oriented strategies. Direct poverty alleviation measures have little effect if overall policies are not directed toward efficient growth; efficient growth demands high utilization of the factors of production, notably labour. Rapid employment growth is the most important factor in poverty alleviation. The efficient utilization of public goods, such as education is also an aspect of efficient growth. If such growth takes place, direct poverty alleviation measures are usually redundant and often wasteful. It is not surprising that the most rapidly growing East Asian countries have an excellent record of poverty alleviation, have income distribution patterns close to those of industrial countries and lead in physical indicators of health and education. But, in contrast to the 'doom and gloom' schools of economic development, the evidence indicates that even the low rates of growth most developing countries had, led to quite significant improvements in health and the expectation of life at birth. Jere Behrman and Anil Deolalikar concluded (1988:633) that the changes in health, nutrition and expectation of life indices

... in recent decades in the developing countries have been enormous, and in many cases the absolute gaps between the developing countries and developed countries have been reduced. ... Thus, while significant gaps remain in health and nutritional status across country groups defined by their level of development, by a number of indices such gaps have been reduced more rapidly in recent decades than has been the reduction in gaps, for example, in per capita income.

Drawing on the wider evidence of the debate about the causes of development, economic performance appears to be primarily determined by a country's domestic economic policy framework. Economic policy objectives and administrative 'rules of the game' are moulded by political systems. The economic climate, however, is affected to an important degree by the content and the vigour of the debates that usually begin in university classrooms and how these debates are reflected in the media. The political decisions taken about economic issues in the 'corridors of power' reflect a community's intellectual perceptions about the economics of development.

The discussion about development began with many common characteristics in Asia and Latin America. Gradually, detailed perceptions about economic growth and development have come to vary within and among countries until nearly half a century of development experience has led to fundamental differences of view about the process of development. Three principal models have emerged: the statist South Asia-China model; the outward- and private-enterprise oriented rapid growth North-east and South-east Asian model; and the *dependencia* Latin American model. Adherence to these three models appears to account to an appreciable degree for differences in performance among the three broad groupings of countries.

The three models of development overlap in various ways. There is something of *dependencia* thinking in all developing countries, and the statist and *dependencia* models encompass growth objectives. Export growth, efficiency in private and public enterprises and macro-economic prudence receive lip service in most countries. However, there are also major differences between the statist and *dependencia* models on the one hand and the growth model on the other. In South Asia and Latin America, economic debate is still strongly influenced by 'development economics,' which argues that the behavioural characteristics of developing countries are different from those of industrial countries and that industrial countries' economic relations are biased against developing countries and different from those of industrial countries' relations with each other. In the growth model producers and consumers in developing countries are thought to behave similarly to those in industrial countries, and the international economic environment is neutral. These fundamental differences of perception have influenced economic policy formulation and hence economic performance.

## The role of government direction and regulation

In the spectrum of attitudes represented by the theorists and practitioners of development models, the conviction that national government must play a key role in economic development is fairly pervasive. A government's role may be evident by default; non-intervention in the economy has major economic effects. Government is generally regarded as having a role to play in establishing a development culture in which policies promoting growth with equity can thrive. Human resource development is also widely regarded as an essential public responsibility, particularly at early stages of development. Macro-economic stability, long ignored by many developing countries, is now widely recognized as an essential component of growth. But further views on the role of government in development diverge widely.

At one extreme, growth model proponents consider that the principal directions within an economy can be set by macro- and micro-economic policies that act on the prices facing individuals, households and (private or public) enterprises. The need for administrative intervention is minimized and public employment is limited. Macro-economic and micro-economic policies that seek price stability and openness to international competition result in appropriate resource and factor allocation and utilization. In an open economy there is little danger of 'market failure' in tradeables. Where market failure is evident in tradeables, for example in persistent 'dumping', countervailing action can be taken or in a small economy, such as Hong Kong, dumping may be welcomed. The opening up of service industries to international competition reduces the share of 'non tradeables' in the economy. It is central to the growth model approach that increasing employment opportunities at rising productivity levels will ensure that growth will be accompanied by equity. The avoidance of unproductive public employment by limiting direct and indirect public intervention in the economy is an essential component of this model.

Openness is a key concept of the rapid growth model, but it entails uncertainty and risk. Experience of development suggests that government intervention more often adds uncertainty than reduces risk. The proper role of government is to maintain competitive market 'rules of the game' and provide information to reduce uncertainty so that economic units – producers and consumers – can take advantage of a competitive environment. The production of goods and services should be left to private enterprise because public enterprises cannot manage risk. Many private enterprises will succeed by taking risks in the face of uncertainty, but some will fail. Bankruptcy is thus an essential component of an open economic system. Producers also fail in closed systems, but the failed enterprises – public and private – are usually permitted to go on existing by budget subsidies at great cost to the economy. Fiscal policies start to collapse and monetary policies are distorted, undermining the stability that is essential to growth.

Market failure is highly correlated with the degree to which an economy is closed. As soon as a part of the economy is protected, it becomes necessary to regulate entry, prices, volumes of output and quality so that monopolistic and oligopolistic exploitation may be avoided. Attempts to stabilize export prices to avoid uncertainty for farmers and governments usually destabilize incomes and revenues. The market has been made to fail. Regulation has unanticipated 'by-product' effects (Corden 1974) and encourages rent seeking (Krueger 1974). Administrative costs grow. Administrators join private enterprise rent seekers. Over time, intervention grows until the policy and regulatory framework becomes pervasive. Rules change constantly and their administration becomes increasingly arbitrary and uncertain. The policy framework, far from achieving its objectives, places heavy taxes on economic activities. At worst, combined with macro-economic instability (marked by double or even treble digit inflation), the economy disintegrates into chaos.

*Dependencia-* and statist-oriented analysts argue that the high growth of the Republic of Korea and Taiwan was the result of government regulation and intervention (Hamilton 1986 and Wade 1988) while the proponents of the rapid growth, open economy model consider that if regulation had been even more limited, growth would have been faster and more equitably distributed with consequent improvements to the quality of life. Taiwan and the Republic of Korea had highly protectionist regimes at the end of the 1950s when they turned toward exploiting their comparative advantage through trade. In both countries, protectionist views were strongly entrenched among the manufacturers who benefited from quantitative import restrictions and tariffs. These entrepreneurs were able lobbyists for protection. They had the strong support of administrators whose employment, promotion and power rested on their control over production. The government's willingness to maintain protection was also greatly boosted by the prevalence of protectionist views in the universities and other intellectual forums. The minority of entrepreneurs who were interested in exports for reasons of profitability and those technocrats who saw export orientation as essential to growth, were not powerful enough politically to implement the 'first best' policy of removing protection by creating a policy framework that was neutral between production for the domestic market and exports. Such a regime would have meant greater shifts in production than those that occurred. Hundreds, if not thousands, of privileged public servants would have had to move to the private sector. Such employment changes were not acceptable. A more rapid growth of employment and greater public resources availability were sacrificed for the comfort of a privileged minority.

The technocrats favouring outward orientation recognized these problems, and even exaggerated them. They therefore introduced policies which would offset the high costs of protection. Exemptions from non tariff barriers, drawbacks and exemptions from tariffs on inputs into exports, and export processing zones, were the principal direct offsets to protection. They introduced private costs for the entrepreneurs and social costs for the economy, but they were essential if manufacturers were to export, and they had relatively small negative 'by product' effects. But entrepreneurs argued, and the regulators agreed, that such offsets were not sufficient to counter all the costs of protection. A considerable range of export incentives, that is subsidies, was introduced. Clearly, for rent seekers, risk avoidance, combined with subsidies for protection for domestic markets and for exports, may be preferable to higher profits in international markets. The social costs of such policies are, however, very high. The range of subsidies included privileged access to the domestic market (such as controls on entry into manufacturing, 'wastage' allowances, and cartel arrangements) credit subsidies and tax holidays. The positive effect of these measures was doubtful. Some, such as tax subsidies, were generally redundant (Hughes 1972). All of these measures had major distortionary effects, and thus high indirect costs to the economy. In the Republic of Korea, for example, subsidies to foreign credit undermined the domestic production of machinery, and the subsidies to domestic credit stimulated the establishment of large unwieldy conglomerates which threatened the stability of the economy as well as creating a serious bias against small and medium-sized firms. The government is now trying to assist the small and medium sized firms by removing the biases it created against them. In Taiwan export subsidies created many costs but were largely ineffective (Herderschee 1990). Sometimes the subsidies were so ineffectual that the main beneficiaries were the public servants who devised and implemented the subsidy policies.

The resources wasted by the failure to introduce a neutral policy regime directly denied the populations of even rapidly growing countries of public goods and services. If manufacturing had been less wasteful, there could have been a greater contribution to improving housing, urban and rural facilities.

## Public versus private ownership and management

Government intervention in the economy through public ownership of enterprises has economic characteristics that tend to reduce the utility of public enterprises in offsetting market failure. Public ownership is widely used to take direct responsibility for those components of social and physical infrastructure which are either 'natural monopolies' or where the external benefits cannot be captured by producers, particularly in early stages of development. Public investment in social and physical infrastructural facilities to produce 'public goods' is an important component of development.

The *dependencia* and statist models postulate that governments not only have to supply 'public goods', particularly at the early stages of development, but also have to intervene where private entrepreneurs are not available (or of the correct ethnic group). Government is thought to be able to improve the allocation and utilization of scarce resources where private entrepreneurs might otherwise 'waste' them by failing in business. By 'capturing the commanding heights of an economy' governments are thought to be able to avoid monopolistic practices by private firms. By participating directly in natural resource development, governments are thought to be able to capture all the resource rents instead of allowing foreign interests to do so. In most developing countries the public ownership of goods and services has thus not been confined to 'public goods' that have major externalities. With the exception of a few small economies, notably Hong Kong, where public ownership is confined to the production of such public goods as power, transportation and land development/housing that have large external economies, developing countries built up wide reaching public sectors between the 1950s and 1980s. In addition to public utilities, public sectors include mineral exploitation, some manufacturing and such services as banking. In Singapore, where the public sector has been reasonably well managed, direct intervention in wage setting, compulsory savings through the Provident Fund, planning of tourism and excessive public housing construction led to a totally unnecessary income fall in the mid-1980s. There are some examples of efficient public enterprises in developing countries, but in the main, public ownership is characterized by political intervention, nepotism, managerial inefficiency and high costs to the central budget.

Improving the efficiency of public enterprises has become a major policy issue. But 'privatization' is not a quick and easy option. Once an economy is distorted by public ownership it is very difficult to liberalize. The Republic of Korea and Taiwan are both examples.

In Taiwan private enterprise began to swamp public investment in manufacturing in the 1960s. As the pace of private investment accelerated in the 1970s and 1980s, the relative role of public enterprise in manufacturing shrank further. Public enterprises mainly continued to play an important role in 'natural monopoly' public utilities. In the Republic of Korea defence arguments bolstered a broader predilection for public ownership, ironically dating ideologically from the Japanese colonial era. The Republic of Korea thus retained some public investment in manufacturing in addition to that in public utilities when it was changing its policies in the 1960s. In the 1970s there was a fresh spurt of public investment in manufacturing, combining defence considerations with a desire to build up 'basic' metal and engineering industries. The investment in these industries was heavily subsidised. Only one of these enterprises, POSCO steel, has been commercially successful. The financial returns on capital and social returns have never been revealed even for this enterprise. The other plants have not been able to compete commercially: in addition to the initial investment costs they have drawn heavily on current capital subsidies. By the time they ceased to require subsidies, they were obsolete (cf. Auty 1990).

Achieving efficiency in 'public goods' natural monopolies such as railways is an intransigent problem even in advanced industrial countries. Public ownership and public management both tend to be inefficient, but so does private ownership and management in a monopolistic situation. Monopolies, whether public or private, tend to exploit consumers. Privately- and publicly-owned utilities can appear to be efficient by earning high profits and distributing dividends. But in a monopolistic situation such profits may be earned despite great inefficiency. In the monopolistic situations that exist in some areas of telecommunications or in power supply and similar industries, private and public ownership and management has to be subject to surveillance and regulation if it is not to be exploitative.

Investment by public utilities tends to be large scale. If ownership is public, it can embarrass the government through high public borrowing requirements. Utilities, however, do not have high borrowing requirements because they are publicly owned, but because they are capital intensive. The macro-economic impact on the economy is the same whether borrowing is by the private or public sector. The economic issues concern the efficiency with which investment funds are used, the returns that they earn and how capital as well as other resources are managed to produce high quality products at low cost.

The principal argument for privatisation is concerned more with management than ownership. Private management tends to be more efficient than public management because it is usually less hampered by limits on hiring and firing and by seniority rules. But private management also only tends to be efficient in the competitive sectors of the economy. There are many examples of poorly managed private firms in monopolistic situations.

The principal advantage of the private ownership and management of enterprises lies in the sanctions imposed by the threat of failure. For this reason alone it usually makes sense to privatize public enterprises that do not produce public goods. Existing enterprises, however, may be difficult to privatize because their asset base is exaggerated by past management failures and would have to be written down severely to make private investors interested in purchasing the enterprise. This usually proves very difficult politically. Privatizing public utilities in addition requires a review of the regulatory environment to ensure that the new private enterprise will not be able to exploit consumers.

Privatization is thus not a panacea, but a major policy issue, particularly for the South Asian countries. Statist policies have led to monumental public enterprise problems which are likely to take years to resolve. In China and Vietnam the appropriate form of ownership and organization for manufacturing, services and even for agriculture is still far from clear. In the rest of East Asia and in Latin America an enterprise-by-enterprise approach may prove to be the least difficult course of reform. Typically, the greater the distortion from a competitive and open environment, the greater the current operating costs are likely to be and the greater will be the costs of reform.

### Macro-economic policies

Macro-economic policies are the 'sleeper' of economic development. If domestic prices and the price of foreign exchange remain stable and if the exchange rate is in equilibrium, there is little concern with macro-economic issues. If inflation reigns so that real interest rates fluctuate and the national currency becomes overvalued, sustained economic growth becomes impossible. But prudent fiscal policies are only possible if there are no major subsidies such as those for import substitution.

Price stability was recognized by the East Asian countries to be an essential step to outward orientation, competitiveness and growth. In Taiwan and the Republic of Korea price stabilization and devaluation were regarded as key policies when these countries 'unshackled' their exports (Riedel 1988) respectively in the late 1950s and early 1960s. In South Asia price and exchange rate stabilization became important targets in the 1960s. Malaysia and Thailand complained in the late 1960s that the imprudent price policies of the industrial countries were leading to the export of inflation to developing countries that had opted for sound macro-economic policies. Indonesia was the last of the East Asian countries to stabilize its prices in 1965. Thereafter, when Asian countries experienced episodes of double digit inflation, sometimes up to 20 per cent, notably as petroleum prices rose rapidly in the 1970s, they brought prices under control quickly each time, often at considerable short-term cost, because they recognized that sustained growth was impossible with inflation. The industrial countries failed to deal with increasing inflation as an aftermath of petroleum price increases. They then had to adopt highly restrictive policies in 1981-82 to bring inflation down to modest levels. Several Asian countries preferred recession to continuing inflation. The 1981-82 recession had a marked impact on standards of living, but was thought worth the cost because price stability cleared the way for a prolonged period of growth from 1982 to date.

Price stability has important social welfare effects. It is essential to growth with equity. In Asia it is thus widely perceived that taxation through inflation is a sophisticated form of stealing from the poor.

The instruments of macro-economic policy vary among developing countries. Financial markets are less developed than in industrial countries and the use of monetary and financial policy instruments is more limited than in industrial countries.

Most developing countries, notably in South Asia and Latin America, have 'repressed' financial systems which reduce the usefulness of interest rate and other price signals. Inward oriented trade policies tend to result in chronic balance of payments difficulties, so that capital movements must be carefully controlled. Monetary and financial policies then become distorted and are likely to have little effect on price stabilization.

The other principal instrument of macro-economic policy – fiscal policy – thus has to carry the main burden of stability in developing countries, requiring strong political will and a considerable command of efficient procedures both in revenue raising and in the management of public expenditures. Fiscal policies lie at the heart of effective government intervention in many developing economies. Asian countries (even one as large as India) have been successful in prudent fiscal management so that in spite of repressed financial systems (in India, Pakistan, Sri Lanka, Indonesia and the Republic of Korea) they have managed, by and large, to maintain price stability while expanding their infrastructural sectors. In contrast to most Latin American countries, most Asian countries were able to maintain stable exchange rates and thus avoid the devaluation-followed-by-imported-inflation-and-further-devaluation  cycles  that undermined macro-economic stability in Latin American countries.

Small economies such as Hong Kong and Singapore were not able to use either monetary or fiscal policies effectively because of their openness. They accordingly controlled migration so that labour policy became a principal macro-economic instrument. Immigrants were welcomed in boom periods of high wage pressure and restricted in downturns.

### Micro-economic policies

The critical difference between the East Asian countries and the other regions lies in overall growth rates, particularly in the 1980s. However, there is also an important difference between the Latin American and South Asian countries. Whereas Latin American growth rates fell steeply in the 1980s, South Asian countries showed a small but steady increase in the 1970s over the 1960s, and a marked growth increase in the 1980s in comparison to the 1970s. Accelerated growth largely reflected the gradual improvement in agricultural growth rates following marked liberalization of agricultural policies. Agricultural growth was made possible by underlying macro-economic stability. South Asia, like East Asia, became largely self-sufficient in grains. In Latin America, by contrast, the stop-go swings of the 1970s continued the *dependencia* inspired policy pattern of the 1950s and 1960s. The ability to borrow freely in international capital markets exacerbated the amplitude of economic swings, leading to the very poor performance of the 1980s.

Ideological rigidities were not eased by the adoption of some of the economic aspects of the growth model in countries such as Argentina, Chile and Uruguay. While financial liberalization replaced repression in some countries, fiscal balance could not be achieved overnight in countries that had practised taxation through inflation for decades.

Although the major differences in economic performance among the three regions under consideration appear to lie in manufacturing, the importance of agriculture also stands out. The East Asian countries steadfastly enjoyed a higher rate of agriculture as well as manufacturing growth than either the South Asian or Latin American countries. The principal explanation lies in the stimulus to agriculture in East Asia from the 1950s, culminating in the application of the new technology of the 'green revolution' by 'getting the prices right' and making appropriate infrastructure available. The lower levels of protection for manufacturing throughout the period not only encouraged a more efficient and less inward-oriented structure of manufacturing, but also permitted a more rapid rate of agricultural growth. Useful service sector data are unfortunately not available, but it seems that the North-east and South-east Asian countries also had a relatively rapid, outwarfi-oriented and efficient growth of services, notably in such areas as tourism, banking and in internal as well as external trade.

By the mid-1980s the actual policies facing farmers, manufacturers and other producers and consumers in the three regions had drawn together. While Hong Kong and Singapore remained the two principal liberal economies, Taiwan and the Republic of Korea and Chile were approaching 'openness'. Thailand and Malaysia had always been fairly open, growth oriented economies with relatively low levels of protection and hence of bias against agriculture. A contrasting structure of production between East Asia and the other regions acquired differing characteristics as a result of some 30 years of different government signals. Levels of effective assistance were lowest and had the least variance in open economies such as Singapore and Hong Kong. Taiwan and the Republic of Korea are moving in the same direction. The effect over the years was to stimulate entrepreneurs to be efficient and outward-looking.

In the South-east and North-east Asian countries the business culture has developed strongly outward-oriented targets for the individual firm, for industries and for the economy as a whole. In South Asian and most Latin American countries, (with the exception of Chile), in contrast, export orientation remains the exception. The major rewards are still for import substitution. The regulatory frameworks appear to be similar, whether in the form of protection for import substitution or export incentives, but the effectiveness of regulations in openness terms is different: the ratio of exports to GDP is far higher in most East Asian countries than in other developing countries. Real rate of export growth is similarly higher in East Asia. When China changed its economic outlook in the late 1970s, high export growth typically became one of the first objectives.

The combination of prudent macro-economic policies with growth oriented micro-economic policies has been reflected in relatively high savings and investment ratios in East Asian countries. All three country groupings raised investment in the 1970s with East Asian countries registering the largest increases.

Investment in South Asia stabilized in the 1980s. Once the major changes in agricultural policy were completed, there was little incentive to increase investment in the stagnating manufacturing and service sectors and public resources were not available for increased infrastructural investment. In Latin America slow growth and instability led to a decline of the ratio of investment to GDP. In the East Asian

Table 2.3   *Real average annual growth of value added, by sector (% in 1980 $US)*

|  | 1960–70 | 1970–80 | 1980–88 | 1960–88 |
|---|---|---|---|---|
| *Agriculture* | | | | |
| Latin America | — | 3.4 | 2.5 | — |
| (Brazil) | — | (4.2) | (3.5) | — |
| South Asia[a] | 2.6 | 1.8 | 2.5 | 2.5 |
| (India) | (2.1) | (1.8) | (2.3) | (2.4) |
| South-east and East Asia (excluding China) | 4.4 | 4.0 | 3.1 | 4.3 |
| China, People's Republic of | 9.1 | 2.6 | 6.8 | 5.4 |
| *Industry* | | | | |
| Latin America | — | 6.0 | 1.1 | — |
| (Brazil) | — | (9.4) | (2.6) | — |
| South Asia[a] | 5.6 | 4.8 | 7.4 | 5.1 |
| (India) | (5.1) | (4.5) | (7.6) | (4.9) |
| South-east and East Asia (excluding China) | 9.6 | 10.6 | 6.2 | 10.1 |
| China, People's Republic of | 8.5 | 7.9 | 12.4 | 10.1 |
| *Services* | | | | |
| Latin America | — | 6.6 | 1.6 | — |
| (Brazil) | — | (8.0) | (3.1) | — |
| South Asia[a] | 4.9 | 4.8 | 6.2 | 5.0 |
| (India) | (4.7) | (4.5) | (6.1) | (4.8) |
| South-east and East Asia (excluding China) | 6.1 | 8.0 | 6.0 | 7.5 |
| China, People's Republic of | −2.9 | 4.3 | 11.3 | 6.3 |

*Note*
[a]Excludes Myanmar.
*Source:* International Economic Data Bank, Australian National University.

countries investment ratios jumped again, reflecting booming economies and rapid public revenue growth. In China the freeing up of private and co-operative initiatives, notably in agriculture, led to very high investment ratios.

Relatively high investment ratios only explain part of high sectoral and overall growth rates in East Asia. Policies that led to relatively small distortions in the production structure meant better resource allocation and utilization. Capital/labour intensity was lower and employment growth was therefore higher. Shift work tended to be more common, so that although relatively little capital was used, it was used more intensively. Paradoxically, in the export-oriented economies production tended to be less imported input intensive than in import substituting ones. Thus not only were more dollars invested, but for each dollar invested the social returns were higher in East Asian than in other developing economies.

Macro-economic policies have many micro-economic effects. For example, competitive financial policies stimulate savings and price stability encourages investment. Micro-economic policies at the same time have macro-economic effects. Outward-oriented policies in agriculture, manufacturing and services ease balance of payments constraints and require lower levels of monetary policy intervention. Rapid growth

Table 2.4    *Average gross domestic investment as a percentage of GDP, 1960-70 to 1980-86 (%)*

|  | 1960–70 | 1970–80 | 1980–88 | 1960–88 |
|---|---|---|---|---|
| Latin America | 16 | 22 | 15 | 19 |
| (Brazil) | (19) | (24) | (15) | (20) |
| South Asia | 19 | 22 | 18 | 20 |
| (India) | (19) | (23) | (18) | (21) |
| South-east and East Asia (excluding China) | 19 | 26 | 25 | 25 |
| China, People's Republic of | 19 | 28 | 28 | 26 |

*Source:* International Economic Data Bank, Australian National University.

increases public revenues and reduces budget constraints. Macro-economic and micro-economic policies are thus mutually reinforcing and it is the policy framework as a whole that affects growth. The experience of such rapidly growing countries as Japan and the Republic of Korea suggests that individual policies can diverge quite considerably from optimal directions without bringing growth to a halt, provided essential directions of competitiveness and efficiency are stimulated by the overall policy framework.

### The international environment

The international environment plays a role in explaining inter-temporal differences in global growth. The protectionism of the 1930s undermined growth while the unprecedented openness of the industrial countries' economies since World War II stimulated it in developing countries as well as industrial countries. Trade, capital and labour flows among and into industrial countries have been remarkably free of barriers in comparison to previous eras. Protection against imports from developing countries is largely limited to clothing and textiles despite the burgeoning of new protectionism in the late 1970s and early 1980s. After expanding markedly in the 1960s and 1970s migration opportunities declined in the 1980s. Overall, however, the 1980s have presented considerable export growth opportunity for developing countries. The barriers that do exist are mostly directed against the 'gang of four' (Hong Kong, Singapore, Taiwan and the Republic of Korea) and yet the latter continue to expand their exports more vigorously than most other developing countries. It seems that the principal obstacles to export growth do not lie in biased 'rules of the game', but in the perceptions of the statist and *dependencia* models that the 'rules' are biased and in subsequent export pessimism. Uncertainty is engendered, investment is undermined and exports fail to take place.

The statist and *dependencia* models focused on the movement of the barter terms of trade rather than on income terms of trade as indicators of long run as well as short run export potential and achievement. Barter terms of trade are useful short term macro-economic indicators. But for the long run, even if barter terms of trade could be measured accurately, they have little analytical value. Countries seeking to increase exports of agricultural, mineral and manufactured goods and services must be concerned with their income terms of trade, that is, not with relative movements in prices, but in what export earnings will buy. To increase export earnings a country must be highly competitive. This often means reducing prices through high productivity, that is, deliberately worsening barter terms of trade. This was the approach adopted by the 'gang of four' and other highly motivated exporters such as Thailand and Malaysia. All these countries focused on efficiency within export sectors to be able to drop prices against their competitors.

From the 1950s, the 'gang of four' played a seminal role in 'unshackling' the exports of manufactures. By disproving the hypothesis that developing countries could not compete in manufactures against industrial countries they opened the way to rapid growth. Specializing in highly productive agriculture and in labour intensive manufactures along lines of comparative advantage, East Asian countries expanded exports and employment rapidly and reduced balance of payments and government budget constraints on economic growth. Indonesia, Malaysia and Thailand continued to export primary products, but all the East Asian countries diversified into exports of manufactures, mostly (more than 60 per cent) to industrial countries. The penetration of industrial country markets by the four newly industrializing countries and the other ASEAN countries is much higher than that of Latin American countries (Panoutsopoulos 1990).

By limiting levels of protection Hong Kong and Singapore were able to welcome private direct foreign investment without incurring high costs. The Republic of Korea, in contrast, eschewed private direct foreign investment at considerable cost to its technological development, to avoid high costs of inward oriented foreign investment.

Most of the South-east and East Asian developing countries, like the Latin American countries, borrowed heavily in international capital market in the 1970s when world capital markets were liquid and the real cost of capital was low. Borrowing by the South Asian countries and by China was, however, very limited. As an extension of their prudent macro-economic policies these countries understood that having chosen repressed financial systems and high protection with concomitantly low and slowly growing exports, they had to limit private capital inflows of all types. In most South-east and East Asian economies relatively high rates of borrowing did not cause problems. In the Philippines with highly distorted macro- and micro-economic policies, a debt crisis followed. Several of the other South-east and Asian countries experienced liquidity problems when real interest rates rose just as commodity prices fell in the early 1980s, but they did not have solvency problems. After the difficulties of the 1981-82 recession export earnings rose rapidly from a high base. The highly productive investments of the 1970s brought the benefits of increasing productivity and income. Apart from the Philippines, Asia has not experienced debt problems in the 1980s.

Most Latin American countries' experience was more akin to the Philippines than to the other Asian countries. Repressed financial systems, high protection with low export levels and low export growth were compounded by capital flight. Inflation continued unabated. Borrowed capital had been used for consumption and, worse still, for unproductive private and public investment. Liquidity problems soon turned into solvency crises.

Table 2.5 *Exports of manufactures by leading developing country exporters of manufactures,*[a] *1965 and 1987*

| | 1965 | | | 1987 | | | 1965-87 | | |
|---|---|---|---|---|---|---|---|---|---|
| | Exports | Share | Per capita | Exports | Share | Per capita | Exports | Share | Per capita |
| | $ million | % | $ | $ million | % | $ | Average annual real growth % | | |
| Taiwan | 189 | 3 | 15 | 49,360 | 17 | 2,509 | 20.4 | 6.4 | 25.4 |
| Hong Kong | 995 | 15 | 277 | 44,780 | 15 | 8,173 | 10.7 | −1.2 | 16.5 |
| Korea, R. of | 104 | 2 | 4 | 43,580 | 15 | 1,037 | 23.9 | 9.5 | 29.5 |
| China, P.D.R. | 1,021 | 16 | 1 | 27,622 | 9 | 26 | 9.6 | −2.0 | 15.8 |
| Singapore | 339 | 5 | 180 | 20,477 | 7 | 7,846 | 15.3 | 3.2 | 22.4 |
| Brazil | 134 | 2 | 2 | 11,750 | 4 | 83 | 18.5 | 5.1 | 23.5 |
| Mexico | 165 | 3 | 4 | 9,774 | 3 | 119 | 10.7 | −1.3 | 15.5 |
| Yugoslavia | 617 | 9 | 32 | 8,942 | 3 | 382 | 6.4 | −4.3 | 14.2 |
| India | 828 | 13 | 2 | 8,658 | 3 | 11 | 3.3 | −6.1 | 10.4 |
| Pakistan | 191 | 3 | 4 | 2,801 | 1 | 27 | 2.3 | −7.1 | 8.4 |
| Argentina | 84 | 1 | 4 | 2,013 | 1 | 65 | 6.2 | −3.6 | 14.2 |
| Chile | 28 | * | 3 | 448 | * | 36 | 12.2 | −4.3 | 13.2 |
| Total | 4,679 | 71 | 3 | 230,205 | 78 | 99 | 12.2 | 0.4 | 18.3 |
| Other developing countries | 1,875 | 29 | 3 | 65,952 | 22 | 53 | 11.0 | −1.1 | 16.0 |
| All developing countries | 6,572 | 100 | 3 | 296,157 | 100 | 83 | 11.9 | — | 17.7 |

*Note*
[a]SITC 5 to 9 less 68.
*Source:* International Economic Data Bank, Australian National University.

Typically of *dependencia* postures, policy makers in Latin America blamed international conditions for their debt difficulties and turned towards 'socializing' debt as solution to their problems. Taxpayers in industrial countries have not been enthusiastic about paying for the debts incurred by extravagant bank and developing country policies. The Latin American debt posture was, not surprisingly, unsuccessful. Major lenders, whose lack of prudence had contributed markedly to the high level of debt, have finally begun to write off some of their assets, but action was late and limited. There have been some aid flows to enable countries (notably Bolivia) to write off debt, but the international initiatives on which much hope has been placed from time to time have not eventuated. 'Socializing' debt or helping to reduce it by aid flows would at least partly be at the cost of the prudent borrowers of Asia. The cost of the debt burden would thus be transferred from imprudent to prudent borrowers. Attitudes to the accumulation and servicing of debt differ considerably on the two sides of the Pacific.

## Conclusions

If all developing countries had followed the outward and private-enterprise-oriented rapid growth North-east and South-east Asian model, their average annual growth rate of GDP per capita would have been around 7 per cent per annum. Standards of living would have doubled every decade. Extremes of poverty would have been largely eliminated. Most people in the world would be living longer, they would have greater access to education and other public goods and they would be living lives of modest comfort.

The failure of the majority of developing countries to achieve reasonable growth rates is ascribed to a variety of causes by the followers of the statist and *dependencia* models: exploitation by industrial countries (their trading cartels, transnational enterprises and banks), by their own elites (through corruption, cartels and monopolies) and by political dictatorships. Most developing countries, however, have not missed out on growth because of policies imposed on them by others. Under the influence of development ideologies of the 1950s they have freely chosen policies that are inimical to rapid and equity oriented growth. Statist and *dependencia* views have been of great assistance to political and economic elites in choosing policies that maintain their power and impose it on the mass of the population.

## References

Auty, R.M. (1990), 'The Korean heavy industry drive re-evaluated'. Paper presented at the conference 'The Impact of Policy Reform on Trade and Industrial Performance in Developing Countries', 22 June 1990, University of Bradford (mimeo).

Behrman, J.R. and Deolalikar, A.B. (1988), 'Health and Nutrition' in H. Chenery and T.N. Srinivasan, *Handbook of Development Economics*, vol. 1, North Holland, Elsevier Science Publishers, Amsterdam, pp. 631-712.

Balassa, B. and Hughes, H. (1969), 'Statistical indicators of industrial development', Economics Department Working Paper No. 45, May 1969, World Bank, Washington, DC.

Chen, E.K.Y. (1989), 'Trade policy in Asia' in S. Naya, M. Urrutia, M. Shelley and A. Fuyentes, *Lessons in Development: a comparative study of Asia and Latin America*, International Center for Economic Growth, San Francisco, pp. 55-76.

Chenery, H.B. and Syrquin, M. (1975), *Patterns of Development*, 1950-1970, Oxford University Press, London.

Corden, W.M. (1974), *Trade Policy and Economic Welfare*, Oxford University Press, London.

Fields, G.S. (1989), 'Changes in poverty and inequality in developing countries', *The World Bank Observer*, 4(2) pp. 167-85.

Haggard, S. (1988), 'The politics of industrialization in the Republic of Korea and Taiwan', in H. Hughes (ed.), *Achieving Industrialization in East Asia*, Cambridge University Press, Sydney, pp. 260-82.

Herderschee, J. (1990), *Incentives for exports: a case study of Taiwan and Thailand*, unpublished PhD thesis, National Centre for Development Studies, Canberra (mimeo).

Hamilton, C. (1986), *Capitalist Industrialization in Korea*, Westview Press, Boulder, Colorado, p. 193.

Hughes, H. (1972), 'Assessment of policies towards direct foreign investment in the Asian-Pacific area' in P. Drysdale (ed.), *Direct Foreign Investment in Asia and the Pacific*, Australian National University Press, Canberra, pp. 313-43.

Kravis, I.B. (1986), 'The three faces of the International Comparison Project', *The World Bank Research Observer*, 1(1) January, pp. 3-26.

Krueger, A.O. (1974), 'The political economy of the rent seeking society', *The American Economic Review*, 64(3), June, pp. 291-303.

Mackie, J.A.C. (1988), 'Economic growth in the ASEAN region: the political underpinnings' in H. Hughes (ed.), *Achieving Industrialization in East Asia*, Cambridge University Press, Sydney, pp. 286-326.

Maddison, A. (1982), *Phases of Capitalist Development*, Oxford University Press, New York.

Panoutsopoulos, V.D. (1990), *The supply determinants of the developing countries' penetration of the United States market for manufactures*, unpublished PhD thesis, National Centre for Development Studies, Canberra (mimeo).

Riedel, J.R. (1988), 'Economic development in East Asia. Doing what comes naturally?' in H. Hughes (ed.), *Achieving Industrialization in East Asia*, Cambridge University Press, Sydney, pp. 1-38.

Syrquin M. (1988), 'Patterns of structural change' in H. Chenery and T.N. Srinivasan (eds.), *Handbook of Development Economics*, vol. I, Elsevier Science Publishers, Amsterdam, pp. 203-27.

Tawney, R.H. (1926), *Religion and the Rise of Capitalism: A Historical Study*, John Murray, London.

Wade, R. (1988), 'The role of government in overcoming market failure: Taiwan, Republic of Korea and Japan' in H. Hughes (ed.), *Achieving Industrialization in East Asia*, Cambridge University Press, Sydney, pp. 129-63.

Weber, M. (1922), *Sociology of Religion*, Methuen, London.

# Trade policy reform: recent evidence from theory and practice*

Trade policy reform has become essential for developing countries to keep up with global technological advances and to compete in an increasingly integrated world economy. Expanding trade should help developing countries to improve resource allocation, economy-wide efficiency and economic growth. Yet most developing countries (as well as industrial countries) still have serious trade barriers. Also, trade reforms have confronted objections, scepticism and obstacles. As a result, considerable uncertainty remains about the potential effectiveness of trade reforms, how well they have been carried out and their outcome.

This chapter draws upon the results of a recent study of the experience of trade policy reforms in developing countries, particularly those carried out with the support of World Bank adjustment lending during the 1980s (Thomas and Nash, forthcoming). It synthesizes results of this study with conclusions from the existing literature. By focusing on adjustment programs of the 1980s, by examining statistical evidence from large samples as well as case studies of individual countries, and by considering the links between trade policy reform and adjustment lending, this study extends and complements the results of studies of reforms in earlier periods (for example, Krueger 1978; and Michaely and others, 1991).

The overall goal of this survey is to bring together all of this evidence to clarify what are the important unanswered questions in trade policy reform and which ones can be resolved so as to give guidance in obtaining stronger and more effective results. It considers the issues in four major topic areas, corresponding to the sections of the paper. First, it reviews the expected gains from trade reforms. Second, it considers the experience of developing countries that have undertaken reforms to determine how much reform actually has taken place and how effective it has been in promoting the desired outcomes. Third, it discusses major trade policy reforms (exchange rate, import policy and export policy), their expected benefits, and issues of sequencing and pacing. Fourth, it examines issues of the links of trade liberalization with macro-economic stabilization and with other domestic reform measures.

## Why reform trade policy?

'Trade policy reform' has many meanings. Here it covers measures that move the trade regime toward a more neutral incentive framework for foreign trade, toward a more liberal trade regime, or toward both. Neutrality refers to incentives among and between exportables and importables, between sales to domestic and export markets, and between tradables and non-tradables. A more liberal trade regime refers to the reduction of controls and to the replacement of direct interventions by price mechanisms.

*Expected gains from trade policy reforms*

In the traditional static and partial equilibrium framework, the direct costs of resource misallocations caused by the misalignment of domestic and international prices are generally estimated to be a few percentage points or less of GDP a year. The costs are much larger, however, when the likely effects of trade restrictions on market structure are also considered (Condon and de Melo 1986). Protection has been empirically linked to excessive entry of firms into the protected domestic markets in some countries, meaning that firms operate at an inefficiently small scale. The insulation of domestic producers from international competition has also been linked to oligopoly behaviour in the domestic market. Caves (1980) and Jacquemin (1982) conclude that greater openness restricts oligopoly power. Bergsman (1974) estimates losses of 5 to 7 per cent of GDP from oligopoly rents and inefficiencies associated with non-competitive behaviour in Pakistan and Brazil.

Indirect costs include the waste of resources in income-generating but unproductive activities associated with protection, such as smuggling, lobbying, evading tariffs, and building plants with excess capacity to get import licences. The indirect costs of foreign exchange controls and non-tariff barriers tend to be large because they involve allocations based on discretion rather than efficiency grounds and because they support price controls and investment licensing. These rent-seeking costs have been estimated to be as high as 30-45 per cent of GDP in India and 15 per cent in Turkey (Grais, de Melo, and Urata 1986; Krueger 1974; Mohammad and Whalley 1984). These studies, however, assumed that all rents are consumed in competitive efforts to capture them, so that the efficiency cost can be estimated by the size of the rent: consequently, the estimates should be regarded as upwardly biased.

Reducing protection should raise GDP, but what explains the significant and sustained differences in rates of growth between inward- and outward- oriented economies? Chenery, Robinson and Syrquin (1986) provide evidence of a link between outward orientation and total factor productivity growth. Country studies have found productivity growth to be significantly higher in periods of liberal trade policy, for example Kim (1987) on Korea, Krueger and Tuncer (1982) on Turkey, and Nishimizu and Page (1982) and Havrylyshyn (1990) on Yugoslavia.

Traditional growth theories are inadequate for explaining the relation between trade regimes and growth rates, but some recent approaches are more promising (Edwards, 1989a). Some new growth models have replaced the traditional assumption of constant returns to scale with one of increasing returns to scale and different types of external economies. If the return to capital does not decline over time – it is assumed to decline in traditional models – the incentive to accumulate capital does not disappear automatically. So if trade policy reforms raise the marginal return to capital, they can generate a higher equilibrium growth rate.

Other models have focused on the role of technological change: the more open the economy, the greater its ability to adopt the wide range of innovations taking place around the globe, and increase its long-run growth rate. Romer (1989) developed a model based on this effect, tested for its significance in a sample of 90 countries, and found that such effects of economic openness were important in encouraging growth. Other research has shown how an openness to trade increases incentives to undertake research and development domestically by widening the potential market and increasing the returns to such expenditures (Grossman and Helpman 1989). Pack (1988) takes a different approach. He argues that factor productivity growth in manufacturing sectors has not been conclusively linked to the trade regime. Rather, he posits that outward-oriented regimes grow faster because they can absorb the continual transfer of factors from sectors of low productivity (e.g., agriculture and the informal sector) to sectors of high productivity without reducing the terms of trade in the latter, as would be the case if the production had to be absorbed in the domestic economy.

More recently, research has also documented the effects of trade policy on income distribution. In a sample of 37 developing countries, Bourguignon and Morrisson (1989), holding other variables constant, found that protectionism (an average effective protection rate higher than 30 per cent) was associated with a rise in the Gini coefficient of distributional inequality of 5 points, a 4 to 5 percentage point fall in the income share of the poorest 60 per cent of the population and a fall of 20 per cent in the mean income of the poor. They point out that this result is consistent with predictions of the Stolper-Samuelson theorem: freer trade benefits the relatively abundant factor, which in developing countries is the relatively poor factor, labour.

Trade and domestic restrictions also have macro-economic implications that are exposed when a country faces severe shocks. Economies that maintained protectionist restrictions were largely divorced from the international price structure and failed to readjust production in response to relative price changes such as higher oil prices. Protective regimes also isolated their economies from technological progress abroad, ultimately hurting competitiveness. When the terms of trade shifted against them, many countries with restrictive and inflexible trade regimes were unable to increase exports rapidly and had little further scope for efficient import substitution. Large trade deficits and macro-economic imbalances were the results.

Policy makers and economists express a variety of reservations about trade policy reform, most related to inconsistency with stabilization efforts or to transitional costs (see for example Rodrik 1988; Sachs 1987; and Taylor 1988). Conflicts do arise between trade and other reforms. But the evidence in this paper suggests that proper sequencing of reforms can help minimise these conflicts. The evidence also shows that trade reforms generally improve economic performance (exports and income growth) when they are credibly implemented and complementary actions taken.

Short-term transitional costs are usually expected from resource reallocation. But the findings of the Bank's previous research (Michaely and others, 1991) indicate no clear relationship between trade liberalization and unemployment. Although unemployment sometimes increased in the period immediately following reform episodes, the study concluded that this increase usually resulted from causes other than the reforms, such as the stabilization measures that were needed to resolve macroeconomic crises.

## Experience with reform and its implications

### Conditions preceding reform episodes

Most reforming countries in the 1980s had financial support from the World Bank and the International Monetary Fund (IMF). Based on evidence from a number of sources[1], 40 countries that received trade policy-related loans from the World Bank in 1980-87[2] were grouped into three broad categories of average anti-export bias (low, medium, or high) relative to the other groups at the outset of adjustment lending. Only Chile and Korea had a relatively low level of restrictions, 60 per cent of the countries had a high level, and 35 per cent had a medium level prior to adjustment lending (the early 1980s in most cases).

While data on effective rates of protection (ERP), which show the joint effects of tariffs and non-tariff barriers, are available for only a few countries, it is clear that developing countries as a whole have far more restrictive trade regimes than do developed countries. Furthermore, protection tends to be highest for goods in which other developing countries have the greatest comparative advantage, creating a greater bias against South-South trade than against North-South trade (Erzan 1989). First, the average import tax for 50 developing countries, weighted by imports, was 34 per cent at the end of 1985 (Erzan and others, 1988). For many countries, average rates were much higher (about 90 per cent in Bangladesh, Costa Rica, and Pakistan, and 118 per cent in India), and within each country rates were very dispersed, with top rates much higher than the average. By contrast, average tariffs on industrial goods in OECD countries were estimated to be about 5 per cent (GATT 1980 and Finger and Laird 1987). Second, non-tariff import barriers – usually a more serious restriction than tariffs – in the 50 developing countries were estimated to cover 40 per cent (unweighted) by number of all tariff positions (product categories in the tariff code) at the end of 1985. A World Bank study of eight developing countries for which data on production by tariff position were available found that six had non-tariff barriers covering products representing 35 per cent or more of production. Finger and Laird (1987) give a similar estimate for 38 developing countries in 1982. They also estimate that in 1984, 15 per cent of the industrial product categories of the 11 industrial countries in their sample were subject to non-tariff barriers.

### Policy changes

In the context of the loans to the 40 developing countries, the most common reforms covered the exchange rate (38 countries), export promotion (33 countries), and protection studies (28 countries).(2) Proposed reform measures (Table 3.1) for exports and quantitative restrictions were generally stronger than those related to the level and dispersion of tariffs (Halevi 1989; Thomas 1989).

Actual implementation of the reform proposals varied considerably among the trade loan recipients.[3] Some made little progress or even reversed their reforms (Guyana, Yugoslavia, Zambia and Zimbabwe), while some undertook substantial

Table 3.1  *Intensity and distribution of major trade policy reform proposals among 40 countries receiving World Bank trade adjustment loans, 1979-87*

| Area of reform | Present | Not present | Strong | Moderate | Mild or absent |
|---|---|---|---|---|---|
| Exchange rate[a] | 38 | 2 | | | |
| Export promotion[b] | 33 | 7 | | | |
| Protection studies | 28 | 12 | | | |
| Overall export policy | | | 15 | 15 | 10 |
| Imports for exports | | | 17 | 15 | 8 |
| Overall import policy | | | 14 | 15 | 11 |
| Non-protective quantitative restrictions | | | 14 | 16 | 10 |
| Protective quantitative restrictions[c] | | | 14 | 15 | 11 |
| Tariff level[c] | | | 7 | 21 | 12 |
| Tariff dispersion | | | 7 | 24 | 9 |
| Schedule of future action | | | 6 | 29 | 5 |
| Overall reduction in anti-export bias | | | 17 | 12 | 11 |

*Notes*

[a] Often these were not written conditions, but important understandings in the program – usually in conjunction with the IMF.

[b] Removal of restrictions, provision of export credits, insurance, guarantees, institutional development, and the like.

[c] Where reforms replaced QRs by tariffs, they are counted in both lines. Sometimes the changes reduced protection and sometimes not.

*Source*: World Bank data.

reform (Chile, Mexico and Turkey). While nearly all countries that planned or implemented major trade policy reforms did so with adjustment loan support from the World Bank, a few countries, notably Bolivia and Haiti, also reformed their trade policies considerably during 1979-87 without such support.

Progress has been made in correcting misaligned exchange rates (Figure 3.1) and in reducing impediments to exports, including restrictions on imports needed by exporters. Several countries have substituted tariffs for quantitative restrictions. Joint reductions of quantitative restrictions and tariff levels (and therefore progress in reducing protection) have been more modest, with several exceptions, including Bolivia, Costa Rica, Chile, Ghana, Korea, Mexico, and until recently, Turkey. The

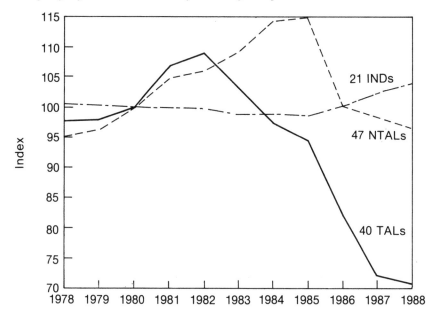

21 INDs = twenty-one industrial countries.
40 TALs = forty trade adjustment loan recipient countries.
47 NTALs = forty-seven non-recipients of trade adjustment loans.

*Note*
Multilateral index of the real exchange rate measured against a basket of currencies of trading partners. Increase in index indicates a real appreciation.

*Source*: Based on ICJF data.

Fig 3.1 Real exchange rate indices for selected country groupings, 1978–88 (unweighted averages; 1960 = 100)

measured ratios of imports to GDP (in current and constant prices) in the recipients of trade adjustment loans have risen relative to the ratios for non-recipient countries, indicating the influence of both increased financing and import liberalization.[4]

*Performance outcomes*

Researchers have often found a positive association between export growth and overall economic growth (Balassa 1982, 1985, World Bank 1987b), although the robustness of this result in low-income countries has been weaker (Kavoussi 1986; Ram 1985). Figure 3.2 indicates the tendency of higher export growth and GDP growth to go together. Admittedly, exports are part of GDP but this does not necessarily mean the correlation is a statistical artifact and a similar picture emerges if exports are excluded from GDP as well.[5] None of this proves causality, however. Tracing the influence of specific policies behind superior export and GDP growth is complex because the potential causes for the changes are many, making the direction of causality between exports and growth difficult to test rigorously. (Findlay 1984 and

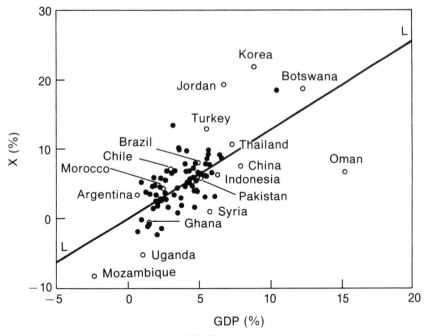

GDP = Average GDP growth rate during 1965–88.
X = Average growth rate of exports of goods and manufacturer services during 1965–88.
LL = Fitted line based on least square regression.

*Source*: Based on World Bank data.

Fig 3.2    GDP and export growth for developing countries, 1965–88

Jung and Marshall 1985 discuss some of the issues). It also takes time for policy reforms to produce the expected improvements in resource allocation, efficiency and growth.

The adjustment episodes of the 1980s and longer-term experience suggest that trade policy and structural reforms have contributed positively to the growth in output and exports. Real exchange rate depreciation and commercial (import and export) policy reform are linked to such improved performance. The additional financing and policy reforms connected with adjustment lending have each been found to have contributed to relative improvements in the 1980s. After controlling for some other factors, trade adjustment lending is associated with a mild improvement in GDP, exports, and other economic variables (Thomas and Nash, forthcoming). The results are stronger and statistically more significant when the comparison is between trade policy reformers and non-reformers rather than simply between trade loan recipients and non-recipients.

The response of output to policy change, although varying considerably, has not been as great as expected. Country studies identify several factors that may have constrained the supply response. First, failing to give enough attention to the institutional and infrastructural needs of exporters has often been a problem (weak systems for providing duty-free and restriction-free access to imported inputs; inadequate port, transport and telecommunications facilities; poor information and market services for exporters). In addition, when entrepreneurial and managerial capacities are relatively underdeveloped, the supply response is inevitably slower. Shortages of trained labour and poorly developed input supply lines have also been serious problems in many cases.

Second, domestic regulatory and public sector policies influence the supply response by determining whether incentives actually change in response to reform (in the case of price controls) and by affecting the mobility of factors of production in response to changes in incentives (labour regulations, market entry and exit regulations, foreign investment controls). Some public sector policies have impeded rapid adjustment to a changed incentive structure and so have inhibited the supply response (allocation mechanisms in centrally planned economies; state monopolies or domination of agricultural markets, as for many export crops in Africa).

Third, growing protectionism in international markets in the late 1980s has depressed world prices and blocked market access, thereby reducing the export response to trade policy reforms, particularly in agriculture. For manufactured exports, industrial countries represent more promising markets because of low tariffs, but non-tariff barriers in some important product categories (for example, textiles, clothing, steel) have hurt developing country export growth.

Finally, the response to reforms is crucially influenced by perceptions concerning their sustainability. Reforms that are not expected to last will not generate the investment and supply response needed to ensure long-term political support for the reforms. Expectations of failure and reversal become self-fulfilling prophecies. The credibility of reform depends on the country's previous track record in policy reform, the effectiveness and forcefulness of the initial reform steps, macro-economic stability, and consistency with other reforms (financial sector reform and agricultural pricing, for example).

## Trade policy measures

### *Liberalization versus targeted trade policy*

Some countries have reached greater neutrality in incentives through a relatively hands-off approach, but some through selective and judicious government assistance. Thus relatively liberal, non-interventionist regimes such as in Hong Kong and Chile have successfully promoted trade and growth, and so have regimes based on export-promoting market intervention and state assistance as in South Korea and Taiwan during their earlier stages of development. However, with the exception of Korea's policies from 1973 to 1979 (see below), intervention in these two cases was more neutral and less distortionary than has been the case in most developing economies and also more effective than elsewhere. Moreover, in these and in other countries where trade policy was successful in the 1980s (such as in Ghana, Indonesia, Mexico, and Turkey), the direction of reform has been toward liberalization.

From 1973 to 1979 Korean export development policies included targeted support for petrochemicals, steel, metal products, shipbuilding, machinery and automobiles. Measures included substantial subsidies through long-term lending, tax holidays, accelerated depreciation and import protection. These policies eventually succeeded for some industries (for example, steel and automobiles) but were expensive failures in others (for example, petrochemicals) and had mixed results in others (for example, heavy machinery). The policies contributed to an economic crisis in the 1980s and, on average, produced low economic returns (World Bank 1986a). Their deficiencies were rapidly recognised, and drastic restructuring of some industries began as early as 1979.[6]

Relying on non-interventionist and neutral policies avoids the susceptibility to misjudgement and abuse to which targeted investment promotion policies are prone. It also helps a country avoid the imposition of countervailing duties, which other countries are allowed to introduce under the General Agreement on Tariffs and Trade (GATT) in response to direct export subsidies. On average, less interventionist regimes have been more effective in promoting exports and growth (Agarwala 1983; Balassa 1988, Easterly and Wetzel 1989; Edwards 1989a; Landau 1983; Marsden 1983; and Scully 1988).

*Exchange rate policy*

The real exchange rate should help ensure equilibrium in the balance of payments and domestic markets and be compatible with growth in tradables and output over the longer term. Edwards (1989b) considers some of the empirical issues associated with estimating an exchange rate that is appropriate in this sense. An overvalued domestic currency indirectly taxes exportables and lightly protected importables while favouring non-tradables and importables protected by binding restrictions. Fluctuations in the real exchange rate also hurt exports because of the uncertainty they engender (Caballero and Corbo 1989).

A real devaluation, accompanied by exchange rate unification where relevant, improves the incentives for production of exports and efficient import substitutes. Macro-economic stability, with low fiscal deficits and inflation rates, and stable and adequate exchange rates have been the hallmark of East Asia's economic success. In Korea, in only two of the years from 1970 to 1986 did the real exchange rate deviate significantly (by over 14 per cent) from its 1980 value (World Bank 1987a). The importance of the exchange rate to trade policy reform is emphasised by the experience of Cote d'Ivoire, whose currency, and that of other countries in Francophone Africa, is pegged at a fixed rate to the French franc. Côte d'Ivoire's reform programme faltered in part because a simulated devaluation based on manipulation of import tariffs and export subsidies, which was not fully implemented, proved to be a poor substitute for devaluation (O'Connell 1989).

*Export policy*

Two prerequisites for a successful export policy are a stable macro-economic policy and low protection for imports. A few East Asian economies have been successful exporters despite protective import policies (Korea and Taiwan) by avoiding exchange rate overvaluation and by using export subsidies and other measures to offset the anti-export bias from import protection. This approach would be difficult to replicate elsewhere, however, since Korea's policies during the 1960s and 1970s included export subsidies, which other countries would countervail (Nam 1986 and Balassa 1982), and vigorous government suppression of rent-seeking activities viewed as incompatible with export growth, implemented in ways that many governments would be unwilling or unable to undertake.

In general, export subsidies – including income tax rebates, which have long been used in Latin America – have not had the desired effect on exports. High subsidies have usually resulted in cheating, fictitious claims of export production in order to get the subsidies, and wasteful rent-seeking, as experience in Turkey, Yugoslavia and other countries illustrates (World Bank 1986b). Furthermore, the heavy fiscal burden of the high subsidies needed to offset a strong anti-export bias may generate macro-economic disequilibrium and an external debt problem, as Havrylyshyn (1990) found in Yugoslavia, or burden efficient export sectors, as Nogues (1989) found in Argentina. Policies involving special treatment of exporters, including subsidies, foreign exchange retention allowances, and favourable exchange rates, have also been a problem in socialist countries. For example, China's dramatic success in achieving rapid aggregate export growth may be less than meets the eye, because a significant but unknown proportion of exports may have been economically inefficient due to excessive incentives (resulting from competitive subsidies offered by provinces and regions) and its highly distorted price system (World Bank 1988a). Fitzgerald and Monson (1989) investigated subsidy programmes administered by seven developing countries and found no evidence that they were cost effective.

A number of other export policies of the East Asian countries could be usefully applied elsewhere. Giving direct exporters and their suppliers restriction-free access to inputs at duty- and tax-free international prices avoids wide variations in effective incentives between different exports that use inputs subject to different import controls and tariffs. Also, such measures are not subject to the countervailing duties that importing countries are increasingly applying to direct or indirect export subsidies. Duty-free schemes also involve costs, however. Resources may be drawn away from more efficient activities, such as resource-based export sectors, which are taxed. Other costs include temporary increases in the fiscal deficit[7], disprotection of domestic suppliers of importable inputs, and the creation of new opportunities for rent-seeking. These costs need to be balanced against the likely economic gains.

Efficient infrastructure, telecommunications, export credit, and quality control help exporters of manufactures to be more competitive to meet exacting and frequently changing requirements, and to deliver orders reliably and on time. Some countries have tried to promote exports by setting up export development (or free trade) zones to insulate exporters from the infrastructural or policy-based inadequacies of the economy at large. A comparison of successful East Asian exporters with other countries that have tried this shows that the zones tend to be successful where they are part of an overall favourable environment, rather than a substitute for such an environment, as in Malaysia, the Philippines and Thailand (Linn and Wetzel 1990). The East Asian experience also suggests the value of adjusting restrictive labour regulations affecting lay-offs, fringe benefits, minimum wages, and collective action, to reduce labour costs and increase flexibility. Assisting exporters to secure technical assistance services from consultants and information suppliers of their choice has also been shown to be helpful, in contrast to the disappointing record of official export promotion organisations (Keesing and Singer 1989). Establishing an environment attractive to foreign investors, such as macro-economic stability, protection of property rights, a stable and transparent regulatory environment, and liberal access to foreign exchange for profit remittances and imported inputs and services is also valuable (World Bank 1989b). Since foreign direct investment is a useful source of technology, capital and connections to world markets, such policies are likely to be superior to special incentives, such as tax holidays, which may attract footloose industries that leave when the holiday is over.

Other policies are needed to counteract the bias against exports from primary sectors, which are frequently discouraged by overvaluation, taxes, low administered prices, and inefficient government monopolies, as well as by industrial protection and restrictions on foreign investment. In Argentina, for example, where agriculture provides about 75 per cent of exports, the anti-export policy bias keeps agricultural exports at half their potential level (Sturzenegger, forthcoming). Malaysia in the 1960s and Chile in the later 1970s created a positive policy environment for primary exports, with good results. Chile's reforms helped reinvigorate the export-oriented mining sector, based to a large extent on foreign private initiative. They also led to a spectacular increase in agricultural and wood product exports, which grew from US$44 million in 1972 to US$1,102 million in 1986 (World Bank 1986b, 1988b).

Balassa (1986, 1988) found an exchange rate elasticity for primary exports almost as large as that for all merchandise (including primary) exports, and even larger for a sample of Sub-Saharan African countries. Similarly Jaeger (1989) found a significant positive supply elasticity of export crops (and total value added in agriculture) to the producer price in a sample of Sub-Saharan African countries.[8] This evidence, together with the presence of severe distortions that depress producer prices, confirms Binswanger's (1989) conclusion that policy reform can quickly increase primary exports from individual countries and that non-price institutional issues are also important. In the agenda for primary agricultural policy reform in Africa (recommended in World Bank 1989a), some of the most important reform proposals aim at increasing the role of the private sector in pricing and marketing agricultural imports and outputs, for example, by reducing or eliminating the power of state marketing boards.[9]

Other obstacles may not be under the control of developing country governments, however. Export growth for some key agricultural products that compete with temperate zone agriculture has been constrained by protection in industrial countries, while growth in demand and in prices for tropical primary products has also been low. Consequently, for exporters of primary products as a whole, a significant growth in exports will also require export diversification (Koester, Schafer and Valdes 1989).

*Import policy*

Non-tariff import barriers (import licensing, prohibitions, exemptions, quotas, official reference prices and foreign exchange allocation) make the structure of protection less transparent and the import system more uncertain, they sever the link between domestic and international prices, and they encourage lobbying, rent-seeking and corruption. For these reasons, a reduction in non-tariff barriers, even if protection levels remain roughly the same, can have important beneficial effects on the economy. One simple reform is to switch from a positive list of permitted imports, which creates high levels of uncertainty and strong lobbying pressures, to a negative list, which allows unlicensed import of all non-listed items. This was the first major step in Korea's liberalization programme in 1967.

Other barriers, such as quotas or licensing requirements, can also be reduced or phased out. For example, quotas can be auctioned, and the size of the quota increased until the auction bids (and their protective value) fall to zero, at which time imports can be freely allowed. Or a tariff could be imposed on imports in excess of the quota, with the level of the tariff reduced over time. With the exception of recent experiments in Columbia, such schemes have been tried only in developed countries, which have tended to rely more on quotas than have developing countries, in which discretionary licensing procedures (without explicit quotas) are more prevalent. A more common import reform measure in developing countries is to impose tariffs providing approximately equivalent protection on product categories as non-tariff controls are eliminated. This change re-establishes the link between domestic and international prices, ensuring that they move in the same direction and diverge by no more than the amount of the tariff.

Tariffs are a more transparent form of protection and frequently have a revenue-raising function as well. However, tariffs on finished products are usually higher than on intermediates and raw materials, and tariff exemptions are common, causing effective protection to vary greatly across industries. One of the goals of reform is generally to reduce this dispersion, with the expected result being greater efficiency in allocation of resources.

A relatively low and uniform tariff structure reduces dispersion of effective protection and is preferred among feasible options on both efficiency and political economy grounds. It is impossible to predict with certainty that resource allocation will become more efficient as effective protection becomes more uniform (Bhagwati and Srinivasan 1973). Studies of optimal tariff structure (see, for example, Chambers 1989 and Panagariya 1989) are sensitive to the underlying model assumptions and to the presumed objectives of the tariffs. Nevertheless, the general conclusion favours uniformity. The economic justification is that relatively low and uniform tariffs minimize distortions in production incentives for a given level of overall protection to importables. They also have the practical advantage of being less subject to lobbying and political influence. One qualification is that uniform tariffs may need to be supplemented with consumption taxes on final products to minimize consumption distortions. Also, raising low rates as a step towards unification encourages domestic production of products whose effective tariff rates are raised, perhaps drawing resources from exports and any 'under-protected' import substitutes. For this reason, exporters would need to be insulated from paying prices above world levels for these protected inputs. Some of the more successful reformers (Bolivia, Chile, Mexico) have converged their tariff structures toward 15 per cent, in addition to nearly eliminating quantitative restrictions, while some others have reduced tariffs to below 30 per cent.

In most countries, increasing production efficiency requires a reduction of effective protection and rationalization of protection among imports, taking into account the protective effect of the domestic tax system. The effect of the tax system can be quite important; for example, domestic tax rates in Ghana varied so much across sectors that a uniform tariff of 30 per cent would result in effective protection rates ranging from 0 to 50 per cent (Shalizi and Squire 1986). In such cases, it is especially important to co-ordinate tariff and domestic tax reform, a step often overlooked in World Bank policy recommendations (Rajaram 1989). Also, by co-ordinating tariff reform with domestic tax reform, deeper reductions in tariffs are possible than under a regime in which tariffs have an important revenue-raising role. The goal would be a low, equal rate of tax on imports and domestic production for each product, possibly administered as a tax on consumption.

## Design and sequencing of trade reforms and complementary policies

### *Trade policy reforms and macro-economic stabilization*

One important issue is whether trade liberalization and stabilization are incompatible and whether the fiscal deficit and inflation should be reduced before trade policy reform is introduced. Tariff reduction can lead to revenue losses, exacerbating a fiscal deficit and inflation.[10] Devaluation raises the price of tradables and can, in the short run, at least, increase inflation, while import liberalization can aggravate balance of payments problems.

Another issue is whether trade policy reforms are productive under macro-economic instability. Where inflation has been very high and variable Fischer (1984) points out that leads and lags in the movement of individual prices have made the resulting relative prices a poor guide for economic decisions. Furthermore, the exchange rate is often used instead of adequate macro-economic policies as an anti-inflationary tool in such situations, thereby reducing the effectiveness of trade reform, as occurred in a number of Latin American countries (Corbo and de Melo 1987; Kiguel and Liviatan 1988). Under these conditions, trade reform measures whose effectiveness depends on relative price changes are unlikely to be successful, and they should be delayed until very high rates of inflation are brought down.

But apart from countries with extremely high inflation, experience in the 1980s corroborates Krueger's (1981) conclusion that in general, trade policy reform and stabilization can proceed in parallel successfully. Whatever the potential conflicts, in practice strong trade policy reformers have also generally managed to reduce the fiscal deficit, inflation, and the balance of payments deficit more than have weaker reformers (Table 3.2). One reason for this is that some reforms increase revenues, while other fiscal instruments can be used to offset any declines in tariff revenues (see below). Where the fiscal deficit has been sufficiently reduced, the current account deficit has also declined under import liberalization, and inflation has declined even with devaluation. Furthermore, import liberalization can also lower domestic prices by providing much needed competition in domestic markets. A real depreciation can usually be achieved by using a crawling peg and correction of the underlying fiscal imbalance, as in Brazil (in some periods), Chile, Colombia and Turkey (Edwards 1989b).

Table 3.2　*Macro-economic indicators before and after reform in trade adjustment loan countries (unweighted average for each group in percentages)*

| Indicator | 3 years before | 2 years before | 1 year before | Year of program | 1 year after | 2 years after | 3 years after |
|---|---|---|---|---|---|---|---|
| *Inflation rate* | | | | | | | |
| Significant reform | 31.5 | 34.3 | 30.6 | 55.5 | 25.9 | 22.9 | 22.6 |
| Significant reform[a] | 30.6 | 33.0 | 26.6 | 48.9 | 20.3 | 17.4 | 17.0 |
| Moderate reform | 12.4 | 11.8 | 12.3 | 9.83 | 8.9 | 8.1 | 7.6 |
| Mild reform | 15.5 | 15.7 | 15.3 | 17.4 | 14.8 | 16.9 | 19.3 |
| *Fiscal balance/GDP* | | | | | | | |
| Significant reform | −4.8 | −6.4 | −7.8 | −7.2 | −6.1 | −4.4 | −4.6 |
| Significant reform[a] | −5.1 | −6.4 | −6.5 | −7.1 | −5.9 | −3.6 | −2.6 |
| Moderate reform | −7.2 | −7.8 | −6.0 | −5.8 | −5.4 | −5.1 | −4.7 |
| Mild reform | −8.0 | −6.8 | −8.6 | −8.9 | −8.4 | −8.0 | −13.8 |
| *Resource balance/GDP* | | | | | | | |
| Significant reform | −5.2 | −3.4 | −2.5 | −1.5 | 0.4 | −0.7 | −1.1 |
| Significant reform[a] | −5.6 | −3.5 | −3.6 | −3.1 | −0.7 | −1.5 | −1.9 |
| Moderate reform | −8.8 | −8.6 | −7.1 | −6.4 | −7.1 | −6.0 | −4.4 |
| Mild reform | −6.2 | −9.9 | −7.5 | −7.8 | −6.4 | −6.4 | −3.2 |

*Note*
Group includes 24 countries for which implementation data are available. The extent of reform (1980-87) is based on a combination of changes in policies (high, moderate, or low) with respect to the exchange rate (depreciation) and commercial policy. Countries in each group are as follows: *Significant* (high in both categories or high in one and moderate in the other): Chile, Colombia, Ghana, Jamaica, Korea, Mauritius, Mexico, and Turkey; *Moderate* (moderate and moderate, or high and low): Bangladesh, Madagascar, Morocco, Pakistan, Panama, the Philippines, and Thailand; and *Mild* (others): Côte d'Ivoire, Guyana, Kenya, Malawi, Senegal, Togo, Yugoslavia, Zambia, and Zimbabwe. (Mild includes countries that reversed reforms.)
[a] Excludes Mexico, for which changes in operational deficit is a more meaningful measure of fiscal effort.
*Source*: World Bank data.

Many trade policy reforms are not inconsistent with fiscal adjustment. Eliminating non-tariff barriers – especially converting them to tariffs – and eliminating tariff exemptions can increase revenue (Jamaica, Kenya, Mauritius). So can reducing very high tariff rates if this causes tariff evasion rates to fall or if import demand is price elastic (that is, if actual tariff rates exceed maximum-revenue tariff rates).

But such increases in tariff revenue cannot always be relied on. For a sample of countries that reformed primarily non-tariff barriers, tariff revenue increased from 2.7 per cent of GDP to 3.4 per cent. But for a sample of tariff reformers – among them Mexico, Morocco, the Philippines and Thailand – revenue fell on average from 2.8 per cent of GDP to 2.3 per cent (Matin 1989). Of course, how important this decline in revenue is, depends on how significant trade taxes are in the government's revenue base. As a percentage of total revenue, explicit trade taxes ranged from 4 per cent in Brazil to 58 per cent in Gambia, averaging 36 per cent in low-income and 19 per cent in middle-income countries (World Bank 1988d). Implicit taxes – the difference between what state marketing boards pay producers for an exportable and the price at which they sell it – are sometimes more important than explicit taxes, as Schiller (1988) found in Côte d'Ivoire. Also, the fiscal effects of a devaluation depend on whether the government is a net buyer of foreign exchange (Ghana, Sierra Leone, Somalia, Uganda and Zaire) or a net seller (Nigeria). Governments that are net buyers can combine a devaluation with tariff reform to prevent any decline in revenue in terms of foreign currency from being reflected in domestic-currency revenue.

Efforts to evaluate the likely revenue effects of specific trade reforms before implementation deserve more attention that they sometimes receive. Measures to reduce expenditure or increase revenue from other sources may need to be implemented along with trade policy reform to avoid harmful effects on the budget deficit. For example, Mexico generated additional revenue through tax reform when import liberalization lowered trade taxes; by contrast, Morocco did nothing to offset the revenue losses, leading to a partial reversal of reform. Shalizi and Squire (1986) point out that fiscal policy can also complement trade reform by making tax rates on domestically produced final goods equal to tariff rates on their imports, thereby reducing protection, raising revenue, and allowing tariff rates to be reduced further, as in Malawi, Nigeria and Togo. Another way in which fiscal policy can support trade reform is by ensuring that public investment helps the reforms succeed. Public investment budgets have borne the brunt of expenditure cuts needed for stabilization and adjustment in many countries (Côte d'Ivoire, Mexico, Morocco, the Philippines). But efficient investments in infrastructure and expenditures for research and extension services are important for deriving full advantage from increased trade incentives. Infrastructural inadequacies create serious constraints in low-income economies.[11]

*Trade policy and domestic sector reforms*

External and domestic reforms are best carried out simultaneously because of their complementary effects. The benefits of trade policy reforms have usually been greater when accompanied by domestic economic reforms (Pursell 1989). If market exit or entry is difficult, inefficient firms may remain, and new firms may never get started. Hachette (1988) concluded that Chile's elimination or reduction of many regulatory interventions, particularly in the labour market, and controls inhibiting firms' ability to restructure or close down, were important for the success of the 1974–79 trade reforms. By contrast, regulations that made it costly for firms to restructure or shut down have been a factor in failed liberalization attempts in Poland, Turkey (in the early 1970s), and Yugoslavia. Regulations governing entry of new firms and expansion of established ones apparently slowed the pace of adjustment in other countries such as Mexico, until 1988 (as analysed in World Bank 1988c). Price or wage controls are incompatible with trade policy reforms whose purpose is to alter relative prices. In the presence of rigid labour market controls, firms may have to shed labour or close down in response to import competition even though the workers could have been profitably employed at lower wages. Similarly, industries trying to expand may be unable to bid labour away from contracting sectors with high minimum wages. Financial sector regulations that encourage banks to continue to lend to bankrupt enterprises may dry up the supply of new credit to firms that should be expanding. Regulatory reform in these areas, combined with support for restructuring in the financial and industrial sectors, could magnify the benefits of trade policy reforms.

In some circumstances it is better to introduce external and domestic reforms in sequence. Some domestic reforms are best deferred until the business and financial communities realise that import protection will be reduced. If investment or price controls are removed in highly protected sectors, for example, increased investment and production might be encouraged in the wrong sectors. Sometimes, reforms have generated needs for subsequent infrastructure investments to support export-oriented industries, whose growth could not have been foreseen. Conversely, trade policy reform in some cases may need to wait until a domestic policy is changed. For example, removal of export controls on products that are still heavily subsidised could cause the subsidy budget to balloon or domestic supplies to run short as the products are sold into higher priced world markets.

Since there can be no universal rule for sequencing, analysts need to be sensitive to the potential for complementarity and conflict between various trade and domestic reform measures in the design of reform packages. In particular, because of the importance of the supply response to trade reforms, any domestic policies that create significant bottlenecks ought to be considered for simultaneous reform.

*Public sector policy*

Protection of state-owned manufacturing enterprises has interfered with liberalization programmes in some countries (Argentina, Bangladesh, Chile). Nogues (1987) notes that the first reversals in the 1980 attempt at trade policy reform in Peru came in re-protecting state-owned enterprises. In other cases, buyers have insisted on guarantees of high protection when governments have privatised unprofitable firms (as with Togo's steel mill). Liquidation would probably be preferable to privatisation in these cases. In socialist countries, trade liberalization needs to be accompanied by a phasing out of the central planning and allocation mechanisms, thus allowing the new market signals to be effective at the firm or farm level (Havrylyshyn 1989). Domination of crop output markets by state enterprises may mean that the effects of devaluation on producer prices are realised very slowly, while input prices rise quickly. Meaningful trade liberalization in such cases may entail abolition of the state enterprise (Ecuador, Nigeria) or elimination of its legal monopoly in the import market (Mexico).

A corrupt or inefficient customs service can also reduce the response of the trade sector to reforms, and it would need to be improved as greater reliance is placed on tariffs. The Indonesian government transferred the entire staff of the customs administration to other positions and contracted with a foreign firm to provide a customs service (Barichello 1988). In many cases, administrative deficiencies have led to delays in introducing tariff reforms, export tax rebates, duty relief systems for exporters, and bonded warehouses.

*Sequencing and pacing of trade policy reforms*

In countries with a substantially overvalued exchange rate, priority should go to measures to achieve and maintain a real devaluation, while countries with multiple exchange rates in the goods market can benefit by unifying them at this time. A large real devaluation can make quantitative import restrictions redundant and facilitate their rapid removal (Bolivia, Chile, Ghana, Laos, Mexico, Nigeria, Sri Lanka and Zaire). This shift from commercial policy protection to 'exchange rate protection' is a major step toward neutrality in incentives between exportables and import substitutes and among import substitutes.

Issues related to the sequencing of export and import reforms have also received attention (Corden 1987, Michaely 1986). Introducing export policy reforms (such as temporary admissions or duty drawback schemes) before, or at least at the same time as, import reforms permits an earlier export supply response and allows unification of the tariff structure to proceed without burdening exporters as low tariffs on inputs are raised. One way to start import policy reform is by replacing non-tariff barriers with tariffs providing roughly the same protection and eliminating tariff exemptions. These measures ought to be followed by moves to make tariff rates lower and more uniform. If revenue is not a serious concern, however, non-tariff barriers could be phased out without introducing equivalent tariffs.

An expeditious reform program is preferable to a prolonged one because the benefits are greater and emerge sooner. Furthermore, long-drawn-out execution of the reform allows opponents time to organise, establish ties with officials carrying out the reforms, and lobby for reversal (Nelson 1989). And partial or indecisive reforms are likely to arouse substantial opposition from those whose protection is being removed, while receiving little support from potential gainers. For these reasons weak reforms have often been reversed, as in Colombia in the mid-1970s and Peru in the late 1970s and early 1980s.

Two factors may, however, argue against rapid reforms. One concerns the losses from transitional unemployment, which could be larger with radical programmes than when changes are pre-announced and phased in over time. In theory, the gradual approach would allow enterprises and individuals to begin to adjust before the reforms are implemented, thereby reducing transitional unemployment. However, there is evidence that labour has in fact been absorbed quite rapidly into expanding industries

(Michaely and others 1990), especially when they had excess capacity, were labour intensive, and required little or easily obtained capital equipment. This finding raises at least some doubt about the severity of transitional unemployment, whether change is rapid or gradual. Also, when import regimes are dominated by quantitative restrictions, introducing import reforms gradually could worsen temporary unemployment because firms wishing to expand would continue to face the delays and procurement problems in inputs and capital equipment typical under such regimes, which greatly delays their response to new opportunities.

A second argument concerns the credibility and likelihood of reversal of reforms. Gradual reforms may be preferable if they are more likely to be sustained than radical reforms, which concentrate the disruption of existing patterns within a short time period. In some countries, this may be politically more difficult to handle than a less concentrated disruption that is spread out over time.

In practice, the optimal pace and intensity of import reform varies from country to country. Some successful reforms have been comprehensive, intensive and fast, as in Bolivia, where non-tariff barriers were eliminated and a strong tariff reform was started virtually overnight. Mexico quickly reduced the coverage of quantitative restrictions and reduced tariffs in about two years. Chile's phasing out of quantitative restrictions was rapid, while tariff reductions took place over five years. Korea has carried out its comprehensive reforms over twenty years, with substantial import liberalization occurring since 1980. It is desirable to announce trade reforms in advance, as Chile and Korea did, even though implementation is spread over a period of years, to give affected activities time to adjust and improve credibility. Whatever the individual circumstances, however, experience in the 1980s indicates that along with decisive, unequivocal actions in the first year to enhance the programme's credibility, five to seven years from the initiation of reforms is sufficient for a substantial liberalization. This should allow time for quantitative restrictions to be phased out, and for tariffs to be reduced to about 15–25 per cent. Further tariff reductions could come in later stages of reform.

## Conclusion

This chapter, by intention, did not focus on the important issues of the international economy that are relevant for developing country policy. Most important, industrial countries' own trade restrictions limit the benefits of developing country reform. Progress in multilateral negotiations affects the gains from unilateral reforms by developing countries. These considerations, however, do not alter the basic conclusions of this chapter.

From the review of theoretical and empirical research on trade policies and reform, three broad conclusions can be drawn. First, developing countries are more open and their trade regimes are more efficient today than a decade ago. But progress in reform has been slower than anticipated in many countries. In particular, while progress has been considerable in reducing quantitative restrictions, much remains to be done in reducing nominal and effective protection levels in a large number of countries. Second, where significant reforms have been credibly implemented along with other complementary reforms, the results in the external sector and economy-wide have been positive. And third, the outcomes have often fallen short of expectations. Macro-economic instability and the absence of complementary policies and conditions have sometimes weakened the supply responses to reforms.

The evidence strongly supports further reform of trade policies. In the future, however, three issues need particular attention. First, trade reforms need to focus on reducing nominal and effective protection levels, and on steeper tariff reductions in order to enhance competition and competitiveness. Second, for increased effectiveness, trade reforms ought to be supported by measures to achieve and maintain macro-economic stability. More weight may need to be given to the consequences of trade and other policy reforms on the fiscal deficit. Furthermore, when the inflation rate is very high and variable, stabilization efforts should precede other reforms. Third, greater attention to complementary policies, investments, and institutions would have a large pay-off. Sometimes, internal sector distortions may be so severe as to block the benefits from trade reforms. In such cases, domestic deregulation and infrastructural and institutional complements must accompany trade reforms. These recommendations should improve the economic response to trade reforms and in so doing enhance their acceptability.

## Notes

*This paper is based on a larger study entitled 'Strengthening Trade Policy Reform' from the Trade Policy Division containing contributions by Sebastian Edwards, Nadav Halevi, Thomas Hutcheson, Andras Inotai, Donald Keesing, Ramon Lopez, Kazi Matin, Garry Pursell, and Alexander Yeats, under the overall guidance of Stanley Fischer and John A. Holsen, and with major inputs, detailed comments, and assistance from many others.

1   Loan recommendation reports; country memoranda; country briefs; audit reports; mission reports; background work for the World Bank (1988a and 1989); IMF reports; and the draft paper from a Ford Foundation project on 'Trade Policy and the Developing World'.

2   Through June 1989, there were 98 adjustment loans from the World Bank to 44 countries that contained significant trade policy components.

3   Among the 40 trade loan recipients, implementation data were available for 24. Detailed findings on implementation refer to the 24, while aggregate data were also considered for the 40 recipients, as well as for 48 non-recipients.

4   Four sets of domestic factors have constrained stronger and more sustained reform efforts. In Kenya, Peru, Yugoslavia and Zimbabwe, vested interests against reform and weak convictions about its benefits combined to undermine commitment to reform. Administrative and institutional bottlenecks and inadequate implementation capacity contributed to implementation setbacks in Bangladesh, Côte d'Ivoire, and Malawi, where reforms to strengthen public sector institutions received inadequate attention. Weak macro-economic performance and conflicts between policy reform and stabilization goals slowed trade liberalization in Morocco and the Philippines and led to its reversal in Argentina and Zambia. And finally, a slow supply response to reform, by reducing the apparent benefits, has undermined the enthusiasm for reform, especially in the low-income countries of Sub-Saharan Africa. These factors were derived from background studies to Thomas and Nash (forthcoming), interviews

with World Bank economists, and case histories of reform (Bhagwati 1978; Krueger 1978; Little, Scitovsky and Scott 1970).

5   Since the export and non-export sectors normally compete for resources, there is a trade-off between the growth rate of exports and non-exports. Consequently, a higher growth of exports does not necessarily mean a higher growth of GDP as an identity. But the evidence indicates that higher export growth is usually associated with higher growth even of the non-export sector. A simple regression of growth of GDP, excluding exports, on export growth shows a highly significant coefficient (0.51, t-statistic = 3.26), though not as large as that of GDP growth, including exports, on export growth (1.29, t-statistic = 8.38).

6   According to a former deputy Prime Minister, these problems influenced the new liberalising policy direction followed in the 1980s (Kim 1987).

7   Short-run negative revenue effects may occur when protection of inputs is principally provided by tariffs. Tariff revenue should increase, however, as expanding exports increase the supply of foreign exchange for imports.

8   He also found a negative effect of exchange rate overvaluation, over and above the effect of the exchange rate on producer price. He interpreted this as indicating that overvaluation is an indication of other distortions in the trade regime that are detrimental to exports (such as scarcity of imported inputs).

9   Public sector marketing boards, especially in Africa, have almost always depressed producer prices, but they have rarely been effective in stabilizing prices, as they were intended to do (Knudson and Nash 1990).

10   Although there is no one-to-one analytical link between fiscal deficit and inflation, large budget deficits do, sooner or later, tend to create high inflation. For an analysis, see Fischer (1989); for some evidence, see World Bank (1988d).

11   For example, a World Bank (1989c) study found that virtually all firms in Nigeria are hooked to (and pay for) the public power grid, yet every one with more than 20 employees has its own generator. In some African countries, fewer than 20 per cent of all telephone calls and 10 per cent of international calls are completed. Lack of road maintenance increases costs to vehicle owners and shippers by up to 50 per cent on paved roads and even more on unpaved roads.

## References

Agarwala, R. (1983), 'Price distortions and growth in developing countries', World Bank Staff Working Paper no. 575, Washington, DC.

Balassa, B. (1982), 'Development strategies and economic performance' in *Development Strategies in Semi-Industrialized Countries*, Oxford University Press, London.

Balassa, B. (1986), 'Economic incentives and agricultural exports in developing countries', paper presented at the Eighth Congress of the International Economic Association, New Delhi, India.

Balassa, B. (1988), 'Incentive policies and agricultural performance in Sub-Saharan Africa'. World Bank PPR Working Paper no. 77, Washington, DC.

Baldwin, R.E. (1989), 'The political economy of trade policy', *Journal of Economic Perspective* (Fall).

Baldwin, R.E. (forthcoming) 'High technology exports and strategic trade policy in developing countries: The Case of Brazilian Aircraft' in G. K. Helleiner (ed.) *New Trade Theory and Industrialization in Developing Countries*, Oxford University Press, New York and London.

Barichello, R.R. (1988), 'Indonesia trade reforms in the mid-1980s: policies, processes and political economy' (mimeo).

Bergsman, J. (1974), 'Commercial policy, allocative efficiency, and X-Efficiency', *Quarterly Journal of Economics*, 88 (August), pp. 409-33.

Bhagwati, J. (1978), *Foreign Trade Regimes and Economic Development*, National Bureau of Economic Research, New York.

Bhagwati, J. and Srinivasan, T.N. (1973), 'The general equilibrium theory of effective protection and resource allocation', *Journal of International Economics*, 3, pp. 259-81.

Binswanger, H. (1989), 'How agricultural producers respond to prices and governments', paper presented at First Annual World Bank Conference on Development Economics, April 27-28, Washington, DC.

Bourgignon, F. and Morrisson, C. (1989), *External Trade and Income Distribution*, Development Centre Studies, OECD, Paris.

Caballero, R.J. and Corbo, J. (1989), 'How does uncertainty about the real exchange rate affect exports?' World Bank PPR Working Paper no. 221, Washington, DC.

Caves, R.E. (1980), 'International trade and industrial organization: introduction', *Journal of Industrial Economics*, 29 (December), pp. 113-118.

Chambers, R. (1989), 'Tariff reform and the uniform tariff', CECTP, World Bank, Washington, DC.

Chenery, H., Robinson, S. and Syrquin, M. (1986), *Industrialization and Growth: A Comparative Study*, Oxford University Press, New York.

Condon, R. and de Melo, J. (1986), 'Industrial organization implication of QR trade regimes: evidence and welfare costs'. Paper prepared for meetings of Applied Econometric Association, Istanbul (December 10-12), World Bank, Washington, DC.

Corbo, V. and de Melo, J. (1987). 'Lessons from southern cone policy reforms', *World Bank Research Observer* 2, no. 2.

Corden W.M. (1974), *Trade Policy and Economic Welfare*, Clarendon Press, Oxford.

Corden, M. (1987), *Protection and Liberalization: A Review of Analytical Issues*, IMF, Washington DC.

Easterly, W.R. and Wetzel, D.L. (1989), 'Determinants of growth: survey of theory and evidence', World Bank PPR Working Paper no. 343, Washington, DC.

Edwards, S. (1989a), 'Openness, outward orientation, trade liberalization and economic performance in developing countries', World Bank PPR Working Paper no. 191, Washington, DC.

Edwards, S. (1989b), *Real Exchange Rates, Devaluation and Adjustment: Exchange Rate Policy in Developing Countries*, MIT Press, Cambridge, Mass.

Erzan, R. (1989), 'Would general trade liberalization in developing countries expand south-south trade?' World Bank PPR Working Paper no. 319, Washington, DC.

Erzan, R., Kuwahara, H., Marchese, S. and Vossenaar, R. (1988), *The Profile of Protection in Developing Countries*, UNCTAD Discussion Paper no. 21, New York.

Findlay, R. (1984), 'Growth and development in trade models' in R. Jones and P. Kenen (eds.) *Handbook of International Economics*, vol.I, North-Holland, Amsterdam.

Finger, J.M. and Lair, S. (1987), 'Protection in developed and developing countries – an overview', *Journal of World Trade Law* 2, no. 6.

Fischer, S. (1989), 'The economics of government budget constraint', World Bank PPR Working Paper no. 224, Washington, DC.

Fischer, S. (1984), *Real Balances, the Exchange Rate, and Indexation: Real Variables in Disinflation*, NBER Working Paper no. 1497, Cambridge, Mass.

Fitzgerald, B. and Monson, T. (1989), 'Preferential credit and insurance as means to promote exports' *World Bank Research Observer* (January) 4, pp. 89-114.

GATT (1980), *The Tokyo Round of Multilateral Trade Negotiations – II Supplementary Report*, Geneva.

Grais, W., de Melo, J. and Urata, S. (1986), 'A general equilibrium estimation of the effects of reductions in tariffs and quantitative restrictions in Turkey in 1978' in T. N. Srinivasan and J. Whalley (eds.), *General Equilibrium Trade Policy Modeling*, MIT Press, Boston.

Grossman, G.M. and Helpman, E. (1989), *Comparative Advantage and Long-run Growth*, National Bureau of Economic Research Working Paper 2809, Cambridge, Mass.

Hachetts, D. (1988), 'Chile: trade liberalization since 1974', paper prepared for conference in São Paulo, April 1988, World Bank, Washington, DC.

Halevi, N. (1989), 'Trade liberalization in adjustment lending', background paper for *Strengthening Trade Policy Reform*, Sec. M89-1454/1, CECTP, World Bank, Washington, DC.

Harberger, A.C. (1974), 'Notes on the dynamics of trade liberalization', prepared for conference on trade liberalization (October), Santiago, Chile.

Harberger, A.C. (1988), 'Issues in the design of tariff reform', CECTP, World Bank, Washington, DC.

Harberger, A.C. (1989), 'Applications of real exchange rate analysis', *Contemporary Policy Issues* 7 (April), pp. 1-25.

Havrylyshyn, O. (1989), *Poland: Policies for Trade Promotion*, UNDP/World Bank Trade Expansion Program, Washington, DC.

Havrylyshyn, O. (1990), *The Timing and Sequencing of Liberalization: Yugoslavia*, Basil Blackwell, London.

Jacquemin, A. (1982), 'Imperfect market structure and international trade: some recent research', *Kyklos*, 35 (Fasc.1), pp. 75-93.

Jaeger, W. (1989), 'The impact of policy on African agriculture: an empirical investigation' (December 14), mimeo, World Bank AFTTF, Washington, DC.

Jung, W and Marshall, P. (1985), 'Exports, growth and causality in developing countries', *Journal of Development Economics*, 18, pp. 1-12.

Kavoussi, R (1984), 'Export expansion and economic growth: further empirical evidence', *Journal of Development Economics*, 14, pp. 241-50.

Keesing, D and Singer, A. (1989), 'How to provide high-impact assistance to manufactured exports from developing countries', CECTP, World Bank, Washington, DC.

Kiguel, M. and Liviatan, N. (1988), 'Inflationary rigidities and orthodox stabilization policies: lessons from Latin America', *World Bank Economic Review*, 2 (September), pp. 273-98.

Kim, M. (1987), 'Korea's adjustment policies and their implications for other countries' in V. Corbo, M. Goldstein and M. Khan (eds.), *Growth Oriented Adjustment Programs*, IMF and World Bank, Washington, DC.

Kim, Y.C. and Kwon, J.K. (1977), 'The utilization of capital and the growth of output in a developing economy', *Journal of Development Economics*, 4, pp. 205-78.

Knudsen, O and Nash, J. (1990), 'Domestic price stabilization schemes in developing countries', *Economic Development and Cultural Change* (January).

Koester, U., Schafer, H. and Valdes, A. (1989), 'External demand constraints for agricultural exports – an impediment to structural adjustment policies in Sub-Saharan African countries', *Food Policy*, 14 (February), no. 3.

Krueger, A.O. (1974), 'The political economy of the rent-seeking society', *American Economic Review*, 64 (June), pp. 291-303.

Krueger, A.O. (1978), *Liberalization Attempts and Consequences*, Ballinger, Cambridge, Mass.

Krueger, A.O. (1981), 'Interactions between inflation and trade objectives in stabilization programs' in W. Cline and S. Weintraub (eds.), *Economic Stabilization in Developing Countries*, Brookings Institution, Washington DC.

Krueger, A.O. and Tuncer, B. (1982), 'An empirical test of the infant industry argument', *American Economic Review*, 72(5), pp. 1142-52.

Krugman, P.R. (1987), Is Free Trade Passé?', *Economic Perspectives*, 1(2), pp. 131–44.

Landau, D. (1983), 'Government expenditure and economic growth: a cross-section study', *Southern Economic Journal*, 49, pp. 783-92.

Linn, J.F. and Wetzel, D.L. (1990), 'Public finance, trade and development: what have we learned?' in V. Tanzi (ed.), *Fiscal Policy in Open Developing Economies*, IMF, Washington DC.

Little, I.M.D., Scitovsky, T. and Scott, M.F. (1970), *Industry and Trade in Some Developing Countries: A Comparative Study*, Oxford University Press, New York.

Lopez, R (1989), 'Trade Policy, Growth and Investment', background paper for *Strengthening Trade Policy Reform*, Sec M89-1454/1, CECTP, World Bank, Washington, DC.

Marsden, K. (1983), 'Links Between Taxes and Economic Growth: Some Empirical Evidence', World Bank Staff Working Paper no. 605, Washington, DC.

Matin, K. (1989), 'Macro-economic environment and trade policy' in *Strengthening Trade Policy Reform*, Sec M89-1454/1, CECTP, World Bank, Washington, DC.

Michaely, M (1986), 'Guidelines for Country Economists for the Review and Evaluation of Trade Policies', World Bank CPD Discussion Paper no. 1986-7, Washington, DC.

Michaely, M., Papageorgiou, D. and Chokso, A. (1991), *Liberalizing Foreign Trade: Lessons of Experience in the Developing World*, Basil Blackwell, London.

Mohammad, S. and Whalley, J. (1984), 'Rent-Seeking in India: Its Costs and Policy Significance', *Kyklos*, 37, pp. 387-413.

Nam, Chong-Hyun (1986), *Export Promoting Policies Under Countervailing Threats: GATT Rules and Practices*, World Bank Discussion Paper no. VPER59, Development Policy Issues Series, Washington, DC.

Nau, H.R. (1989), *Domestic Politics and the Uruguay Round*, Columbia University Press, New York.

Nelson, N.M. (1989), 'The Politics of Long-Haul Economic Reform' in J. M. Nelson, *et. al.* (eds.), *The Politics of Economic Adjustment*, Washington, DC.

Nishimizu, M. and Page, J.M.Jr. (1982), 'Total factor productivity growth, technological progress and technical efficiency change: Yugoslavia 1965-78', *Economic Journal* (December), pp. 920-36.

Nogues, J. (1987), 'The timing and sequencing of trade liberalization – Peru', mimeo, World Bank, Washington, DC.

Nogues, J. (1989), 'Latin America's Experience with Export Subsidies', World Bank PPR Working Paper no. 182, Washington, DC.

O'Connell, S.A. (1989), 'Uniform trade taxes, devaluation and the real exchange rate', World Bank PPR Working Paper Series no. 185 (April), Washington, DC.

Panagariya, A. (1989), 'On the theory of tariff reforms' (mimeo), CECTP, World Bank, Washington, DC.

Pursell, G. (1989), 'Issues in import policy reforms' in *Strengthening Trade Policy Reform*, Sec M89-1454/1, CECTP, World Bank, Washington, DC.

Rajaram, A. (1989), 'Tariff and tax reforms: do bank recommendations adequately integrate revenue and projection objectives?', CECTP, World Bank, Washington, DC.

Ram, R. (1985), 'Exports and economic growth: some additional evidence', *Economic Development and Cultural Change*, 33, pp. 415-25.

Rodrik, D. (1988), 'Liberalization, sustainability and the design of structural adjustment programs', CECPT, World Bank, Washington, DC.

Romer, P.M. (1989), 'What determines the rate of growth and technological change?', World Bank PPR Working Paper Series no. 279, Washington, DC.

Sachs, J. (1987), 'Trade and exchange rate policies in growth-oriented adjustment programs', Department of Economics, Harvard University, Cambridge, Mass.

Schiller, C. (1988), *The Fiscal Role of Price Stabilization Funds: The Case of Côte d'Ivoire*, IMF Working Paper, Washington, DC.

Scully, G.W. (1988), 'The political economy of free trade and protectionism', paper prepared for Conference on the political economy of neo-mercantilism and free trade, June 9-11, Big Sky, Montana.

Shalizi, Z. and Squire, L. (1986), 'Tax policy for Sub-Saharan Africa', Country Policy Department, Resource Mobilization Division, World Bank, Washington, DC.

Sturzenneger, A. (forthcoming), 'The political economy of price discrimination in the Argentine pampas' in A. O. Krueger, M. Schiff and A. Valdez (eds.), *The Political Economy of Agricultural Pricing Policy in Selected Latin American Countries*, World Bank, Washington, DC.

Taylor, L. (1988), *Economic Openness: Problems to the Century's End*, World Institute for Development Economics Research, Helsinki.

Thomas, V. (1989), 'Developing Country Experience in Trade Reform', World Bank PPR Working Paper no. 295, Washington DC.

Thomas, V. and Nash, J. (forthcoming), *Best Practices Lessons in Trade Policy Reform*, Oxford University Press, New York.

UNCTAD (1986), *Protectionism and Structural Adjustment, Introduction and Part I*, TD/B/1081, Geneva.

Valdes, A. and Zietz, J. (1980), *Agricultural Protection in OECD Countries: Its Costs to Less Developed Countries*, International Food Policy Institute, Washington, DC.

Wade, R. (1988), 'Taiwan, China's duty rebate system', CECPT, World Bank, Washington, DC.

World Bank (1986a), 'Korea: managing the industrial transition', Report no. 6138-KO, Washington, DC.

World Bank (1986b), *World Development Report*, Washington, DC, pp. 106-9.

World Bank (1987a), 'Trade and industrial policies in the developing countries of East Asia', Report no. 6952 Washington, DC.

World Bank (1987b), *World Development Report 1987*, Washington, DC.

World Bank (1988a), *Adjustment Lending: An Evaluation of Ten Years of Experience*, Policy and Research Series no. 1, Washington DC.

World Bank (1988b), 'Chile – agricultural sector brief', LA4AG (May 25), Washington, DC.

World Bank (1988c), 'Mexico: trade policy reform and economic adjustment', Report 7314-ME (August 23), LATTF, Washington, DC.

World Bank (1988d), *World Development Report 1988*, Washington, DC.

World Bank (1989a), 'The long-term perspective for Sub-Saharan Africa: a strategy for recovery and growth', Washington DC.

World Bank (1989b), 'The role of foreign direct investment in financing developing countries', Board Memorandum (July 11), Washington, DC.

World Bank (1990), 'Report on Adjustment Lending II', Board Memorandum (March), Washington, DC.

# Trade policy reform and economic performance in developing countries: assessing the empirical evidence

## Introduction

Trade policy reforms are a significant component of the structural adjustment efforts undertaken by many developing countries in response to the economic difficulties of the 1980s, and have featured prominently in the conditionality attached to World Bank lending for structural adjustment, as well as IMF stabilization agreements. By the end of fiscal year 1989, the Bank had concluded 143 structural loan agreements with 62 countries and structural adjustment lending was accounting for a third of all IBRD lending. Almost 70 per cent of structural adjustment loans (SALS) contained trade policy reform conditionality: of the 143 loans made up to mid-1989, 98 contained significant trade policy components (World Bank, 1990).

The structure of conditionality, defined as the proportion of loans containing one or more conditions in various policy areas, is shown in Table 4.1 for a sample of 51 adjustment loans made to 15 countries during the period 1980-87. Trade policy reforms were required in almost 80 per cent of the sample programmes; in the highly indebted middle income countries, the share increases to 90 per cent. Table 4.2 shows the specific areas of trade reform included in SALs, for a sample of 40 countries that received loans with a significant trade component during 1980-87. Exchange rate flexibility, export incentives, liberalising imported inputs for exports, and substitution of quantitative restrictions by tariffs were widely used conditions.

Trade policy reform can take several forms and may involve a move towards neutrality, or liberalization, or both. There is an extensive and well-known literature which provides a theoretical rationale for trade policy reform.[1] A lowering of the general level of protection is expected to reduce the costs of protection resulting from the misallocation of resources in production, and the consumer welfare losses due to the divergence between the domestic and world prices of traded commodities. A shift towards greater neutrality by equalising the incentives for export and import substitution production, is expected to improve the allocation of resources in production of traded goods. In addition to the static efficiency gains, trade policy

Table 4.1   *Content of World Bank structural adjustment lending operations, 1980-87 (total number of loans with conditions in various policy areas (%))*

| | Sub-Saharan Africa | Highly indebted middle income countries | Other developing countries | All countries |
|---|---|---|---|---|
| *Item* | (13) | (22) | (16) | (51) |
| 1. Exchange rate | 30.8 | 18.2 | 0.0 | 15.7 |
| 2. Trade policies | 76.9 | 90.9 | 62.5 | 78.4 |
| 3. Fiscal policies | 61.5 | 72.7 | 56.3 | 64.7 |
| 4. Budget/public expenditures | 69.2 | 50.0 | 37.5 | 51.0 |
| 5. Public enterprise | 61.5 | 54.5 | 43.8 | 52.9 |
| 6. Financial sector | 38.5 | 36.4 | 43.8 | 39.2 |
| 7. Industrial policy | 58.3 | 9.1 | 25.0 | 25.5 |
| 8. Energy policy | 7.7 | 13.6 | 50.0 | 23.4 |
| 9. Agricultural policy | 76.9 | 40.9 | 37.5 | 9.05 |
| 10. Other | 23.1 | 9.1 | 12.5 | 13.7 |

*Source:* World Bank, *Adjustment Lending: An Evaluation of Ten Years of Experience* (Washington, DC, 1988), Table 4.2.

reform is expected to generate productivity growth effects. Exposure to international competition forces domestic producers to raise their productivity performance to international levels, and the expansion of market size through exports allows scale economies to be realised.

The relationship between trade policy orientation and economic performance in developing countries continues to be the subject of professional debate and argument.[2] There is an absence of consensus about the appropriate analytical framework within which to estimate the effects of trade policy reform. As noted by Michalopoulos (1987, pp. 46-7):

the analytical framework . . . falls short of providing a quantitative structure for linking inputs (policy action) and output (macro-economic performance) . . . Indeed, the framework has little to say about the quantitative impact of key components of policy reform (e.g. trade reform, improvements in pricing, public investment reviews and the like) on medium term economic performance . . .

Consequently, disagreements arise over the interpretation of the empirical evidence on the impact of trade policy re-orientation.

Early studies of the potential efficiency gains that would result from trade liberalization concentrated on estimating the size of the 'Harberger triangle' costs associated with protection. Typically, the estimated figures were small, often less than 5 per cent of GNP.[3] More recently, attempts to estimate the efficiency gains associated with trade liberalization have used computable general equilibrium models

Table 4.2   *Main components of trade policy in 40 adjustment loan countries*

| Area of reform | Significant | Less significant | Negligible | Total | Present | Not present | Total |
|---|---|---|---|---|---|---|---|
| *Overall import policy*[a] | 19 | 10 | 11 | 40 | — | — | — |
| QRs on noncompetitive imports | 12 | 16 | 12 | 40 | — | — | — |
| Protective QRs | 12 | 17 | 11 | 40 | — | — | — |
| Tariff level | 7 | 20 | 13 | 40 | — | — | — |
| Tariff dispersion | 8 | 22 | 10 | 40 | — | — | — |
| Protection level | 13 | 26 | 1 | 40 | — | — | — |
| Schedule of future reduction | 6 | 29 | 5 | 40 | — | — | — |
| Protection studies | — | — | — | — | 28 | 12 | 40 |
| *Overall export policy*[a] | 15 | 14 | 11 | 40 | — | — | — |
| Exchange rate[b] | — | — | — | — | 38 | 2 | 40 |
| Export promotion[c] | — | — | — | — | 33 | 7 | 40 |
| Imports for exports | 17 | 15 | 8 | 40 | — | — | — |

*Notes*

The assessments refer to proposals supported by the Bank. They do not necessarily refer to policy implementation.

[a] Based on judgement on the significance of the overall reform proposals.

[b] Often these were not explicit conditions, but constituted understandings, frequently made under the programme.

[c] Includes such schemes as export credits, insurance, guarantees, and institutional development.

*Source:* World Bank *Adjustment Lending: An Evaluation of Ten Years of Experience* (Washington, DC, 1988), Table 3.1.

which employ calibration counterfactual experiments to trace out the effects of policy changes. Most of these studies aggregate the effects of imperfect competition, scale economies and unproductive rent-seeking activities and it is difficult to separate out the contribution of each effect.[4]

It has been equally difficult to establish strong empirical evidence of a link between trade liberalization and productivity growth.[5] The major NBER project conducted by Krueger and Bhagwati in the 1970s failed to find any firm support for the hypothesis that trade liberalization will stimulate productivity growth (Bhagwati 1978, Chapter 5). Pack (1988, p. 327) concludes a comprehensive review of the empirical evidence on the relationship between trade policy orientation and manufacturing productivity growth in developing countries, thus:

comparisons of total factor productivity growth among countries pursuing different international trade orientations do not reveal systematic differences in productivity growth in manufacturing, nor do the time-series studies of individual countries that have experienced alternating trade regimes allow strong conclusions in this dimension.

This chapter focuses on a separate body of empirical evidence on the relationship between trade policy orientation and economic performance in developing countries, by examining the impact of adopting structural adjustment programmes containing a significant trade policy reform component. The objective of the paper is two-fold. The first is to review the evidence that is available on the effects of trade policy reform programmes, paying particular attention to the methodologies used in the various studies undertaken so far. The second is to present some new evidence on the impact of trade reform SALs, on various indicators of economic performance. The results are obtained using the generalised evaluation methodology, applied to a sample of 80 developing countries covering the period 1981-88.

## Empirical studies of the effects of trade policy reform programmes on economic performance

Three alternative empirical approaches have been used in the literature to analyse the effects of trade policy reform programmes on performance.[6] The 'before-after' approach compares the economy's performance before and after adoption of the programme. While this approach is easy to apply, a major problem with it is that all observed changes are attributed to the programme. Since non-programme determinants of performance will be changing during the observation period, the before-after estimates of programme effects will typically be biased.

The second procedure, known as the 'control group' approach, was designed in part to overcome the inability of the before-after approach to distinguish between programme and non-programme determinants of performance. Pooled time series cross section data are used to compare the performance of countries with programmes to those without. The basic assumption is that programme and non-programme countries are subject to the same external environment, so that by comparing performance changes in the programme countries with the control group of non-programme countries, the effect of the external environment is cancelled out, leaving the difference in group performance to reflect the impact of the programme's trade policy reforms. The problem with this approach is that programme countries differ systematically from non-programme countries prior to the programme period, and bias is introduced, therefore, by the fact that the countries with programmes are not randomly selected.

The third, less direct, approach is to use econometric simulation models to analyse the effects of trade liberalization on performance. One variant of this approach relies on individual country modelling to analyse the effects of trade policy reform programmes on economic performance. Here, the simulations of economy models are used to infer the hypothetical performance of programme policy packages. Comparison of actual outcomes with simulated outcomes can provide insight into the degree to which programme policies have been implemented. A further advantage of this approach is the focus on the relationship between policy instruments and policy targets, which provide information on how policy changes affect the workings of the economy, rather than the final performance outcome. The application of this approach is limited, however, to single country studies where each model incorporates economy-specific structural characteristics.[7]

An alternative simulation approach is an elaboration of the control group methodology and is known as the generalised estimator procedure. In this procedure a regression is carried out with the change in the target variable as the dependent variable, and measures representing external conditions, lagged targets and a dummy for the existence or not of a programme, are used as independent variables. A reaction function is assumed so that the change in a country's policy instruments between the current period and previous period is a function of the difference between the desired values of macro-economic variables in the current period and their actual values in the preceding period. Thus the implicit policy vector generated by the reaction function represents the counterfactual – the policies that would have been undertaken in the absence of a programme. The fundamental assumption made in this procedure is that there is a stable reaction function linking target outcomes in one year with the values assigned to policy instruments in the next. The lagged targets are a proxy for the values of policy instruments in the current year in the absence of a programme. The methodology thus depends on the stability of the policy reaction functions, both across countries and through time – a debatable proposition to say the least. However, it is a sufficient condition for meaningful results to be obtained that the deviations in the reactions of instruments to targets should be random through time and across countries. Provided this condition is met, the margin of error in estimating the counterfactual is likely to be considerably smaller than under the before-after and with-without approaches.

In the discussion that follows, the existing empirical studies of the impact of trade policy reform programmes on economic performance are grouped according to these different approaches.

*Before – after studies*

The study by Michaely *et. al.* (1991) contains detailed case studies of the impact of foreign trade liberalization in nineteen countries over the past twenty years. The synthesis volume (vol. 7) provides a cross country tabulation of the individual country study findings. The impact of trade liberalization is calculated by averaging individual countries' performance during the three year pre- and post-liberalization periods.[8] For real GDP, the data show the average annual growth to be higher in the post-liberalization periods. Data on output growth in the tradable and non-tradable sectors shows accelerated growth in both sectors after liberalization. In periods of 'strong' trade liberalization (when the real exchange rate depreciated), the tradable sector grew much faster than the non-tradable sector in the post-liberalization period. The manufacturing output growth rate fell in the immediate post-liberalization period, and then recovered, with growth slightly higher than before the liberalization. The study does not test for the statistical significance of the differences in performance.

World Bank (1988) examines performance in 40 countries that received structural adjustment loans with a trade policy component. The weighted average of the external balance changed from −3.2 per cent of GDP in 1978-81 to +1.4 per cent in 1982-87. In more than half of the same countries, the growth of exports in 1982-87 was more rapid than in 1965-81.

The before-after impact of trade reform is further tested in World Bank (1989), applying regression analysis to a sample of 40 trade loan countries. The dependent variable is the change in average GDP growth rate after the adjustment loan compared to the growth rate before the loan, relative to the average change in 47 non-trade loan countries. The independent variables are changes in imports, terms of trade and the real exchange rate. Trade liberalization is represented by a dummy variable that assumes a value of 1 during a period of trade loan, and 0 otherwise. The results show the coefficient of the dummy to be positive but statistically insignificant.

*With-without studies*

World Bank (1989) compares export and GDP growth in a sample of 40 countries with loans containing a significant trade reform component, with 47 non-trade loan countries. It is found that the difference in growth performance between the two groups of countries during the adjustment period, was statistically significant.[9]

The impact of trade reform on performance is further tested in World Bank (1989) using a hybrid methodology combining the with-without and before-after approaches. Using a sample of 26 countries that received trade adjustment loans before 1986, and comparing average changes in nine performance indicators for the three year periods before and after the trade loan, it is shown that performance was superior, on average, in the trade loan countries. Calculated across all nine indicators, it was found that trade adjustment countries performed better than the others in 71 per cent of cases. However, the difference of the change in mean values was statistically significant for only one of the indicators, namely import growth.

*Econometric simulation*

Estimates of the impact of trade reform measures on economic welfare can also be made using computable general equilibrium models in which changes in economic welfare are used to measure the impact of trade liberalization. In most cases, estimates are made of the effect of increased import competition on domestic manufacturing in conditions of economies of scale and oligopolistic markets. Rodrik's (1988) estimate for Turkey suggest that the ease of entry and exit is likely to be an important determinant of the size of welfare gain from liberalization: restrictions on market entry lead to a lowering of aggregate welfare gains. Gunasekera and Tyers' (1991) study is a general equilibrium analysis of industrial protection in Korea, which incorporates imperfect competition and scale economies. Simulations of the long-run effects of trade liberalization indicate substantial gains, measured in terms of percentage changes in the main macro variables, from liberalization, with much of the gain accruing as a result of rationalization in the manufacturing sector. The study by Bertola and Faini (1991) simulates the impact of trade liberalization using Moroccan data and shows that the removal of quantity restrictions would have a significant impact on the imports. Devarajan and Rodrik (1989) is a general equilibrium study of tariff removal in Cameroon. The inclusion of scale economies significantly raises the welfare gains from liberalization.

The results of the model simulation approach to estimating the effects of trade liberalization appear to lend support to the case for trade reform. However, the limitation of the techniques need to be recognised. The results are often highly sensitive to assumed values of the model parameters. The procedure of maintaining rather than testing hypotheses provides less definite results than econometric, data-based methods, and may be regarded therefore as more of an art than a science (Richardson, 1989).

The generalised estimator procedure has been used recently to examine the impact of World Bank structural adjustment lending (World Bank, 1990) and the International Monetary Fund's stabilization programmes (Khan, 1990). However, we are not aware of any study that applies this approach to the evaluation of trade policy reform.

In summary, the existing literature does not offer convincing empirical evidence on the impact of trade liberalization programmes on economic performance. The results of applying the 'before versus after' method of evaluation are statistically insignificant. Furthermore, this approach is methodologically weak, in that changes due to extraneous influences cannot be separated from the impact of the programme reform measures. Consequently, 'the before-after approach can be useful to show what happened in programme countries, but not why it happened' (Goldstein 1986, p. 3, quoted in Mosley *et. al.* 1991). The 'with and without' approach offers more opportunity for separating out the influence of programme reforms, however, the results obtained from cross-country comparisons for the first half of the 1980s failed to reveal evidence of a statistically significant difference in average performance between the programme and non-programme samples. The single country simulation exercises generally showed positive gains from trade liberalization, but the results obtained from applying this approach are highly sensitive to the assumed values of the model parameters.

In an attempt to overcome some of the deficiencies of previous empirical studies, it was decided to carry out estimations of the effects of trade adjustment programmes using a modified control group methodology. The results of this exercise are reported in the next section.

## Econometric evaluation of trade adjustment programmes

The advocates of trade adjustment policies suggest that among their effects are the following: an increase in the rate of growth of exports; an improvement in the balance of trade; an increase in the rate of growth of output, particularly in the manufacturing sector; and an increase in the rate of growth of productivity. These variables were thus chosen as the principal target, or performance, indicators to be analysed. The methodology employed essentially implies estimating an equation of the form:

$$\delta y_t = \beta_0 + \beta_i Y_{i,t-1} + \beta_j W_{jt} + \beta^{prog} D + e_t$$

Where, for a given country in time period t, $\delta y_t$ represents the change in the target variable y, $Y_{i,t-1}$ is the vector of lagged targets (including, of course, the dependent target), $W_{jt}$ is a vector of world economic variables, and D is a dummy variable representing programme status.

To carry out the analysis a group of 80 low and middle-income developing countries was selected. The choice of these countries was basically determined by the availability of data for most of the macro-economic variables considered during the period of the study (1981-88). Many, although not all, of these countries implemented trade adjustment programmes as part of agreements with either the World Bank or the IMF in some years of the period. The data on the 80 countries for 8 years were pooled to generate 640 observations. A dummy variable was created and assigned a value of 1 for country years in which a programme was in operation and 0 otherwise.

Following the methodology of Goldstein and Montiel (1986), we estimated equations of the form described above. However, it was necessary to make two changes to the methodology to make it more relevant to the problem of trade policy. The first concerns the time period over which it is expected that these programmes might have their desired effects.

The original methodology implicitly assumes that most of the effect of a programme will be observed during the first year of operation. For an IMF stabilization programme this is not necessarily unreasonable. In the case of trade policy reform, however, it is more likely that the effects will tend to accumulate over two or three years. To take this into account we constructed two alternative formulations of the programme dummy by taking weighted averages of its values in the current year with those of the previous year and the previous two years respectively. In the latter case, for example, the dummy would take the value 0.33 in the first year of a programme, 0.67 in the second, and 1.0 in the third and subsequent years. The cumulative effects of the programme would then be picked up by the increments in the value of the dummy in the initial years of a programme. Furthermore, programmes implemented for only one or two years would be given less weight than those applied for three or more years.

The second innovation required to adapt the methodology to trade policy was concerned with the calculation and treatment of the real exchange rate. When one considers the nature of trade adjustment strategies it is clear that the real exchange rate cannot be considered as either purely a target or as purely an instrument. It is in fact a bit of both. On the one hand it is a target in that its level is not directly controlled by the authorities and it is a result of the interaction of a number of policy instruments with social, political and economic structures. On the other hand, it is an instrument in that the level of the real exchange rate will be one of the main determinants of the outcome of the target variables of a trade adjustment policy – growth, of income, imports, exports and productivity. The dual nature of the real exchange rate was reflected in its treatment in our analysis.

The real exchange rate is included as a target, although the nature of the analysis is such that the effect of policy instruments is captured by the lagged targets and the programme dummy, and indeed we were able to analyze the effect of programmes on the real exchange rate. In order to incorporate a useful analysis of the real exchange rate it is inadequate simply to use the traditional formula

$$\frac{E.P_F}{P_D}$$

in which E represents the nominal exchange rate, $P_F$ some external price index and $P_D$ a domestic price index, all expressed as an index based on an arbitrary year for all countries. When measured in this way it is meaningless to compare the level of the real exchange rate across countries.

Since the level of the real exchange rate was to be considered as a target/instrument in the study it was necessary to be able to compare levels across countries. One possible solution would have been to calculate a real exchange rate measured relative to a purchasing power parity equilibrium. However, this would have had two major problems. The first is that a purchasing power parity does not necessarily measure an equilibrium exchange rate, since this is also dependent on the overall stance of other policy instruments, as well as external conditions and non-trade currency flows. Secondly it is in practice very difficult to calculate purchasing power parities for many countries due to a lack of detailed data.

It was decided to adopt a measure of exchange rate disequilibrium which took into account the overall structure of the balance of payments, including the capital account, but which was easily calculable from relatively aggregate balance of payments data. The basic idea is that the balance of payments may be divided, very broadly, into three types of flows: variable, fixed and residual.

Variable flows are all those which might, in principle, be sensitive to exchange rate movements. The main examples of these are imports and exports of goods and non-factor services, and short term capital movements, including errors and omissions. Fixed flows would basically consist of factor payments and direct foreign investment. Finally, residual flows would largely be other foreign indebtedness and changes in the reserves. The estimation of the exchange rate disequilibrium is then made by calculating the exchange rate change required to make residual flows equal to zero, assuming a unit price elasticity for the variable flows. It can easily be shown that this deviation is given by the formula:

$$d = \frac{F + \sqrt{F^2 + 4EI}}{2E} - 1$$

where E is the sum of variable inflows, I the sum of variable outflows, and F is net fixed outflows. A positive d suggests an overvalued exchange rate, and a negative value an undervalued rate.

The above result shows that, without reference to other data, it is possible to calculate a crude measure of overall balance of payments disequilibrium. This calculation was made for all the country and year observations. For each country, the year in which the value of the deviation from equilibrium was smallest in absolute terms was chosen as the base year for the calculation of the real exchange rate index,

using the traditional formula noted above.
The value of the index in the base year was calculated by the formula:

$$\frac{100}{(1 + d)}.$$

Thus if, in the base year, the exchange rate was judged to be undervalued by 5% ($d = -0.05$), the index would take the value 105. This real exchange rate index was thus broadly comparable in levels across countries, but for each country was consistent with movements of prices and nominal rates from year to year.[10]

### Estimation and results

Following this methodology, regression equations were estimated on the pooled data. The variables used to represent external conditions were the growth in the volume of world trade (gWD) and the change in the terms of trade of the country concerned (gTOT). The performance variables analysed were:

| | |
|---|---|
| Growth of GDP | (gGDP) |
| Growth of exports of goods | (gXG) |
| Level of the real exchange rate | RER |
| Growth of labour productivity | gPROD |
| Balance of trade as a % of GNP | BOT |
| Growth of imports of goods | gIMP |
| Growth of manufacturing value added | gMAN |

The dummy variables included, as alternatives, were DUM1, which took a value of 1 if a programme was in operation and 0 otherwise, DUM2 which was an average of DUM1 over two years, and DUM3, which was an average of DUM1 over three years. A typical equation estimated was of the form:

$$\delta g GDP_t = \beta_0 + \beta_1 gWD_t + \beta_2 gTOT_t + \beta_3 gXG_{t-1} + \beta_4 BOT_{t-1} + \beta_5 RER_{t-1} + \beta_6 gGDP_{t-1} + \beta_7 DUM1$$

where $\delta$ is the first difference operator. The results of the estimations are summarised in Table 4.3.

The lagged performance and world demand variables in most cases show expected signs and were usually significant. Thus acceleration in GDP and export growth were found to be positively associated with the growth of world trade.

An improvement in the terms of trade tended to reduce export growth and increase import growth, the effect being more statistically significant in the case of exports. Also, as might be expected, an improvement in the terms of trade tended to be associated with a revaluation of the real exchange rate.[11] Finally, an improvement in the terms of trade is also reflected in an improvement in the trade balance as a proportion of GNP.[12]

The lagged targets were useful in explaining changes in the performance variables. In every equation the lagged value of the target variable showed a statistically

**Table 4.3** *Regression results: programme dummy*

| Dependent | gWD$_t$ | gTOT$_t$ | gXG$_{t-1}$ | BOT$_{t1}$ | RER$_{t1}$ | gGDP$_{t-1}$ | gIMP$_{t-1}$ | gMAN$_{t-1}$ | gPROD$_{t-1}$ | DUM1 | DUM2 | DUM3 |
|---|---|---|---|---|---|---|---|---|---|---|---|---|
| δgGDP | 0.13152 (2.27307) | −0.02274 (−1.49866) | 0.02014 (1.75267) | −0.00018 (−1.41410) | 0.00926 (1.45525) | −0.74883 (−19.30439) | | | | 0.00393 (0.83475) | | |
| δgGDP | 0.13040 (2.25232) | −0.02314 (−1.52384) | 0.01997 (1.73775) | −0.00018 (−1.41853) | 0.00919 (1.44450) | −0.74931 (−19.32394) | | | | | 0.00483 (0.91215) | |
| δgGDP | 0.12831 (2.21001) | −0.02334 (−1.53536) | 0.01985 (1.72639) | −0.00018 (−1.41985) | 0.00924 (1.45355) | −0.74968 (−19.33451) | | | | | | 0.00540 (0.91263) |
| δgXG | 0.54600 (2.24141) | −0.42786 (−6.74636) | −0.87352 (−18.06713) | −0.00154 (−2.87885) | 0.02585 (0.96485) | 0.46490 (2.84841) | | | | 0.00399 (0.20172) | | |
| δgXG | 0.54191 (2.22322) | −0.42916 (−6.75942) | −0.87384 (−18.07496) | −0.00155 (−2.89559) | 0.02483 (0.92694) | 0.46483 (2.84922) | | | | | 0.01015 (0.45718) | |
| δgXG | 0.53589 (2.19253) | −0.42978 (−6.76519) | −0.87420 (−18.07927) | −0.00155 (−2.90132) | 0.02463 (0.92068) | 0.46404 (2.84469) | | | | | | 0.01322 (0.53135) |
| gRER | −0.17604 (−0.95849) | −0.18353 (−3.81015) | −0.07197 (−1.97264) | −0.00013 (−0.32393) | −0.11594 (−5.73744) | −0.19022 (−1.54483) | | | | 0.00786 (0.52591) | | |
| gRER | −0.17286 (−0.94025) | −0.18302 (−3.79513) | −0.07207 (−1.97479) | −0.00012 (−0.28799) | −0.11430 (−5.65587) | −0.19185 (−1.55814) | | | | | −0.00006 (−0.00358) | |
| gRER | −0.16339 (−0.88652) | −0.18134 (−3.75862) | −0.07157 (−1.96138) | −0.00010 (−0.24932) | −0.11265 (−5.58230) | −0.19177 (−1.55800) | | | | | | −0.01074 (−0.57132) |
| δgIMP | 0.09912 (0.54053) | 0.12425 (2.62210) | 0.01650 (0.45400) | 0.00107 (2.66625) | 0.08727 (4.35717) | 0.59407 (4.52063) | −0.97721 (−23.08028) | | | −0.00725 (−0.49102) | | |
| δgIMP | 0.09875 (0.53805) | 0.12426 (2.61855) | 0.01662 (0.45724) | 0.00106 (2.64997) | 0.08649 (4.31896) | 0.059464 (4.52444) | −0.97662 (−23.07505) | | | | −0.00398 (−0.24026) | |
| δgIMP | 0.09580 (0.52047) | 0.12345 (2.59957) | 0.01644 (0.45217) | 0.00105 (2.63087) | 0.08562 (4.28022) | 0.59469 (4.52466) | −0.97640 (−23.07323) | | | | | 0.0009 (0.0509) |
| δgMAN | 0.25016 (2.23995) | 0.45649 (1.59870) | 0.03524 (1.65882) | −0.00028 (−1.13437) | 0.01293 (1.04994) | | | −0.77999 (−18.27287) | (1.45768) | 0.01332 | | |
| δgMAN | 0.24665 (2.20895) | 0.04561 (1.56806) | 0.03491 (1.64425) | −0.00028 (−1.13923) | 0.01234 (1.00010) | | | −0.78092 (−18.29895) | | | 0.01633 (1.59932) | |
| δgMAN | 0.24070 (2.15080) | 0.04539 (1.55802) | 0.03447 (1.62229) | −0.00028 (−1.12698) | 0.01278 (1.03462) | | | −0.78178 (−18.29815) | | | | 0.01598 (1.40303) |

Table 4.3 (contd)

| | | | | | | | | |
|---|---|---|---|---|---|---|---|---|
| $\delta g$PROD | 0.13441 (0.56460) | 0.00718 (0.08825) | 0.06340 (1.09985) | 0.00034 (0.48121) | −0.02814 (−0.89634) | 0.13350 (1.37513) | −1.02244 (−13.50645) | 0.01286 (0.67348) |
| $\delta g$PROD | 0.11105 (0.46264) | 0.00488 (0.05997) | 0.06070 (1.05203) | 0.00034 (0.48175) | −0.02821 (−0.89999) | 0.12945 (1.33276) | −1.02427 (−13.54230) | 0.02064 (0.95779) |
| $\delta g$PROD | 0.08076 (0.33180) | 0.00135 (0.01660) | 0.05869 (1.01721) | 0.00033 (0.47486) | −0.02821 (−0.90115) | 0.12581 (1.29504) | −1.02661 (−13.57746) | 0.02881 (1.17826) |
| $\delta$BOT | 9.93720 (1.46658) | 0.54678 (5.90475) | −0.10248 (0.42583) | −1.27718 (−7.20698) | −4.26122 (−1.79643) | (−0.98326) | 0.22317 (0.42543) | |
| $\delta$BOT | 9.32174 (1.44145) | 9.88522 (5.86840) | 0.53259 (0.41488) | −0.10277 (−7.23023) | −1.31149 (−1.84555) | −4.27597 (−0.98724) | | 0.44165 (0.74976) |
| $\delta$BOT | 9.14689 (1.41042) | 9.87543 (5.85859) | 0.52194 (0.40648) | −0.10277 (−7.22880) | −1.30483 (−1.83808) | −4.31047 (−0.99522) | | 0.47688 (0.72230) |

*Note*

t ratios are in brackets

meaning of symbols is given in the text

$\delta g$ is the first difference operator

significant negative correlation with the change in the dependent target. However, this relationship is not economically significant as it only reflects the fact that growth rates tend to decelerate when they are high and accelerate when they are low. The same relationship would be found for any bounded random variable. Among the economically significant relationships found was a positive association between lagged GDP growth and the acceleration of export growth. This would be consistent with the idea that in the short run export growth may be inversely correlated with output growth as increased internal demand tends to draw resources away from the export sector. The positive coefficients on the lagged real exchange rate in the import equation are also to be expected, as they suggest that imports are inversely correlated with the real exchange rate. There is also a surprising significant positive coefficient on lagged GDP in the import equation. This implies a negative relationship between GDP and import growth, contrary to almost all empirical studies. However, it is possible that the result is only the consequence of collinearity between lagged imports and lagged GDP included as independent variables in the equation.

The most surprising result of the whole exercise, however, was that for none of the performance variables were any of the dummies representing trade reform programme status found to be statistically significant. This might suggest, then, that such programmes have no impact on performance. However, such a judgement would be premature. Among the performance variables we included changes in the real exchange rate. This implies that there is no apparent relationship between programme status and movements in the real exchange. However, as has been pointed out previously, devaluation of the real exchange rate is almost always a central feature of a trade adjustment strategy. We cannot then conclude that trade reform policies have no effect, since our results suggest that countries which embark on reform programmes under the auspices of the multilateral lending institutions are no more likely to adopt trade policy reforms than those which do not.

This is obviously an important conclusion as far as the lending agencies are concerned. It might be a reflection of the fact that conditionality is difficult to enforce. On the other hand it might also be the result of the generalised adoption of trade reform policies by countries with no formal agreement with the lending institutions. If our intention is to judge the effectiveness of trade reform policies, the previous results indicate the importance of identifying programme countries on the basis of the policy packages adopted rather than by statements of intent.

Such an approach is obviously fraught with difficulties. The first of these is how one identifies a country implementing a trade reform strategy. The main problem is how the combination of instruments can be weighted to make the judgement about whether a country is reforming or not. The criteria adopted inevitably introduce a large degree of subjectivity into the assignation of countries into the categories of reformers or non-reformers.[13]

As a first step in this direction we attempted to identify reforming countries purely on the basis of exchange rate undervaluation. This is not to suggest that trade reform only consists of maintaining a certain real exchange rate. Simply that, given the central importance of exchange rate policy for trade adjustment strategies, it is highly probable that countries with undervalued exchange rates will also be reforming countries. The degree of undervaluation of the exchange rate could then be used as a more general indicator of policy stance.

In order to maintain the consistency of the methodology a dummy variable was created with a value of 1 for country-year observations when the exchange was undervalued by 10% or more, on the basis of the calculation described previously.[14] This dummy variable was then used as an indicator of reform programme status. As in the case of the programme dummy in the first part of the study, two alternative versions -averages over two and three years to pick up lagged effects- were calculated. The equations described previously were then re-estimated with the real exchange rate dummy in place of the programme dummy. The results are shown in Table 4.4. In this case the results are only reported for the equations in which the unlagged dummy is included, since in no case were more significant results obtained with the 2- and 3-year lagged versions.

Broadly speaking the effects of the two external condition variables (gWD and gTOT) and the lagged target variables on the changes in the targets were very similar to those obtained in the previous set of estimations. The differences occurred with the coefficient of programme dummy. This was statistically significant in two cases. In the first it was positively associated with changes in the real exchange rate (with a t-statistic of 12.95). This was hardly surprising, given the way in which this dummy had been calculated originally. The other significant result was a negative coefficient of the growth of imports (t-statistic 3.42), suggesting that import growth tends to be reduced by trade reform programmes. This, also, is not a surprising result. The immediate reason why many countries adopt trade reform programmes is a fundamental disequilibrium in the balance of payments. If the policy does not reduce import growth, at least in the short and medium term, it will be unsustainable. It might also be interpreted more simply to mean that real devaluation slows import growth. It is important to note that the effect of the programme dummy on imports does not extend to the overall balance of trade.

Although the expected positive sign was found in this equation the coefficient was not statistically significant. It is not even certain that a trade reform programme based upon an undervalued exchange rate will improve the balance of trade in the short term. This is probably the result of the relatively low price elasticities of both import and exports of developing countries. The programme dummy had no significant effect on any of the other target variables.

## Conclusions

The overall conclusion of this study must be that there is no empirical evidence to suggest that economic performance benefits from trade reform strategies. This is consistent with the rather ambiguous evidence from other sources presented in the first half of this chapter. This conclusion must, however, be qualified for a number of reasons.

The first of these is that, by their nature, if trade reform strategies are going to be successful their effects will not be immediate. While the different specifications

Table 4.4  *Regression results: exchange rate dummy*

| Dependent | $gWD_t$ | $gTOT_t$ | $gXG_{t-1}$ | $BOT_{t-1}$ | $RER_{t-1}$ | $gGDP_{t-1}$ | $gIMP_{t-1}$ | $gMAN_{t-1}$ | $gPROD_{t-1}$ | DUM-RER |
|---|---|---|---|---|---|---|---|---|---|---|
| $\delta gGDP$ | 0.13234 (2.28684) | −0.02196 (−1.44318) | 0.02023 (1.75901) | −0.00017 (−1.31754) | 0.00778 (0.97894) | −0.74913 (−19.30331) | | | | 0.00260 (0.47378) |
| $\delta gXG$ | 0.55511 (2.28227) | −0.41677 (−6.51603) | −0.87600 (−18.12229) | −0.00156 (−2.90855) | 0.03444 (1.03138) | 0.46804 (2.86949) | | | | −0.00968 (−0.41952) |
| $\delta RER$ | −0.23018 (−1.41474) | −0.14260 (−3.33286) | −0.06156 (−1.90393) | 0.00026 (0.71757) | −0.29089 (−13.02063) | −0.15254 (−1.39807) | | | | 0.19989 (12.94664) |
| $\delta gIMP$ | 0.11150 (0.61654) | 0.12685 (2.68703) | 0.01532 (0.42683) | 0.00092 (2.31250) | 0.13667 (5.53730) | 0.59083 (4.55211) | −0.98534 (−23.55478) | | | −0.05831 (−3.422701) |
| $\delta gMAN$ | 0.25123 (2.24252) | 0.04793 (1.63981) | 0.03468 (1.62854) | −0.00026 (−1.05084) | 0.01774 (1.14245) | | | −0.77963 (−18.21451) | | −0.00178 (−0.16147) |
| $\delta gPROD$ | 0.13356 (0.55930) | 0.01524 (0.18569) | 0.06726 (1.16738) | 0.00038 (0.53132) | −0.04089 (−1.05824) | | | 0.13991 (1.44380) | −1.02281 (−13.48281) | 0.01369 (0.54958) |
| $\delta BOT$ | 9.25164 (1.4372) | 10.01778 (5.90358) | 0.59341 (0.46272) | −0.10002 (−7.03582) | −2.10191 (−2.37229) | −4.10422 (−0.94845) | | | | 0.99416 (1.62355) |

*Notes*

t ratios are in brackets

meaning of symbols is given in the text

$\delta g$ is the first difference operator

of the programme dummies did try to take this into account, there existed an implicit assumption that any time lags involved would be similar across countries. If this were not the case, we could not expected the methodology employed to show any clear results. Indeed, in such a case no cross country study would be likely to yield unambiguous results. This points to an even more profound problem associated with the design and evaluation of trade adjustment strategies.

If we cannot be sure about the speed of the effects of adjustment strategies we must also doubt the universality of their 'beneficial' effects. The theoretical basis of such strategies – the efficiency of competitive markets driven by price signals– makes no reference to either institutional structures or relative levels of development. It might well be that at certain levels of development, countries with an appropriate institutional structure could benefit from a more liberal trade strategy, whereas others will not. This might explain the difficulty in obtaining clear results from large cross-country studies.

The very absence of results is in itself important. It points towards the need for more case-by-case analysis, in order to identify the conditions under which trade liberalization strategies may be successful. This would also pave the way towards a clearer understanding of the mechanisms whereby foreign competition stimulates or retards the process of development.

## Notes

1   For recent examples, see World Bank (1987), Bhagwati (1988), and Thomas and Nash in this volume. In this chapter, the terms 'trade liberalization' and 'trade policy reform' are used interchangeably.

2   Compare, for example, Bhagwati's (1987, p. 257) claim that 'the question of the wisdom of an outward-oriented (export promoting) strategy may be considered to be settled' with Helleiner's (1990, p. 879) view that 'The World Bank, in particular, has recently directed major research attention to trade and industrialization policy issues, reporting the gist of its conclusions, favoring outward orientation and liberal trade regimes for all, in the 1987 World Development Report. But this research failed to address many of the most interesting questions; was suspect in many circles from its outset because of the known predilections of its organizers; and has ultimately proven unconvincing'.

3   The seminal example of this approach is Harberger (1959).

4   The earlier calibration models of trade liberalization applied to developing countries are summarised in Krueger (1984, pp. 545-7). More recent contributions are reviewed in Havrylyshyn (1990) and Richardson (1989).

5   For a detailed assessment of the empirical evidence see Kirkpatrick and Maharaj (1991).

6   Goldstein and Montiel (1986) provide a detailed description of these approaches.

7   This approach is subject to the so-called 'Lucas critique' of *ex ante* econometric policy evaluation, namely that the model parameters may not remain invariant to policy changes.

8   The time periods differ between the countries, and are determined by trade liberalization 'episodes' in each country.

9   As the authors of the report acknowledge, the results are not surprising, since performance was typically poorer among trade adjustment loan recipients at the outset of the lending than among non-recipients.

**10** It should be noted that the higher the value of the index the more devalued is the real exchange rate.

**11** Clearly, in this case the causality is not well defined. If world markets are imperfectly competitive a devaluation (revaluation) of the real exchange rate may cause a decrease (increase) in export prices.

**12** There is no contradiction between the results for imports and exports and that for the balance of trade, as the former are expressed in volumes and the latter in values. It does suggest, though, that price elasticities for both imports and exports are less than one.

**13** For example, many studies group countries into outwardly- or inwardly-oriented economies or intensive or moderate reformers, for reasons assumed to be obvious but not always completely explained.

**14** 10% is obviously an arbitrary figure. It reflects the tendency particularly in the early stages of reform programmes, to 'overshoot' the devaluation necessary to maintain currency equilibrium.

## References

Bertola G. and Faini, R. (1991), 'Import demand and non-tariff barriers: the impact of trade liberalization', *Journal of Development Economics*, vol. 34, pp. 269-86.

Bhagwati, J. (1978), *Foreign Trade Regimes and Economic Development: Anatomy and Consequences of Exchange Control Regimes*, Ballinger, Cambridge Mass.

Bhagwati, J. (1988), 'Export-promoting trade strategy: issues and evidence', *The World Bank Research Observer*, vol. 3 (January).

Devarajan, S. and Rodrik, D. (1989), 'Trade liberalization in developing countries: do imperfect competition and scale economies matter?', *American Economic Review, Papers and Proceedings* (May).

Goldstein, M. (1986), *The Global Effects of Fund-Supported Adjustment Programmes*, Occasional Paper 42, IMF, Washington DC.

Goldstein, M. and Montiel, P. (1986), 'Evaluating fund stabilization programs with multi-country data: Some methodological pitfalls', *IMF Staff Papers*, vol. 33, no.2.

Greenaway, D. and Read, G. (1990), 'Empirical evidence on trade orientation and economic performance in developing countries' in C. Milner (ed.) *Export Promotion Strategies*, Harvester Wheatsheaf, Hemel Hempstead.

Gunasekera, D. and Tyers, R. (1991), 'Imperfect competition and returns to scale in a newly industrialising economy', *Journal of Development Economics*, vol. 34, pp. 223-47.

Harberger, A. C. (1959), 'The fundamentals of economic progress in developing countries – using the resources at hand more effectively', *American Economic Review*, vol. 49, p. 134ff.

Havrylyshyn, O. (1990), 'Trade policy and productivity gains in developing countries: a survey of the literature', *World Bank Research Observer*, vol. 5, no. 1.

Helleiner, G. (1990), 'The macroeconomic effects of Fund-supported adjustment programs', *IMF Staff Papers*, vol. 37, no. 2.

Khan, M. (1990), 'The macro-economic effects of Fund-supported adjustment programs', *IMF Staff Papers*, vol. 37, no. 2.

Kirkpatrick, C. and Maharaj, J. (1991), 'The effects of trade liberalization on industrial sector productivity performance in developing countries' in J.M. Fontaine (ed.), *Libéralisation du Commerce Extérieur et Strategies de Développement Economique*, Presses Universitaires de France, Paris.

Krueger, A. (1984), 'Trade policies in developing countries' in R. W. Jones and P. B. Kenen (eds.) *Handbook of International Economics*, vol. 1, Elsevier, New York.

Michaely, M., Papageorgiou, D. and Choksi, A. (eds.) (1991), *Liberalizing Foreign Trade: Lessons of Experience in the Developing World*, Basil Blackwell, Oxford.

Michalopoulos, M. (1987), 'World Bank programs for adjustment and growth' in V. Corbo, M. Goldstein and M. Khan (eds.), *Growth-Oriented Adjustment Programs*, IMF and World Bank, Washington, DC.

Mosley, P., Harrigan, J. and Toye, J. (1991), *Aid and Power: the World Bank and Policy-based lending in the 1980s*, Routledge, London.

Pack, H. (1988), 'Industrialization and trade' in H. Chenery and T. N. Srinivasan (eds.), *Handbook of Development Economics*, vols. 1 and 2, Elsevier, New York.

Richardson, J.D. (1989), 'Empirical research on trade liberalization with imperfect competition: a survey', *OECD Economic Studies*, no. 12 (Spring).

Rodrik, D. (1988), 'Imperfect competition, scale economies, and trade policy in developing countries' in R. E. Baldwin (ed.), *Trade Policy Issues and Empirical Analysis*, University of Chicago Press, Chicago.

Thomas, V. and Nash, J. (this volume), 'Trade policy reform: recent evidence from theory and practice'.

World Bank (1986), Structural Adjustment Lending: A First Review of Experience, report no. 6409, World Bank Operations Evaluation Department, Washington, DC.

World Bank (1988), Adjustment Lending: An Evaluation of Ten Years of Experience, Policy and Research Series, no. 1, World Bank, Washington, DC.

World Bank (1989), Strengthening Trade Policy Report, vol. II (November), Country Economics Department, Washington DC.

World Bank (1990), Report on Adjustment Lending II, Country Economics Department (March), Washington DC.

# Impact of trade policy reform in the shadow of the debt crisis

The professional discussion of trade policy reform has been conducted in the general context of its impact on economic efficiency, growth and development performance. This is reflected in the papers collected in this volume. However, in actual fact, many of the current trade policy reforms have to be carried out, not just in a context of general adjustment and development, but in the context of the much more specific requirement of increasing capacity to service external debt obligations. The basic requirement is to achieve an export surplus over and above what would be needed to obtain essential consumption goods or intermediate and capital goods needed for development and devote this surplus to debt servicing. The alternative is to achieve a measure of import substitution in order to save foreign exchange over and above what would be needed or advisable for strictly developmental purposes.

The starting point for any discussion must be the fact that debt service involves for the debtor country a secondary burden, in the form of worsened terms of trade, on top of the primary burden of mobilising and transferring savings at the expense of domestic investment or domestic consumption. This was originally pointed out by Keynes (1936) (based on John Stuart Mill) in connection with the reparations imposed on Germany after World War I. It became a matter of great controversy, Keynes being supported, in different ways, by Pigou, Harry Johnson and Samuelson, but opposed by Ohlin (based on Ricardo), denying the existence of a double burden. On the whole, the facts, as well as analytical logic, are on the side of Keynes and the double burden.

What does this mean for trade policy reform? If either exports or efficient import substitution must be further expanded – it means, for example, that the devaluation which is suggested in the reform package in order to encourage the production of tradables at the expense of non-tradables must be sharper – say by 30% instead of 15%. Since devaluation, as a side effect to the encouragement of tradables, has an inflationary impact and also tends to move the terms of trade against the devaluing country, both these effects will also be increased. This is a particularly serious matter for the indebted countries of Latin America and Africa, since they already suffer from inflationary pressures and deteriorating terms of trade.

The additional exports which are needed to pay debt service, and which hopefully will be produced by the additional devaluation, carry the double burden argued by Keynes. It can, in fact, be shown empirically in the case of the Latin American countries that the quite successful expansion of their volume of exports, particularly in manufactures, has been achieved at the price of deteriorating terms of their trade in manufactures, as well as primary products (Singer 1989), Since, obviously, with their increased exports the debtor countries have to compete with other non-indebted countries, this may result in general price pressures and deteriorating terms of trade for developing countries in general (Sarkar and Singer 1989). Theoretically this secondary pressure on the non-indebted countries should equally affect the developed industrial countries in their exports of manufactures, but their manufactured exports are largely of different types – high-technology manufactures – protected by techno-logical monopoly rents. So the overall effect is that of a deterioration of South-North terms of trade in manufactures, with price pressures affecting most harshly the highly indebted countries, the non-indebted developing countries less harshly and the industrial countries least of all.

To the extent that the additional exports are forced exports, almost literally exports 'at any price', it will be seen that this situation falls within the category of 'immiserizing' growth, made familiar by the writings of Jagdish Bhagwati (Bhagwati 1981). If the deterioration in terms of trade outweighs the increase in volume of exports the situation can become self-defeating. In the words of Irving Fisher, when supporting Keynes in 1933: 'The liquidation of debts cannot keep up with the fall in prices which in causes. In that case, the liquidation defeats itself. While it diminishes the number of dollars owed, it may not do so as fast as it increases the value of each dollar owed . . .' (Fisher 1933). The same result will be obtained if the rate of inflation, as a result of devaluation and import strangulation due to debt service, offsets, or more than offsets, the currency devaluation. Then a new devaluation may be necessary and a vicious circle develops in which Irving Fisher's dictum also comes true.

These effects may not be very important as long as we deal with a single country, particularly if the country involved has only a small share of world markets. The situation is different if the condition of indebtedness extends to a large number of countries and they are all simultaneously forced or advised to expand their exports for the sake of attaining a capacity to service their debts. This clearly can involve a fallacy of composition, and will result in a situation where the Keynes/Fisher argument comes true. Unfortunately, this is the actual situation at the present time, with the many debtor countries among the developing countries simultaneously asked to implement virtually identical adjustment packages, practically all of them involving devaluation and other export-promoting measures.

So far, we have put the case in terms of export expansion rather than import substitution. In current adjustment packages this is where the emphasis lies. Import substitution is treated with suspicion because it is ideologically associated with development strategies of planned industrialisation to which the currently fashionable ideology is opposed. However, in the more thoughtful expositions of the current doctrine, import substitution is accepted as a possible alternative to export expansion, but it is usually qualified as '*efficient* import substitution'. There can be no objection to this. Of course, import substitution should be efficient rather than inefficient. However, exactly the same is true of export expansion. What we want is *efficient* export expansion. An export expansion which is bought at the price of deteriorating terms of trade is not efficient, but immiserizing. Presumably the reason why export expansion is not qualified by the adjective 'efficient' in the same way as import substitution, is that the current ideology treats exports as intrinsically efficient because of world competition. However, it has been argued here that there is such a thing as inefficient export expansion.

It should be obvious that the doubts expressed above regarding trade policy reform in the service of debt payment apply with particular strength, or perhaps exclusively, to a situation of slow world growth, associated protectionism and a generally unfavourable international environment. In fact, there is a good deal of empirical evidence to show that the kind of trade policy reform, in the direction of more outward orientation, now recommended to developing countries has worked better in earlier years of rapid economic expansion during the Golden Years of, say, 1960-73, and that it is far less successful in the unfavourable external environment of more recent years. This precondition of a more favourable international environment for the success of the trade policy reforms is at last beginning to be recognised also by the IMF and World Bank. The logic of this is that trade policy reform and structural adjustment must not be limited to the developing debtor countries, but must also extend to the creditor countries to which the additional exports are to be sold and the powerful industrial countries which determine the international environment.

### References

Bhagwati, J. (1981), *The Theory of Commercial Policy*, vol. 1, MIT Press, Cambridge, Mass.

Fisher, I. (1933), 'The debt-deflation theory of great depressions', *Econometrica*, vol. 1(4), October.

Keynes, J.M. (1936), 'The German transfer problem', *Economic Journal*, vol. 39.

Sarkar, P. and Singer, H.W. (1989), 'Manufactured exports and terms of trade movements of less developed countries in recent years (1980-87)', IDS Discussion Paper, no. 270 (November).

Singer, H.W. (1989), 'The relationship between debt pressures, adjustment policies and deterioration of terms of trade for developing countries (with special reference to Latin America)', Institute of Social Studies, The Hague, Working Paper Series no. 59 (July).

*S. M. Shafaeddin**

# The effectiveness of nominal devaluation: the influence of the level of development

## Introduction

The literature on the impact of devaluation on export earnings and the supply of tradable goods is inconclusive both at the theoretical and empirical level.[1] Much of the confusion in the literature on devaluation is related to the different assumptions made concerning the nature and characteristics of the devaluating economy. One common weakness of the standard approaches to devaluation is their lack of differentiation between various economies in terms of their level of development, stage of industrialisation, and socio-economic and structural features.

The impact of devaluation on the production and export of manufactured goods depends on: the extent to which devaluation of the nominal exchange rate can be translated into real changes; the impact of real exchange rate devaluation on relative prices, costs and profitability of tradable and home goods; the supply response to changes in relative prices, through capacity utilisation in the short run and the expansion of productive capacity through reallocation of resources to exportables in the longer run; the exchange rate policy of competing countries; and the 'terms of trade effects' of devaluation.

This chapter is limited to an examination of the extent to which nominal exchange rate devaluation is translated into real devaluation in both the short and long run, and to an investigation of whether an economy's level of development influences this process of translation.

## Devaluation in developing countries in the 1980s

In the 1980s a large number of developing countries undertook exchange rate devaluations simultaneously. In fact, 73 out of 111 countries and territories for which data are available, devaluated their nominal exchange rate during the 1980-87 period.[2] The majority of these countries, 70 per cent, began devaluating in 1980-81, and devalued repeatedly thereafter.[3] Simultaneous devaluations by a large number of countries (henceforth collective devaluation) makes improving price competitiveness more difficult for any one country.

Developing countries differ significantly in terms of their level of development and industrial capacity. One would expect, *ceteris paribus*, that the translation of nominal into real devaluation would be higher, at a higher level of development and industrialisation. Higher technological capacity, larger capacity for production of capital goods, and the availability of skilled human resources would tend to contribute to a more flexible production capacity and higher supply elasticities and thereby lessen the inflationary impact of devaluation.

Under ideal conditions, nominal devaluation will result in an equivalent real devaluation. As time passes, however, the real effect of the devaluation may be eroded by inflation.

There is some limited evidence in the literature on the inflationary impact of devaluation for the 1960s and 1970s. This evidence is mostly concerned, however, with single devaluations, rather than the series of discrete devaluations which took place in the 1980s. Harberger (1964), for example, concluded that in Latin American countries a devaluation of about 50 per cent would result in increases in the price level of 20–30 per cent. Cooper (1971), examining the short term (one year) effect of devaluation in more than 30 developing countries in the 1950s and 1960s, concluded that devaluation led to price increases less than the rate of devaluation. A number of other studies for the 1970s have also shown that nominal devaluations were partially translated into real devaluation in the subsequent one to two year period.(4) Nevertheless, it appears that this impact has been gradually eroded over time. Edwards (1989) analysed 29 devaluations between 1962 and 1979 and found that on average, nominal devaluation of 10 per cent resulted in real devaluation of about 7 per cent in the first year after devaluation, declining to about 5 per cent after three years. Not surprisingly, the erosion was found to have been less severe in countries where macro-economic restraint policies had been implemented.

There is, however, little comprehensive evidence, to our knowledge, on the inflationary impact of devaluation in developing countries for the 1980s. Nor are we aware of any empirical study on the influence of the level of development on the translation of nominal into real devaluation.[5]


## Methodology, definitions and data

To investigate the extent of translation of nominal exchange rate (NER) devaluation into real exchange rate (RER) devaluation, the index of 'effectiveness of nominal devaluation' used by Edwards (1989) is employed, where:

$$I = \frac{\text{percentage change in RER}}{\text{percentage change in NER}} \times 100$$

This index is measured for two periods: short run – between one year before the first devaluation and the year of devaluation ($I_1$); long run – between one year before the first devaluation and the year of the last devaluation ($I_2$). The period covered is 1980-87.

The value of I ranges between 0 and 100. $I = 100$ would imply that normal devaluation is fully translated into real devaluation, and $I = 0$ means that no real exchange rate devaluation was achieved. I takes a positive value.[6]

The real exchange rate is measured as the nominal exchange rate deflated by the consumer price index (CPI), corrected for the changes in the United States wholesale price index (WPI). Neither index is an ideal measure for estimating the competitiveness of exports. Moreover, the data on both consumer price indices and exchange rates, based on IMF sources, are unreliable for many developing countries, particularly for Sub-Saharan Africa and the low income economies. Only official prices are used in compiling the index, and coverage is often poor.

As far as the short term is concerned, $I_1$ could be distorted in cases where inflation was already high in the year of the devaluation and devaluation was used to adjust to rising domestic prices. Hence, as an additional indicator, the changes in the rate of inflation in the year of the first devaluation and the subsequent year are measured to investigate whether devaluation led to additional inflation. Obviously, the inflationary pressure or its acceleration might not necessarily be caused by devaluation alone since there are a large number of other factors influencing inflation.

The choice of sample countries was governed by the availability of data. The sample covered a total of 60 countries, which were grouped into four income categories.[7] Because of their particular exchange rate arrangements, the Francophone countries were excluded.

## Empirical results

Table 6.1 provides data on the distribution, in different per capita income groups, of the countries whose inflation accelerated during the year of the first devaluation in the 1980s and/or the subsequent year. For the sample countries as a whole the acceleration of inflation is more widespread in the first year of devaluation than in the following year. Inflation accelerated in about two thirds of the countries concerned in the year of devaluation, as against 45 per cent in the subsequent year. In over a quarter of countries, inflation accelerated in both years, but these countries, with three exceptions (Jamaica, Sri Lanka and Nepal) had already shown very high rates of inflation in the year before the first devaluation and it is very likely that 'other factors' played a significant role in the acceleration of inflation. The proportion of countries where inflation accelerated also varies across per capita income groups. Judged by the magnitude of this proportion, the highest income group shows the lowest inflationary impact in the year of devaluation. While the inflationary impact of devaluation in this year increases sharply at the second and third income level, it declines, through moderately, for the lowest income group.[8]

Table 6.1  *Distribution of sample countries whose inflation accelerated during the first and second year of the first devaluation, 1980–87*

| Per capita GDP group | Total no. of sample countries | Countries where inflation accelerated in: | | | | | |
| | | first year | | second year | | both years | |
| | | No. | % | No. | % | No. | % |
|---|---|---|---|---|---|---|---|
| greater than $1500 | 13 | 6 | 46 | 7 | 53 | 5 | 38 |
| $1500 – $800 | 13 | 10 | 77 | 5 | 38 | 4 | 31 |
| $800 – $400 | 8 | 6 | 75 | 2 | 25 | — | — |
| less than $400 | 17 | 10 | 59 | 9 | 52 | 5 | 29 |
| *Total* | 51 | 32 | 62 | 23 | 45 | 14 | 27 |

*Note*
Excludes Francophone Africa.

According to Table 6.1, in the year following the first devaluation, the inflationary impact declines significantly in the middle income group, and slightly in the lowest income group, but increases in the highest income group. For the highest income group, the proportion of countries whose inflation rate accelerated in the year of the first devaluation as well as the subsequent year, is the highest.

In short, following the first devaluation of the 1980s, acceleration of inflation appears less widespread in the highest and the lowest income group in the year of devaluation. In the subsequent year more countries in the highest income group show acceleration of inflation, and the proportion of countries whose inflation accelerated reduces slowly in the lowest income group while it declines sharply in the other income groups. Possible explanations for such patterns of inflationary impact will be discussed later in the chapter.

The index of effectiveness of nominal devaluation shows a somewhat similar pattern in the short run. According to Table 6.2, $I_1$ was on average highest in the higher income group, 74%, as against 60% for the lowest income group and almost 30% for the other two groups. This indicates that a nominal devaluation of 10 per cent would lead to real exchange rate devaluation of between 3 and 7.4 per cent in the first year of devaluation.[9]

As far as the effectiveness of devaluation is concerned, $I_2$ is obviously more relevant, since as mentioned already, the depreciation of the real exchange rate should be maintained in order to secure the desired changes in the incentive structure. To investigate the effectiveness of nominal devaluation in the long run, a comparison was made between $I_1$ and $I_2$ at various income groups, as shown in Tables 6.2 and 6.3. Table 6.2 compares for various income groups, the incidences of $I_2$ greater than $I_1$. It also compares the average magnitudes of $I_2$ and $I_1$ for various income groups. Table 6.3 provides the distribution of the sample countries according to the magnitude of $I_2$ at various income groups.

Table 6.2  *Comparison of short-term ($I_1$) and long-term ($I_2$) indices of effectiveness of nominal devaluation, 1980-87*

| Descriptions | Per capita income groups | | | |
| --- | --- | --- | --- | --- |
| | *Greater than $1500* | *$800-1500* | *$400-800* | *less than $400* |
| $I_2$ smaller than $I_1$ | 7 | 4 | 1 | 10 |
| $I_1$ equal to $I_1$ | 1 | — | — | — |
| $I_2$ greater than $I_1$ | 5 | 7 | 4 | 2 |
| Not clear due to the lack of data for both indices | 1 | 2 | 2 | 3 |
| Total number of countries | 14 | 13 | 7 | 15 |

| | *Average magnitude of indices (1)* | | | |
| --- | --- | --- | --- | --- |
| $I_1$ | 74 | 2.87 (42.8) | 29.3 | 59.7 |
| $I_2$ | 46.6 | 34.3 (57.2) | 58.7 | 29.6 (33.6) |

*Countries with $I_2$ greater than $I_1$[b]*

| | | | |
| --- | --- | --- | --- |
| Cyprus, Malta Argentina, Republic of Korea, Malaysia | Mauritius Colombia, Turkey, Ecuador, Jamaica, Botswana Thailand | The Philippines, Nigeria, Indonesia, Ghana | Zambia, Zaire |

*Notes*

[a] = $I_1$: short-term index; $I_2$ = long-term index as defined at the bottom of table.

[b] Figures in brackets exclude cases of appreciation of the real exchange rates, i.e., cases where I was negative.

The evolution of the effectiveness of nominal devaluation in the long run confirms the continuation of the tendency noticed in the short term. With a few exceptions, shown at the bottom of Table 6.2, for the majority of countries in the highest and the lowest income group $I_2$ was smaller than $I_1$ indicating that in the majority of countries in these two income groups the effectiveness of devaluation declined in the long run. By contrast, for the second and particularly the third income group, $I_2$ is greater than $I_1$ in most cases, indicating that the effectiveness of devaluation increased over time in these cases.

Moreover, according to Table 6.2 for the income group $400-800 the magnitude of $I_2$ is also, on average, the highest among various groups concerned. For four countries in this group $I_2$ exceeded 60 per cent. Otherwise, if one excludes this group, cross-comparison of the average magnitude of $I_2$ (Table 6.2) and its distribution across income groups (Table 6.3) indicates that in the long run there is an inverse relation between per capita income and the effectiveness of nominal devaluation.

Table 6.3  *Distribution according to the magnitude of the indices of effectiveness of devaluations* ($I_2$) *for various income groups in the sample of countries during 1980-87*[a][c]

| Magnitude of $I_2$ | Per capita income groups ($) | | | | No. | Total countries % |
|---|---|---|---|---|---|---|
| | greater than $1500 (1) | $1500–800 (2) | $800–400 (3) | less than $400 (4) | | |
| | | | Number of countries | | | |
| 100–90 | 1 | — | 1 | — | 2 | 4 |
| 90–80 | — | — | — | — | — | — |
| 80–70 | 2 | 1 | 2 | 1 | 6 | 12 |
| 70–60 | 2 | 3 | 1 | 1 | 7 | 14 |
| 60–50 | — | 3 | — | — | 3 | 6 |
| 50–40 | 2 | 2 | 1 | 3 | 8 | 16 |
| 40–30 | 3 | 2 | 1 | 2 | 8 | 16 |
| 30–20 | 2 | — | 1 | 2 | 5 | 10 |
| 20–10 | 1 | — | — | 4 | 5 | 10 |
| 10–0 | 1 | — | — | 1 | 2 | 4 |
| negative | — | 2 | — | 1 | 3 | 6 |
| *Total* | 14 | 13 | 7 | 15 | 49 | 100 |

*Notes*
[a] The percentage change in the real exchange rate divided by the percentage change in the nominal exchange rate between the year of the last devaluation and one year before the first devaluation in the 1980-87 period.
[b] Appreciation of the real exchange rate despite devaluation.
[c] Does not add up because of rounding.
[d] Excludes Francophone countries.

To study the possible time lag effect of inflation on the magnitude of I, a new index ($I_3$) is calculated and compared with $I_2$ for those countries with high $I_2$ values, as well as a number of other countries, as shown in Table 6.4. As defined at the bottom of the table, $I_3$, unlike $I_2$, takes into account the impact of the inflation rate up to one year after the last devaluation. It is clear from the table that in almost all cases where the magnitude of $I_2$ has been significant, the decline in the magnitude of the index over time, represented by the ratio of $I_3$ to $I_2$, is sharper than the cases where $I_2$ shows smaller magnitude (Botswana and, to some extent Morocco, are two notable exceptions). In other words, the inflationary impact of devaluation increases (the effectiveness of nominal devaluation declines) sharply as time passes.

It should be noted that in some of the countries where the magnitude of $I_2$ is high, the depreciation of the currency was partially caused by 'passive' rather than 'active' devaluation. In cases where the local currency is defined in terms of a composite of currencies, as a result of appreciation of the US dollar against other currencies between 1980-85, the local currency concerned depreciated *vis-à-vis* the

Table 6.4   *Comparison of different long-term indices of effectiveness of devaluation for a limited number of sample countries, 1980–87*

| Country and per capita income group ($) | Indices[a] $I_2$ | $I_3$ | Ratio $I_3 : I_2$ |
|---|---|---|---|
| **Greater than $1500** | | | |
| Cyprus | 72.8 | 46.2 | 0.63 |
| Trinidad | 76.6 | 57.5 | 0.75 |
| Hong kong | 47.3 | 37.3 | 0.79 |
| Republic of Korea | 47.0 | 33.4 | 0.71 |
| Malaysia | 28.1 | 27.4 | 0.97 |
| **$1500 – 800** | | | |
| Mauritius | 53.5 | 30.1 | 0.89 |
| Jamaica | 65.2 | 48.9 | 0.75 |
| Botswana | 68.2 | 53.3 | 0.78 |
| Thailand | 67.3 | 43.7 | 0.64 |
| **$800 – 400** | | | |
| The Philippines | 23.2 | 22.2 | 0.95 |
| Morocco | 74.8 | 57.2 | 0.76 |
| Mauritania | 44.5 | 26.7 | 0.60 |
| **Less than $400** | | | |
| Kenya | 48.3 | 37.4 | 0.77 |
| India | 14.1 | 13.9 | 0.99 |
| Nepal | 14.8 | 3.8 | 0.25 |
| Gambia | 45.9 | 3.0 | 0.65 |

*Note*

[a] $I_3$ = percentage change in the real exchange rate between the year before the first devaluation in the 1980s and one year after the last devaluation (over 1980-87 period), divided by the percentage change in the nominal exchange rate over the same period.

dollar. We define the resulting depreciation as 'passive devaluation'. In the case of 'active' devaluation the local currency would also be devalued *vis-à-vis* the composite basket. Good examples of passive devaluation are Malaysia, Cyprus and Malta in the first income group, Botswana and Mauritius in the second income group, and Kenya, Tanzania and Zaire in the last income group.

## Summary and conclusions

This chapter has examined the difficulties of translation of nominal devaluation into real exchange rate changes in developing countries in four different per capita income groups during 1980-87. It refutes the assumptions of homogeneity of countries usually made in the traditional approaches to devaluation and attempts to investigate the influence of the level of development on the ability to translate nominal devaluation into real devaluation. It concludes that devaluation has involved a significant inflationary impact in most developing countries. For the first year following devaluation, the index of effectiveness of nominal devaluation ranged from 30 to 74 for various per capita income groups, indicating that a nominal devaluation of 10 per cent leads to real devaluation of 3 to 7.4 per cent. As time passes, the long-run index of effectiveness of devaluation (the period between the year before the first devaluation and the year of the last devaluation in the 1980-87 period) declines, reflecting a decline in the effectiveness of devaluation.

Taking per capita income as a rough indicator of the level of development, a distinction was made between the short- and the long-term impact of devaluation. In the short term, the highest income group showed the highest degree of effectiveness of nominal devaluation, and the lowest income group took the second position. As time passed, however, the effectiveness of the nominal devaluation eroded faster in the lowest income group as compared with the highest, but it increased for the two middle income groups. In the long run, in the period between the year before the first devaluation and the year of the last devaluation there appeared to be an inverse association between the per capita income and the indices of effectiveness of devaluation for various income groups, excluding the third one.[10] This group showed the highest degree of effectiveness of devaluation, both over time and in relation to other income groups in the long run.

The unreliability of the data used, and the limited size of the country groupings, mean that the findings of the study – of a positive relationship between the level of development and the effectiveness of nominal devaluation – should be interpreted with caution. Further research on this issue is required.

### Notes

*This study is a modified version of a part of a longer study being published by UNCTAD. The author is a member of the UNCTAD secretariat. The views expressed in this chapter are those of the author and do not necessarily reflect the views of the UNCTAD secretariat.

1   Unless stated otherwise the exchange rate is defined as US$ per unit of currency, and devaluation is defined as the decline in the average value of currency in terms of the dollar.

2   Devaluations of less than 5 per cent are excluded.

3   For more details, see Shafaeddin (1991a).

4   For a review of these studies, see Edwards (1989).

5   Killick (1990) refers to the possible influence of these factors, but does not discuss the point empirically.

6   I will normally assume a positive value. It will be negative if the nominal devaluation (reduction in NER) leads to an appreciation to the real exchange rate (i.e., an increase in RER).

7   The following income per capita grouping were used: (i) greater than US$1500 – 15 countries, (ii) $800-$1500 – 16 countries, (iii) $400-$800 – 9 countries, (iv) less than $400 – 21 countries.

**8**  The fact that the African countries, whose CPI data is highly unreliable, constitute the bulk of this group suggests that the results for the lowest income groups may reflect the unreliability of the data.

**9**  These estimates of the inflationary impact of devaluation in the 1980s are rather higher than the figures suggested by Edwards (1989).

**10**  Shafaeddin (1991b) discusses some of the factors that might account for this inverse association.

## References

Bhagwati, J. (1978), *Foreign Trade Regimes and Economic Development, Anatomy and Consequences of Exchange Control Regimes*, Ballinger, Cambridge, Mass.

Cooper, R. N. (1971), 'Currency Devaluation in Developing Countries', *Essay in International Finance Series*, no. 86, Princeton University (June).

Diaz Alejandro, C.F. (1965), *Exchange Rate Devaluation in a Semi-industrialized Country*, MIT Press, Cambridge, Mass.

Edwards, S. (1989), 'Exchange Rate Misalignment in Developing Countries', *Research Observer*, vol. 4, no. 1 (January), pp. 3-21.

Harberger, A. (1964), 'Some notes on inflation' in W. Baer and I. Kertenctzky (eds.), *Inflation and Growth in Latin America*, C. D. Irwin, Homewood, Ill.

Kaldor, N. (1978), 'The effects of devaluations on trade in manufactures' in *Further Essays on Applied Economics*, Duckworth, London.

Katseli, L. T. (1986), Discrete devaluation as a signal to price setters: suggested evidence from Greece', in S. Edwards and A. Liaquat (eds.), *Economic Adjustment and Exchange Rate in Developing Countries*, University of Chicago Press, Chicago.

Killick, T. (1990), *The Adaptive Economy: Adjustment Policies in Low-income Countries*, Overseas Development Institute, London, Ch. 4.

Krueger, A. O. (1978), *Foreign Trade Regimes and Economic Development: Liberalization Attempts and Consequences*, Ballinger, Cambridge, Mass.

Shafaeddin, M. (1988), 'Agricultural price policies and the oil boom, wheat and meat in Iran', *Food Policy* (May), pp. 185-98.

Shafaeddin, M. (1990), 'Investment, imports and economic performance of developing countries' in H. W. Singer, N. Hatte and R. Tondon (eds.), *Adjustment and Liberalization in the Third World*, New World Order Series, vol. VII, Ashish Publishing House, New Delhi.

Shafaeddin M. (1991a), 'The impact of devaluation on cost, profitability and competitiveness of manufacturing exports of developing countries' (forthcoming).

Shafaeddin M. (1991b), 'The role of imports and direct contribution of devaluation to inflation in effectiveness of nominal devaluation' (forthcoming).

Taylor, L. (1978), 'Contradictory effects of devaluation', *Journal of International Economics*, (August), pp. 445-57.

Taylor, L. (1981), *Structuralist Macro-economics*, Basic Books, New York, Chaps. 1, 3 and 7.

# New wine in new bottles: an evaluation of evolving industrial policies and performance in developing countries

## Disillusionment

Disillusionment with the failure of many aid projects in the industrial sector, beginning a decade or more ago, led many aid donors to reconsider their policies for the sector, and to introduce new types of aid to meet new situations . . . new wine for new bottles.

Hitherto, aid for industry had been directed mainly at helping the large-scale capital-intensive, western-technology centred, often public sector or parastatal, enterprises. But the results had generally been disappointing, involving for example, under-utilisation of capacity, poor employment generation, unsatisfactory economic rates of return, high costs of production behind protective walls, inappropriate technology, and poor sustainability. It was a dismal catalogue of failure.

A few examples, drawn from evaluation studies of the mid 1980s, will serve to illustrate how serious the situation had become. Among the projects in the Caribbean evaluated by the German Development Institute at that time, were two major industrial projects, both of which had turned out to be virtual failures (German Development Institute 1985). The first was a large forestry/sawmill project in Guyana. After four years the power station was still not completed and therefore the sawmill was not operating. But even if the power station had been finished, the evaluators commented that the local staff probably would not have been able to handle the complicated technology, and if it had broken down the foreign exchange situation was so desperate that probably spare parts could not have been imported. The other one was a complicated integrated livestock project in St Lucia, which involved the processing of manure into organic fertiliser, and the production of biogas to supply electrical energy. It involved advanced technology, and each component of the project was highly dependent upon the others being successful. In the event it was an almost total failure: the milk was sold fresh, whilst the milk processing facility and abattoir lay idle, and the biogas installation had broken down and had not been repaired. Other examples are easy to come by. One relates to a boat building project in Somalia evaluated in 1985 (SIDA 1986a). The project was to build 6.4 metre, and later on

8.5 metre, motorised fishing vessels for the Somalian fishing industry. Some boats were built, but their price, in relation to the value of the fish that could be caught, was such that it would have been uneconomic for anyone to have bought them. Somalia fishermen have therefore continued to catch fish in the traditional ways, and the boat-building factory has largely turned over to the manufacture of other quite unrelated products (such as water tanks and latrine covers). After ten years of effort, this factory had achieved virtually nothing towards helping the Somalian fishing industry become more economically productive. All three projects quoted were in small developing countries, and these are the ones where the industrial record has hitherto been least satisfactory.

It is not safe to generalise from examples such as these to all developing countries, because the experience of the larger countries of Asia and Latin America has been rather different. These countries are more urbanised and more industrialised, and industrial projects have had a greater degree of success there than in the smaller agriculture-dominated countries of Africa, the Caribbean and the Pacific (the ACP countries). Even in Africa, there are a few examples where industrial policies have been highly successful. Outstanding among them is Mauritius, where manufactured exports have now superseded sugar in what was until recently virtually a monocrop economy. Botswana is another country that has pursued a successful industrialisation policy, based largely on the boom in the diamond industry, but thanks also to prudent and enlightened policies favouring industrial development at all levels. The Ivory Coast also has achieved a highly effective industrial sector. So even in the relatively small economies of Africa there have been success stories. Furthermore, there is at least one industrial sector, energy, where economies of scale are so dominant that small enterprises are unlikely to be successful.

Nevertheless, despite the above caveats, it remains a fact that most industrial projects in the ACP countries have yielded very disappointing results, and this is consistent with the findings of a number of influential evaluation syntheses in the early 1980s. Foremost among these was the International Development Association's review of its activities over a long period, which concluded that 'industrial growth strategies have only been successful in a few countries which possessed either a large resource base or a highly skilled work force' (IDA 1982). A similar conclusion was reached by Gerard Egnell, group leader of the Rehabilitation Working Party at the Institut de l'Entreprise in France (UNDP 1988). He found that of 353 industrial projects in developing countries that had been examined, only one-fifth were using what could be regarded as a satisfactory percentage of their installed capacity, whilst about a quarter had virtually ground to a halt, and about 60 per cent were working badly and making very inadequate use of their productive potential.

By the beginning of the 1980s it had become painfully obvious that industrial projects in the smaller developing countries were falling far below what had been expected of them. Although technically there were not many problems (except for the fact that modern technologies were generally being used, with excessive dependence on expatriate skills), they failed badly when it came to marketing and economic return, so that in many cases their net contribution to the economy was either very small or negative.

## Change in aid policy

Many donors decided that the time had come for a fundamental change in aid policies. It had been realised by that time that for the ACP countries in particular the emphasis on large-scale industrial projects was misplaced. What was required was assistance towards small and medium sized enterprises (SME).[1] These would usually be located in rural areas, and serve the needs mainly of rural people, whose purchasing power would have to be boosted by policies favouring agriculture, fisheries and forestry. This integral link between improving agricultural/fishery/forestry productivity, and fostering SMEs, was now seen to be the key to the success of this new policy. Virtually all donors at this time had begun to introduce structural adjustment policies to help the developing countries revise their macro-economic policies in such a way as to give more incentives to agricultural producers. In addition, many aid donors, among them the EEC, the Netherlands, UNDP, ILO and UNIDO, to name only a few, began to introduce new and more flexible kinds of aid aimed at helping SMEs in the private sector, for example by improving their access to credit, providing much needed vocational training in basic business skills, improving marketing, and tackling infrastructural bottlenecks wherever possible. These new policies have only been operational for a few years, but already some important evaluation syntheses have been carried out. The rest of this chapter is an attempt to summarise the main lessons that have been learned from them, and to give some pointers as to the directions in which this kind of industrial aid policy should be moving in the years ahead.

## The new industrial policies: some lessons learned

The main lessons that emerge from this recent evaluation work are as follows:

1. Because SMEs can only flourish in rural areas if agriculture, fishing or forestry are reasonably prosperous, priority has to be given to macro policies that foster the growth of rural incomes. This can be even more important than measures aimed directly at helping the SMEs themselves. However, some caution needs to be exercised in deciding what such a policy should be. It may not necessarily be the case that a policy of trade liberalization, for example, will automatically help SMEs; it could have the opposite effect. This is illustrated by a study carried out by ILO in Sri Lanka (quoted in UNDP 1988), which found that on balance the impact of a trade liberalization policy on SMEs had been adverse, although this may have been partially due to the fact that the policy was not one of complete liberalization and some distortions remained which tended to favour large-scale industries. Nevertheless, it indicates the need for caution as to what macro-economic policies should be followed, and what is right for one country may not be right for another.

2. An evaluation of 15 agro-industrial projects found that none of the industrial estates examined (nor indeed the smallholder plantations) were self-sustaining in the sense of being able to finance the re-planting and re-equipment over time. It

concluded that agro-industrial projects are very likely to fail if they are conceived and implemented as isolated one-off projects without regard to the wider needs of the sector of which they are a part. Thus in designing agro- industrial projects full consideration has to be given to upstream and downstream linkages, vertical and horizontal integration, pricing and marketing policies, and physical location. No doubt the typical agro-industrial enterprise such as a sugar factory, an oil palm estate, or a jute mill, may be considerably larger than the typical SME, but even so the need for any enterprise to be planned in relation to the needs and potential of the sector of which it forms a part, cannot be over-emphasised.

3. Because SMEs provide such a vitally important supplementary source of income to women engaged in agriculture their needs must be specifically catered for.

4. Sub-contracting from larger-scale industrial enterprises to SMEs can help the latter develop. The Bapak Angkat (Foster Father) Scheme in Indonesia is an interesting example of how large enterprises, public or private, have been able to foster the supply of components they need from small-scale industries. This scheme is now being further developed so that the fostering firms can assist small companies producing other articles not directly associated with their own.

5. Government-financed agencies for fostering SMEs, such as Small Industries Development Agencies and the like, should be approached with some caution as they often end up being more concerned to perpetuate their own existence than to meet the needs of their SME clients. Donors should make use of existing institutions as much as possible rather than create new ones, and it should be borne in mind that often, self-help organisations sponsored by industry itself, or by Non-Government Organisations, can be more effective than Government ones.

6. Contrary to what is sometimes believed, it seems from recent evaluation work that shortage of credit is not often a major problem, at least so far as the smaller enterprises are concerned. A World Bank study of rural non-farm activities in Thailand, for example, found that credit was seldom a major problem; and the joint UNDP, ILO, UNIDO and Government of Netherlands evaluation found a similar result (UNDP 1988). However, this is not to say that suitable credit institutions are not needed; they are, especially in those countries where the commercial banks have not developed a network of rural branches, or where rural co-operative banking institutions have not yet been developed. In these circumstances special credit institutions aimed at meeting the needs of the SMEs may need to be created, but if so they should be as decentralised as possible and based on local knowledge of the borrowers and lenders.

7. Training is a vitally important need, but it should be as practical as possible, and given by people who have had first-hand experience of running a small business. But such people are hard to find. Most staff of training institutes lack this kind of experience, and are fearful that their ignorance will become obvious, so they tend to concentrate on theoretical aspects which will serve to enhance their 'superiority' over their students. There are many examples of rural training institutes that may appear on the surface to be ideal for this purpose, but which in practice are of little use. For example, the teachers in the Village Polytechnics in Kenya lack personal experience of small business management, and they tend

to produce trainees and graduates whose first objective is to get away from the rural areas and into the towns in search of jobs. Even teachers in the main co-operative training colleges have often come straight from school or university and have had no personal experience of actually running a co-operative.

8. The World Bank Thailand study referred to above found that the overriding problem, so far as manufacturing and handicrafts enterprises were concerned, was the marketing of the product, and this is also a key lesson from the other evaluations of SMEs. In Kenya, for example, the Industrial Development Programme stimulated the production of a range of products of small artisans, but without first conducting any proper surveys to make sure that there was a market for the products. The artisans knew that they would be very unlikely to be able to sell what they had produced and so they lost interest (UNDP 1988). A synthesis evaluation of 19 DANIDA-funded fishery cooling and cold-storage projects in 1989, found that 14 of them were at least partial failures, and the main reason was that the market for frozen fish was so small in most developing countries, and processing costs so high, that the product could not be marketed successfully (DANIDA 1989). The existing chilling techniques were more appropriate for the people's needs, as any market survey would have revealed if it had been made beforehand. Far greater attention needs to be given to marketing problems if SMEs are to be successful, and this should be a priority in training, and in project design.

## Pointers to the future

The preceding review of the main lessons from evaluation studies throws up a number of pointers as to the direction in which industrial aid policies should be moving.

1. It is important that the needs of SMEs in rural areas should no longer be looked at in isolation but always as a component part of the general problem of how best to foster a more productive and prosperous rural economy. Macro-policies need to cover SMEs as the other side of the coin of agricultural, fisheries or forestry projects. The case may seem fairly obvious, stated like this, but the fact is that at present this kind of comprehensive macro-planning is sadly lacking in most developing countries, and policies for SMEs are all too often drawn up as if they were an isolated sector, independent of any other. Governments will set up a Small Industries Development Agency or something similar, hoping that this isolated initiative will solve the problem. One synthesis report on a major evaluation of SMEs goes so far as to assert that SMEs should not be regarded as a special sector calling for special policies, but rather as the norm on the basis of which everything should be ordered, and to which everything else should be related.

2. Backward and forward linkages are clearly of vital importance for the development of SMEs. Such linkages were often minimal so far as large-scale industries were concerned, since the non-agricultural inputs were mostly imported, and the production mostly exported, and many of the skilled staff were expatriates.

However, with SMEs the potential for forward and backward linkages is much greater, and this merits more detailed study. As the rural economy develops, of course, the needs of agriculture, fisheries or forestry become more sophisticated, (for example, for fertilisers, machinery, transport) and the tendency is for the supplying and using businesses to grow larger and to move towards the towns and cities. This is bound to happen eventually, but for the time being there is still great scope in the ACP countries for deriving more spin-off benefits in rural areas from linkages.

3. There is increased scope for the setting up of joint ventures involving both enterprises of the developing countries (especially the ACP countries) and those of the developed countries. The Centre for the Development of Industry, set up under the EEC-ACP Convention, could well step up its present role in this context. The Swedish aid agency, SIDA, has developed the concept of 'sister industries', that is, Swedish firms working with their counterparts in the developing countries. It has established a 'Sister Industry Programme' in Tanzania. A recent evaluation of this programme (SIDA 1988a) found that there had been a mixed experience: some Tanzanian companies had benefited greatly from the association and had developed into well-established and growing enterprises, but others had run into considerable difficulties, especially on the management front, and had experienced serious restructuring problems. The evaluation concluded that the key to future success lay mainly in the strengthening of management capability.

4. Small size had led to some of the smaller SMEs experiencing problems, such as coping with the legal constraints in setting up a business, dealing with bureaucracy, and sometimes obtaining credit. The synthesis report on SMEs referred to earlier emphasizes the importance of these problems as obstacles to the development of small businesses, whose owners may be scarcely literate and are likely to be unaccustomed to handling legal or bureaucratic matters. An imaginative new approach to the problem of helping small businesses cope with the problems of bureaucracy is the 'One Stop Office'. This comprises just one office serving a district, housing all the government officials that small entrepreneurs are likely to need to contact, so they can deal speedily with their business rather than having to make the rounds of a number of government offices. This is just one example of how, with a little imagination, developing countries can make their administrations 'SME-friendly'. In the credit field also, special credit programmes geared to the needs of SMEs are required. New ways of mobilising rural savings (which, it is now realised, are far more important than they were previously thought to be) need to be worked out along the lines of the Grameen Bank in Bangladesh, or the Credit Union and Savings Associations in Zambia, and donors might consider incorporating provision for compulsory regular savings in more of their rural credit projects.

5. Another crucial area of SME development is basic education and training, especially vocational training. Hitherto this kind of training has been mostly ineffective: formalised and irrelevant curricula; teachers that lack SME background or experience; an overemphasis on modern know-how and approaches. Above all else, there is a need to select trainers who have a real empathy for SMEs, and

who can begin their training from the point at which the small entrepreneurs are now, building on the resource base they already have (especially their own acquired experience), and enabling them to see that within their own collective experience they already have the means for their own economic improvement.

6. If small enterprises are to be seriously encouraged there can be no avoiding the need to improve the basic education of women, and particularly their access to credit, because that is an area where they are particularly disadvantaged. Women also need to have their sense of self-esteem and self-confidence boosted to enable them to hold their own in societies that are often male dominated. The organisation 'Women in Development' has done some excellent work in this context and more still is needed: this should be an integral part of all SME planning.

7. An important conclusion is that if this kind of aid is to be fully successful changes are needed on the aid administration front. Such aid tends to be labour-intensive, and more donor agency staff will be needed, especially in the field; aid administration will need to be decentralised even more than at present; and there will need to be far more opportunities, from the project identification stage onwards, for participation by the beneficiaries.

8. The view is gaining ground that there has been excessive emphasis in the past on the role of industrial estates as a means of encouraging SMEs, and the tendency now is to move towards a more geographically dispersed programme of training and business extension services, as exemplified by the Botswana Enterprises Development Unit which was recently evaluated by SIDA (SIDA 1986b).[2] Kenya Industrial Estates (KIE) has also found that its most successful clients have been in the small towns rather than in the industrial estates, and they are therefore emphasizing extension work and industrial promotion there rather than adding to the existing estates. An evaluation of NORAD aid to Kenya recommended that KIE should strengthen its support to extension services to entrepreneurs, develop KIE as a resource centre for women entrepreneurs, and develop training in basic business skills (Christian Michelsen Institute 1987). These are surely the directions in which industrial promotion agencies should now be moving, rather than simply adding to the existing industrial estates. An outstanding example of a successful programme along these lines is the 'Improve your Business' project set up by SIDA and evaluated in 1988 (SIDA 1988b). It is now in use in over 20 countries, and ILO has persuaded several other donors to adopt it. It comprises a very simple and down-to-earth system of learning by doing for small enterprise managers, a kind of self-instruction. It brings the training to the trainee, rather than the other way round, and it starts where the trainee is now. This is the kind of training programme that will have to be fostered if SMEs are to be further encouraged.

9. One of the motivations underlying the new policy of bringing the services to the entrepreneurs, rather than the other way round, is the growing need to stem the migration from the countryside to the towns and cities. In China, for instance, rural non-agricultural development has become a key component of the policy of stemming rural-urban drift, and the current slogan is 'leave the land, but not the countryside; enter the factory, but not the city' (UNDP 1988). Such a policy

strengthens the case for a widely dispersed business extension service, meeting the needs of the entrepreneurs where they happen to be.

## Conclusion

The switch in emphasis from large-scale industry to small and medium sized enterprises, usually located in rural areas, calls for a sea change in policy, at least as far as the ACP countries are concerned. It requires a fundamentally changed approach to industrial projects on the part of both the developing countries and also the donors. The evaluations of what have been achieved so far, in this direction, are very encouraging, and the new policies have proved successful and should be pursued. If there is a problem it is not with the policies themselves, but the degree of vigour with which they are implemented, many developing countries still have not accepted the need to switch the emphasis from larger industrial projects to smaller ones.

If SMEs are to be seen henceforth as the norm in most ACP countries, rather than large-scale, export-oriented, urban-based industries, macro-policies will need to be adjusted so as to foster directly this kind of development, whereas in the past such policies have usually had an adverse effect. Above all, a fundamental change of attitude to entrepreneurship on the part of the bureaucrats is called for. They need to adopt a much more positive, co-operative and supportive approach to the needs of small and medium sized enterprises, viewing them collectively as a major springboard for economic growth. A two-pronged policy of encouragement to the farmer, combined with the establishment of a climate conducive to the investment of rural savings in SMEs, helped by well directed infusions of aid, could give many depressed ACP economies the boost they need so that the resourcefulness of the people can be released and put to productive use. This is the heady new wine, and it must continue to be poured into new policy bottles.

## Notes

1 There is no generally accepted definition of what comprises small and medium-sized enterprises. Most studies use definitions based on the number of employees. The maximum number for such enterprises can vary from 25 workers to as many as 200.

2 The present writer visited most of the industrial estates in Botswana, during 1988, and apart from those in Gaberone, few of them had been very successful in stimulating the growth of SMEs.

## References

Christian Michelsen Institute (1987), *Kenya: Country Study and Norwegian Aid Review*.

DANIDA (1989), *Cooling, Coldstorage and Distribution of Fish, Sector Evaluation, Synthesis Report* (May).

German Development Institute (1985), *Evaluation of the Co-operation between the European Community and the Caribbean ACP States, V. Final Report* (November).

IDA (1982), *IDA in Retrospect*, Oxford University Press, Oxford.

SIDA (1986a), *Manufacturing Fishing Vessels: an Evaluation of SIDA-Supported Industrial Rehabilitation in Somalia, Evaluation Report* (written by S. Larsson and J. Valdelin).

SIDA (1986b), *Developing Entrepreneurs: An Evaluation of Small Scale Industry Development in Botswana, 1974-84, Evaluation Report* (written by J. O. Agrell, B. D. Bergman, P. Hallerby and K. Ring).

SIDA (1988a), *Sisterhood on Trial: An Evaluation of the Performance and Linkages of the Sister Industries in Tanzania, Evaluation Report* (written by S. Carlsson, S. Alange, K. Forss, S. Malai and S. Scheinberg).

SIDA (1988b), *Improve your Business: An Evaluation of an ILO-SIDA Regional Small-Scale Business Promotion Project in Africa* (written by C. Lindahl and R. Dainow).

UNDP (1988) with Government of Netherlands, ILO, UNIDO, *Development of Rural Small Industrial Enterprise: Lessons from Experience*.

# II: Sub-Saharan African perspectives

# Policy reform or industrialisation? The choice in Zimbabwe

**Abstract**

Zimbabwe has experienced one of the highest economic growth rates in Africa in the 1980s, about 4 per cent annually, despite breaking with the IMF in 1984 over foreign-exchange controls and the level of the budget deficit, and with its main bilateral aid donor, the USA, in 1987. It has nevertheless met all its debt-servicing obligations without rescheduling, entailing an annual capital outflow equal to about 5 per cent of GDP.

Although in some respects Zimbabwe has always had 'reformed policy', it has retained tight trade controls, and industry has continued to develop behind high protective barriers. Not only is the volume of output of manufacturing industry some 35 per cent higher than in 1980, but output is more diversified, with a significant share of exports. It earns about 20 per cent of foreign exchange, or 40 per cent including ferro-alloys, steel and cotton lint. This has been achieved in a tightly controlled economy in which foreign exchange constraint has held down investment and employment.

It is argued that structural adjustment packages need 'depackaging'; some policy reforms such as restoration of markets, the provision of incentives to farmers, and in some cases devaluation, may be necessary for the restoration of minimum conditions for economic development in some countries. It does not follow that all subsides must be removed, that the state's role must be minimized or that trade controls should be abandoned. While it is agreed that the former set should improve static efficiency, it is argued that the latter would damage prospects for industrialization, and thereby chances of developing comparative advantage in new areas.

There is, nevertheless, near unanimity in Zimbabwe that reforms are now needed, and the government began implementing a reform package in October 1990. This could result in the abandonment of price controls, reductions in subsidies, budget cuts, and the replacement over a five-year period of nearly all quantitative import controls by tariffs. It is not yet clear to what extent this programme represents an abandonment of the earlier policy, or a pragmatic attempt to obtain more aid whilst protecting industry by other means.

## Introduction

### *The debt crisis*

The pressure for 'structural adjustment' in developing countries is related to the debt crisis. This itself was a direct consequence of earlier advice, tendered by the international financial institutions and authorities in the rich countries in the 1970s, when high international liquidity followed the first major oil price rise. Their message in effect was: borrow cheaply to invest, and buy more of our capital goods in the process. The crisis arose in its present severe form because of the way in which the rich countries then chose to solve their own crisis after 1979, that is, through deflation, which forced a collapse in world commodity prices, so lowering their import costs.

The earlier advice to borrow of course fitted in with developing countries' desire to industrialise and break away from primary commodity-price instability or secular falls, and although many countries may have followed poorly conceived industrialization strategies which involved too large a bias against agriculture and exporting, the advice to borrow was hard to resist with the high negative real rates of interest that ruled in the mid to late 1970s. The observation, therefore, is that a dramatically more hostile external environment was the dominant factor in causing the debt crisis.

### *The World Bank position*

The World Bank position, on the contrary, as set out in the Berg report[1] and only modified slightly since, is that it is internal policies that have been wrong in almost all cases. Their advice is now to 'Get the Prices Right', to follow existing comparative advantage. They claim that the countries that are doing this are succeeding, and those which are not are continuing to fail. This is dubious even on the evidence they present;[2] they ignore cases like Zimbabwe which are successful despite adverse external impacts.

### *Adjustment to what?*

The term 'structural adjustment' is ambiguous: it implies the adjusting of wrong structures and so implies development. In fact it means the abandonment, not of inappropriate structures, but of earlier state-oriented policies that were themselves designed to change those structures; that is, it is really a policy to preserve the essence of the old colonial structures by reversing the (usually failed) policies that had been introduced in an effort to change them. But these policies may have failed in many cases more because of the change in international environment than for internal reasons: South Korea and Taiwan earlier, and in a more favourable environment, adjusted their structures radically through a package very different from that of the World Bank; and Zimbabwe, in a more modest way, and under much harsher external constraints, has been attempting something similar. It may, however, now be about to abandon the attempt in favour of something more akin to the World Bank model.

## Zimbabwe's policies

### Transformation

Soon after independence the new government of Zimbabwe published its broad economic strategy,[3] in which it proposed to move away from colonial economic structures, reducing the extreme inequalities without cutting the living standards of the rich (initially almost entirely white), through high economic growth. This was an attempt to eat its cake and have it; it was soon shown to be unrealistic under the impact of drought and South African destabilisation. Nevertheless a significant 'basic needs'-oriented social programme has survived in an environment of reduced growth rates and continuing wealth and income inequality. Protection of this programme and the development of an economic base that can reduce the continuing over-dependence on exports of primary products are still (even after the 1990 reforms) seen in Zimbabwe as depending on government initiative, and the development and protection of key industries in both import substitution and exporting. Conversely, calls for liberalization of the World Bank variety are viewed by many as coming from the over-privileged, who derive their wealth and income from the inherited structures based on exploitation of primary commodities for export.

### Debt policy

Zimbabwe borrowed heavily after independence in a context of willing lenders (the IMF had pronounced that Zimbabwe was 'underborrowed') and heavy rehabilitation needs. This borrowing was, however, later than that of most developing countries, and the consequences of the changed world environment become obvious by 1982, before the country was too deep in debt. Nevertheless, there was a severe balance-of-payments crisis in that year which led to devaluation and an IMF programme.

The payments deficit, however, persisted and the government decided in March 1984 that the more open policies were neither equitable nor functional, even on their own terms. It therefore attacked the payments problems by direct measures, including the reinstatement of strict controls on dividend and profit remittances and raised government spending, leading to a suspension of the programme (which had not been resumed by mid-1990). Despite the near suspension of factor income payments for three years, the government took care to meet all debt obligations in full, without any rescheduling, and has now established a high (and rising) credit rating. It continues to borrow selectively. It has reduced the debt-service ratio from almost 40 per cent to 25 per cent, but does not intend to attempt to reduce it further, given the obvious need for further development funds not only in industry, but also in rural electrification and water supply. Once again the IMF is reported as saying that Zimbabwe is 'underborrowed'.

Currently proposed liberalization measures in many ways represent a more cautious attempt to return to the relatively open policies of 1981-82, although if they go to completion (over a planned five-year period) they could include full trade liberalization. However, in the short run the main impact will be felt to external borrowing facilitated by the commitment to liberalization.

*State and market*

Zimbabwe has a government-dominated economy, with a number of parastatals involved in infrastructure, marketing and production. The government dominates in investment, and also constrains private capital through a battery of controls on prices, minimum and maximum wages, job protection, foreign exchange and trade. Nevertheless, the private sector is dynamic, and the majority of production arises in commercial farms, foreign-owned mines, and industrial companies, There is a stock exchange with about 50 companies listed (plus several new flotations in 1990 and 1991), whose industrial index outperformed all other in 1988 and 1989. It has shown uninterrupted growth since 1989 and grew a further 162 per cent in 1990. This performance reflects not only the high liquidity in the 'hothouse' atmosphere of a protected economy, but also high profitability, both in the domestic and foreign markets.

Two or three basic components of structural adjustment packages have been part of Zimbabwean economic policy all along. These include maintenance of an appropriate exchange rate, with the Zimbabwe dollar depreciating by about the inflation rate differential. The World Bank and other observers have generally not thought the currency overvalued by more than 20 percent.[4] Secondly, markets exist in most areas, allowing for the small size of the economy (a number of economic activities are necessarily monopolistic or oligopolistic in the absence of imports). In particular, a structure of incentives has brought an increasing number of agricultural producers into the market, and the structure of agricultural production has steadily shifted since independence in favour of communal area farmers. This, however, has only been achieved at the cost of guaranteed prices and government and aid-financed investment in infrastructure, including depots, silos and other storage facilities. As a result, subsidies reached a high level soon after independence, and policy for the seven years since has been to reduce them, although the outcome in most cases has merely been to contain them.

When coupled with high educational and health expenditure and the cost of maintaining the sixth largest army in Africa, it is not surprising that the budget deficit has struck at around 10 per cent of GDP. The collapse of the IMF programme in 1984 was partly because of failure to make progress towards 5 per cent. However, it has been argued by Green that Zimbabwe has had to maintain armed forces at a level (50,000) which is about five times higher per caput than the average for Africa, entirely because of South African destabilization, and in particular the need to guard the Beira corridor to Zimbabwe's nearest port.[5] Removing this excess expenditure from the accounts would reduce the budget deficit to only 2 or 3 per cent of GDP (Green claims zero). In relation, therefore to a normal, non-destabilized situation, Zimbabwe is following a set of economic policies that are very conservative for a country in the process of development. To require a reduction of the actual deficit would, therefore, be equivalent to demanding either that the country cease defending itself in a geopolitical situation that has seen a neighbouring country brought to its knees by destabilization, or to run a budget surplus in relation to social and developmental components of government expenditure, i.e. to abandon efforts to improve the standard of living.

It may be argued that unlike the case of some countries such as Ghana, Mozambique, Tanzania and Zambia, where markets had largely ceased functioning, exchange rates were overvalued, and subsidies were at unsustainable levels, Zimbabwe is not in need of further adjustment. Indeed, it is arguable that its policies are in some respects inward-oriented in relation to the need for economic transformation. Nevertheless, as in almost all African countries, a standard package is being made a condition for multilateral and bilateral support programmes. There is ritual pressure to devalue and to reduce the budget deficit: 'Find out what it is and tell them to halve it irrespective of its causes' would not seem to be particularly unfair to the IMF's methodology in this respect; and to reduce subsidies would mean destroying the incentives to small producers for which, at other times, Zimbabwe is praised. This is where most of the pressure has come in Zimbabwe's case: the final components of a typical conditionality package are urges: rapid liberalization of the trade and foreign exchange regimes; and privatisation and general reduction of the government's commercial role. These have direct implications for industrialization and long-run development.

### Industrialisation

The development of manufacturing industry is seen in Zimbabwe as the key to future growth. This, however, has not led to a debilitating bias against agriculture and mining, which are valued for their foreign exchange earnings and contribution to self-sufficiency. But policies have not been tailored to meet the demands of these primary sectors. Industry and its short-run protection are the bottom line, with ambitious plans in train to redevelop and expand the iron and steel industry, selective downstream engineering activities, including the production of machine tools and diesel engines, and chemical, fertiliser and pulp and paper production.

### Exporting

Export promotion has always been seen as important, and has increasingly moved in the direction of manufactured goods as the easier consumer-goods import substitution has run out of steam. But such export promotion is distinguished from export-led growth, which has hitherto been explicitly disavowed. Direct measures to promote manufactured exports include a 9 per cent cash subsidy; an export pre-financing facility; and a supplementary allowance in foreign exchange for inputs for production for the domestic market for companies with rising exports. In addition, in October 1990 a foreign exchange retention scheme was introduced. These measures have operated in the context of more appropriate exchange rate management, which has prevented the serious overvaluation of the currency.

A number of institutional measures have been made to improve earnings from trade; however, they have so far produced mixed results. The Minerals Marketing Corporation of Zimbabwe was established in 1985, marketing all mineral products (except gold), iron and steel, and ferroalloys. But for most minerals it merely seems to have become another middle-man in the old sanctions-busting chain. A wider state-trading organization was established in 1987, with monopoly only in barter trade. Recently, the formation of a Zimbabwe Export Council and a Zimbabwe International Trade Organization have been proposed after two years of work through the Zimbabwe Export Promotion Programme under EC funding.

### Zimbabwe's record

#### GDP growth

Since independence there has been a compound annual rate of GDP growth of about 4.2 per cent.[6] Although this does not appear remarkable, it is perhaps in the context of Africa in the 1980s with many other countries showing declines, and South Africa barely averaging 1.5 per cent. The average is about the same for the second half of the decade as the first, so does not depend on the post-independence boom (whose effects were largely eliminated in any case by the 1982-84 slump). It is noteworthy that current fashion in Zimbabwe is to quote only sub-periods showing 3.2 percent growth (compared with population growing at 2.9 per cent).

#### Self-sufficiency

Zimbabwe is self-sufficient in most foodstuffs, and is usually an exporter of maize. Although wheat demand has tended to rise faster than production, the gap closed in 1989 and 1990; beef, sugar, coffee and horticultural products are all major exports. A big stimulus to import substitution of manufactured goods was given by international sanctions following UDI in 1965, and the number of distinguishable products made by local industry rose from 600 to 6,000 between 1965 and 1975: it is now about 8,000.[7] As a result, overall consumption demand is 96 per cent met locally, although with an average import content of about 20 per cent.[8] In energy, only oil has to be imported, with electricity-generating capacity coming from hydroelectric power and thermal generation in coal-burning plant, despite the availability of excess regional hydroelectric capacity.

#### Exports

The consequence of direct export-promotion measures has been that after stagnation in the volume of exports from 1977 to 1985, 1986 saw a 25 per cent rise, 1987 a further 7 percent, and although volume figures are not yet available, 1988 saw a 10 per cent rise in US$ terms. Although this record owes much to the rise in base metal and tobacco prices, it also contains a major contribution from 'non-traditional' manufactured exports, which rose 10 per cent to over Z$1 bn. about 30 per cent of the total in 1988, led by textile and clothing manufacturers, with rolling stock and light-metal manufacturers also prominent.

This success record has been held back by World Bank refusal to extend the export-revolving fund loan it made in 1982. Negotiations for a larger loan began in 1985 and were near agreement in 1987, when new stringent IMF-type macro-economic policy pre-conditions were imposed, requiring trade liberalization and other politically unacceptable measures. As a consequence, Zimbabwe resorted to renewed commercial borrowing (at higher interest rates) to finance its export programme. It is worth emphasizing that the political nature of this intervention is particularly transparent in view of the success of the policies being followed by Zimbabwe. In cases where a country's difficulties can plausibly be ascribed to its policies, IMF and World Bank conditionality can more credibly appear to be purely technical. In this case, a government policy measure was succeeding in raising exports (very much what the World Bank wants to see happen). Increased support for the measure was denied because success would probably have been in a context of little 'structural adjustment'.

*Investment*

The rate of investment since 1980 has been only about 17.5 per cent. The growth achieved so far has been largely through the raising of capacity utilization and capital consumption. An investment ratio of 25–30 per cent would be needed for sustained GDP growth of 4–5 per cent.

*Employment*

The record in employment has been even worse than that in investment, with only about 100,000 new jobs created over the ten years since independence. The annual increment to the labour force has been about 100,000 and is now at least double that. Calls for liberalization and foreign investment so as to improve this job creation record are increasingly heard; simple calculations show, however, that with internationally competitive technology, the needed investment ratio to employ even half the increment would be 60 per cent of GDP.[9] State intervention and protection of labour-intensive production is thus a more plausible alternative.

**The World Bank model**

Countries gain from trade with each other, and the gains are greatest where countries are exploiting their comparative advantage, rather than dumping goods they are making inefficiently. We can agree with these propositions without thinking, as the neo-classicists in the World Bank and elsewhere seem to, that that is all there is to it. The slogan 'Get the prices right' is an expression of this view, implying the use of international price structures in internal markets. It follows from this that the World Bank will generally advocate a package that includes devaluation of the local currency, a reduction in the government budget deficit, liberalization of the trade regime, privatization and general reduction of the government's commercial role. Furthermore, it claims that these are purely technical recommendations and that whether a country follows capitalist or socialist policies is of no concern to the Bank.

Even if one were to accept that such a package was appropriate for a country, like Zambia, in serious trouble after a commodity collapse and failed industrialization strategy, it does not necessarily follow that it would be appropriate for a country with a significantly successful industrial record. In Zimbabwe's case some of the policies are already in place and would be harmful if taken further, as they would simply bring about deindustrialization.

One would, therefore, be tempted to ask how successful Zimbabwe's policies would have to be before the World Bank would be obliged to alter its prescription. How would success be registered for the World Bank? Zimbabwe's modest success may be compared with the recent record of Ghana, which is judged by the World Bank to be a success story on the basis of average annual growth of 5 per cent with capital inflows amounting to over 5 per cent of GDP. The growth can be explained largely by the inflows alone, not by any particular policies.[10] It has, in fact, been explicitly stated that these inflows are available because of Ghana's compliance with structural adjustment measures.[11] It is pertinent, then, to ask what Ghana's record would be with a 6 per cent outflow and structural adjustment policies, or conversely, what Zimbabwe's record would be with a 5 per cent inflow and its relatively unadjusted (on the World Bank's own assessment) policies. It is not clear that Ghana is laying the basis either for long-term development (the recent Ivory Coast or Kenyan experience shows the dangers of intensifying the exploitation of existing comparative advantage), or even for escaping from the debt-trap, for as the loans from the first five years of the programme fell due, the IMF fell over itself to offer favourable terms for rescheduling (public debt rose from 26 per cent of GDP in 1980 to 45 per cent in 1987, and is now almost certainly much higher).

But one must go further and point out that Ghana and other structural adjusters are being asked to take on trust the future effectiveness of a policy package which to date has not a single developmental success to point to. Stabilization of a country's economy at a level of general poverty may be desirable as a base from which an advance may be planned; a stabilization which systematically undoes the bases previously laid for such an advance is another matter.

Thus the World Bank strategy seems to be deficient at both conceptual and quantitative levels. Conceptually, it pays insufficient evidence to the conditions for industrialization, so that even when it advocates further industrialization, it continues to support macro-economic policies which make it difficult, if not impossible. At the quantitative level, in concentrating on making marginal efficiency improvements it loses sight of the sources of dynamic growth. Undoubtedly, raising efficiency in agriculture is desirable, in fact necessary, but nothing proposed suggests the possibility of growth rates of more than 5 per cent per annum, and that only in recovery periods from deep economic crisis. Nations which have become rich have done so through structural change involving industrialization, experiencing growth rates of 8-12 per cent for a decade or so. This was the case not only for the NICs and Japan, but also for the Soviet Union and many East European countries when they were making the transition from predominantly peasant societies to middle-income ones.

In the early 1960s Kwame Nkrumah developed the concept of neo-colonialism. He argued that colonial economic structures had been developed to provide cheap commodities to the metropolitan powers. Because of the instability of most commodity prices, and an argued tendency for a secular underlying decline, economies dependent on them were unstable and lacked prospects of developing beyond a state of being more efficient 'hewers of wood and drawers of water'. Both Ghana and Tanzania attempted to transform their economies by industrialising; unfortunately, both have failed miserably and are now implementing IMF programmes. Yet Nkrumah and Nyerere were right in their analysis, although their policies were seriously flawed, because countries which followed a version of World Bank advice in the 1960s and 1970s reaped the whirlwind in the 1980s, just as forewarned. The economies of the Ivory Coast and Kenya have been devastated by the winds of commodity price instability and decline, precisely the phenomenon Nkrumah said it was necessary to escape from. Present World Bank triumphalism is imposing the policies that have led to such disaster in these countries, onto other countries, which tried but failed to escape from the trap. Furthermore, it is imposing them on a country like Zimbabwe, which has made a greater success of industrialization and self-reliance. According to the orthodoxy, failed protectionist policies (Tanzania) prove the need for liberalization; but so apparently do failed liberal policies (Ivory Coast); and so do successful protectionist policies (Zimbabwe)!

## Zimbabwe's alternative in context

Zimbabwe's economic strategy has in fact been a variant of a tried and tested one. There is scarcely a successful country in the world which did not use protection of infant industries as a key element in development strategy.[12] We can go back to Germany in the early part of the nineteenth century, to France, Italy and Japan a bit later, or to the 1960s and South Korea and Taiwan. In all these cases and many others, the state played a strategic, stimulating role, helping to 'pick winners' and supporting them, sometimes investing itself. It usually operated restrictive trade and foreign exchange policies, and frequently ran a budget deficit. Furthermore, it should be noted that the latter two countries began liberalizing their foreign exchange controls only in 1989, as did Italy, and many are aware of the important role of trade barriers (mainly non-tariff) in Japan.[13] Amsden's (1989) study shows that while South Korea was comparable to other late industrialisers in its use of low-wage labour, borrowed technology and industrial subsidies, it has pursued such policies in conjunction with others that are quite contrary to the World Bank's advice to other countries. These mainly relate to a key state role in directing investment, both for exporting and import-substitution. She concludes that South Korea's success refutes the market theory on several basic issues.

Nevertheless, the World Bank and the IMF are telling countries with per caput incomes of only a few hundred dollars per annum that they will not escape from poverty unless they remove protection, whilst countries that have escaped from poverty, and now have per caput incomes measured in thousands of dollars (sometimes over ten thousand), are only now in the process of removing protection to deal with the problems not of poverty but of wealth, wealth created under protectionist regimes.[14] Like the NICs, Zimbabwe has positive measures to promote trade, whilst not allowing the external trade 'tail' to wag the whole economic dog. It would certainly be desirable to reduce the high budget deficit, but the seriousness of the situation should not be exaggerated: Italy, one of the most dynamic economies in Europe, has also been running a budget deficit of about 10 per cent of GDP.

*Is there a Zimbabwean model?*

The example of Zimbabwe's relative success story clearly cannot be transferred automatically to many other countries. Few have the combination of endowments of minerals, good agricultural soils and climate, industrial base, and the highly educated and experienced managerial and technical classes.

As against these advantages, Zimbabwe has also suffered from serious disadvantages, principally those arising from destabilization by South Africa, both directly and through the Mozambican National Resistance (MNR or Renamo) in Mozambique, which cut the natural trade routes. Contributory problems have been four years of drought out of the last nine, and the communal troubles in Matabeleland (also fanned by South Africa). A heavy defence burden has, as mentioned earlier, been another major cause of the budget deficit.

Nevertheless, Zimbabwe's economy has been growing at about 4 per cent year despite an average capital outflow of about 5 per cent of GNP in recent years, which has had to be financed by a large trade surplus requiring severe import constraints.[15]

But it is also clear that Zimbabwe's present policies are far from ideal, considering the inefficient use of some resources. In particular we may refer to the waste of personpower, as shown by the lack of jobs for qualified school leavers on top of a pool of unemployment of about a million people; and the waste of land resources, with about half the best land underutilized in the commercial farms whilst peasant farmers cultivate land suitable mainly for grazing purposes. There is thus considerable potential for faster growth following redistribution of wealth and income. More open policies, following orthodox structural adjustment, would be liable to worsen rather than improve the existing misallocations.

Overall, it may be argued that although all countries have a high degree of specificity and cannot therefore provide easy solutions for each other, Zimbabwe's experience may have some valuable lessons to offer. Its relative success cannot be explained by an unusually favourable set of circumstances or highly efficient policy implementation; it has suffered from very serious disadvantages, and it has used key resources inefficiently. Where it has differed from many other countries is in guarding its limited freedom of manoeuvre against liberalizing pressure so as to maintain some elements of a long-term industrialization strategy.

### The World Bank victorious?

During 1988 and 1989, with rapidly rising exports and a falling debt-service ratio,[16] calls for liberalization lost much of their force. However, it was also clear that the existing system was operating less and less efficiently, in that there were increasing delays in making decisions, and increasingly widespread corruption (the evidence from the Sandura Commission[17] was only the tip of a large iceberg) and this was throwing the rationality of the foreign-exchange allocation system into doubt.

Nevertheless, this was still the system that had delivered positive results, and the most obvious diagnosis should have been for reform. This is what was argued by the Ministries of Industry and Technology, and Labour and Manpower Development. The more orthodox Ministry of Finance, Economic Planning and Development, however, plainly wished to reach an accommodation with the World Bank so as to raise the sources of concessionary finance.[18] (An event seen as highly symbolic by the press – the marriage of the Finance Minister's daughter to the son of the World Bank's resident representative in Zimbabwe – also took place in 1988). The compromise eventually reached has produced a Zimbabwe-designed trade liberalization to be phased in over five years; this effectively began on 1 October 1990, with the transfer to open general import licence of plastic granules and tin plate; dyes, dyeing chemicals, binders, colourants and pigments; and clinker for the cement industry. Very careful monitoring will take place, so that firms will not become unviable simply because of an earlier inability to retool caused by foreign exchange shortage, or because of closure of local sources of supply. Nevertheless, the basis is a switch from quantitative controls to a tariff-based system, which will remove from government a major potential instrument for planning industrialization policy.[19] Since such instruments have not actually been used to a significant extent, it is possible that the net result may yet be beneficial, if control is retained over strategic parameters of policy, including the tariff structure (this will mean resisting World Bank demands for lower and flat-rate tariffs).

Zimbabwean policy-makers, however, have a reasonable understanding of the sources of growth in the NICs, and reject the free-market interpretation of the World Bank. And they plainly have an ambition to make of Zimbabwe 'an African NIC', despite its manifest range of disadvantages (of which being landlocked may be added to the earlier list). A plausible explanation of why they may be abandoning the strategy now, is that the NICs themselves are also doing so; however, in the latter's case it is because they are now strong enough to benefit from freer trade; that is, they are moving into a new phase. It is arguable that such a policy shift is very premature for Zimbabwe. It may thus be one of history's ironies that the African country which best showed the viable alternative to World Bank structural adjustment policies for countries in an early phase of development, itself embraced them just before they became widely discredited.[20]

## Conclusion

As the World Bank strategy is ill-founded conceptually, and has no track record, its chances of success in bringing about structural transformation leading to self-sustaining industrialization in African countries are negligible. By contrast, Zimbabwe has shown that the time-honoured approach of industrialization through government intervention and protection still works.

Growth can, of course, be engendered by capital inflows, and for a time sufficient funds may flow to maintain growth in some of the World Bank's 'showpiece' countries. Countries rendered unviable by a combination of mismanagement and external shocks may, of course, start growing again from a very low level if policy reform (as represented by what I have referred to as the basic components in a structural adjustment package) leads to the development of incentives and if markets start to function again. However, an emphasis on static comparative advantage, for all that it may raise the efficiency of use of present resources, diverts attention away from the fundamental changes that are necessary if a country is to grow out of a range of caput income in the low hundreds of dollars. The other components in the structural adjustment package – liberalization, and minimization of the state's role – far from aiding an advance from the position of stabilization or adjustment to world realities, which may be achieved by application of the basic elements, seem likely to destroy such agents for transformation as currently exist. It may, therefore, be necessary to offer critical support to the basic components in the package, but to reject the later elements for most countries.

The intention of Zimbabwe's 'home-grown' trade liberalization programme is clearly to attempt to raise efficiency by introducing a wider role for market forces. At the same time it is undoubtedly realised that many firms would be destroyed by rapid liberalization; some because they are infants, other because past import constraints have prevented them from reinvesting adequately. The purpose of a tightly monitored five-year transition is to give them time to become competitive. Nevertheless, the influence of the World Bank is obvious in the ultimate aim to remove all quantitative restrictions (something not yet achieved by South Korea or Taiwan, let alone the USA or the EC) in five years, and may represent an over-estimation of the level of development already achieved by the country. It is submitted that a more realistic assessment would be to place it roughly where the NICs were in the early 1960s, that is, ready for a shift of emphasis from import-substitution strategy to export-oriented industrialization, but without abandoning all domestic market protection.

## Notes

This paper was written in early 1990 and revised in late 1990.

1   World Bank (1981).

2   World Bank and UNDP (1989). On page 27 they claim that '... evidence suggests that reforms and economic adjustment generally have led to better economic performance in the

region' (sub-Saharan Africa). Their evidence for this statement is that growth of GDP in 1980-84 was 1.4% with reform, 1.5% without; in 1985-87 it was 2.8% with, 2.7% without. Meanwhile Zimbabwe was achieving 4.1% and 3.4% (and 4.2% for 1985-89). Clearly, these figures offer no support whatsoever to their contention, so they excluded from the samples countries said to have suffered (or benefited from) significant external impacts. This produced the desired result, with adjusters growing faster that non-adjusters – 1.2% and 3.8% as compared with 0.7 and 1.5% (*ibid.* p. 30). However, the criteria for categorisation and the definition of 'external impact' are dubious, and the exclusion of Zimbabwe from the non-adjusters is perverse, given the large negative impact of drought and South African destabilization.

3   Initially in *Growth with Equity*, but also in the papers for the 'Zimcord' conference, both in 1981, and later in the *Transitional National Development Plan, 1982/83 - 1984/85* (TNDP).

4   See the discussion in Riddell 1990.

5   R. H. Green, personal communication.

6   The statistics quoted in the following sections are from the Economist Intelligence Unit, *Country Report: Zimbabwe, Malawi* (quarterly) or *Country Profile Zimbabwe* (annually); most of these derive from the Central Statistical Office (Harare), *Quarterly Digest of Statistics*.

7   See Confederation of Zimbabwe Industries, *Register and Buyers Guide* (annual).

8   See Knox *et al.* 1988, pp. 52-53; also Riddell 1990, pp. 348-9.

9   Of course, the multiplier might result in the creation of more jobs at low investment cost, but unfortunately, the record since 1980 shows little evidence that this has a value significantly greater than unity, and it would need to be 3, with an investment ration of 30 per cent, before full employment became a realistic aim on this strategy.

10   See the chapter on Ghana by Jeffrey Haynes in Parfitt and Riley 1989.

11   Thus in the words of the joint World Bank/UNDP report (1989)'Reforming countries have nevertheless benefited in other respects. Multilateral and bilateral donors have gradually but significantly shifted their aid flows to give greater support to countries with strong sustained adjustment programmes, while aid to non-reforming countries has begun to decline in real terms' (p. 27).

12   For a definition of the infant industry argument, see Corden 1989.

13   'Direct foreign investment in South Korean equities is to be allowed from 1992 ... the government's first clear commitment to financial liberalization'. (*Financial Times*, March 1989). 'South Korea is also opening and liberalizing its market more quickly and at an earlier stage that Japan did' (*Financial Times*, 5 April 1989). A US report in 1989 singled out the following countries for alleged unfair trading practices: Japan, Korea, the European Community, Taiwan, Brazil and India' (*Financial Times*, 2 May 1989).

14   Compare: 'The US yesterday rejected Third World demands for exemptions from trade liberalizing action under the GATT ... Trade liberalization promoted rather than hindered economic growth and was sound policy for countries at all levels of development' (according to Mr. Michael Samuels, US deputy trade representative at GATT meeting, quoted in *Financial Times* 9 November 1988).

15   Net transfers on debt as percentage of GNP, taken from World Bank *World Debt Tables, 1990-91*, vol. 2, *Country Tables*, p. 426

16   From 35 per cent in 1987 it has now fallen to about 20 per cent.

17   A commission appointed in January 1989 to investigate evidence of corruption by ministers and civil servants in motor vehicle marketing.

18   'In the light of Britain's insistence that economic assistance should be confined to those countries such as Nigeria, Ghana, Kenya and Malawi which are firmly committed to

serious and far-reaching economic reforms. Zimbabwe cannot expect very much ... aid and investment inflows will increase substantially only when Zimbabwe follows the majority of other African states down the road to structural adjustment' (*Financial Times*, 29 March 1989).

19  See Evans 1989, p. 15.
20  See Colin Stoneman 1990, pp. 18-23.

## References

Amsden, A. (1989), *Asia's Next Giant: South Korea and Late Industrialization*, Oxford University Press, New York.

Central Statistical Office (Harare), *Quarterly Digest of Statistics*.

Corden, W.M. (1989) in G.M. Meier and W.F. Steel (eds.), *Industrial Adjustment in Sub-Saharan Africa*, Oxford University Press for the World Bank, Oxford.

Economist Intelligence Unit, *Country Profile Zimbabwe* (annually), London.

Economist Intelligence Unit, *Country Report: Zimbabwe, Malawi* (quarterly), London.

Evans, D. (1989), 'Visible and invisible hands in trade policy reform', mimeo, Institute of Development Studies (July).

Haynes, J. (1989) in T.W. Parfitt and S.P. Riley (eds.) *The African Debt Crisis*, Routledge, London.

Knox, J., Robinson, P. and Stoneman, C. (1988), 'Zimod: A Simple Computer Model of the Zimbabwe Economy', *Social Science Computer Review*, vol. 6, no. 1.

Riddell, R.C. (ed.) (1990), *Manufacturing Africa: Performance and Prospects of Seven Countries in Sub-Saharan Africa*, James Currey and Heinemann, London.

Stoneman, C. (1990), 'Zimbabwe opens up to the market', *Africa Recovery*, vol. 4, no. 3-4 (October-December), pp. 18-23.

World Bank (1981), *Accelerated Development in sub-Saharan Africa*, World Bank, Washington, DC.

World Bank and UNDP (1989), *Africa's Adjustment and Growth in the 1980s*, World Bank, Washington, DC.

World Bank (1991), *World Debt Tables, 1990-91*, vol. 2, *Country Tables*, p. 426.

*John Weiss*

# Industrial policy reform in Mozambique in the 1980s

## Introduction

With the recent policy shifts in Eastern Europe it is timely to consider recent changes that have also taken place in some socialist developing economies. China and Vietnam are examples of countries that have introduced significant economic reforms. Less well-documented is the major policy shift in the small war-torn African economy of Mozambique. This chapter discusses the key reforms since the mid-1980s affecting industry, and comments on the limited policy options open to the government.

## Industry in Mozambique after independence

Some of the key facts of Mozambique's recent economic history need to be stated briefly.[1] Prior to independence in 1974 the colony had been a supplier of raw materials to the colonial power Portugal, of labour to the mining sector in South Africa, and of transit services to the inland colonial states of the southern Africa region. A limited industrial development occurred in the 1940s and 1950s, chiefly to serve the needs of the settler community or to provide inputs to export processing. During the 1960s the Portuguese administration of the colony attempted to encourage further industrial development, including the promotion of foreign investment by non-Portuguese firms, as a means of strengthening its position against the emerging nationalist movement of FRELIMO. The settler community increased significantly during the decade, providing a growing market for local consumer goods.

Independence in 1974 came after a protracted campaign by FRELIMO. The circumstances of the transfer of power left the economy weakened significantly. In the three years after 1974 there was a major exodus of settlers, depriving the new state of skills and capital. Portuguese capitalists who left the country often sabotaged the industrial assets they left behind. A significant consequence was that with many enterprises abandoned by their owners, the state stepped in to assume responsibility for their operation. Although not formally owned by the government, these 'intervened enterprises' came to form a major part of the state industrial sector.

The new state inherited an industrial sector relatively small, by international standards, in terms of value-added per head of total population, and heavily skewed towards the traditional manufacturing activities of food processing, beverages and tobacco. Table 9.1 illustrates this, showing these branches with a higher share of manufacturing value-added in Mozambique than in other countries of the region for which comparable data are available.

The disruption of the transfer of power, combined with the effects of the oil price shock and drought, created a major decline in industrial output with 1975 production around 60 per cent of the pre-independence figure.[2] During the second half of the 1970s production recovered steadily, to around 75 per cent of the 1973 peak by 1981. However, that year saw an intensification of the insurgency campaign by the 'armed bandits' RENAMO, which began to create major economic disruption through sabotage of power and transport facilities and general dislocation of life, particularly in rural areas. The first half of the 1980s saw a very major decline in economic activity, with industrial production halved between 1980 and 1985. Severe scarcities of both local and foreign goods emerged, leading to barter systems of exchange in some parts of the country as money ceased to be an acceptable form of exchange. Scarcity led to the emergence of parallel markets for goods and foreign currency at prices very much above official levels. Table 9.2 gives production figures for selected goods 1980-86 to illustrate the extent of the downturn. The crisis of the mid-1980s led to the rethinking of economic policy that is the subject of this chapter.

Table 9.1  *Composition of manufacturing value-added, selected low-income African economies, 1973*

| % share of | Manufacturing value-added per capita ($US 1975 prices) | Food, drink tobacco | Textiles, wearing apparel leather, footwear | Metal products, equipment |
|---|---|---|---|---|
| | | (31)[a] | (32) | (38) |
| Ethiopia | 11 | 29 | 39 | 2 |
| Kenya | 29 | 27 | 10 | 23 |
| Madagascar | 29 | 22 | 40 | 10 |
| Tanzania | 18 | 28 | 24 | 11 |
| Zaire | 15 | 17 | 17 | 15 |
| Zambia | 86 | 11 | 11 | 31 |
| Zimbabwe | 138 | 12 | 16 | 21 |
| Mozambique | 48 | 44 | 15 | 12 |

*Note*
[a] Numbers in brackets refer to ISIC divisions.
*Source:* All countries except Mozambique, UNIDO (1984). For Mozambique, National Planning Commission, *Informação Estatistica*. Maputo.

Table 9.2    *Production of selected industrial commodities, 1980–86*

|  | 1980 | 1981 | 1982 | 1983 | 1984 | 1985 | 1986 |
|---|---|---|---|---|---|---|---|
| Textiles (mill. metres) | 6.0 | 10.1 | 9.5 | 8.4 | 8.8 | 5.8 | 4.6 |
| Garments (mill. pieces) | 7.6 | 7.8 | 7.1 | 8.9 | 9.2 | 6.7 | 4.7 |
| Paints (mill. litres) | 1.0 | 0.6 | 1.0 | 0.9 | 0.7 | 0.4 | 0.2 |
| Tyres and tubes (thousand pieces) | 197.0 | 301.0 | 228.0 | 195.0 | 89.0 | 162.0 | 123.0 |
| Glass containers (mill. pieces) | 24.0 | 21.9 | 19.9 | 16.5 | 20.6 | 9.3 | 6.9 |
| Oils and soaps (thousand tons) | 36.8 | 47.5 | 40.6 | 34.1 | 21.4 | 12.6 | 13.2 |
| Flour (thousand tons) | 98.4 | 109.5 | 95.0 | 82.0 | 74.4 | 73.6 | 57.5 |
| Cement (thousand tons) | 236.0 | 261.0 | 270.0 | 188.0 | 105.0 | 77.0 | 73.0 |
| Timber thousand cubic metres) | 164.0 | 140.0 | 92.0 | 62.0 | 74.0 | 68.0 | 72.0 |

*Source*: National Planning Commission, *Informação Estatistica* (1986).

## Industrial policy and planning after independence

FRELIMO officially adopted Marxism-Leninism as party ideology at its third congress in 1977. This position was only reversed at the 1989 congress, in favour of a looser form of socialism. In the late 1970s, in line with the party's new ideological stance, a central planning system was introduced. The formal sector of the economy was obviously more susceptible to central control than were peasant agriculture or informal urban activities, and the controls and directives of the plan were influential in relation to the larger industrial enterprises. In principle all industrial enterprises of 'national importance', whether publicly or privately owned, were included in the plan. The system operated through a hierarchical network of controls. Enterprises were controlled by different ministries, depending on their type of products, for example, engineering goods and industrial intermediates were the responsibility of the Ministry of Industry and Energy, agro-processed goods the responsibility of the Ministry of Agriculture, light consumer goods the responsibility of the Ministry of Light Industry and building materials the responsibility of the Ministry of Construction. Operational supervision of enterprises was provided by co-ordination units or directorates, under the authority of the various Ministries, that specialised in particular types of enterprise. For example, under the Ministry of Light Industry there were separate directorates for textiles, clothing and beverages, and under the Ministry of Industry and Energy, separate directorates of light and heavy engineering.

Annual enterprise production targets were set by the Planning Commission, with an attempt to balance overall production and requirements for categories of industrial products. Detailed controls over enterprises were operated by the directorates, who allocated foreign exchange and raw materials, and directed enterprise outputs to the users identified in the plan. Official sales under plan allocations were at controlled prices. In consultation with directorates, enterprises prepared annual plans and estimates of their input requirements, and in an iterative procedure, attempts were made to reconcile national targets with what was feasible for enterprises. However, even for private sector firms, enterprises autonomy was strictly limited.

This tight control system for industrial enterprises was introduced in 1979 and lasted in the form described to around 1987. However, with the difficulties faced by the economy in the 1980s the planning system operated in a rapidly deteriorating environment, so that there were increasingly less resources to allocate. For many enterprises heavy financial losses emerged, which were covered directly by the Central Bank.

In terms of industrial strategy, the government briefly considered a form of heavy industry strategy, similar to that partly pursued in Tanzania in the 1970s, and often associated with socialist industrialisation. In 1981 a ten-year development plan was drawn up which included investment in larger-scale industrial projects, in activities like iron and steel, aluminium, chemicals, engineering and vehicle assembly. The basic premise of the plan was a 'large project approach' for both industry and agriculture. However, the plan's requirements in terms of financing and implementation were such that it was finally judged impractical and was never formally published, By 1983, with the deteriorating economic situation, the FRELIMO congress officially reversed the emphasis on large projects, emphasizing instead the need to utilize and rehabilitate existing capacity and to encourage the small-scale sector. The need to promote small-scale industry using local resources for local consumption was recognized. Since then the objectives of policy have not altered significantly, with encouragement to new initiatives by small industries combined with rehabilition of the existing larger enterprises. Within this latter category, priorities for rehabilitation have not been set out explicitly.

## Industrial policy reform from the mid-1980s

The central planning system had a major impact on resource allocation in industry, since it allocated the key resource of foreign exchange and controlled enterprises prices for official sales. However, the economy in general was far from planned, given the difficulties of planning the peasant sector, the external shocks emanating from the world market, and the internal dislocation and sabotage caused by the insurgency.

As early as 1983 the government appears to have been rethinking the central aspects of policy. This was reinforced by the entry into Mozambique of the major international agencies. The country joined the IMF and World Bank in 1984, and started to receive significant bilateral donor assistance from USAID around the same time.[3] Up to 1987 reform mainly involved some decontrol of prices, particularly for fruit and vegetables. However, the main set of reforms came in January 1987 with the launch of the Economic Recovery Programme (ERP). This attempted to both adjust for major macroeconomic imbalances through a package of reforms familiar from structural adjustment elsewhere in the region, and to alter the institutional framework of the economy through a virtual dismantling of the central planning system.

For industry the key focus of the ERP is on plant rehabilitation, with financing and technical assistance provided through bilateral and multilateral donor programmes. The new policy has three broad objectives for industry:

- greater enterprise autonomy through the use of commercial criteria in decision-taking;
- greater encouragement for new private investment, both local and foreign;
- greater efficiency in resource use through a shift in relative prices.

Greater enterprise autonomy is being introduced in recognition of the rigidity of the system of central control at the enterprise level. It has been implemented through a major diminution of the role of the central plan. Plan targets are no longer binding, and are based on a bottom-up procedure from enterprises' own estimates. Enterprises are free to sell their output where they choose, and can set their own prices using a cost-plus pricing formula. Most industrial prices are 'conditional', in that the directorates of the controlling Ministries have the authority to check increases *ex-post* to see they are in line with the agreed formula. However, *de facto*, there is now little administrative check on prices. Directorates still have the role of allocating foreign exchange, and given the import-intensive nature of industry in Mozambique, access to foreign exchange is a key determinant of output growth.

As a result of the large increases in aid financing, foreign exchange is now much more readily available than in the early 1980s, and there are now alternative mechanisms for obtaining foreign exchange that do not involve the directorates. First, an export retention scheme was introduced in 1983 to allow exporters the right to purchase foreign currency up to an agreed proportion of their export sales. Second, where there is an aid programme for a particular enterprise, foreign exchange made available under that programme goes directly to the enterprises concerned. Third, since September 1989, a relatively small proportion of foreign exchange has been set aside for a non-administered fund whereby for selected products, registered enterprises can have automatic access to foreign exchange and the guarantee of an import licence. However, for most imports, a licensing system still applies so that even after enterprises have obtained access to foreign exchange, permission must be obtained to import specific products.[4] Finally, a potentially significant reform designed to increase enterprise autonomy is the change in labour legislation in 1987, which allows payment of performance-linked incentive payments and gives greater scope for enterprises to declare redundancy on commercial grounds.

The greater encouragement to private investment can be seen as a continuation of the emphasis of the 1983 FRELIMO congress, which drew attention to the importance of encouraging private initiative. The government has shown a willingness to sell off some of the intervened industrial enterprises under its control. Further, two relatively generous investment incentive laws have been passed, one in 1984 dealing with foreign investors, and the other in 1987 with new domestic investors. These give holidays from profits taxation for periods of three to ten years, plus various tax deductions. Also, in December 1988 the basic structure of enterprise taxation was modified, with the removal of all tax on distributed dividends and the restriction of the maximum rate of profits tax to 50 per cent. The government has made serious efforts to attract foreign investors, although as yet little foreign capital has come into industry. Given the importance of investor confidence in decisions on location for foreign investment, one would not expect heavy foreign investment prior to a resolution of the insurgency.[5] Emphasis has also been given to encouraging the small-scale private sector, with finance and technical assistance provided under aid programmes.

In terms of the relative price changes generated by the ERP, the key parameter for industry is seen as the price of foreign exchange. During the first half of the 1980s, whilst the official exchange rate was fixed, its growing scarcity saw the emergence of an unofficial market where foreign exchange was priced at many times its official value. The ERP introduced a series of step devaluations with the aim of bringing the official rate closer to the black market rate. The rationale is the familiar one: that this will price foreign exchange at its opportunity cost and thus encourage exports, discourage the use of imports and encourage the use of local non-traded inputs by industrial enterprises, whilst also bringing foreign exchange back from the parallel into the official market. The nominal official exchange rate has moved from around 40 metical per US dollar in late 1986 to over 800 metical per dollar in late 1989. The exact degree of real devaluation is difficult to measure given the lack of an accurate internal price index, but it almost certainly has been very substantial. At present, with the continuation of licensing restrictions, most enterprises that compete directly with imports receive protection through a combination of quota restrictions, import tariffs and movements in the real exchange rate. The system of import controls and tariffs is under review and it is likely that in future, with some loosening of import controls, a greater part of protection will be through tariffs and the exchange rate.

These policy changes are part of a wider programme of reform and have been accompanied by a major increase in aid financing. Given the dependence of Mozambique industry on imported inputs and the very low capacity utilization in 1985 and 1986, one would expect that production would rise significantly with the availability of more foreign exchange. However, changes in the security situation can easily offset these positive effects. What can be said is that the ERP's own targets are extremely optimistic and will not be met. The original aim was to bring production back to 1980 levels by 1990. Very approximate estimates for 1988 put industrial output at no more that 50 per cent of the 1980 level. This is a modest increase over the 1985-87 period, but clearly recovery to the 1980 level will not be achieved in the short run. In comparison with reform programmes elsewhere in Africa, preliminary estimates suggest a more dramatic decline prior to the introduction of the reforms, but a somewhat more rapid recovery that in the Ivory Coast, Zambia and Nigeria (see Table 9.3). Initial results have been less favourable than in Ghana.

## Alternative industrial strategies

The security question and the country's geo-political position as a front-line state make the Mozambique situation different from that elsewhere. However, for any small, low-income economy with a poor infrastructure and weak industrial base, strategic choices are limited. For Mozambique there is a sense in which the recent policy shift represented the only viable alternative. The move from a system of central direction to one of enterprise autonomy, with greater use of market allocation, is paralleled in other socialist developing economies in response to the difficulties of devising and implementing detailed directives for industry. Even without the obvious dislocations caused by the insurgency, there would have been a strong case for greater use of market rationality in industrial policy, even if the market was guided by central plan priorities.[7] Also, there is doubt as to whether state industrialisation alone could have led the rehabilitation drive now under way. State entrepreneurs are required if the public sector is to play a leading role, whilst the state is seriously short of qualified professionals. The encouragement to private investment can be seen as an attempt to tap the initiative of those potential entrepreneurs who could otherwise have emigrated or engaged in service or trade activities.

Table 9.3 *Comparative performance of manufacturing in selected African economies before and during economic reform programmes*

| | Manufacturing output[a] | |
| Country | Before | During |
| --- | --- | --- |
| Ivory Coast | −1.8 (1981–83) | 5.8 (1984–86) |
| Ghana | −17.1 (1980–83) | 15.0 (1984–87) |
| Nigeria | −7.8 (1982–85) | 0.2 (1986–87) |
| Zambia | −3.1 (1982–84) | 4.0 (1984–86) |
| Mozambique | −15.5 (1980–86) | 7.8 (1987–88) |

*Note*
[a]Average annual growth of real output.
*Source*: For Mozambique *Informação Estatística*, and for the other countries World Bank (1989), box 5.4, p. 117.

In terms of priorities within industry, as yet no clear view has been taken. The broad strategic choice of inward-looking import substitution versus outward-looking export promotion seems over-simplified in the Mozambique context. Although there is a tendency to treat all manufactures as internationally traded goods, this can be misleading in low-income, industrially backward economies. If one sees traded goods as products manufactured to world standards with an internationally recognized technology, non-traded or local manufactures will be those whose quality makes them inadequate substitutes for imports and non-exportable.

In Mozambique, apart from agro-processed goods, manufactured exports are a very small proportion of production with the vast majority of goods sold in the home market. In the 1980s the situation was one of general scarcity, with both imports and local manufactures in excess demand. There are some import-competing traded activities where domestic goods serve a similar market to imports. These include items like paints, boxes, cement and tyres. Without re-equipping and modernisation, these activities are unlikely to be internationally competitive. However, for such goods, some protection is likely to be justified well into the medium term, not on specific infant industry grounds, but more in terms of an infant economy argument based on the general backwardness of skill and infrastructure. There is nothing radical or socialist about protecting inefficient, technically-outmoded industry on a permanent basis, and experience elsewhere has demonstrated the need to combine protection with incentives to reduce costs and improve efficiency. There is a need, therefore, to ensure that protection of this type is not a major obstacle to improvements in operating performance.

Exportable manufactures are currently largely agro-processed goods like sugar, timber and cashews. Despite the significant real devaluation, there can be little expectation that exports will play a major role in Mozambique's industrialisation, given the unfamiliarity of producers with export markets and the need to adapt production to internationally competitive standards.[8]

At present, a significant part of industry in Mozambique falls under the category of non-traded goods, since quality is so much below world levels. These include products like beer, garments, footwear, drums, cans, soap, some building materials and some light engineering products. Casual observation suggests that in the late 1980s some of these goods were selling at prices below the c.i.f. price of import alternatives. Their low quality and cheaper price meant that they served a different segment of the market to imports. In some branches, these goods involve small-scale production and draw on local raw materials.

One can argue that in a low-income economy, there are limits on the extent to which industry should aim at producing international standard products, and that in Mozambique efforts should be made to develop relatively efficient products that serve the local, low-income market. This view finds support from diverse intellectual positions. It is in the spirit of the socialist industrialisation strategy for small economies set out in the early 1970s by Clive Thomas, that argues that industry should meet local needs based on local resources and utilizing local technology.[9] Further, it is in line with the emphasis on small and medium industry that the World Bank is advocating for African industrialisation, since in many cases this type of good can be produced at output levels that are low by international standards, using an adapted version of foreign technology.[10]

The implication of this argument is that whilst there may be some place for import substitution production that replicates import standards, and for export promotion aimed at foreign demand, neither are likely to be central to a successful industrial strategy for Mozambique. In the more liberalized environment following the ERP, survival simply on the basis of government protection will no longer be a viable option, so that local industry will need some specific advantages over foreign producers, if it is to survive in the long-term. Low labour costs and use of local raw materials are potential advantages for some domestic producers, but for others, knowledge of, and proximity to the local market, and an ability to modify products to the requirements of this market, are likely to be crucial.

## Notes

1  Useful sources are Hanlon (1984) and Isaacman (1983).

2  Production data come from National Planning Commission, *Informação Estatistica*.

3  Disentangling the relative significance of external pressure and internal decisions in explaining the government's policy shift is difficult. Ottoway (1988) suggests the initial impetus for reform was internal.

4  The question of the relationship between directorates and enterprises was under discussion in the late 1980s. One possibility is to convert the larger directorates into holding companies.

5  There has been press speculation that there may be political motives behind the government's attempts to attract South African capital. The argument is that this could create a group in the South African business sector with an interest in discontinuing support for RENAMO.

6  Based on data from *Informação Estatistica*.

7  Mackintosh (1985) argues for the greater use of prices and markets in agriculture as part of a socialist agricultural transition. White and Wade (1988) discuss the concept of a 'guided market' in the context of price reform in China.

8  In examining export performance in sub-Saharan Africa, Balassa (1990) finds the real exchange rate to be a statistically significant explanatory variable. However, the vast majority of African exports remain non-manufactures, and growth of manufactured exports in the 1980s has been slower than in other developing regions.

9  Thomas (1974) also focuses on the need for an integrated industrial structure, which implies investment in a range of basic industries supplying industrial inputs.

10  World Bank (1989; p. 137) discusses the importance of fostering entrepreneurship and argues that 'The paucity of business that can link imported and local technologies – 'the missing middle' – is a major impediment to Africa's development'.

## References

Balassa, B. (1990), 'Incentive policies and export performance in sub-Saharan Africa', *World Development*, vol. 18, no. 3.

Hanlon, J. (1984), *Mozambique: the Revolution under Fire*, Zed Books, London.

Isaacman, A. and Isaacman, B. (1983), *Mozambique: from Colonialism to Revolution*, Westview, Boulder, Colorado.

Mackintosh, M. (1985), 'Economic tactics: commercial policy and socialization of African agriculture', *World Development*, vol. 13, no. 1.

Ottoway, M. (1988), 'Mozambique: from symbolic socialism to symbolic reform', *Journal of Modern African Studies*, vol. 26, no. 2.

Thomas, C (1974), *Dependence and Transformation*, Monthly Review, New York.

UNIDO (1984), *Handbook of Industrial Statistics*, UN, New York.

White, G. and Wade, R. (1988), 'Developmental states and markets in East Asia: an introduction', in G. White (ed.), *Development States in East Asia*, Macmillan, London.

World Bank (1989), *Sub-Saharan Africa: From Crisis to Sustainable Growth*, World Bank, Washington, DC.

# Bias overkill? Removal of anti-export bias and manufacturing investment: Ghana 1983–89

This chapter analyses the impact upon the activity of the manufacturing sector in sub-Saharan African countries of attempts to remove anti-export bias through devaluation and foreign-trade liberalization policies. It is argued that these will modify incentives in such a way as to discourage private investment. The conclusion drawn is that, even if one accepts the view that restoration of efficiency in the manufacturing sector implies de-protection of domestic manufacturing through devaluation and trade liberalization, the private sector cannot be relied upon to invest in manufacturing while these rationalisation policies are being pursued, so that the expected efficiency gains will not materialise unless the state comes in either as a direct investor, or by engaging in an active industrial policy. Such a policy would entail either interference with market through incentive-modification, or resorting to a policy of 'managed macro-disequilibrium', especially concerning the exchange rate.

The first part of the chapter expounds the general argument, while the second provides an illustration based on Ghana's recent experience.

## The general argument

There is a general agreement on the necessity to develop industrial sectors in Africa. The Berg report (World Bank 1981), although held to be the first articulation of policies directed more towards agriculture than industry, states:

Industry has a crucial role in long-term development; it is one of the best training grounds for skill development; it is an important source of structural changes and diversification; and it can increase the flexibility of the economy and reduce dependence on external forces.

But it goes on to warn:

Although these development benefits justify incurring some additional costs to promote industry, they do not justify the promotion of industry at any cost. ... Excessive investment in industry can starve other sectors of capital, foreign exchange and high-level manpower, while expensive manufactured products can raise costs in other sectors and limit their growth. (World Bank, 1981; pp. 91-2)

Although there is a consensus on the need for industrialisation, the nature of industrialisation, as well as the means required to promote it, are still open to debate. The structuralist view, as expressed for instance by Singh (1982), stresses the benefits to be reaped from industrialisation in the future, even if these do not materialise in the present, and recommends state intervention to promote it.

On the contrary, the view which has gained strength during the 1980s considers that the form of industrialisation which has been either directly promoted by the state (Nellis 1986), or has developed under indirect public intervention (Balassa 1980), has proved inefficient. The World Bank view, as expressed in the World Development Report (1987), or in Meier and Steel (1989, p. 14) is that efficient industrialisation will best be promoted by de-protection of domestic industrial sectors, leading to outward orientation and a withdrawal of the state from interference in both internal and external trade.

This view is clearly reflected in structural adjustment programmes and justifies a number of measures, among which foreign trade liberalization and withdrawal of the state from industrial activity figure prominently together with devaluation. Such measures promote changes in the economic environment, but, as noted by Riddell (1990), do not define an industrial policy.

The main concern of these measures appears to be less the short-term evolution of industrial activity than the medium-term evolution of efficiency, which suggests the possibility of a trade-off between aggregate output and efficiency, resulting in a case for short-term positive de-industrialisation in African countries. In so far as some industrial enterprises are net absorbers of scarce resources, including foreign exchange, closing them down would improve overall resource availability.

Hopefully, if supply-side reforms are effective enough to allow domestic manufacturing to gain new markets, especially for exports, industrial expansion will occur eventually. This scenario is however a rather long-term one, which depends on a lengthy sequence of events starting from overall reform and ending with the conquest of new markets. This transition involves two crucial stages: an effective increase in industrial efficiency and a positive reaction by the private sector to new investment opportunities.

One paradoxical element in the sequence is that, although industrial output might be left to contract in the short term, investment (preferably private in this view) would have to take place simultaneously, following possible opportunities created by devaluation and trade liberalization. Independently of the effectiveness of liberalization in terms of industrial efficiency, this requirement placed upon private investors points to a delicate sequencing policy.

The traditional crowding-out argument suggests that withdrawal of the state will ease the domestic credit situation, improving private investors' access to funds and hence allowing new investment (Marsden and Belot 1987). Assuming that crowding-out is the general case, investment will take place only if and where opportunities are attractive enough. However, there are no a priori reasons why these opportunities should materialise in manufacturing.

One way of approaching this question is to look at the manufacturing sector in terms of its international competitiveness and then investigate the effects of devaluation, before considering trade liberalization. One can start by noting the *de facto* non-traded position of manufacturing sectors, which cater mainly for domestic markets and export only a small part of their output. In principle, they produce import-substitutes, and as such ought to be considered as tradable sectors, but they are not import-competing, because of protection policies such as protective tariffs and quantitative restrictions,[1] Following Schydlowsky (1982), one can then characterise goods produced by such sectors as 'tradables made non-traded by policy fiat', or more briefly as 'policy-induced' non-traded goods.

This problem in classification introduces some ambiguity regarding the manufacturing sector's reaction to devaluation and trade liberalization. Since one of the aims of devaluation cum liberalization is to revive production of tradables as opposed to non-tradables, one can speculate which characteristic will dominate: that of 'tradables' or 'non-traded' goods.

## Impact of devaluation

If we look at the effects of devaluation first, one notes that, as non-traded activities, domestic prices of manufactures do not obey the 'law of one price', and do not follow the simple equation $DP = OER \times WP$ (where DP is the domestic price, OER is the official rate of exchange and WP the World price of a similar good). There is then a possibility that they will react as non-tradables, so that relative price movements turn against them.

At 'best' (if protection results solely from protective tariffs, TM) domestic prices of manufactures will be constrained so that DP is less than or equal to $(OER \times WP) + TM$. At 'worst', if protection is enforced through quantitative restrictions, they will bear no simple direct relation to the world price.[2] Consequently, domestic prices need not change by the full amount of devaluation.

Given that in contractionary conditions, especially under import-substitution, manufacturing sectors exhibit large excess capacity, they will typically follow a fixed-price pattern, based on a cost-plus mark-up, and react to shifts in domestic demand through output variations in a 'stagnationist' fashion (Taylor 1988; p. 30). Such appears to be the case in Ghana (Green 1987). In such a situation, output prices will not increase by the full amount of devaluation, but will react to cost increases.

On the cost side, with an above-average import content, manufacturing activities will have a higher post-devaluation inflation than other activities, pushing up their relative prices and possibly inducing a fall in domestic demand. *De facto* non-tradability will then result in something like a scissors' crisis where, at best, mark-ups or margins in the manufacturing sector remain constant.

On the resource allocation side, non-traded manufactured goods will complete with true 'tradables', that is exports, whose prices will fully reflect devaluation. If investment opportunities materialise after devaluation they will tend to appear more in export and export-related sectors than in domestic-oriented manufacturing.

The co-existence of a 'true' tradable sector in exports, and a 'policy-induced' non-traded manufacturing sector will then turn to the advantage of the truly tradable sector, and correction of anti-export bias through devaluation will in effect introduce an anti-domestic bias. This asymmetry between tradables and policy-induced non-traded activities will result in a movement of incentives against manufacturing, unless it can be turned into a truly tradable sector.

## Impact of trade liberalization

Since protection is responsible for this 'non-tradability', the answer must lie in liberalization. If de-protected, manufactured goods would become truly tradable; competing effectively with imports, their domestic price would be determined by the world price times the rate of exchange and fully reflect devaluation, which would then enhance investment opportunities. However, liberalization of external trade *pari passu* with devaluation will spark another sequence of events, most probably aggravating the anti-domestic bias.

Regarding price differentials, liberalization will seek to weaken overall protection and equalise it among various goods. This means that the differential between world prices and domestically produced competing goods will diminish, lowering the upper boundary on domestic output prices. (The TM element will fall in the constraining equation $DP < (WP \times OER) + TM$). Simultaneously, domestic prices of imported inputs will tend to increase relative to that of output if tariffs tend toward equality, that is, if tariffs on imported inputs (traditionally low in import-substituting strategies) rise, closing the gap between rates of protection on inputs and output. The downward adjusting element will then be domestic value-added, cutting profit margins.

Availability of inputs might also suffer as a result of trade liberalization. Imported inputs will probably be substituted against in favour of imports of consumer goods, following the release of pent-up demand previously repressed through import controls (Ocampo 1987).[3] Domestic input availability might also be reduced, if domestic inputs are equally exportables. It might prove more profitable to sell them directly on the world market than to local producers, or, manufacturers might find then too costly if they have to pay the export-price, which comes to the same thing. This will lead to an absolute or perhaps relative fall in the availability of industrial inputs, inducing import-strangulation in the manufacturing sector.

Finally, on the demand side, domestic demand will partly shift in favour of imported goods, while, on the resource allocation-side, trade liberalization will open a new range of profitable opportunities, attracting investment outside the manufac-turing sector.

The overall result is that investment opportunities will not be good in the domestic manufacturing sector, which might be part of the explanation for the decrease in investment under Structural adjustment programmes noted by Mosley, Harrigan and Toye (1991).

Now, granted that a combination of devaluation, liberalization and de-protection is necessary to improve efficiency in manufacturing and that investment will be necessary to take advantage of opportunities opened by the prospects of increased efficiency, the question is, who will choose to invest, under such circumstances?

The aim of greater efficiency and the movement of incentives then appear to contradict each other; de-protection leads to greater efficiency, but by depressing profit opportunities weakens investment. One can then think of two ways out. One is to invest despite adverse incentive movements, which means substituting public for private investment. The other is to alter the incentive scheme so as to restore private profitability. In both cases, we fall back on interventionist policies, either direct interventionism, by engaging in public investment, or indirect, by interfering with the incentive system in order to induce private investment.

### Ghana under structural adjustment

The workings of the bias created by devaluation cum liberalization bias is illustrated by the case of Ghana. Although presented as a major success by the World Bank (World Bank 1989a and 1990), Ghana's is a rather untypical experience.

Its adjustment programme was supported by a vast transfer of external resources. Net transfers from 1983 to 1987 totalled US$1,179 million, which is roughly as much as Benin, Niger, Senegal and Togo received together during the same period. Official capital inflows moved from US$126.9 million in 1981 to US$302.9 million in 1984 and US$412.7 million in 1987, while private direct investment fell from US$16.3 million to respectively US$2.0 million and US$4.7 million in the same years (IMF 1988).

Exports showed a marked recovery with year on year growth rates, in current dollars, ranging from 7 per cent to more than 37 per cent between 1984 and 1987. This trend showed most markedly in the export/GDP ratio, which was increased more than six-fold between 1983 (3.3 per cent) and 1988 (21.2 per cent).

On the domestic side, demand was restored by an increase in nominal aggregate wages and salaries both in the public and private sectors, as well as an increase in agricultural producer prices. Between 1983 and 1987 the total government wage bill increased 11.8 times, cocoa producer prices by 12.5 times, while the consumer price index increased only 3.5 times, all inducing an increase in demand for consumer goods (Leenhardt and L'Heriteau 1989). Private consumption, after falling by roughly 5 per cent and 10 per cent per annum in 1982 and 1983, regained momentum, reaching the 1981 level in 1984 and increasing steadily from then on to reach a cumulative increase of 24 per cent between 1983 and 1987, and 33.3 per cent between 1983 and 1988.

The impact on industry was quite marked, with the overall production volume index increasing by 53 per cent between 1983 and 1987, with an even more marked growth in manufacturing volume of 71 per cent. Wholesale and retail trade increased by 60 per cent over the same period. The external constraint was relaxed, with imports increasing by 33 per cent (in 1980 values) between 1983 and 1987, and the import to GDP ratio rising from 9.2 per cent in 1983 to 25 per cent in 1988.

Table 10.1   *Ghana: selected indicators, 1980–88*

| | 1980 | 1981 | 1982 | 1983 | 1984 | 1985 | 1986 | 1987 | 1988 |
|---|---|---|---|---|---|---|---|---|---|
| GNP (million cedis 1908 prices) | 42,670 | 41,452 | 38,761 | 37,063 | 40,215 | 41,955 | 43,994 | 45,910 | 48,633 |
| Annual rate of change | 0.3 | −2.9 | −6.5 | −4.4 | 8.5 | 4.3 | 4.9 | 4.4 | 5.9 |
| Private Consumption (million cedis 1980 prices) | 35,953 | 33,941 | 30,564 | 30,461 | 33,973 | 35,755 | 37,055 | 37,919 | 40,606 |
| Annual rate of change | 2.4 | −5.6 | −9.9 | −0.3 | 11.5 | 5.2 | 3.6 | 2.3 | 7.1 |
| Gross Fixed Investment (million cedis 1980 prices) | 2,613 | 2,309 | 1,783 | 1,742 | 1,985 | 2,476 | 2,395 | 2,907 | NA |
| Annual rate of change | −5.7 | −11.6 | −22.8 | −2.3 | 13.9 | 24.7 | −3.3 | 21.4 | NA |
| Export (million US$) 1980 prices 1,257 | 1,247 | 1,214 | 638 | 648 | 809 | 1,198 | 1,270 | 1,395 | |
| Annual rate of change | 32.6 | −0.8 | −2.6 | −47.4 | 1.6 | 24.8 | 48.1 | 6.0 | 9.8 |
| Imports (million US$) 1980 prices) 1,128 | 1,071 | 726 | 643 | 699 | 808 | 898 | 856 | 920 | |
| Annual rate of change | 8.8 | −5.1 | −32.2 | −11.4 | 8.7 | 15.6 | 11.1 | −4.7 | 7.5 |
| Agricultural output (million cedis 1980 prices) 24,821 | 24,183 | 22,865 | 21,270 | 23,335 | 23,486 | 24,259 | 24,267 | 25,140 | |
| Annual rate of change | 2.2 | −2.6 | −5.5 | −7.0 | 9.7 | 0.6 | 3.3 | 0.0 | 3.6 |
| Industrial output (million cedis 1980 prices) | 5,086 | 4,273 | 3,546 | 3,125 | 3,404 | 4,006 | 4,313 | 4,802 | 5,291 |
| Annual rate of change | 0.3 | −16.0 | −17.0 | −11.9 | 8.9 | 17.7 | 7.7 | 11.3 | 10.2 |
| Manufacturing output (million cedis 1980 prices) 3,346 | 2,700 | 2,147 | 1,909 | 2,153 | 2,677 | 2,974 | 3,270 | 3,575 | |
| Annual rate of change | −1.4 | −19.3 | −20.5 | −11.1 | 12.8 | 24.3 | 11.1 | 10.0 | 9.3 |
| Imports as a proportion of GNP | 9.2 | 5.3 | 3.0 | 9.3 | 7.9 | 11.9 | 23.1 | 24.3 | 25.1 |
| Exports as a proportion of GNP | 8.5 | 4.8 | 3.3 | 6.2 | 7.5 | 9.8 | 19.6 | 21.2 | 19.0 |

*Note*
Share of exports and imports in national income calculated from current cedi values.
*Source:* World Bank *World Tables*, various issues, Washington DC.

A closer examination reveals that this increase in output was most marked in sectors producing consumer goods (such as food products, beverages and tobacco, which together have a weight of 73 per cent in the national consumer price index, and represent close to 45 per cent of manufacturing output), and export goods (such as sawmill and wood products). Production of intermediaries, such as cement and non-metallic minerals, iron and steel and non-ferrous metals tended to grow more slowly.

Output increases brought about a rise in capacity utilization, which according to the World Bank, rose on average from 19 per cent to 32 per cent between 1980-83 and 1984-87 (World Bank 1989a). Here, the same pattern as for output is revealed, with capacity utilization increasing more markedly in domestic consumer and export-related sectors.

Table 10.2  *Index of manufacturing production, 1981–87 (1977 = 100)*

| Sectors | 1981 | 1982 | 1983 | 1984 | 1985 | 1986 | 1987 | A | B |
|---|---|---|---|---|---|---|---|---|---|
| Food | 58.8 | 38.2 | 46.3 | 29.3 | 41.8 | 40.6 | 50.5 | 1.09 | 0.95 |
| Beverages | 78.2 | 50.7 | 42.5 | 60 | 59.3 | 75.1 | 85.2 | 2.00 | 1.40 |
| Tobacco | 50.8 | 38.1 | 33.7 | 63.4 | 61.3 | 57.6 | 54.6 | 1.63 | 1.37 |
| Textile | 32.1 | 15.7 | 10.6 | 15.9 | 19.2 | 22.9 | 26.1 | 2.46 | 1.26 |
| Sawmill & wood Products | 52.4 | 36 | 45.6 | 60.3 | 75.4 | 79.5 | 79.3 | 1.74 | 1.77 |
| Chemicals excluding petroleum | 34.7 | 17.1 | 18.6 | 40.4 | 31.8 | 38 | 51.8 | 2.79 | 1.91 |
| Cement and non-metallic minerals | 71.4 | 46.5 | 50.3 | 42.4 | 63.6 | 47.4 | 49.7 | 0.98 | 0.86 |
| Iron and steel | 69.8 | 30.9 | 12.8 | 26.3 | 46.2 | 38.8 | 42.9 | 3.35 | 1.08 |
| Non-ferrous Metals | 104.5 | 113.8 | 25.6 | na | 28.4 | 72.5 | 90.3 | 3.53 | 1.00 |
| *Total* | 63.3 | 50.4 | 35.3 | 39.3 | 49.3 | 54.2 | 56.8 | 1.61 | 1.12 |

*Note*
A is the ratio of the output index of 1987 to that of 1983, the year in which the Adjustment
 Programme was started.
B is the ratio of average index for 1986-87 to the average index for 1981-83.
*Source*: Government of Ghana, Central Bureau of Statistics.

Table 10.3  *Trends in capacity utilization (%)*

| Sector | 1983 | 1984 | 1985 | 1986 | 1987 | 1988 | A |
|---|---|---|---|---|---|---|---|
| Textiles | 16.0 | 17.3 | 19.7 | 17 | 24 | 33 | 2.0 |
| Chemicals | na | 20 | 21 | 26 | 28 | 30 | 1.5 |
| Wood products | 20 | 28.1 | 32.5 | na | 43 | 70 | 3.5 |
| Rubber | 22 | 15 | 16 | 23 | 28 | 38 | 1.7 |
| Plastics | 35 | 30.4 | 28 | 30 | 39 | 39 | 1.1 |
| Paper and printing | 30 | 17.3 | 14.5 | na | 30 | 42 | 1.4 |
| Pharmaceuticals | 35 | 27.4 | 16.6 | 25 | 33 | 29.6 | 0.85 |
| Electricals | 44 | 8.3 | 33.2 | 30 | 36 | 40 | 0.9 |
| Leather | 26 | 12 | 21 | 14 | 15 | 20 | 0.8 |
| Garments | 25 | 20 | 25.5 | 27 | 25 | 35 | 1.4 |

*Note*
A is the ratio of capacity utilisation in 1988 to that in 1983.
*Source*: Government of Ghana, Ministry of Industry, Science & Technology and UNIDO.

The reaction of private investment, on the other hand, was extremely sluggish.
The ratio of gross domestic investment to GDP rose from 6.9 per cent 1984 to an
estimated 12.5 per cent in 1988 (with a projected figure of 16.5 per cent for 1991),
but most of the increase was due to public investment, whose ratio to GDP rose
roughly 3.5 times from 2.5 to 8.3 per cent between 1984 and 1988, while that of
private investment actually fell from 4.4 to 4.2 per cent between these two dates,

with most private investment going into rehabilitation of gold mines (World Bank 1989b).

This point was raised in at least in two meetings of the IMF's reviews of ESAF in November 1989 and June 1990, where disappointment was expressed in the weak reaction of the private sector to devaluation.[4] An indication of the sectors which have attracted private investment is given by data from the Ghana Investment Centre (Table 10.4)

Table 10.4   *Total proposed investments in projects approved by Ghana Investment Centre ($US millions)*

| Area of activity | 1986 | 1987 | 1988 | 1989 | Total |
| --- | --- | --- | --- | --- | --- |
| *1. AGRICULTURE* | 55.4 | 74.7 | 43.4 | 31.0 | 204.5 |
| *2. MANUFACTURING* | 208.2 | 283.5 | 117.4 | 137.9 | 747.0 |
| Food | 33.3 | 33.4 | 16.9 | 10.8 | 94.4 |
| Beverages | - | 0.8 | 32.3 | 3.2 | 36.3 |
| Tobacco | - | - | - | 4.5 | 4.5 |
| Textiles, garments, and leather | 0 | 4.8 | 0.6 | 0.1 | 5.8 |
| Wood and wood products | 128.6 | 174.3 | 35.1 | 66.8 | 404.8 |
| Non-metallic minerals | 1.6 | - | 0.6 | 4.1 | 6.3 |
| Fabricated metal products | 20.3 | 13.8 | 11.0 | 2.4 | 47.5 |
| Machinery and electricals and transport equipment | 0 | 0 | 3.4 | 0.2 | 3.6 |
| *3. BUILDING AND CONSTRUCTION* | - | 5.2 | 3.3 | 5.8 | 14.3 |
| *4. TOURISM* | 109.9 | 3.9 | 2.4 | 16.7 | 132.9 |
| *5. SERVICES* | 2.2 | 0.2 | 7.8 | 7.4 | 17.6 |
| *TOTAL* | 375.7 | 367.5 | 174.3 | 198.8 | 1116.3 |

*Source:* Ghana Investment Centre *Annual reports.*

Is this behaviour explained by the reversal of bias following devaluation and trade liberalization? The limited indications we have fit in with our earlier analysis.

As regards relative price movements, the expectations set out earlier are consistent with the data (See figure 10.1 and 10.2). Figure 10.1 gives the price indices in dollar terms (1980 = 100) of imported manufactured goods (MpMnf), imported non-petrol primary products (MpPrimary) and domestically manufactured goods (MnfDom$). The price index of domestic manufacturing reverses its upward trend from 1981 onwards, falling back to its pre-1977 level from 1984, while the price of imported goods remains above this level, confirming a 'scissors' hypothesis. In figure 10.2, the domestic manufacturing price index is seen to rise faster than that of both domestic absorption and agricultural goods from 1982 onwards, reflecting the high import content of manufacturing activity.

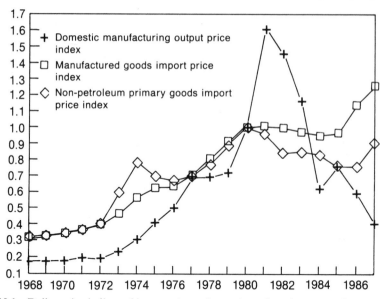

Fig 10.1   Dollar price indices of imports (manufactured goods and non-petroleum primary products), and of domestic manufacturing output

One should note that liberalization has not been conducted thoroughly in Ghana. Imports have been liberalized with import scheduling first eased and then abolished, and access to foreign exchange widened, first through an auction system, and later through the operation of exchange-bureaus. However, there has been little reform of nominal protection, and import duties in particular have not been amended significantly (although this is on the agenda for 1990-91). One of the mechanisms noted earlier, by which mark-ups in the manufacturing sector would be squeezed due to a convergence in import taxes on inputs and outputs, will therefore not have operated.

The other phenomenon, however, relating to import liberalization and crowding out of industry, has probably occurred. Although we do not have figures tracing the composition of imports, the changes in the allocation of foreign exchange through the auction system suggests that a 'liberalization bias' has operated against industry; the proportion of foreign exchange going to industry fell markedly from 1986 to 1988, from more than two-thirds to less than half of the total, while that attributed to trading purposes increased markedly from less than 2 per cent to more that 17 percent (Leenhardt and L'Heriteau 1989; p. 78).

All these elements suggest that an anti-manufacturing bias is at work at least as far as manufacturing for the domestic market is concerned. If this 'anti-domestic' bias allowed export diversification, export markets would then substitute for domestic ones, initiating the optimistic sequence described above where export-diversification prospects would make up for low investment in domestic-oriented manufacturing activity, However, this does not seem to have been the case.

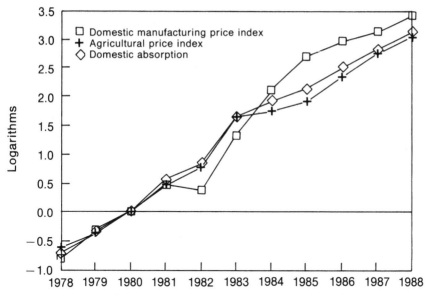

Fig 10.2   Domestic deflators: manufacturing, agriculture and domestic absorption

## Problems of export diversification

A three-year plan for non-traditional exports was launched in 1987 with the aim of bringing their share of total exports up to 15 per cent by 1990. However, an assessment carried out in June 1990 indicates pessimism (Kulatunga 1990). The conclusions it presents are worth looking into here, since the obstacles this report identifies are those bearing upon all manufacturing activities, but are magnified by the necessity of breaking into new markets.

Figures on external trade show an increasing share of non-cocoa exports in the total (from about 30 per cent in 1986 to around 52 per cent in 1989, and a projected 64 per cent in 1990). However, this rise does not mean very much. First, most of it is due to the absolute fall in the value of cocoa exports in spite of a quantity increase and second, because most of the shortfall in cocoa exports are made up by another traditional export, timber. Non-traditional exports have increased from US$. 27.9 million in 1987 to 34.7 million in 1989. However, in the latter year they were still no more than 4 per cent of total export receipts.

Many reasons seem to account for this failure, and these can be grouped under four headings:

- institutional problems (such as infrastructure, and lack of training).
- inadequate domestic productive basis.
- macro-economic environment.
- inadequate incentives.

We shall not consider the first of these since its solution is supposed to be addressed by the three-year export development plan. Suffice it to say that the lack of institutional support could be a reflection of the emphasis put upon a cocoa-based export strategy and on the expectation of attracting new foreign capital in large enterprises.

Analysis of the three other headings is more relevant here. Inadequacy of domestic productive basis is an important starting point. This has been analysed in great detail in reports produced by the Ghana Export Promotion Council in 1987, and more recently in early 1990, and constraints have been clearly identified. Prominent among these are two points: lack of credit facilities – either for investment or working capital – and the difficulty of obtaining inputs, either local or imported. This is where macro-economic factors come in.

Lack of credit is a direct result of credit ceilings established from 1983 onwards, that is from the time the first stand-by agreement was signed with the IMF. This problem is not particular to non-traditional export industries, as it affects the whole manufacturing sector. However, export-oriented sectors, especially non-traditional ones, are at a disadvantage because of the higher risks involved than in producing for the home market, or engaging in domestic trade.

Concerning the availability of material inputs, again export-diversifying ventures bear the same disadvantage as most manufacturing regarding access to imported inputs. Given the fast turnover in processed consumer goods activities, any productive activity which entails time and therefore incurs financial costs, is at a disadvantage when competing for foreign exchange with consumer goods importers. This was clear in the operation of the auction system, but the bias is still operating, and is probably enhanced by anticipations of further devaluations.

Some export-oriented industries also suffer from 'export competition' as far as domestic supplies are concerned. The wood-processing industry, for one, finds it hard to get an adequate supply of timber, either because timber is actually sold to exporters, or because it is priced at export prices, which are seen as prohibitive for domestic processing industries. In other words, the removal of 'anti-export bias' might well have introduced an 'anti-export-diversification bias'.

Incentives for export diversification are fairly standard, that is tax rebates, duty-free importation of raw materials for export production, and a 35 per cent retention scheme for foreign currency earned in non-traditional exports. Three points ought to be made here.

The first is that the reform programme assumes that the non-traditional export sector already exists, rather than having to be built up from scratch. This has many consequences, one of which concerns credit. New export business cannot be established unless some risk-takers are ready to venture their capital. As stated earlier, the relative profitability of various activities points more to financing trade than production, and to either traditional export or domestic-oriented production than to new exports. Whatever the incentives offered, they can only be drawn on once the export enterprise has proved successful; for example, tax rebates or foreign exchange retention can only operate if you have made a profit and managed to break into export markets. No proper risk-guaranteeing scheme is in operation, since the Bank of Ghana is extremely reluctant to bear any risk connected with variations in the rate of exchange, preferring to devolve this to commercial banks (L'Heriteau 1990).

The second point concerns import-duty rebates, which are more attractive the higher the tariff. Foreign trade reforms that bring down the tariff rates obviously weaken this instrument, so that two measures of economic policy – exemption from import duties and lowering import duties – seem to contradict each other.

The last point concerns the foreign exchange retention scheme. This scheme cannot operate unless one is interested in holding dollars rather than cedis. This amounts to the implicit assumption that there is a disequilibrium in foreign trade, with an overvaluation of local currency or import restrictions. In such a case one gains from the scheme either by getting the true value of dollars, or by being allowed to import restricted goods which will sell domestically at a premium.[6] However, with a market-clearing rate of exchange and no restriction on imports, such a scheme yields little positive incentive to exporters, apart from perhaps psychological comfort.

## Conclusions

In spite of its successes, the Ghanaian economy suffers from two important weaknesses, a lack of private investment in the manufacturing sector, and a lack of export diversification. Although these weaknesses are historically rooted in the economy of Ghana[7], one can wonder whether the failure of SAP policies to redress them is purely accidental, arises from misprescription, or is somehow built into some elements of these policies, namely the management of the external sector.

We saw how an active devaluation policy combined with external trade liberalization influenced the incentive structure in favour of short-term investments and traditional exports and against manufacturing investments and export diversification.

This in itself is not surprising: the removal of a bias is in effect a *reversal* of that bias. De-protection of domestic industry, which is part of the removal of anti-export bias, will necessarily introduce an anti-domestic bias. Similarly, the revival of traditional exports will introduce a bias against the development of new exports. If one considers that the two weaknesses mentioned above are important, one will agree that some corrective action has to be taken. This leads us to ask what corrective policy instruments are at the disposal of the state within the structural adjustment policy framework.

In principle, economic liberalization is opposed to the utilization of sector-specific policy instruments. All activities should be treated on the same footing, no specific advantage should be granted to any sector, with incentives resulting spontaneously from the setting of macro variables (such as the rate of exchange or the rate of interest) at their equilibrium level, and the removal of distortions (such as import controls).

In this perspective, any corrective action has to be an exception to strict liberal principles, and will take the form of either direct (through public investment or public enterprise) or indirect (through subsidies) state intervention within a macro-economic framework, where fundamental variables (such as the rate of exchange) are set at their equilibrium value and distortions are removed. The main criticisms of this form of intervention are their budgetary costs, the possible effect on overall allocation of resources (following the idea that the cost of the intervention might exceed that of the distortion) and rentier attitudes (with subsidies treated as regular income receipts).

One should then perhaps weigh the disadvantages of this form of intervention against those of an alternative course where consciously maintained macro–economic disequilibria and distortions would be played upon in order to enhance the power of incentives. By allowing operators to take advantage of a distortion, a privilege is granted them which can be suppressed if it does not achieve its aim. In other words, such a 'controlled distortion approach' allows one to move from a 'passive incentive' scheme to what could be called an 'active incentive' scheme, i.e. an incentive system which can operate both as incentive and sanction.

Regarding export diversification, an overvalued rate of exchange would allow exporters to retain highly prized foreign currency earned through diversifying exports, and thus grant them a potent motive for exporting.[8] Import restrictions would enhance the effectiveness of such an incentive scheme by allowing exporters to freely import goods subject to quantitative restrictions. Similarly, some overvaluation coupled with import restrictions could restore relative incentives in favour of investment in manufacturing activity.[9]

Under such a scheme, budgetary costs would be lower than under corrective interventions within a macro equilibrium framework. Exemptions from distortions do not entail subsidies, but are a privilege 'in kind', and do not draw on the budget.

The comparative impact of such a scheme in terms of overall misallocation of resources is more difficult to sort out, and ought to be investigated more precisely. However, one should note first that the policy framework proposed here is a variant of domestic protection and that the major criticism made of protective policies is that they fail to induce 'maturity' in protected activities, inducing 'rentier' attitudes (Balassa 1980). This implies that the main question is one of the accountability of the procedure. This is a question of adequate monitoring, with the possibility of abolition in case of failure to attain some pre-defined target, acting as a potent sanction.

One should note also that such a scheme can be made flexible; if the notion of reversibility of privilege is accepted, then conditions under which it is granted can be modified. For instance, the proportion of retained foreign exchange can be gradually diminished as sectors grow out of infancy, and criteria for eligibility can be changed according to macro-economic strategies, for example, gradually shifting away from foreign exchange earnings to, say, maximising domestic value-added.[10]

Policies based upon the establishment of an equilibrium rate of exchange *pari passu* with external trade liberalization, when applied to previously protected economies, induce a reversal of bias which can accentuate structural weaknesses of these economies. Corrective action is thus necessary. However, corrective interventions will violate the principles of liberalization, and one can speculate what kind of violation will prove both most effective and less costly. What this chapter has argued is that there probably is a good case for controlled distortion, which would allow low–cost interventions, and, given adequate monitoring, flexibility.

The argument for state intervention presented here is not based upon the traditional public versus private dichotomy; the ultimate aim of public intervention is not to promote public investment, but to foster efficient private investment. The basis of the argument is one of timing: short-run adaptations induced by the restoration of an efficiency-inducing environment depress investment opportunities, which have then to be restored by actions insensitive to immediate profit motivations.

The difference with the structuralist position as expressed by Singh (1982) is that the argument in favour of state intervention is based here only on its role in the attainment of the goal of allocation of resources defined by neo-classical analysis. This is a minimal argument for state intervention which does not necessarily oppose Singh's wider case for state activity.

## Notes

1   For an analysis based upon this particular form of non-tradability, see Bevan, Collier and Gunning (1987).

2   In theory there is a tariff equivalent to quotas, however, it is very difficult to calculate this equivalent; see Fontaine and Georgopoulos (1991).

3   See the analyses and estimates in Oyejide (1991) and in Fontaine (1991).

4   Except in gold-mining and cocoa.

5   World bank (1989b) gives a figure of 77%.

6   This was the basis upon which foreign exchange retention schemes operated in Tanzania and Kenya.

7   See Huc (1989, p. 124).

8   Note the self-correcting aspect of a foreign exchange retention scheme; any disequilibrium in the rate of exchange is automatically corrected by the privilege of retaining part of the foreign exchange earned in export-diversifying activities.

9   This would not necessarily mean such drastic action as quantitative restrictions. If, for instance, imports of consumer goods are subjected to advance deposit or import-prepayment schemes – whereby the equivalent in domestic currency is deposited and retained by the Central Bank for a given amount of time – they would incur both financial costs and risk on the rate of exchange, which would equalize financial prospects with home-produced manufactured goods, thus offsetting part of the anti-manufacturing bias.

10   For a description of such a scheme in the case of Korea, see Lanzarotti (1992a and 1992b, Ch. 5).

## References

Balassa, B. (1980), 'The process of industrial development and alternative development strategies', *World Bank Staff Working Paper 438*, World Bank, Washington, DC.

Bevan, D.L., Collier, P. and Gunning, J.W. (1987), 'Consequences of a commodity-boom in a controlled economy: accumulation and redistribution in Kenya 1975-1983', *The World Bank Economic Review*, vol. 1, no. 3.

Fontaine, J.M. (1991), 'Import liberalization in Kenya' in J. M. Fontaine (ed.), *Foreign-Trade Reform and Development Strategies*, Routledge, London (forthcoming).

Fontaine, J.M. and Georgopoulos, M. (1991), 'Protection tarifaire et instabilité des prix internationaux: une note' in J. M. Fontaine (ed.) *Contrôle du Commerce Extérieur et stratégies de Développement Economique*, Presses Universitaires de France, Paris.

Fransman, M. (1982), *Industry and Accumulation in Africa*, Heinemann, London.

Green, R.H. (1987), *Ghana: Stabilisation and Structural Shifts*, Wider, Helsinki.

Huc, M.M. (1989), *The Economy of Ghana: the First Twenty-Five Years since Independence*, Macmillan, London.

IMF (1988), *Ghana: Statistical Annex*, Document SM/88/242, mimeo, Washington, DC.

Kulatunga, S. (1990), *Export development prospects and problems*, UNDP/ITC project GHA/87/004 (June).

Lanzarotti, M. (1992a), 'Exchange rates and subsidies in an export-promotion policy; the case of South Korea' in J. M. Fontaine (ed.), *Foreign-Trade Reform and Development Strategies*, Routledge, London (forthcoming).

Lanzarotti, M. (1992b), *La Corée du Sud: le développement d'un pays sous-développé*, Presses Universitaires de France, Paris (forthcoming).

Leenhardt, B. and L'Heriteau, M.F. (1989), 'Situation Macro-économique et Montaire du Ghana', Caisse Centrale de Coopération Economique (Document de Travail), Paris.

L'Heriteau, M.F. (1990), 'Réforme du secteur bancaire et perspectives de crédit au secteur privée', Caisse Centrale de Coopération Economique (Rapport internel), Paris.

Marsden, K. and Belot, T. (1987), 'Private enterprise in Africa: creating a better environment', *World Bank Discussion Paper no. 17*, World Bank, Washington, DC.

Meier, G. and Steel, W. (1989), *Industrial Adjustment in Sub-Saharan Africa*, Oxford University Press, EDI series in Economic Development, Oxford.

Mosley, P. (1990), 'Structural adjustment: a general overview, 1980-89', IDPM Discussion Paper no. 21, University of Manchester.

Mosley, P., Harrigan, J. and Toye, J. (1991), *Aid and Power: the World Bank and Policy-based Lending in the 1980s*, Routledge, London.

Nellis, J. (1986), 'Public Enterprise in Sub-Saharan Africa', *World Bank Discussion Paper No. 1*, World Bank, Washington, DC.

Ocampo, J.A. (1987), 'The macro-economic effect of import controls: a Keynesian analysis', *Journal of Development Economics*, no. 27.

Oyejide, A. (1991), 'Impact of price-based and quantity-based import control measures in Nigeria' in J. M. Fontaine (ed.), *Foreign-Trade Reform and Development Strategies*, Routledge, London (forthcoming).

Ridell, R. C. (ed.) (1990), *Manufacturing Africa: Performance and Prospects of Seven Countries in Sub-Saharan Africa*, James Currey and Heinemann, London.

Schydlowsky, D. (1982), 'Alternative approaches to short-term economic management in developing countries' in T. Killick (ed.), *Adjustment and Financing in the Developing World*, IMF, Washington, DC.

Singh, A. (1982), 'Industrialisation in Africa: A structuralist view' in M. Fransman (1982).

Taylor, L. (1988), *Varieties of Stabilization Experiences*, Clarendon Press, Oxford.

World Bank (1981), *Accelerated Development in Sub-Saharan Africa: An Agenda for Action*, Washington, DC.

World Bank (1989a), *Sub-Saharan Africa: From Crisis to Sustainable Growth*, Washington, DC.

World Bank (1989b), *Ghana: Public Expenditure Review 1989-91*, mimeo, Washington, DC.

World Bank (1990), *World Development Report*, Oxford University Press for the World Bank, Washington, DC.

*Gérard Chambas and Anne-Marie Geourjon*

# The new industrial policy in Senegal – a highly controversial reform

## Introduction

Senegal overcame the first oil shock and the droughts of 1973 and 1975 thanks in particular to a favourable evolution of the prices of phosphates and groundnut products. However, at the end of the 1970s the country was affected by a combination of unfavourable events, chiefly a fall in the prices of its main exports, new increases in the prices of petroleum products and low crops of groundnuts due to droughts in 1978, 1980 and 1981.

Up to 1978 the growth rate of the agriculture sector, including livestock and fishing, was higher than the growth of population. However, from 1978 onwards groundnut production, which accounts for a large part of export revenues, and which determines to a large extent the level of activity in other sectors, fell sharply.[1] Moreover, at the end of the 1970s, the badly managed marketing network broke down, leaving the state with a considerable debt.

In 1960 Senegal had a manufacturing sector serving the regional market. Its average growth rate fell from 6.2 per cent in 1960-70, to 20 per cent in 1970-81 (World Bank 1980 and 1982), partly as a result of import-substitution policies in other countries of the region. Despite this unfavourable trend, the share of the manufacturing sector in GDP was still 16 per cent in 1979-81, as compared to an average of 8.3 per cent for African countries (Geourjon 1988).

The unfavourable shocks from 1978 to 1981 resulted in serious macro-economic imbalance: in 1980-81, the budget deficit reached 11.5 per cent of GDP.[2] The imbalance and the persisting stagnation of the economy are symptoms of the need for a major adjustment.

At the beginning of the 1980s, the Senegalese manufacturing sector was uncompetitive. Tariffs and non-tariff barriers, which were raised on several occasions at the end of the 1970s and the beginning of the 1980s, are an important cause of this lack of competitiveness (Geourjon 1990). Over-protected import-substitution enterprises often produce poor quality goods at a high price. The export-oriented branches of manufacturing, already penalized by high production costs, cannot develop because of an overvalued currency and the protected domestic market (Barbier 1989).

In order to overcome these problems, in 1980, under several agreements with the IMF, the authorities launched a stabilization policy aimed at reducing the main imbalances. Moreover, after a reform of the agricultural sector, a programme of reform of industrial policy, known as the 'Nouvelle Politique Industrielle' (NPI), was set out in 1986 with the support of the World Bank. Its aim was to lay the ground for a recovery of the industrial sector starting from 1989.

The NPI marked a radical change in the orientation of Senegalese economic policy, and has been implemented only partly, under especially difficult economic and social conditions and its effects have been highly controversial. For some analysts, the NPI has increased decisively the problems of the Senegalese manufacturing sector. For others, the NPI had limited effects because of the limited implementation of the initial plan.

This chapter attempts to analyse and evaluate the impact of this highly controversial reform on the industrial sector.


## The Nouvelle Politique Industrielle

The goals of the reform of trade and industrial policies were defined by the Senegalese government and the funding agencies. Both sides were in agreement on the basic principles of reform, but it was more difficult to decide how and how fast the measures aiming at achieving these objectives were to be applied.

The evaluation made in 1986 by the Ministère de l'Industrie et de l'Artisanat (MDIA) brought out the main consequences of the trade and industrial policies pursued in Senegal in the 1970s. Tariff protection during this period was reinforced, whilst at the same time the number of exemptions was increased. This resulted in a complex and inconsistent system; whereas in 1984 the average nominal tariff rate was in theory about 86 per cent, imported goods were actually taxed at an average rate below 20 per cent, that is at a rate well below the legal minimum tariff.[3]

Tariff policy was circumvented by national producers who exerted pressure on the government to use non-tariff barriers. In the 1970s, like many other developing countries, Senegal resorted increasingly to quantitative restrictions (QRs)(Krueger 1978).[4] The high nominal tariff rates, differentiated according to the stages of production, together with the numerous exemptions and the QRs granted to some firms, mainly in the capital-intensive industries, involved a high level of effective protection (sometimes higher that 825 per cent).

Other businesses, on the other hand, were penalized by the advantages granted to some producers; for example, in 1989, the firms producing biscuits or sweets bought sugar from the Compagnie Sucrière Sénégalaise, which enjoyed the benefit of a 'convention spéciale' (the most favourable regime of the investment code), at a price of 313 CFA.F per kg. (three times the world price). The diversity of incentives arising from the protective system was inconsistent with an efficient reallocation of productive resources in favour of traded goods. The aim of the reform was therefore to reduce protection of the domestic market, and to reinforce export promotion.

The NPI provided for a set of measures aiming at liberalizing trade and restructuring the industrial sector; with a reduction in protection, measures had to be adopted simultaneously to improve the environment for firms and to reduce the cost of some inputs.

The rationalisation of the protection system did not aim at totally removing the protection of Senegalese industry; because of high production costs in this sector, protection is necessary to cover the gap between national and international prices. The reform was meant to allow for a more neutral and better understood trade and industrial policy. This implied a simplification of the system and its evolution towards tariff-only protection, with lower and more harmonised rates, abandoning any practices liable to make its effect less transparent.

It was planned to eliminate progressively all QRs, and to revise tariff rates downwards. To improve the clarity of the system, it was decided that the 'valeurs mercuriales' (reference prices) should not be used any more as a protective tool, and that the 'codes de précisions,' which allowed exemptions to legally determined tariffs, should be abandoned.[5] Any tariff provides import-substitution sectors with a direct advantage and hence creates a bias against other sectors, and in particular the exportables sector. The NPI therefore planned to improve export promotion by rationalising the export subsidy system. Combined with the reduction in protection, this was meant to contribute towards a reduction in the relative disadvantage of the export sector.

Other accompanying measures were aimed at improving the operating environment of firms, for example, a liberalization of prices and marketing. Lastly, the reform planned to changed the labour laws, in order to make hiring and firing procedures and real wages, more flexible.

All the planned measures of the NPI had to be applied between 1986 and 1988 to ensure that, as initially planned, the recovery of the industrial sector would be felt from 1989 onwards. No impact study on the industrial sector had been completed before the introduction of the reform programme. A study by the Boston Consulting Group (BCG) was completed only at the beginning of 1987, that is after the first de-protection measures had been applied. Its conclusions pointed to some important economic and social costs. It should be noted that these costs had been estimated on the assumption that the whole programme would be applied.

The content of the programme itself can be criticised. Many measures were limited to the announcement of the principle of a reform or to the launching of a study on a precise question. In view of the inevitable delays, it was not very realistic to hope that concrete decisions could be taken on these questions within the three-year period planned for the implementation of the NPI. Thus, the details of most accompanying measures aimed at reducing the costs of firms were not made clear (for example, on reform of the labour code). On the other hand, the NPI announced precise measures to reduce protection, for example, through tariff reform and removal of QRs. The Senegalese industry was thus to face international competition without benefiting from the intended measures.

The planned time schedule within the reform programme involved a quick cut in the level of protection of local firms; tariffs were to be modified and QRs removed within two years. The authors of the NPI probably underestimated the time necessary for Senegalese industry to adapt to this new environment. The question of the appropriate speed of protection reduction for an economy is a difficult one. In 1985-86 the view of the World Bank in the field of trade policy was very much influenced by the works of Anne Krueger, who argued in favour of quick liberalization in order to avoid the political problems involved in changes spread out over a long period (Krueger 1985). This argument has merit, but the economic and social costs of an abrupt change are higher, and a fast pace of de-protection is only warranted if there are few rigidities, especially in the labour market (Michaely 1986); this is not the case in Senegal. By underestimating some country-specific constraints, the reformers underestimated the problems, and hence the time necessary to implement such measures. It was not very realistic, for example, to hope to change quickly the conditions for firing workers in a country where the most powerful union is known to be a political force. Similarly, because of the advantages granted by the state when signing contracts with some firms, it was equally predictable that there would be difficulties in re-negotiating investment incentives.

## Positions on the NPI

To understand better the problems of applying reform and its effects, one must examine the conditions under which the programme was negotiated. In discussing the reform of trade and industrial policy in Senegal, the IMF and the World Bank have used the same language and arguments that they have in other LDCs. The IMF focuses more on the balance of public finances and hence on the yearly changes in fiscal revenues, than on the effects of supply-side policies. The World Bank offers a standard, very detailed, structural adjustment package in exchange for its funding. Its experience in the field of trade policy arises mainly from Latin American and Asia. France has played a part in the funding of adjustment since 1978 and remains the main funding partner (Chambas 1989). France does not oppose the aims and main orientation of the World Bank, but is not in favour of an abrupt cut in protection. The French position regarding the NPI is especially delicate because of the important French interests in the Senegalese industrial sector. Among the funding agencies, it was logical that the World Bank would be the main negotiator on the NPI with the Senegalese authorities. A distinction must be made between the position of the Senegalese government and that of the private sector. Although the reform provoked different reactions in various ministries, in 1986 the Senegalese government fully adopted the NPI and the results of the 1987 study by the Boston Consulting Group on the cost of implementation did not lead to a change in its attitude towards reform.

In the 1970s the government had emphasized the development of industry and invested considerably in the sector through subsidies and foregone tax revenue. Disappointed by the results of earlier policy, the government was prepared to try liberalization.

The Senegalese civil service's distrust of the private sector has its roots in the

French colonial administration (Courcel 1987). The resentment of new private entrepreneurs by some civil servants found expression in the NPI, which was to force the firms to become competitive. Moreover, the development of the national private sector has given rise to a renewed nationalism. Introduction of the NPI provided the Senegalese with an opportunity to expose the foreign private sector, especially French firms, which are vulnerable to international competition. Lastly, one of the main reasons for the acceptance of the NPI by the authorities was to draw on the resources whose disbursement was conditional upon the implementation of the reform.

Private sector entrepreneurs admitted that the protectionist policy pursued in the 1970s was excessive, but questioned the NPI measures aimed at reducing this protection quickly. They felt that they had been victims of a complicated and inconsistent system, whose effects were not well known and which benefited firms unequally. Concerned at the high cost of some local inputs, they thought that the accompanying measures should have been implemented before the reduction in protection. The traders' point of view was much less critical of the NPI than that of the industrialists, since the NPI was intended to open borders and thus facilitate the import trade.

It does not appear that any dialogue has taken place during the implementation of the NPI. The urgency of the short-run financial deadlines, because of conditionality, induced the various partners, particularly the government, to reach an agreement quickly. The World Bank negotiates the terms and conditions of adjustment with the government, and depending on the decisions made, offers the funds which help the country to meet short-run deadlines. In such circumstances it is probable that some aspects of industrial policy have been negotiated in a rush, to enable Senegal to benefit more quickly from the Bank's resources.

The private sector has not been much involved in discussing the NPI. Private entrepreneurs were invited on 18 January 1986 to a meeting organised by the MDIA, with the support of UNIDO. They were asked to comment on this occasion, but no written documents were distributed. The local industrialists' association felt that it was not sufficiently consulted, as the inter-ministerial committee officially adopted the NPI on 10 February. Entrepreneurs later made many comments on the NPI to the MDIA. They felt excluded from the policy dialogue and have maintained a very reserved attitude toward a policy which they criticised openly from the start.

## Progress in implementation

Since 1980, taxation of imported goods involves three items: (i) a customs duty at a uniform rate; (ii) a fiscal duty with four different rates; a reduced rate (DFR), an ordinary rate (DFO), a standard rate (DFM), and a special fiscal duty (DFS); (iii) VAT with a variable rate.

The customs duty and the fiscal duty are only applied to imported goods. VAT is a tax on domestic consumption, which is levied both on imports and on locally produced goods, so that it does not affect the level of tariff protection, which depends only on the former two duties.

The customs duty has been revised downwards within the planned time span with reductions in two stages (July 1986, July 1988). The changes in the rates of the import duties are presented in Table 11.1.

In discussion of the tariff reform the effective protection granted to various activities was estimated very crudely by the 'protection differential'; that is, the gap between tariffs on final goods and tariffs on inputs. For example, in 1985 for the category of finished products this gap was approximately 40 per cent (assuming that inputs are subject to the rate of 25 per cent for raw materials and semi-finished goods). However, by 1988, for activities using semi-finished products as inputs, this gap should have been reduced to 10 per cent.

The only aspect of the tariff reform which has not been implemented relates to the 'codes de précision', which allow exemptions to the legal tariff rates. These codes remain in force.

The time schedule to eliminate QRs has also been gradually satisfied. The programme was planned to liberalize imports of products that do not compete with local industry. At the next stage, however, the sector was to be exposed to foreign competition with the strongest industries liberalized first, followed by the most vulnerable (such as textiles, shoes and school stationery). Currently, QRs no longer exist for most industrial goods, except those produced by firms who benefit from special investment incentives.

## The lack of 'accompanying measures'

Although most aspects of the NPI relating to the reduction in protection have been implemented, some of the additional measures designed to strengthen the position of local producers were delayed and others failed to live up to expectations. The 1981 investment code was modified with a new code adopted in 1987; to simplify bureaucratic procedures a single government department was given the responsibility of dealing with investments under the new code. The only new measure adopted regarding the labour market was the removal of the requirement to obtain government permission before hiring new workers. The procedure for obtaining permission to engage in foreign trade was simplified in 1987 and price controls were removed for some products. However, little progress has been made in cutting the cost of inputs like water, energy, transport and telecommunications. The APEX credit line from the World Bank aimed at funding firms has been usable only with a lag, and turned out to be unsuitable for restructuring, as the required criteria could be met only by firms with a sound financial position. The export subsidy system was changed so that the subsidy is computed on the basis of national value-added and not on the f.o.b. value of exports. This reform renders the procedure more logical from an economic point of view, but complicates the estimation of the subsidy and increases delays in its receipt. Also, some firms remain subject to price controls when they sell in the domestic market.

After June 1987, and particularly after July 1988, after the second tariff reduction and the lifting of the QRs, the Senegalese government decided to increase again the

Table 11.1  *Import taxes by categories of products before and after reform*[a]

| | 1985 | | | From July 1986 on | | | From July 1988 on | | |
|---|---|---|---|---|---|---|---|---|---|
| | Customs duty (CD) | Fiscal duty (DF) | Import tax DP = CD + DF | Customs duty (CD) | Fiscal duty (DF) | Import tax DP = CD + DF | Customs duty (CD) | Fiscal duty (DF) | Import tax DP = CD + DF |
| 1 Social goods or assimilated | exempt | suspended | 0 | exempt | suspended | 0 | exempt | suspended | 0 |
| 2 Strategic goods | 15% | suspended | 15% | 15% | suspended | 15% | 10% | suspended | 10% |
| 3 Equipment goods and raw materials | 15% | DFR = 10% | 25% | 15% | DFR = 10% | 25% | 10% | DFR = 10% | 20% |
| 4 Semi-finished goods | 15% | DFR = 10% | 25% | 15% | DFR = 10% | 25% | 10% | DFO = 20% | 30% |
| 5 Locally produced current consumption goods | 15% | DFO = 40% | 55% | 15% | DFO 30% | 45% | 10% | DFM = 30% | 40% |
| 6 Other finished products | 15% | DFM = 50% | 65% | 15% | DFM = 35% | 50% | 10% | DFM = 30% | 40% |
| 7 Luxury goods | 15% | DFS = 75% | 90% | 15% | DFS = 65% | 80% | 10% | DFS = 50% | 60% |

*Note*
[a] From August 1989 the customs duty is increased by 10% to 15%.
*Source:* Loi 86-36, 4 August 1986.

tariff protection granted to some sectors. However, the principle of the need for elimination of QRs was never reconsidered.

The government insisted on a 20 per cent 'protection differential' for all sectors, implying that semi-finished goods be taxed at the DFR rather than the DFO (see Table 11.1). Thanks to the 'Codes de précision', which enables the classification of the goods to be changed for fiscal purposes, in practice the customs administration has maintained a differential of at least 20 per cent. This is not what was planned initially by the Loi 86-36.

On the other hand, some 'emergency' reference prices ('valeurs mercuriales') have been fixed to protect the local firms. They apply to almost all locally produced goods, and aim to weaken the effects of the removal of QRs and of the tariff cuts.

In August 1989, 85 goods for which it was technically difficult to establish a reference price, were the subject of a minimum levy in order to combat under-invoicing.[6] The removal of QRs favoured the import of products with an abnormally low value (for example, due to subsidy in the exporting country, or dumping), which threatened local industry. Controlling the value and quality of such products is difficult and requires mechanisms that Senegal does not yet possess. In these cases a minimum levy provides a counter to under-invoicing the products' values, and hence guarantees some customs revenue. Lastly, the government reinforced tariff protection in August 1989 (Loi 89029) by increasing the customs duty from 10 to 15 per cent.

The use of various techniques like changes in the classification of goods for fiscal duty, reference prices, minimum levy, and the increase in the customs duty rates have reduced the real impact of de-protection. Further firms subject to investment conventions have not been affected by the reforms.

## Impact of the reform on the industrial sector

The NPI aimed at reversing the deteriorating performance of the Senegalese industrial sector. However, it is difficult to evaluate the extent to which this objective has been met, for two reasons. First, many factors impinge on the evolution of the industrial sector. Observing a trend, favourable or unfavourable, during the period of implementation of the NPI is not enough to identify a causal relation between the NPI and a change in performance.

Moreover, and this is often underestimated, the Senegalese economy has been strongly affected by exogenous factors. The 1988 presidential election marked the beginning of a period of uncertainty caused by the 'post-electoral troubles'. The difficulty of forecasting the nature of the economic policy which was to be implemented has certainly favoured a waiting attitude by the industrialists affected by the NPI. Also the departure of Mauritanians from Senegal profoundly upset economic activity in spring 1989. Mauritanians were important in the wholesale and particularly the retail trade; after their departure, many producers met with difficulties because of unpaid invoices. The disputes with The Gambia, resulting in strict controls over trade between Senegal and The Gambia in August 1989, have also contributed albeit to a lesser extent, to an increase in the climate of uncertainty.

The second difficulty in evaluating the impact of the NPI is that the recent trend in industrial activity is not well known. Despite initiatives like the creation of a unit within the MDI to monitor the NPI's effects, and the observation of a sample of firms by USAID, which have supplemented the information usually provided by the Statistics Department and by some confederations of employers, there is still insufficient data available on industry.

Given these difficulties in isolating and assessing the effects of the NPI, here we consider the impact of the NPI on prices alone, and try to analyse the reactions of firms to the NPI from recent survey data.

The removal of tariffs and the lifting of non-tariff barriers have modified the costs of inputs and the prices of imported consumer goods. These measures, which are the main components of the reform, have also affected the size of customs fraud and the level of protection enjoyed by firms depends both on tariff and non-tariff barriers, and on the level of customs fraud. We first consider the impact of the change in the protection system, assuming no fraud, and then analyse the change in the level of protection enjoyed by firms, under alternative assumptions regarding fraud.[7]

### The effects of the reform of firms assuming no fraud

Our aim is to evaluate the consequences of the tariff reductions for a Senegalese firm producing consumption goods: we first analyse the case of a firm which did not benefit originally from non-tariff barriers.

When there are no fraudulent imports a firm must sell at a price lower or equal to that of similar imported goods, in order to be able to market its product. Assuming a consumer comparing two goods, one imported and the other locally produced, with prices inclusive of value added tax (VAT), the condition for selling local goods can be written as;

$$P_{TT} < [P_M(1 + DP)] (1 + VAT) \qquad (1)$$

where $P_{TT}$ is the tax-inclusive selling price for the local firm, $P_M$ is the c.i.f. import price of the competing imported good, DP is the import tax rate [DP = CD + DF, with CD as the rate of customs duty and DF as the rate of fiscal duty], and VAT is the rate of value added tax (we assume here the average VAT rate equal to 20 per cent).

Before the reform, a local firm could compete with an imported good worth 100 CFAFs by producing at a tax-inclusive maximum price of 186 (see Table 11.2); after the reform, its production cost must be below 168, implying a 9.7 per cent cut from the previous net-of-tax cost. This fall is made easier by the favourable impact of the reduction in protection on the costs of imported inputs, whose VAT-exclusive price has fallen by 4 per cent.

If one assumes that before the reform the firm benefited from non-tariff protection measures, it is possible that the removal of QRs entailed in some cases (like textiles) an especially difficult adjustment. Some of the previous barriers, like the application of high reference prices or strict quotas, implied such a high level of protection that

Table 11.2   *Conditions for selling a local product before and after trade liberalization*

| | Selling price all taxes included | | Relative change in selling price (%) (VAT excluded) |
|---|---|---|---|
| | Before reform | After reform | |
| 1 *No fraud* | 196.0 | 168.0 | −9.7 |
| $k_0 = k_1 = 0$ | | | |
| 2 Moderate fraud | | | |
| 2.1 Stable fraud | 168.8 | 154.4 | −8.5 |
| $k_0 = k_1 = 0.2$ | | | |
| 2.2 Reduced fraud* | 168.8 | 161.2 | −4.5 |
| $k_0 = 0.2$ $k_1 = 0.1$ | | | |
| 2.3 Increased fraud** | 168.8 | 147.6 | −12.5 |
| $k_0 = 0.2$ $k_1 = 0.3$ | | | |
| 3 *Large fraud* | | | |
| 3.1 Stable fraud | 143.0 | 134.0 | −6.3 |
| $k_0 = k_1 = 0.5$ | | | |
| 3.2 Reduced fraud* | 143.0 | 137.4 | −3.9 |
| $k_0 = 0.5$ | | | |
| $k_1 = 0.45$ | | | |
| 3.3 Increased fraud** | 143.0 | 130.6 | −10.0 |
| $k_0 = 0.5$ | | | |
| $k_1 = 0.55$ | | | |
| 1 *Quasi-total fraud* | 108.6 | 106.8 | −1.7 |
| $k_0 = k_1 = 0.9$ | | | |

*Notes*
\*   Under the reduced fraud assumption, we assume a fall in fraud after liberalization.
\*\* Under the increased fraud assumption, we assume that fraud had increased as a response
   to the removal of non-tariff barriers and deregulation of foreign trade.
$k$ = fraud rate (before reform $k_0$, after reform $k_1$).
*Source*: Computed from data provided by Direction Generale des Douanes.


a switch to a tariff-only protection system could result in a marked de-protection of
firms, who are not compensated by a temporary tax surcharge on the relevant imported
goods.


### The effects of the reforms on firms, assuming customs fraud.

There seems to be an important, but virtually unknown level of fraud in Senegal;
this fraud reduced the level of protection enjoyed by the firms of the modern sector,
which must fix a selling price below what they could get if there was no fraud. The
reform had opposing effects on the incentive to indulge in fraud. The tariff cuts
have entailed a reduced premium to fraud, by reducing the amount of customs taxes
which can be avoided; for a c.i.f. import value of 100, the gross premium went from

86 to 68.[8] The protection reduction implied by the lifting of QRs on competing products has worked in the same direction.

The liberalization of the commercial network, and in particular the simplification of access to foreign trade, are probably the cause of a strong *de facto* reduction in protection for some local activities, textiles in particular.[9]

Our assumption, which needs to be confirmed by further work, is the following: the amount of fraud by an importer depends on the premium to fraud, the probability of getting caught, the penalty incurred, and the importer's risk aversion.[10]

For traditional importers, representing import-export firms for whom commercial respectability is of the utmost importance, and which are well known by the authorities, risk aversion is high. The liberalization of the conditions for delivery of importer's cards has allowed the emergence of new importers who do not have the same interest in their reputation, and who, being able to import freely, have a weak risk aversion; this liberalization has probably been a fundamental factor contributing to an increase in fraud.[11]

The temporary introduction of reference prices has probably also encouraged fraud as determining such prices is difficult, and also because the scope for interpretation by customs officers has made the latter more vulnerable to illegal offers.

When a local firm is competing with fraudulent imports, the condition for selling the locally produced goods becomes:

$$P_{TT} < P_L - k.P_M.DP - K.P_M.VAT.(1 + DP) \qquad (2)$$

where $P_{TT}$ is the all tax-inclusive price of the local firm, DP is the customs duty (CD plus the fiscal duty DF), $P_L$ the legal import price including all customs taxes ($P_L = P_M(1 + CD + DF)(1 + VAT)$, $P_M$ is the c.i.f. import price, and k the rate of fraud.[12]

According to equation (2), the local firm must get its tax-inclusive price in line with the legal import price PL, less the import taxes escaped ($k.P_M.DP$) and the internal VAT evaded ($k.P_M.VAT.(1 + DP)$), because of the cut in the tax base entailed by fraud.[13]

The adjustment effort required by firms in response to the reform depends both on the importance of, and the change in, customs fraud (see table 11.2). If fraud remains stable, they have a smaller effort to make, although their situation is less favourable than when there is no fraud. Assuming that the rate of fraud is 20 per cent, liberalization implies a price cut of 8.5 per cent, against 9.7 per cent when there is no fraud. If fraud increases, firms must increase their relative effort as compared to the assumption of stable fraud (12.5 per cent instead of 9.7 per cent). On the contrary, if fraud decreases, the required relative effort gets smaller (4.5 per cent instead of 9.7 per cent).

## Changes in the industrial sector and the NPI

Although it is difficult to have appropriate indicators, it is clear that the current trends in the modern industrial sector, with firms closing down, job losses, and massive dis-investment by foreign direct investors, are a cause for concern.

According to some observers, the trend in the informal sector is much more favourable than that in the modern sector. In particular, from a sample of 35 firms, there is evidence that the informal sector has shown a much better capacity to adapt to the new economic circumstances characterised by increased foreign competition (Lowenthal *et al.* 1990). However, despite previous studies on the informal sector (van Dijk 1986, Zarour 1989, Charmes 1989), there are no reliable indicators of trends in the sector.

The accelerated deterioration of the modern sector may result from misadaptation to the NPI, but also from the economic stagnation of the country, from uncertainty, from the ageing production capacity, or even from the previously latent desire of foreign investors to pull out, which manifested itself at the time of unfavourable events. Therefore, rather than imputing all problems to the NPI, it seems preferable to analyse the reactions of firms to the new market conditions.

A survey in January 1990 of the main employers' organisations and a sample of about fifteen firms in the modern sector (Lowenthal *et al.* 1990) suggests a qualified evaluation of the NPI; although the NPI has been implemented in particularly unfavourable circumstances, the surveyed firms have adopted various measures to adapt to the new conditions.[14]

After some difficulty in 1986-87, the firms have re-established relations with the public authorities, notably through the various federations of employers. Sometimes, some of them have managed to obtain specific protection measures. Despite their often weak financial situation, many firms from the sample modernised their plants in order to increase their competitiveness and to diversify their lines of production. Despite constraining labour legislation, many firms have introduced piece-rate wages; others are trying to reduce overmanning. Many Senegalese firms used not to have advertising promotion; however, a large textile firm has improved its sales by using televised advertisements. The necessity for quality improvement has been recognised. However, one must note that firms have adopted these measures within an unfavourable environment, with bad macro-economic conditions, failures in the banking system and high costs of some inputs, like energy and water.

The survey of the informal sector, involving 35 firms, shows that the firms in this sector have benefited from the fall in the cost of intermediate inputs, and from the liberalization of the commercial networks. Metal working (for example, agricultural tools and millet mills) and repair service (for automobiles, refrigerators and television sets,) have developed particularly. One should stress that the informal sector has benefited from fraud much more than the modern sector; moreover, the informal sector manages to escape most of the legal constraints bearing on the modern sector, for example in relation to taxation and labour relations.[15]

## Conclusions

Since the 1970s, the modern industrial sector has been in a phase of decline which was even more marked at the beginning of the 1980s. The industrial sector was protected by high tariff and non-tariff barriers. As this protective system was modified over time, it became increasingly more inconsistent and complex, with negative effects on industrial producers, on consumers, and on public finances.

In order to reduce these negative effects and to adjust the industrial sector to a competitive environment, the Senegalese government introduced the NPI. The NPI involved a consistent system of incentives; non-tariff barriers were lifted, and all protection was to be based on tariffs. Various 'accompanying measures' were to allow firms to adjust to this reduction in protection. However, the reform project, which probably underestimated the rigidities of the Senegalese economy, was implemented without a study of its global impact being available initially. The de-protection planned by the NPI has been applied in conformity with the original time schedule, whereas most of the accompanying measures were not implemented. This fact has induced the Senegalese government to adopt some measures to reverse the tariff reduction, such as reference prices and a minimum levy.

The effects of the NPI are difficult to evaluate as many factors determine changes in the industrial sector, and as serious external events have affected the economy. Moreover, precise indicators are not available on recent trends in both the formal and informal sectors. Under the no-fraud assumption, industrialists have had to make an important adjustment to face up to the shock of tariff reductions and particularly, in some cases, the removal of non-tariff barriers. Nevertheless, the cuts in input costs entailed by tariff reductions and return of some protective measures have helped to dampen the shocks. Although the tariff and non-tariff liberalization have reduced the incentive to customs fraud, it seems plausible that the latter has increased because of trade deregulation and the withdrawal of QRs. The probable expansion of fraud has been an important source of problems for the modern industrial sector. On the other hand, some firms of the informal sector have had access to cheaper inputs.

After a difficult period firms in the modern Seneglaese sector have nevertheless, started to adjust despite particularly bad conditions, such as the internal economic position, the failure of the banking sector, and the high cost of some inputs. On the other hand, the NPI has permitted an improvement in the relations between the public authorities and the private sector, which is the main actor in the reform programme. This is an indispensable precondition for a positive reaction of entrepreneurs to the new industrial incentives policy.

### Notes

* This paper was written after various missions in Senegal by A-M. Geourjon in June 1989 for Elliot Berg and Associates, and by G. Chambas in January 1990 for Development Alternatives Inc., under a USAID contract. It draws on the work of each team, and in particular on the mission reports (Elliot Berg and Associates 1990, and Lowenthal, J., G. Chambas, J. Lewis and J. Smith, 1990).
The authors wish to thank the members of both teams for very stimulating discussions. They thank also S. Guillaumont for her comments and J. P. Azam for the translation of this text into English.

1   For example, in 1979, a good agricultural year, groundnut products accounted for 41% of export revenues in Senegal. Information provided by Direction de la Statistique, Government of Senegal.

**2** This refers to the conventional deficit, that is net borrowing requirement. Data supplied by the IMF.

**3** All the exemptions, whose management has a high administrative cost, in 1983-84 resulted in lost revenues for the Treasury amounting to 108 billion CFA.F., i.e. to 148% of the whole customs revenues.

**4** In 1984, imports of 160 products were controlled.

**5** The 'valeurs mercuriales' are administratively fixed values which form the basis for computing the duties and taxes levied at the customs. This system is used to combat under-invoicing of goods and to enable the authorities to have an influence on domestic prices. It can equally be used to change the level of tariff protection for the goods involved without changing the rates officially.

**6** The minimum levy amounts to fixing a minimum duty to be levied when a good is imported. It can be used to ensure revenue collection, but it can also be used to protect an industry if it is fixed at a high rate.

**7** We only quantify the price effect of the tariff reform as the impact of the removal of QRs cannot be estimated due to lack of data.

**8** It is a gross premium as we neglect the expenses entailed by any illegal activity.

**9** Since this reform took place, the number of importer cards has increased four fold.

**10** This assumption derives from interviews with economic agents and officials from the customs services and various parts of the government.

**11** It is possible also that a change in the nature of fraud has occurred: former smugglers may have seized the opportunity presented by liberalization of entry to the import trade to transform part of their smuggling activity into fraudulent imports. (We are grateful to C. Vernhes for this suggestion).

**12** Fraud can come from under-invoicing of a fraction 'k' of the value of the good, or from smuggling of the fraction 'k' of the quantity imported, or from a combination of both, or from other methods.

**13** For the sake of simplification, and also because of the lack of empirical information, we do not take in to account here the cost of fraud, which increases the limit price that the local firm can set.

**14** A mission to Senegal in April-May 1990 by D. Logeay, for the Caisse Centrale de Coopération Economique (CCCE), confirms this response of the modern sector.

**15** The informal sector can easily buy via fraudulent networks whereas the modern sector producers normally only buys through legal channels.

**References**

Barbier, J.P. (1988), 'Nouvelles politiques industrielles en Afrique Subsaharienne ou les écueils de la course au large', *Notes et études*, CCCE, no. 15, Paris.

Barbier, J.P. (1989), 'Réflexion sur la competitivité. Comparaison Afrique–Asie'. *Notes et études*, CCCE, no. 26, Paris.

Chambas, G. (1989), 'Aide française et ajustement au Sénégal', Rapport redigé à la demande de Elliot Berg Associates, CERDI.

Chambas, G. (1990a), 'La réforme fiscale au Sénégal (1986-1990)', *Etudes et documents provisoires*, CERDI.

Chambas, G. (1990b), *Note sur la fraude douanière en Côte d'Ivoire et au Sénégal*, CERDI.

Charmes, J. (1989), *Economie enregistreé secteur informel et comptabilité nationale au Sénégal*

*1977-1988*, Direction de la Statistique, PAGD, Dakar.

Courcel, M. (1987), 'Possibilité et conditions d'une intervention plus dynamique du secteur privé au Sénégal', Club du Sahel, Paris.

Edwards, S. (1987), 'Comment programmer les mesures de libéralisation économique dans les PVD?', *Finances et Développement*, vol. 24, No. 1.

Elliot Berg and Associates (1990), *Adjustment Postponed: Economic Policy Reform in Senegal in the Eighties.*, Report prepared for USAID, Dakar, Alexandria.

Geourjon, A.M. (1988), 'La protection commerciale' in P. and S. Gillaumont (eds.), *Stratégies de Développement comparées zone franc et hors zone franc*, Economica, Paris.

Geourjon, A.M. (1990), 'Evaluation de l'experience du Sénégal en matière d'adjustement structurel; la politique commerciale et industrielle'. Rapport redigé à la demande de Elliot Berg Associates, CERDI, Clermont-Ferrand.

Judet, P. (1989), 'La Nouvelle Politique Industrielle au Sénégal: évaluation, ouvertures', *Notes et études*, CCCE, no. 32, Paris.

Krueger, A.O. (1978). *Foreign Trade Regimes and Economic Development: Liberalisation, Attempt and Consequences*, Ballinger, Cambridge, Mass.

Krueger, A.O. (1985), 'Import Substitution versus Export Promotion', *Finance and Development*, vol. 22, no. 2.

Logeay, D. (1990), 'L'industrie sénégalaise: ses perspectives après la Nouvelle Politique Industrielle'. Note de travail, CCCE, Paris.

Lowenthal, J., Chambas, G., Lewis, J., and Smith, J.T. (1990), *Tax Reform in Senegal 1986-1990*, Project Impact Evaluation Report, Dakar.

Michaely, M. (1986), 'The Timing and Sequencing of a Trade Liberalization Policy' in Choksi, A. and Papageorgiou, D. (eds.), *Economic Liberalization in Developing Countries*, Basil Blackwell, Oxford.

Steel, W.F. (1988), 'Adjusting Industrial Policy in Sub-Saharan Africa', *Finance and Development*, vol. 25, no. 1.

Van Dijk, M.P. (1986), *Sénégal: Le secteur informal de Dakar*, L'Harmattan, Paris.

World Bank (1980), *World Development Report, Washington*, World Bank, Washington DC.

World Bank (1982), *World Development Report, Washington*, World Bank, Washington DC.

World Bank (1987), *La Banque Mondiale et le Sénégal 1960-1987*, Report no. 8041, Washington, DC.

Zarour, C. (1989), *Etude du secteur informal de Dakar et de ses environs*, Phases I, II et III, USAID, Dakar.

# III: Asian perspectives

# Malaysian industrial policy in the 1990s – look east?

## 1 Malaysian industrial policy – look West or look East?

The purpose of this chapter is to address the following questions:

- what is the legacy of Malaysia's industrialisation since the 1950s and what are the main policy issues?
- what are the lessons that Malaysia can learn from 'looking East' at South Korean industrial policy of the 1960s and 1970s?
- given the differences in political and economic structure, can Malaysia copy South Korea?

In looking at Malaysian industrial policy in the 1990s, two crucial assumptions will be made, the first concerning the continuation of pro-Malay policies, the second concerning the desirability of a rapid rate of industrial growth.

Firstly I assume that the government will continue to adopt policies which have, as their stated objective a reduction in income and wealth differences between Malays and Chinese. As stated above, it was at the beginning of the 1970s that preferential policies were adopted under the New Economic Policy (NEP) in favour of 'bumiputras' – the Malays and other 'indigenous' groups – who make up roughly half the total 1990 population of about 18 million. The broad aims of the NEP were to eradicate absolute poverty irrespective of race and to reduce the differences in wealth, income and occupation between the races. The NEP was instituted in 1971 and the objectives were to be achieved by 1990. A variety of policy instruments have been used in the attempt to achieve the NEP objectives, including scholarships and other educational preferences, priorities in employment, especially in the public sector, and licensing and other restrictions imposed on companies, particularly under the Investment Co-ordination Act of 1976. There is little agreement about the effects of the NEP but according to official sources, the incidence of absolute poverty in Peninsular Malaysia had been reduced from 49 per cent of households in 1970 to

17 per cent by the end of 1989 (equal to the 17 per cent target for 1990 set by the NEP) and the ratio of the average income of the Chinese household to that of Malays has declined over the past 20 years from 2.2 in 1967 to 1.6 in 1987 (MTR 1989, pp. 42,45).

But although income differences between Malays and Chinese have been reduced, income inequality within the races remains as high as it was 20 years ago. Thus whereas the proportion of total income going to the poorest 40 per cent of households was 14 per cent in 1967, it was still only 13 per cent in 1987. As a result, many observers in Malaysia (Malays as well as non-Malays) have been very critical of the ownership restructuring arm of the NEP. It has been argued that this policy has fostered the growth of a rentier class and of 'money politics'. The policy has been accused of creating a 'parity of millionaires', with there being little incentive for the growing 'bumiputra rentier class' to become efficient entrepreneurs. As two prominent Malay economists (Zainal Aznam Jusof and Kamal Salih) have argued, 'restructuring the ownership of share capital does not add very much to raising the income of the average Bumiputra household and putting more and more financial resources to acquire companies would be misplaced' (MMR 1989, p. 59). Thus it has been argued that there is in Malaysia a weak, divided bureaucracy which is subordinated to vested political interests and that this has combined with a strong rentier class based in the dominant Malay political group. This weakness of the bureaucracy might seem to provide a reason for by-passing it and for advocating free market policies in Malaysia, but, politically, such advocacy is likely to fall on deaf ears. As Alice Amsden has pointed out in her excellent study of South Korean industrial policy, for free market policies to be introduced presupposes a certain form of 'strong' state and political structure (Amsden 1989, p. 147). In this chapter I assume that the introduction of completely free markets is likely to be politically impossible in Malaysia. Thus in spite of widespread criticisms of certain parts of the NEP, I assume that the Malay-dominated government (re-elected in late 1990 with over two-thirds of the seats in Parliament) will continue to implement ethnic preferences under a renewed NEP into 1992 and beyond. I assume, therefore, that the issue in Malaysia is not whether the state will intervene in industrial policy but how.

The second assumption I make is that a rapid rate of growth in Malaysian GDP is desirable to accommodate the competing claims and expectations of the different ethnic groups. Furthermore, it is assumed that this rapid rate of economic growth is dependent on a rapid rate of growth in the manufacturing sector, since the latter has been a major 'engine of growth' in Malaysia over the past twenty years, and with the relative decline in the primary sector, is likely to continue to be so in the future (see Table 12.1).

Thus in looking at Malaysian industrial policy for the future I make two assumptions: firstly that the Malaysian government will continue to intervene in the economy on ethnic grounds, and secondly that a continued rapid rate of industrial growth is desirable. But the basic argument of this chapter is that to achieve a rapid rate of industrial growth and to achieve it in such a way that it yields a high rate of growth in national income as well as output, the Malaysian government should adopt an active industrial policy. This does not mean that there should be wholesale and

Table 12.1   *Malaysia: Gross Domestic Product (%) by sector*

|               | 1955* | 1960* | 1970 | 1980 | 1989 |
|---------------|-------|-------|------|------|------|
| Agriculture   | 40    | 40    | 31   | 23   | 20   |
| Mining        | 6     | 6     | 6    | 10   | 10   |
| Manufacturing | 8     | 9     | 13   | 20   | 26   |
| Others        | 46    | 45    | 50   | 47   | 44   |
| *Total*       | 100   | 100   | 100  | 100  | 100  |

*Note*
*Peninsular Malaysia only.
*Source:* Alavi 1987, p. 14; Malaysia Ministry of Finance, 1989, p. xii, xiii.

indiscriminate state intervention. It is argued that state intervention is a necessary but not sufficient condition for efficient industrial growth. I argue that a model of an 'efficient industrial policy' is provided by South Korea in the 1960s and 1970s.

The strategic question about the roles of the market and of government intervention has been a source of considerable controversy in Malaysia, particularly since the mid-1980s. At that time two major studies of industrial policy were carried out. These studies, some details of which are given in Table 12.2, were the Malaysian Industrial Policy Study (MIPS) and the Industrial Master Plan (IMP).

Table 12.2   *Studies of industrial policy in Malaysia, 1980s*

|                                       | Malaysia Industrial Policy Study (MIPS) | Industrial Master Plan (IMP)                |
|---------------------------------------|------------------------------------------|----------------------------------------------|
| Date started                          | August 1983                              | July 1983                                    |
| Date completed                        | December 1984                            | February 1986                                |
| Cost (US$'000)                        | 320                                      | 2,025                                        |
| External financing/ executing agencies | UNDP/World Bank                         | UNDP/UNIDO                                    |
| Study carried out by                  | IMG Consultants, Australia               | Individual experts under Dr. Seongjae Yu     |

*Source:* Chee Peng Lim (1987).
MIPS (1984).

These two studies advocated quite different approaches to industrial policy in Malaysia. In its executive report, the IMP contrasted three 'philosophical assumptions' on which a Malaysian industrial development plan could be based. These were;

• the free market rationale modelled on the USA;
• the state rationale modelled on the centrally-planned economy; and
• the plan rationale modelled on Japan and many other newly-industrialised countries and for which the premise is that while the competitive market-mechanism is

indispensable, rational planning is fundamentally important in achieving industrial development objectives.

In planning for Malaysia, the IMP opted for the plan rationale whereas the MIPS emphasized the free market model. Thus whereas the IMP 'looked East' towards the model of Japan, South Korea and state direction, the MIPS 'looked West' towards the USA and the market. Perhaps these differences are not surprising when it is considered that the chief consultant for the IMP was a prominent South Korean economist (Dr Seongjae Yu) and the agency for the IMP was the pro-state-interventionist, United Nations Industrial Development Organisation (UNIDO). By contrast, the MIPS was carried out by a firm of Australian consultants with the agency being the 'free market' oriented World Bank.

It is fair to say that the IMP achieved more influence than the MIPS for two reasons:

- firstly, because its budget was bigger and it covered more aspects of industrial policy (including research and development), whereas the MIPS study was limited to industrial trade and tax incentives;
- secondly, it overlapped chronologically with the MIPS so that it could and did 'absorb' the MIPS study.

The IMP had also followed on from the 'Look East' policy of the Malaysian government which had been launched at the beginning of the 1980s. This meant, according to the Prime Minister, Dr Mahathir, 'emulating the rapidly-developing countries of the East in order to develop Malaysia.' (Mahathir (1983) quoted in Jomo (ed.) (1985), p. 305). First announced in 1981, and repeated in 1982 and 1983, Malaysia's Look East policy was launched in the context of strained relations between the Malaysian and UK governments. Relations were strained following the takeover of Guthrie Corporation by PNB, a Malaysian company, in a 'dawn raid' on the London Stock Exchange, after which the procedures for such takeovers were tightened. And they were strained further by the increase in British university fees for overseas students, many of whom came from Malaysia.

These skirmishes with the British government were, to some extent, a belated reflection of changing power relationships. In switching towards the East, the Malaysian government was recognising that the sun had long set on the British Empire, that it was setting on the American 'empire', and that the world's economic centre of gravity had shifted in the direction of the Pacific Rim.

Thus since the early 1980s Malaysia's foreign policy has been re-oriented towards the East, but industrial policy has been somewhat confused. On the one hand, the rhetoric of industrial policy looks towards the East. In the mid-1980s, the government announced its acceptance of the IMP and the free-market-oriented MIPS was ignored. More recently, in 1990, the Ministry of Trade and Industry (MTI) became the Ministry of International Trade and Industry (MITI), and there was talk of the Malaysian MITI directing industry along the forceful lines of the Japanese MITI. But while the rhetoric of industrial policy has 'looked East', the implementation of industrial policy has been a confused mixture of state-promoted import substitution, privatisation of profitable infrastructure and utilities, and the promotion of foreign investment in the export processing zones.

## 2 The legacy of Malaysia's industrialisation – from the 1950s to the present

Since Malaysia became politically independent in 1957[1], the rate of growth in manufacturing output has been rapid, with the share of manufacturing in total Gross Domestic Product rising from less than 10 per cent in the late 1950s to 26 per cent thirty years later (see Table 12.1). But in spite of a rapid rate of growth since independence, the Malaysian manufacturing sector was still marginally underdeveloped in 1984 given the level of its Gross Domestic Product per capita. According to the World Bank (1987, p. 51), in 1984 the proportion of Malaysia's GDP contributed by manufacturing was slightly under 20 per cent whereas it 'should' have been a little over 20 per cent to match a 'normal' pattern of development. Malaysia's less-than-20 per cent of GDP in manufacturing was in sharp contrast with the 30 per cent of South Korea.

This 'backwardness' of Malaysian manufacturing has its roots in British colonialism, the first of five stages of industrial development that can be identified in Malaysia.

### 2.1 The 1950s – British colonialism and 'backward' manufacturing

In terms of the manufacturing sector, Malaysia was a latestarter. The encouragement given to industrial development since independence in 1957 has contrasted sharply with a lack of encouragement under British colonial rule. The British colonial government was reluctant for two reasons to give any preference to domestically-produced manufactured goods. Not only would the substitution of imported manufactures by protected domestic production reduce the import duty revenue to the government, but it was also likely to raise the prices of some of the goods consumed by plantation workers on the (mostly) British-owned rubber estates, thereby adding to the upward pressure of wages, and reduction of profits, on the estates (see Edwards 1975, p. 288).

Thus at the time of independence, Malaysia was an economy still heavily geared to the production of primary commodities (see Table 12.1). But dependence on primary commodities was not the only legacy of colonialism. At Independence, Malaysia was also an ethnically-segmented society, with the population being ethnically divided both spatially and in terms of occupation. In a very real sense this was a product of colonial rule, for the British had done little to integrate the society.

Thus there were two legacies of British colonialism which have a bearing on later industrial development – an 'underdeveloped' industrial sector and a racially-segmented society.

### 2.2 The 1960s – rapid growth in the import-competing sector

With independence came a different policy emphasis towards industry. Slowly at first, and then more intensively, manufacturing was encouraged. As a result during the 1960s net output in the manufacturing sector in Malaysia grew rapidly from 9 per cent of GDP in 1960 to 13 per cent in 1970. Since 1958, tax incentives had been offered to pioneer industries but from the beginning of the 1960s, import-substituting industries (ISI) were encouraged by giving them protection through import duties and quotas. The average effective rate of protection (ERP) was only 25 per cent in 1962 but by the end of the decade it had risen to more than 65 per cent (see Edwards 1975, p. 98). The ERP was equivalent to very large subsidies. The subsidy-equivalent of protectioŋ in 1969 was about M$400 mn., equivalent to more than 4 per cent of GDP or just under one-fifth of total government operating expenditure. This subsidy of M$400 mn. was equivalent to an ERP when calculated on profits of over 1,000 per cent.

Given such a potential gearing-up of profits through protection, what Anne Krueger has called 'rent-seeking' (the expenditure of resources to get such government-endowed rents) became widespread in Malaysia (see Edwards, 1975, p. 295). But rent-seeking was not the only problem to stem from this ISI phase. There were four other problems. First, there was no pressure on the companies to seek out exports. In 1970 exported manufactures were only 4 per cent of all exports (Edwards 1975, p. 298). This meant that for those industries subject to economies of scale (e.g. automobile assembly), production was limited to a small domestic market and was therefore high cost. Second, import-substitution tended to be limited to final consumer goods with the protection being higher on those goods than on intermediate manufactures. The protection given to consumer goods set up a lobby against protection being given to intermediate industries. Third, the majority of the ISI industries were set up by foreign owned companies. By 1970, more than three-fifths of all manufacturing and mining output in Malaysia was under the control of foreign companies. Finally, there was a regional concentration of industry. The bias in favour of consumer goods and the domestic market, together with the lobby effect, meant that production tended to be set up by large plants near the large towns on the west coast of the Peninsula, in translations always referred to as 'Peninsular Malaysia'. Regional dispersion was unprofitable. This meant that after 1963, when East Malaysia was incorporated into the Federation, the East Malaysians paid higher prices for the protected manufactured goods while getting few of the industrialisation benefits. The net result of this first phase of industrialisation was that the mass of the population in Malaysia was being charged (as consumers) above-world prices, and receiving little or no benefits from the industrialisation. The infant industries were not being forced or 'induced' to grow up. There was little pressure to transfer technology or skills. There was admittedly some growth in manufacturing employment between 1957 and 1970, but it was small – the increase of about a quarter of a million in manufacturing employment was only about one-eighth of the 2 million increase in the total Malaysian labour force over the same period.

By the end of the 1960s the 'easy stage' of ISI had run its course but the industrial development had done nothing to prevent the build-up of racial tensions which were reflected in the riots of May 1969. Income distribution at the end of the 1960s was just as unequal as it had been a decade earlier, with the poorest 40 per cent of households receiving 14 per cent of all income in 1967 compared with 16 per cent a decade earlier. At the beginning of the 1970s, the declaration of the New Economic Policy (NEP) by a new Alliance government under the leadership of Tun Razak, coincided with a new phase of export-oriented industrialisation (EOI).

## 2.3 The 1970s: the NEP and the growth of Export Processing Zones (EPZs)

The introduction of the NEP, with its preferences for Malays coincided with a change of direction in industrial policy from the policy of ISI which had gone through its first easy stage by the end of the 1960s. A policy of promoting export-oriented industries (EOI) was launched. But it is doubtful if this EOI phase contributed much to meeting the NEP objectives.

The promotion of EOIs was initiated with the Free Trade Zone (FTZ) Act of 1971. Under this Act, companies established themselves in FTZs (and Licensed Manufactured Warehouses – LMWs) in Malaysia to export goods assembled or produced by low-wage labour. Exports of manufactures from Malaysia grew rapidly, especially in the second half of the 1970s. By 1980 exports of manufactures accounted for almost a quarter of all exports from Malaysia. Most of the growth was in electronics and electrical machinery and to a lesser extent in textiles and clothing, so that by 1980 about 60 per cent of Malaysia's manufactured exports consisted of these goods.

The development of export processing industries in Malaysia was very fast. In 1987, in a study of export processing zones in Malaysia, Peter Warr stated that:

The importance of EPZs in Malaysia . . . is unique among the developing countries establishing these zones. Nowhere else is their role as significant, either in absolute terms or as a proportion of overall manufacturing activity (Warr 1987, p. 30).

What were the effects of this EOI phase of industrial development? There are three effects that it is important to emphasize here. First, there was little net foreign exchange saving. A major criticism of the ISI phase had been that there was little foreign exchange saving. But in this respect, the record of the EOI sector was worse. According to the MIPS final report, over the period from 1972 to 1982, the net foreign exchange earnings were only a little over 10 per cent of the gross sales if it is assumed that the profits were remitted overseas. Second, although manufacturing employment increased faster in the 1970s than it had in the 1960s, (the total employed in manufacturing rose by more than 400,000 in the decade of the 1970s), wages in the EPZs have been very low. With the increase in low-wage EPZ employment, by 1978 the average real wage in the Malaysian manufacturing sector was below that of 1968. Third, there was little technological transfer or development of skills in the industries established in the EPZs and few linkages with the rest of the economy. As Warr put it: 'The degree of linkage between FTZ firms and the domestic economy, through the purchase of domestically produced raw material and capital equipment, has been disappointing' (Warr 1987, p. 53).

Thus Warr estimated that there was only a very small net benefit to the Malaysian economy from EPZs. In present value terms, over the 25 year period from 1972 to 1997, it was less than 4 per cent of total GDP in the one year of 1982.

By the beginning of the 1980s, therefore, a significant EOI sector had developed in Malaysia, largely separate from the ISI sector which had been promoted through the 1960s. This was the context for the launching of a heavy industrialisation programme – a second phase of ISI – in the 1980s.

*2.4 The early 1980s: the push for heavy industrialisation*

At the beginning of the 1980s, there was a slowdown in the rate of industrial growth in Malaysia. This was the background for the launching of a new phase of industrialisation. This was announced in the early 1980s and was to be carried out through a public sector agency, namely the Heavy Industries Corporation of Malaysia (HICOM). As a result of investments in heavy industrialisation projects such as iron and steel, cement, the national car and small engine plants, the annual public sector investment in commerce and industry rose from M$0.3 bn in 1978-80 to M$0.9bn in 1982 and M$1.5bn in 1984, with most of the investments being financed by external borrowing.

Thus in the first half of the 1980s, as public investment rose, so did long-term external debt. The Federal Government's external debt more than doubled in the two years from 1980 to 1982, from just under M$5 bn. in 1980 to M$12.5 bn. in 1982. As a percentage of GDP at market prices, this external debt doubled from 10 per cent in 1980 to 20 per cent in 1982, and continued to rise to more than 38 per cent in 1986.

Between 1980 and 1985, these foreign borrowings more than offset the deficits on the current account. As a result the Central Bank's foreign exchange reserves increased in 1981 and 1982 and 'pressure to depreciate the exchange rate was temporarily diverted' (World Bank 1989, p. 14). Thus the external financing gave support to Malaysia's real effective exchange rate so that it appreciated through the first half of the 1980s, rising by about 10 per cent between 1980 and 1984.

Malaysia's effective exchange rate rose in real terms through the first half of the 1980s, in spite of a deficit on the external current account, and as it did, so the export-oriented manufacturing sector became increasingly less competitive. This was reflected in an increase in the trade deficit on manufactures from US$5.3bn in 1980 to US$6.8bn in 1982. Manufactured exports more or less stood still over this period while manufactured imports increased substantially (World Bank 1989, p. 144). But it is important to emphasize that this appreciation of the real exchange rate was not a Malaysian equivalent of the 'Dutch disease', that is, it was not due to a surge in primary commodity prices forcing up the exchange rate and making the manufacturing sector less competitive internationally. In fact, Malaysia's barter terms of trade declined from 1980 to 1982.

As foreign financing helped to more than sustain the real exchange rate, Malaysian manufacturing became less competitive, and manufacturing growth slowed. But at the same time the performance of the heavy industrialisation programme itself was weak. Being capital-intensive, it was expected to have long gestation and pay-back periods, but, even relative to these expectations, its performance was disappointing, as was pointed out in the Mid-Term Review of the Fifth Malaysia Plan (MTR 1989, p. 196).

Malaysian industrial policy in the early 1980s started with a big push for heavy industrialisation, but by the middle of the decade there was little prospect of that programme succeeding at least within the 1980s and when, in the mid-1980s, Malaysia's external terms of trade fell sharply, the economy was in crisis.

*2.5 Crisis, adjustment and industrial reappraisal*

The mid-1980s were a period of crisis for Malaysia, with the government, led by Dr Mahathir, being enmeshed in a series of political controversies. Underlying the political crisis was an economic one. In 1986 real Gross Domestic Product was at about the same level as it had been in 1984. There was a particularly severe recession in manufacturing in 1985. Real manufacturing output in that year dropped by over 3 per cent. Manufactured exports were lower in 1985 than in 1984. A World Bank report on Malaysia attributed this partly to a recession in the global semi-conductor industry and partly to a loss in Malaysia's competitiveness (World Bank 1989, p. 17).

The recession was accompanied by an outflow of capital. In 1984 and 1985 there was a surge in the outflow on the investment account. Under these circumstances, the exchange rate either had to be protected by further overseas borrowing or by exchange controls or it had to fall. It fell sharply. In 1986, the exchange rate of the Malaysian dollar to the US dollar fell by a little over 7 per cent but in terms of the IMF's Special Drawing Rights (a basket of currencies), the Malaysian dollar fell by 20 per cent, and the real effective exchange rate fell by about the same percentage. Exports and imports of manufactures responded quickly to this real depreciation. In terms of US dollars, manufactured exports in 1987 were 15 per cent higher than in 1985, while manufactured imports (again in terms of the US$) had risen by only 6 per cent over the same two year period (World Bank 1989, p. 144). As a result there was a transformation in the balance of payments: whereas in 1982 there had been a deficit on the current account of about 14 per cent of GNP, in 1987 this had been transformed into a surplus of 8 per cent.

At about the same time as the Malaysian dollar was being sharply devalued, the Malaysian Government was also relaxing the regulations on the ownership of subsidiary companies established in Malaysia by foreign investors. In 1986, new subsidiary companies established in Malaysia by foreign investors could be 100 per cent foreign-owned provided that they were export-oriented. A sharp increase in direct foreign investment took place, and in the second half of the 1980s, the growth rate of the export-oriented manufacturing sector once again rose sharply.

*2.6 The legacy of the past and the major policy issues*

After this brief review of the past development of the Malaysian manufacturing sector, it is important to ask: what is the legacy? The most striking characteristic is the dualistic structure of Malaysian manufacturing. Superimposed on the resource-based industries of palm oil refining, and wood- and rubber-based industries are the separate ISI and EOI sectors (see Table 12.3). The ISI sector produces mostly for the domestic market and is therefore limited by the small size of that market, while the EOI sector has little contact with the domestic economy outside the EPZs and generates a small ratio of retained value added to gross output.

This dualism was recognized in a World Bank study on Malaysia published in 1980 (see Young, Bussink and Hasan 1980, p. 189) but it was not recognized by the World Bank in its 1987 World Development Report. In that Report, the World Bank

Table 12.3   *Malaysian manufacturing, 1987*

| Industry descriptions | Gross output | Exports (M$m) | % of Gross output exported | Value added (M$m) | VA as % of gross output |
|---|---|---|---|---|---|
| *Resource-based industries,* Consisting of: palm-oil refining, rubber remilling (off-estate), wood products and rubber products | 13,263 | 9,561 | 72 | 2,527 | 19 |
| *Import-substituting industries,* consisting of: food, bev., tobacco, paper and paperboard, chemicals and petroleum products and plastics, non-metallic mineral products, iron/steel, metal products, and transport equipment | 23,186 | 4,135 | 18 | 7,153 | 31 |
| *Export-oriented industries,* consisting of: textiles/garments and electronics and electric m/c | 13,606 | 13,054 | 96 | 3,405 | 25 |
| *Others* | 641 | 385 | 60 | 232 | 36 |
| *Totals* | 50,696 | 27,135 | 54 | 13,317 | 26 |

*Source:* Malaysia Ministry of Finance, 1989, various.

labelled Malaysia as moderately outward-oriented for the 1963-73 and 1973-85 periods (see World Bank 1987, p. 83). But averaging the ISI and EOI sub-sectors of Malaysian manufacturing in this way makes little sense. Indeed it makes about as much sense to say that a person with one foot in boiling water and one foot in ice cold water is moderately comfortable.

Not only is it important to recognize the present dualism in the Malaysian manufacturing sector, but it is also important to recognize the potential for integrating the two, that is, for linking production for the domestic market with production for the export market. Such an integration was advocated by the IMP, which urged the Malaysian government to adopt a strategy of export targeting whereby companies might continue to receive protection for their sales in the domestic market on condition that they export a certain proportion of their production. The idea behind this is that the protected profits from domestic sales can be used to subsidise the less profitable exports.

In recommending such a strategy, the IMP was adopting a plan rationale. Their model for this was the allegedly interventionist strategy of South Korea and Japan. The IMP's view of industrial development in South Korea is consistent with that of a number of researchers who have looked in detail at the development of the

South Korean economy. But such a view clashes with that of many economists who, in the early 1980s, had claimed that the rapid growth of the South Korean economy had been due, quite simply, to the operations of the free market and to an absence of state intervention in the economy. In view of this controversy it is important to 'look East' to see how the state in South Korea intervened in industrial development. This is what the next section does together with briefly looking at the case for intervention in selected markets.

## 3 'Looking east' and the case for state intervention

Included among the sources that claimed that South Korea had grown rapidly because of the adoption of free market policies was the World Bank's 1983 World Development Report (WDR). The WDR had presented an analysis of development which attempted to show that there was an inverse relationship between 'market distortions' and economic growth, that is the greater degree of state intervention and distortion, the slower the rate of economic growth. In this 'orthodox' view, state intervention was harmful – government was seen to be a hindrance.[2]

One of the countries which had developed rapidly, due supposedly to the adoption of free markets, was South Korea. But subsequent research has shown that in the two decades following the overthrow of Syngman Rhee in 1961, the South Korean state intervened extensively in the economy.[3] Areas of intervention included:

- foreign trade, by granting tariff protection for sales in the domestic market conditional on export targets being achieved;
- finance, by giving concessional loans through the state-owned banking system for approved investments;
- technology, by bargaining alongside the South Korean companies (the Chaebols) with foreign suppliers of technology;
- labour markets, by suppressing trade unions but also by investing heavily in education and skill acquisition;
- infrastructure, where the vast majority of the investment was undertaken by the public sector; and
- ownership, where the government encouraged domestic rather than foreign capital.

It is true, as the World Bank has claimed, that South Korean policy was outward-looking and that industrial policy was geared to the promotion of exports. It had to be, as aid from the US to South Korea dried up in the 1960s. It is also true, as the World Bank claimed, that South Korean economic growth has been outstanding. But the evidence does not support the claim that the growth coincided with, or was caused by, the adoption of free markets in South Korea.

There is a strong theoretical case for intervention in a number of markets and intervention in these markets is a necessary condition for a successful industrial policy. From the experience of South Korea and from the inherent characteristics of markets, it is likely to be desirable for governments to intervene in the following areas:

(i) technology – because of information imperfections in the market. There is a strong chance that for an individual company the cost of gaining information about technology will be high relative to the benefits. Thus there may be a gain to society by the state reducing the risk to the company by meeting the cost of getting the information. This gain may be quite large because of economies of scale in the acquisition of information (see Pack and Westphal 1986).

(ii) finance – because of imperfections in the market stemming from risk and uncertainty. Companies may under-invest in long-term production facilities since the rate of profit required by companies is likely to be higher than that required by society. As a result long-term investment is likely to be smaller than the social optimum unless the state underwrites it.

(iii) the training of labour – because of externality imperfections in the market. Companies which spend money on training are not assured of being able to recoup that cost. As a result, training is likely to be less than the social optimum if left to the free market.

(iv) trade – because of imperfections in the market arising from economies of scale, uncertainty or both. Although companies may find it easier to compete in international markets from a platform of highly profitable domestic sales, a company's profit-maximising output may be less than the level of output which gives a lower rate of profit to the company but one which is nevertheless socially preferable. Thus it may be socially beneficial for the state to step in and impose the 'stick' of export targets in return for the 'carrot' of protection in the domestic market (see Krugman in Keirzkowski (eds. 1984, p. 181).

(v) the environment – because it is rare that pricing systems are such that the polluter meets the cost of pollution. Thus this is an area where governments either need to enforce regulations to prevent 'external diseconomies' or need to modify the market to make the polluter pay.

The theoretical lesson is that just as there are many different types of markets, so there are also many types of imperfections. And the lesson from the experience of South Korea is that state intervention may create the correct market signals by changing the market – in this sense Alice Amsden is correct when she says that the South Korean state was right 'to get the prices wrong' (Amsden 1989).

Although the case for state intervention is strong, it is not a case for indiscriminate intervention. State intervention is a necessary but not sufficient condition for a successful industrial policy, since there are of course numerous examples of state intervention which have held back the growth of efficient industrialisation.

Given this conclusion what should the government's industrial policy look like in Malaysia? How, if at all, can state intervention deal with the problems of industrial dualism?

Firstly, how can the import-competing sector be induced to become internationally competitive and forced into export markets? One way may be to reduce its protection in the domestic market. This was the path recommended by the MIPS but rejected by the government on the grounds that many of the industries would go bankrupt. An alternative which may be more politically acceptable but yield the same efficiency gains is that of export targeting – that is of retaining protection for the domestic market but requiring the protected companies to use the profits from the domestic market to subsidise sales in the export markets. In this way, a targeted company can be forced to expand its production and thereby achieve economies of scale even if the rate of profit is lower than without the targeting. This was the path recommended by the IMP but not yet implemented by the Malaysian government. It was the policy followed in South Korea and if it made sense there, it is likely to make even more sense in the considerably smaller market of Malaysia. Thus for the ISI sector it would seem to make sense for the Malaysian government to impose the 'stick' of export targeting alongside the 'carrot' of protectionism.

In the EOI sector, the problem is essentially one of increasing the value-added retained in Malaysia. The obvious way of doing this would seem to be to impose a profits tax on the companies in the EPZs, but it is likely that the TNCs could avoid such taxes by re-arranging their transfer prices, that is the prices at which they buy and sell products from or to their linked companies operating outside Malaysia. Less obvious routes to increasing retained value added may be more successful. For example, small concessional investment loans provided by the government might be sufficient to promote linkages between TNCs and domestic suppliers. Such promotion has been successful in Singapore. Similarly there is a case for the Malaysian government promoting the upgrading of skills and value-added in both the ISI and EOI sectors by providing training grants. Such grants might be financed through a Skills Development Levy as in Singapore.

In Malaysia there is a strong case for the adoption of an interventionist industrial policy because of the imperfections inherent in some markets. The model for such a set of policies is provided by South Korea. Thus there is a case for Malaysia 'looking East' and modelling its industrial policy on that of South Korea. But even if this argument is accepted, the crucial question is, can Malaysia adopt a more strongly interventionist industrial policy?

## 4 The need for a stronger bureaucracy in Malaysia – but can Malaysia copy South Korea?

There is not the space in this chapter to answer this question in detail. Nevertheless, it is important to raise the question if only to draw attention to the nature of the state. For it is important to recognize that the state is not merely a 'black box' but is part of the problem as well as the solution. It is essential to look at what Evans and Alizadeh refer to as the social structure of accumulation (see Kaplinsky (ed.) 1984, p. 27). Once we begin to do this, an interesting question that immediately arises is: how did the South Korean bureaucracy manage to discipline as well as support business? For, in spite of some corruption in South Korea, the bureaucracy has been able (particularly through the 1960s and 1970s) to promote rapid industrial growth through flexible and highly selective action. It has been able to do this because, as has been emphasized by a number of writers, (especially by Amsden 1989, Hamilton 1986 and Johnson in Deyo (ed.) 1987), the South Korean state has not been 'captured' by particular interest groups or classes.

Amsden, Hamilton and Johnson all emphasize that:

- the landlord class was weakened by the land reform programme undertaken soon after the end of Japanese colonialism;
- the domestic, merchant capitalist class, which was in any case quite small in the 1950s since much of the Japanese capital had been taken over by the state, was weakened further by the campaign against illicit wealth and by the nationalisation of much of financial capital at the beginning of the 1960s; and,
- the growth of a labour aristocracy was impossible because of the repression of organised labour and a substantial labour surplus through the 1960s and 1970s.

As a result, the South Korean bureaucracy, which had been strong under Japanese colonialism, and which had been further strengthened by the large aid programmes of the 1950s, found itself, especially from the second half of the 1960s, with a large 'space' in which to work. Industrial policy, which was increasingly centralised through the Economic Planning Board after the Park coup in 1961, could be, and was, highly selective and effective. Thus with the subordination of financial to industrial capital as represented by the state, the stage was set for a period of rapid industrial accumulation facilitated by wages which were low, due to anti-trade union pressure, low food prices and a labour surplus.

As soon as the industrial policy problem is set within a socio-political and historical context, contrasts between South Korea and Malaysia become evident. Here it is useful to highlight three contrasts. The first is that the colonial experiences were quite different. Under Japanese colonialism, industry was developed in Korea, whereas under British colonialism in Malaysia, it was the plantation sector which was rapidly developed. Second, South Korea gained its political independence a decade or so before Malaysia. Third, the geo-political situation of South Korea differed considerably from that of Malaysia with important implications for land reform and aid. Fourthly, Malaysia is ethnically divided whereas South Korea is ethically homogeneous, and Malaysia's ethnic divisions have coincided with economic roles.

These factors not only have meant that the initial conditions between the two countries differed at independence but that the political conditions for further development differed. Thus the manufacturing sector in Korea was more highly developed in 1945 at the end of Japanese colonialism than it was in Malaysia. Furthermore, import-substituting industry was encouraged in South Korea through the 1950s whereas over the same period there was no attempt to encourage manufacturing industry in Malaysia. As a result, in 1965, even though the Gross Domestic Products of the two countries were about equal, the manufacturing sector's share in South Korea (at 18 per cent) was double that in Malaysia (9 per cent). South Korea's experience of manufacturing industry has thus been longer than that of Malaysia.

In addition, as aid receipts declined in the 1960s, South Korea was forced to export. Unlike Malaysia, it could not rely on primary products to finance its imports. But, also unlike Malaysia, after the first 'easy' phase of import-substituting industrialisation in the 1950s, South Korea did not rely on Export Processing Zones for its manufactured exports. Instead, exports from South Korea were built up from a base of producing for a protected domestic market. Export targeting was the name of the game in South Korea, whereas a dualism developed within the Malaysian manufacturing sector with an ISI sector quite separate from the EOI sector based in the EPZs.

The growth of manufactured exports from South Korea was essential because, as aid declined, there was no other source of foreign exchange to finance imports. But, as has been emphasized, the state was able to play an active role in the promotion of exports through targeting because of the peculiar strength of the bureaucracy *vis-à-vis* other groups. In Malaysia, with its primary product exports, the pressures to export manufactured goods were not present to the same extent. And by contrast with the situation in South Korea, the Malaysian state has not had the same 'autonomy' as that in South Korea. The political structure in Malaysia has consisted of an uneasy alliance between Malay and Chinese elites, with the wealth of the Malays being derived from land ownership and control (including forestry concessions), and with that of the Chinese being derived from trade, finance and the primary export sector (mining and plantations).

The bureaucracy in Malaysia has implemented, therefore, relative to that in South Korea, an inefficient industrial policy. It is a difficult task to trace the links between the industrial policies and the political structure in Malaysia. What seems clear is that the bureaucracy in Malaysia has not had the same 'autonomy' from vested interests as has the bureaucracy in South Korea. Instead the weakness of an inexperienced and divided bureaucracy in Malaysia has combined with a strong rentier class based in the dominant Malay political group to prevent the emergence of an efficient, 'deepening' industrial policy in Malaysia. In other words, the social structure of accumulation in Malaysia has militated against the emergence of an efficient industrial policy administered on South Korean lines. Yet what is needed is an industrial policy which will break down the dualism that has developed in Malaysian manufacturing industry. Thus the conclusion of this chapter is that although it seems desirable for Malaysian industrial policy to emulate that of South Korea, there must be considerable doubts about whether it will be possible, given the differences in the political histories and structures of the two countries.

## Notes

1  Malaysia (or at least West, or Peninsular, Malaysia) gained its political independence in 1957. In 1963, the North Bornean states of Sarawak and Sabah joined the Federation as did Singapore. Two years later, Singapore left the Federation to become a separate republic and since then, Malaysia has consisted of the eleven states of Peninsular Malaysia and the two East Malaysian states of Sabah and Sarawak.

2  A joke went the rounds in Latin America that 'the economy only grows at night – while the government is sleeping'.

3  See, for example Amsden (1989), Deyo (1987), Dornbusch and Park (1987), Enos and Park (1988), Hamilton (1986), Harris (1988), Hong (1979), IDS (1984), Johnson in Scalapino *et al* (eds.) (1985), Lee (1979), Lim (1981), Luedde-Neurath (1986), Michell (1988), Pack and Westphal (1986), van Liemt (1988), White (1988) and Yusuf and Peters (1985).

## References

Alavi, R. (1987), *The Three Phases of Industrialisation in Malaysia – 1957-1980s*, MA dissertation, UEA, Norwich, UK.

Amsden, A. (1989), *Asia's Next Giant: Korea and Late Industrialisation*, Oxford University Press, New York.

Chee Peng Lim (1987), *Industrial Development: An Introduction to the Malaysian Industrial Master Plan*, Pelanduk Publications, Malaysia.

Deyo, F. (ed.) (1987), *The Political Economy of the New Asian Industrialism*, Cornell University Press, Ithaca and London.

Dornbusch, R. and Yung Chul Park (1987), 'Korean Growth Policy', *Brookings Papers on Economic Activity*, no. 2, Washington, DC, pp. 389-454.

Edwards, C.B. (1975), *Protection, Profits and Policy: An Analysis of Industrialisation in Malaysia*, PhD thesis, UEA, Norwich, UK.

Enos, J. and Park, W. (1988), *The Adoption and Diffusion of Imported Technology: The Case of Korea*, Croom Helm, London.

Hamilton, C. (1986), *Capitalist Industrialisation in Korea*, Westview Press, Boulder, Colorado.

Harris L (1988), 'Financial reform and economic growth: a new interpretation of South Korea's experience' in Harris *et al.*, *New Perspectives on the Financial System*, Croom Helm, London.

Hong, W. (1979), *Trade, Distortions and Employment Growth in Korea*, Korea Development Institute, Seoul.

IDS (1984), 'Development States in East Asia', *IDS Bulletin*, April, vol. 15, no. 2, Sussex, UK.

IMP (1985), *Medium and Long Term Industrial Master Plan, Malaysia 1986-1995*, UNIDO, August 1985, Vienna.

Jomo, K. S. (ed.) (1985), *The Sun Also Sets*, Insan, Kuala Lumpur.

Kaplinsky, R. (ed.) (1984), *Third World Industrialisation in the 1980s*, Cass, London (see also the *Journal of Development Studies* (1984), vol. 21, no. 1).

Kierzkowski, H. (ed.) (1984), *Monopolistic Competition and International Trade*, Clarendon Press, Oxford.

Lee, E. (1979), 'Egalitarian peasant farming and rural development: the case of South Korea', *World Development*, vol. 7, pp. 493-517.

Lim Youngil, (1981), 'Government policy and private enterprise: Korean experience in industrialisation', *Korean Research Monograph 6*, Institute of East Asian Studies, University of California, Berkeley.

Luedde-Neurath, R. (1986), *Import Controls and Export-Oriented Development: A Reassessment of the South Korean Case*, Westview, Boulder, Colorado.

Michell, T. (1988), *From a Developing to a Newly Industrialised Country: The Republic of Korea, 1961-82*, ILO, Geneva.

Ministry of Finance, *Economic Reports*, various years, Kuala Lumpur.

MIPS (1984), *Final Report of the Malaysian Industrial Policies Studies (MIPS) Project*, IMG Consultants Pty Ltd, Sydney, Australia.

MMR (1989), *Malaysian Management Review*, journal of the Malaysian Institute of Management, August 1989, vol. 24, no. 2 (special issue on the New Economic Policy), Kuala Lumpur.

MTR (1989), *Mid-Term Review of the Fifth Malaysia Plan, 1986-1990*, Government of Malaysia.

Pack, H. and Westphal, L. (1986), 'Industrial Strategy and Technological Change', *Journal of Development Economics*, vol. 22, pp. 87-128.

Scalapino, A. *et. al.* (eds.) (1985), *Asian Economic Development – Present and Future*, Institute of East Asian Studies, University of California, Berkeley.

van Liemt, G. (1988), *Bridging the Gap: 4 NICs and the Changing International Divisions of*

*Labour*, ILO, Geneva.

Warr, P. G. (1987), 'Malaysia's Industrial Enclaves: Benefits and Costs', *The Developing Economies*, vol. XXV, no.1.

White, G. (ed.) (1988), *Development States in East Asia*, Macmillan, London.

World Bank (1983), *World Development Report*, Oxford University Press for the World Bank, London.

World Bank (1987), *World Development Report*, Oxford University Press for the World Bank, London.

World Bank (1989), *Malaysia: Matching Risks and Rewards in a Mixed Economy*, World Bank, Washington, DC.

Young, K., Bussink, W. and Hasan, P. (1980), *Malaysia: Growth and Equity in a Multiracial Society*, World Bank/Johns Hopkins University Press, Baltimore.

Yusuf, S. and Peters, R. (1985), 'Capital accumulation and economic growth: the Korean Paradigm', *World Bank Staff Working Paper*, no. 712, Washington, DC.

*J. Keith Johnson*

# Timing, speed and sustainability issues in the policy reform process – the Philippine case

## Introduction

The major goal of this paper is to provide an assessment of the forces that have impeded the progress and impact of exchange rate, trade, and industrial policy reforms in the Philippines.[1] This in turn facilitates some general observations on the determinants of incisive and sustainable reform programmes. The 1980s have seen the growth of a formidable literature on the process of adjustment (World Bank, 1985, World Bank, 1987 and Dornbusch and Helmers, 1988). While some progress has been made in defining the appropriate composition and sequencing of reforms, there continues to be a marked shortfall between prescription and action on matters of timing and speed. The World Bank, for example, argues that 'the more rapid and fundamental the policy changes, the greater the immediate benefits to the economy', and claims that 'strong and decisive reforms have carried greater credibility and have been better sustained than more timid reforms' (World Bank 1987, pp. 95, 122). However, as is illustrated by the Philippine case, such statements appear to be more firmly rooted in economic theory than in political reality. In this sense, the World Bank's qualification that 'to sustain trade liberalization beyond its initial stage, economic and political stability has proved essential' (World Bank 1987, p. 108) is less than helpful.

To fully understand the problems that surround the continuing process of policy reform in the Philippines, it is necessary to begin by assessing the policy legacy that was passed to the Aquino government in 1986. The chapter is therefore divided into two major sections. The first provides an overview of the development of foreign exchange, trade and industrial policy structure in the four decades following independence. This period was marked by the progressive entrenchment of inward-looking policies, and by sporadic but ultimately ineffective moves towards exchange rate liberalization. Drawing partly upon the themes that emerge from the historical review, the second section attempts to evaluate current developments in exchange rate policy, trade liberalization and industrial policy. Here it becomes apparent that the process of policy reform is once again threatened by short-term responses to macro-economic exigencies; the persistence of rent-seeking by special interest groups; and a lack of harmony in the initiation, scaling, and phasing of programme elements.

## The legacy of the past

Viewing policy developments in the period 1946-86, it is apparent that four major episodes can be distinguished, centreing on the balance of payments and currency depreciation crises of 1949, 1962, 1970 and 1983. Figures 13.1 – 13.6 provide key macro-economic data series that highlight and link the episodes.[2] Special emphasis is given to evaluating the impact of the enforced adjustment and stabilization measures that were applied in the 1980-86 period.

## Evolution of the policy structure, 1946-80

Prior to independence in 1946, there was a customs union between the Philippines and the United States, and the peso was tied to the US dollar. Tariffs on non-US imports were levied at an *ad valorem* level of 23 per cent with the primary objective of raising revenue. These arrangements were largely retained in the early years of independence under the terms of the Bell Trade Act. However, a foreign exchange crisis developed in 1949 as a result of the accumulation of pent-up demand in the post-war period, exacerbated by election-related deficit spending. Following consultations with the US, the Central Bank imposed exchange controls, and intensified quotas and taxes on non-essential and luxury imports. These actions were successful in defending the exchange rate, and provided the basis for an expanding range of interventions directed at maintaining a low price for foreign exchange and promoting import replacement industries. With the negotiation of the Laurel-Langley Agreement with the US in 1954, the Philippines gained full autonomy in its economic relations and proceeded to entrench its protection of 'new and necessary industries', while readily foregoing preferential access to US markets (Sicat 1986, p. 9). The identification of inward-looking exchange and trade policies with nationalist ideals is therefore a long-standing feature of the political economy of the Philippines.

During the 1950s the real exchange rate *vis-à-vis* the US dollar remained high and there was an intermittent but persistent current account deficit. By 1959, the black-market rate for the peso was double the official rate and pressures for devaluation mounted with the powerful sugar lobby taking the lead in arguing for a more realistic exchange rate. In response the government embarked upon a progressive programme of exchange-rate liberalization, working from multiple exchange rates to a free float in the manner of the idealised Bhagwati-Krueger sequence (Baldwin 1975). By mid-1962, the unified exchange rate had settled at P3.90/US$1.00, reflecting market conditions. This presaged the significant expansion of traditional commodity exports (sugar, coconut products, logs and ore extracts) and the achievement of positive balances in the current account in the period 1963-66. However, the industrial sector

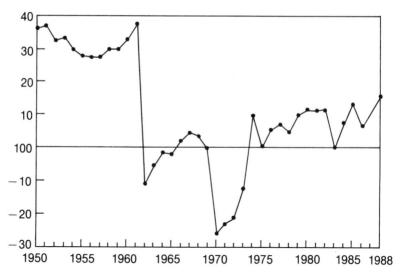

Fig 13.1   Real exchange rate (1975 = 100)

entered a period of retrenchment, confirming the prejudices of those who argued that foreign exchange liberalization would work to the advantage of traditional export oligarchies, at the expense of the modern sectors of the economy (see Figure 13.6)

The inauguration of the first Marcos administration in 1966 marked the adoption of an expansionary macro-economic policy fuelled by a massive credit relaxation. These developments were accompanied by significant rises in the levels of internal and external debt. By 1970 a full-blown exchange crisis had developed, necessitating the restructuring of foreign debts under an IMF stabilization programme and the abandonment of the 'managed float' of the peso that had gradually developed in the late 1960s. This resulted in the depreciation of the peso from P3.90 to P6.40 to the dollar. In the aftermath of the crisis, the current account improved steadily, peaking in the 1973-74 world commodity boom. At the same time, expanding food production stemming primarily from the adoption of high yielding varieties of rice, set the scene for new industrialization initiatives based on steady or declining real wages. The new policy measures that were implemented with World Bank support included the thorough revision of the tariff code to promote import replacement industries, the provision of duty drawbacks on imported inputs under the 1973 Export Incentives Act, and the setting up of the first export processing zone at Mariveles in 1972. Less positively, export taxes were imposed on traditional exports. The developments were therefore also linked to the ascendancy of the import replacement industries lobby over the commodity producer groups.

Following the 1973 international oil crisis, recession in the industrial countries resulted in the decline of commodity prices and the deterioration of terms of trade for most developing countries. However, the policy initiatives of the early 1970s and the declaration of Martial Law in 1972 raised the country's credit standing and made it an attractive target for intermediators seeking to recycle petrodollars. Building

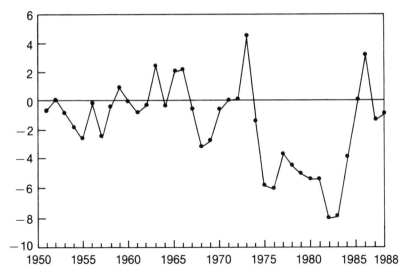

Fig 13.2   Current account balance/GDP ratio (%)

upon the support provided by rice producers and import replacement manufacturers, the government began to promote its own partial vision of export-led growth. While tariffs remained high in comparison to other ASEAN countries, incentives were provided to encourage the development of non-traditional exports (including the opening of enclave industrial processing zones) (Intal 1987, p. 7). However, the government's interventions became increasingly authoritarian and *ad hoc*, as the decade progressed, as business conglomerates were built up on the basis of preferential access to credit, import and trading monopolies, government-backed take overs, and collusive mark-ups on sales and services provided to the public sector. Much of this aggressive and speculative business behaviour was fuelled by the availability of short-term variable interest rate loans from foreign commercial banks, resulting in a rapidly mounting external debt burden (see Figure 13.5).

While the problems associated with the later years of the Marcos administration are readily evident with the benefit of hindsight, it is important to remember that the Philippines was frequently viewed at the time as an exemplar of successful adjustment under the World Bank's tutelage (Broad 1988). Real GDP grew at an average rate of 6.6 per cent in the period 1974-80, compared to 5.7 per cent between 1969 and 1974 (Alburo and Shepherd 1985, p. 92). Over the same period, the contribution of manufacturing to GDP rose from 16.7 to 23.2 per cent and the share of non-traditional manufactures in total merchandise exports rose from around 12.0 to 36.4 per cent. However, total factor productivity in manufacturing fell at an accelerating rate between 1971 and 1983 (UNIDO 1988 p. 77), while the incremental capital-output ratio for the economy as a whole deteriorated from 3.9 in 1979 to 5.2 in 1980 and 8.2 in 1982 (Intal and Pante 1989, p. 23).

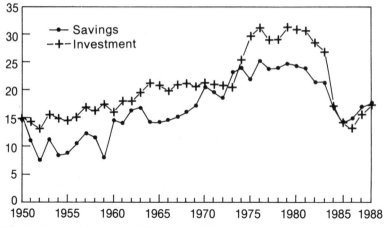

Fig 13.3   Savings and investment/GDP ratios (%)

## Enforced adjustment and stabilization 1980-85

In the aftermath of the 1979-80 oil shock, the Philippines faced deteriorating trade prospects and the tightening of access to external resource flows. Despite an unprecedented adverse shift in the country's terms of trade, the government maintained its counter-cyclical expansion policy. This included plans to equip the Philippines with a heavy industry base through the construction of eleven large-scale processing facilities in key sectors, together with the provision of associated infrastructure (including a costly nuclear power station). As external conditions worsened, the government depended increasingly on short term borrowing from foreign commercial banks to both fund new investment and refinance the deficits of public corporations. With the rapid growth of variable interest rate obligations and the continued slide in the current account balance, the country's debt servicing capacity became precarious.

Against this backdrop, the government instituted a number of important, if uncharacteristic, policy changes, including the liberalization of interest ceilings on banking deposits in 1981 and the commencement of a phased reform of foreign trade policy. The latter included the dismantling of licensing and quota restrictions, the reduction and levelling of tariffs, the elimination of differential sales taxes, and the adoption of strengthened and simplified export promotion measures (as discussed further below). The policy reform initiatives were catalysed by a US$200 million World Bank Structural Adjustment Loan that was disbursed in 1981. In evaluating the government's apparent change of attitude with respect to the protection of import replacement industry, Alburo and Shepherd conjecture that the policy reform initiative was spurred by the country's accession to GATT in 1980, and that its realisation constituted a successful 'palace coup' by technocrats within the bureau-cracy (Alburo and Shepherd 1985, p. 153). More plausibly, it would appear that the government recognized the necessity for reassuring its commercial bank creditors on

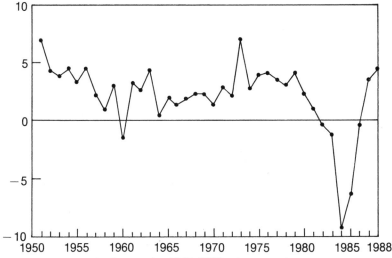

Fig 13.4   Annual growth of per capita GNP (1985 prices, pesos)

its policies, by obtaining the World Bank's imprimatur. Under this interpretation the reforms may have constituted a hostage to fortune, that allowed some scope for delay and selective application.

By 1983 the economy was on the verge of crisis in its current and capital accounts. With an overshoot already evident by mid-year in the balance of payments target agreed under an ongoing IMF stand-by agreement, the peso was devalued from P9 to P11 to the dollar in June. However, the Aquino assassination in August 1983 took the economy into a full-blown debt crisis, on the pattern established by Mexico, as foreign bankers rushed to close lines of credit. A further devaluation to P14 in October 1983 was accompanied by the announcement of the suspension of payments on debt principal. At the same time, negotiations with the IMF on a comprehensive adjustment programme stalled as the government 'revised' its estimate of total foreign debt from $16.3 billion to $24.8 billion between September and November 1983 and it became known that the Central Bank had overstated its foreign exchange reserves by US$800 million (Montes 1987, pp. 3, 13). With devaluation placing huge claims on importers, a scarcity of foreign credits and capital flight, the government required banks to surrender 100 per cent of their foreign exchange receipts and created a ration pool for priority imports. As a further emergency measure, *ad valorem* taxes on imports were raised to generate revenue. Under these circumstances the policy reform process was overwhelmed by waves of emergency and *ad hoc* interventions by government.

As negotiations with the IMF dragged on until December 1984, the government was gradually forced to mould its policies to the IMF's specified 'prior action measures'. These focused on curbing inflation by raising interest rates and taxes. Intensifying the liquidity squeeze, the Central Bank raised interest rates on Treasury bills to over 40 per cent, with the result that commercial banks were deprived of

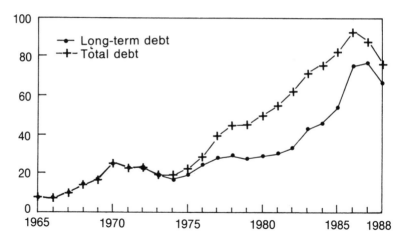

Fig 13.5   External debt/GDP ratio (%)

deposits and industrial firms collapsed as working capital and demand evaporated. The conclusion of the IMF adjustment agreement marked the rescheduling of principal payments over a two-year period, the establishment of a US$3 billion trade facility, and the provision of US$925 million in new money. With the agreement in place and interest rates at unprecedently high levels the government was able to liberalize the exchange regime to meet the IMF's conditions. However, the real exchange rate *vis-à-vis* the dollar continued to appreciate under the resulting managed float.

As described by Montes (1987), the stabilization and adjustment process appeared to meet its targets successfully. The current account balance improved from a deficit of US$2.5 billion in 1983 to a surplus of US$8 million in 1985. Inflation declined to 57 per cent by December 1985, after peaking at 63 per cent in 1984, and debt servicing continued in line with the provisions of the adjustment agreement. However, foreign trade contracted severely, with a decline in exports from US$5.4 billion in 1984 to US$4.6 billion in 1985, and a 40 per cent decline in imports between 1983 and 1985. With concurrent falls in domestic output, investment and employment, the adjustment process resulted in economic immobility rather than stabilization. As a result, the industrial sector suffered chronic dislocation from foreclosures and low capacity utilization. Important questions, therefore, remain relating to the timing and content of the adjustment measures. Early action in the period 1980–81 might have forestalled a crisis, as appears to have been the case with Korea (Aghevli and Marquez-Ruarte 1985). Additionally, the deterioration of relations between the government and the IMF in the period November 1983 to late 1984 led to a critical delay in the flow of external finance and a firming of the explicit and hidden agendas of both parties.

Taking a broad view of the interaction between economic circumstances and internal political developments in the period 1980–86, it appears that the government

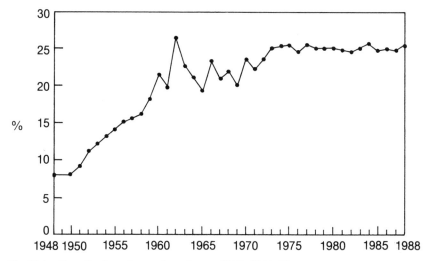

Fig 13.6   Contribution of manufacturing to GDP, 1948–88

gradually disengaged itself from its former alliances with the import replacement and enclave industrialisation lobbies under the pressure of events. According to Snow (1983) the import replacement industry groups became an important element in the political opposition following the commencement of the 1981 import liberalization programme. Subsequently, as the crisis intensified, the government focused upon safeguarding public enterprises and linked business conglomerates by avoiding the curtailment of the public sector deficit. At the same time, the maintenance of the explicit support of the IMF and the World Bank became increasingly essential to allay the fears of foreign creditors (Broad 1988). Under such circumstances, the structural adjustment process can degenerate into a series of short-term trade-offs where 'parts of the agenda that are in the interest of government in power will be implemented; parts that are not will be amended or not implemented at all' and 'the resulting programme will be in the interest of the government, which is not necessarily consistent with any real success in adjustment' (Montes 1987 p. 44).

## Evaluation of current policy developments, 1986-90

The advent of the Aquino administration in February 1986 marked the possibility of a clean start in the process of policy reform. The IMF was quick to state the objectives of the new government as:

- promotion of a more outward looking and competitive economy through appropriate exchange rate and tariff policies
- reorientation of the development process towards the rural and export sectors
- reduction of government intervention in the economy and removal of disincentives to private sector activity.[3]

However, the acceptance and attainment of this manifesto remains in the balance as long-standing constraints and short-term experiences slow the momentum of reform. The following sections attempt to provide an assessment of the progress of policy reform in the areas of exchange rate policy, trade liberalization, and industrial policy. Table 13.1 sets the scene by providing sequences for key economic indicators in the period 1986 to 1989.

Table 13.1   *Key economic indicators: Philippines, 1986–89*

|  |  | 1986 | 1987 | 1988 | 1989 |
|---|---|---|---|---|---|
| Gross Domestic Product | % change | 1.4 | 4.7 | 6.2 | 6.0 |
| Agriculture | % change | 3.3 | −1.0 | 3.5 | 4.0 |
| Industry | % change | −2.1 | 7.8 | 8.5 | 7.1 |
| Services | % change | 2.9 | 6.9 | 6.3 | 6.4 |
| Gross Domestic Investment | % of GDP | 12.9 | 16.0 | 17.3 | 18.8 |
| Gross Domestic Saving | % of GDP | 14.2 | 17.5 | 18.1 | 17.4 |
| Gross National Saving | % of GDP | 16.2 | 16.8 | 17.7 | 16.6 |
| Resource Gap | % of GDP | 1.3 | 1.4 | 0.7 | −1.4 |
| Inflation rate | % change in CPI | 0.8 | 3.8 | 8.7 | 10.6 |
| Merchandise Exports | $ billion | 4.8 | 5.7 | 7.1 | 7.6 |
|  | % change | 4.6 | 18.1 | 23.7 | 8.0 |
| Merchandise Imports | $ billion | 5.0 | 6.7 | 8.2 | 10.8 |
|  | % change | −1.3 | 33.6 | 21.1 | 32.4 |
| Trade Balance | $ billion | −0.2 | −1.0 | −1.1 | −3.2 |
| Current Account Balance | $ billion | 1.0 | −0.5 | −0.4 | −1.4 |
|  | % of GDP | 3.3 | −1.4 | −1.0 | −3.1 |
| External Debt | $ billion | 28.9 | 30.1 | 29.4 | 28.5 |
| Debt-Service Ratio | % | 34.4 | 39.0 | 32.2 | 27.0 |
| Government T ax Revenue | % of GDP | 10.4 | 12.1 | 10.9 | 12.4 |
| Government Budget Deficit | % of GDP | −5.0 | −2.9 | −2.5 | −1.9 |
| Unemployment Rate | % of Labour Force | 11.5 | 9.1 | 8.5 | 7.1 |

*Note:* 1986–88 actuals, 1989 forcast.
*Source:* ADB, *Asian Development Outlook,* 1989 and 1990.

**Exchange rate policy**

Contrary to the expectations of the IMF, the Aquino government placed high priority on maintaining the stability of the nominal exchange rate of the peso *vis-à-vis* the US dollar. In the period 1986 to 1989, the rate depreciated from P20.39 to P21.76, under a managed float which aimed to contain the adjustment within a maximum of three per cent. Following the release of the economy from its artificial compression in 1983-85, both exports and overall output rose as capacity utilization improved. However, the trade deficit widened sharply from US$1.1 billion in 1988 to around US$3.2 billion in 1989, as imports increased by 32 per cent. At the same time inflation accelerated to over 10 per cent per year. With official exchange reserves declining throughout 1989 as a result of defensive sales by the Central Bank, a period of enforced depreciation appears to have commenced resulting in the breaching of the P23 barrier by mid-1990.

While the new government has tended to perpetuate the exchange rate policy of its predecessors, there is a virtual unanimity among economic commentators on the need for a sustained depreciation of the real exchange rate to promote export development and moderate the incidence of balance of payments crises. Firm evidence for this view comes from time series comparison of the purchasing power parity of the peso versus both the US dollar and the currencies of such countries as Thailand and Indonesia (see, for example, Intal and Pante 1989, p. 26, and Medalla 1990, p. 36), and from estimates of divergences between the official exchange rate and the free trade or shadow exchange rate, (see Bautista and Power 1979 p. 79, and Intal and Pante 1989).

Despite universal condemnation by theoreticians, the overvaluation of the exchange rate remains an endemic feature of the macro-economy of the Philippines – a situation that is widely parallelled in the developing world. In attempting to account for the persistent shortfall between the ideal and the actual, three sets of considerations need to be taken into account. These relate to (i) the experience provided by past reform episodes, (ii) the evolving activities of rent-seeking groups, and (iii) the unique features of the current situation.

As has been documented above, the imposition of exchange controls has long been associated with the pursuit of nationalist ideals. Furthermore, the currency depreciation episodes of 1962 and 1970 were born of crisis, such that exchange rate liberalization came to be seen as either a corollary of balance of payments difficulties or the price of support from the IMF. It is also worth noting that few positive benefits can be attributed to these early initiatives, as adjustments to the real exchange rate were soon eroded by accelerated inflation and the bias imparted by an unchanged import substitution trade regime.

The crisis of 1983-85 witnessed the halving of the dollar value of the peso, combined with rapid inflation and a substantial decline in living standards. The depreciation of the peso therefore underlined the erosion of the legitimacy of the government. As the crisis mounted, the Marcos administration lost the support of urban consumers, including the middle class and organised labour groups. As Roemer and Stern comment perceptively on the political economy of devaluation 'this group includes four constituents with considerable political power: trade unions, civil servants, students and the military' (Roemer and Stern 1981, p. 215). It is therefore understandable that the Aquino government has sought to conserve its early political goodwill by defending the exchange rate. Further, it is notable that concurrent actions, such as raising the minimum wage from P15 per day in 1986 to P25 per day in mid-1989, have tended to raise the real exchange rate.

Finally, it is important to note some of the particular features of the current setting. In the first place, the Philippines benefited from the expansion of trade at both the global and regional levels in the second half of the 1980s, while the accumulation of substantial current account surpluses in Japan, and such newly industrialising countries as Taiwan, resulted in the strengthening of private resource flows. These factors reduced the pressure for devaluation. On the other hand, the presence of a substantial debt overhang has led to concern that the depreciation of the peso would inflate the budgetary cost of debt-servicing (Ali 1988, p. 4).

In summary, it is questionable whether the time is ripe for a substantive effort to improve the real exchange rate. Although the government is now presenting the ongoing depreciation as a move to a flexible exchange rate policy to benefit the export sector, this carries the risk that the policy may again be discredited as short-run inflationary pressures are accentuated. In these circumstances, efforts might best focus upon such areas as restraining government expenditures and containing inflation to provide a base for a sustainable real devaluation. At the same time, the continued liberalization of trade policies, and the provision of neutral status to exporters through investment incentive and export credit packages can lay the foundation for export-led growth and the maturation of the exchange rate regime.

## Trade liberalization

In marked contrast to the situation obtaining for exchange rate reform, the history of trade liberalization in the Philippines is comparatively brief. Tariffs and quotas on consumption goods and 'non-essential' items became entrenched in the period 1946-60, resulting in average effective protection rates for import substituting manufactures rising to around 200 per cent (Baldwin 1975, pp. 84-120). Following the unsustained real exchange rate adjustments of 1960-62, trade barriers resumed their role as a major arbiter in resource allocation. In the period 1963-80, effective rates of protection for import substitutes were maintained in the range of 200 to 220 per cent, while taxes on traditional exports widened relative differentials. The trade liberalization programme initiated in 1980 was therefore a break with the past, and it is apposite to consider policy reform in the period 1981-90 as a single act broken into two scenes by the change of government in 1986.

The 1981-85 phase of the import liberalization programme received direct stimulus from the World Bank in the form of two structural adjustment loans (US$ 200 million in 1981, and US$ 302.3 million in 1983). The programme had two major components – the removal of import licences and the reform of the tariff structure. In the period 1981-83 import licences were removed from around 1,000 'non-essential' items, though commercial banks were still required to report letters of credit opened for imports of this type. During 1984-85 plans to liberalize further items were made redundant by the imposition of import controls to conserve foreign exchange. The tariff reform component was to have been phased over five years, resulting in the reduction of the average tariff from 43 per cent to 28 per cent, with a maximum of

50 per cent and a minimum of 20 per cent. The new structure envisaged average rates of 20 per cent for raw materials, 20 to 30 per cent for intermediates and capital goods, and 40 to 50 per cent for consumer goods. By the beginning of 1984 'only' 133 items remained with rates exceeding 50 per cent, but additional *ad valorem* duties had been levied for emergency revenue purposes.

The Aquino administration therefore inherited a half-implemented programme that had been rendered partially ineffective by *ad hoc* measures imposed during the 1983–85 balance of payments crisis. It also inherited political obligations to opponents of the programme. After some wavering, the new government confirmed the maintenance of import liberalization policies in three executive orders and a Republic Act (RA 6647, July 1987). As a result of selective measures implemented by the new government, the number of licensed or regulated import items fell (from 1924 in 1985 to 673 in 1988), and the average tariff on importables was contained at about 30 per cent (Medalla 1990, p. 6). However, export taxes were removed on all items in 1986 (with the exception of logs), to the benefit of the commodity producer lobby.

Tables 13.2 and 13.3 present before and after comparisons of effective rates of protection by sector for the initial and ongoing liberalization exercises. It can be seen that exportables received little relief as a result of the 1981 to 1985 episode, though measurable progress was realised in reducing average levels of effective protection on importable manufactures. As shown in Table 13.3 the differential protection between agriculture and manufacturing based on actual tariffs (book tariff rates) actually widened between 1985 and 1988, suggesting an intensification of protection for import replacement industries. However, the overall picture is one of generally reduced disparities between sectors, which, although not insignificant, were 'not large enough to substantially alter the inherent biases of the protection structure' (Medalla 1990, p. 26).

Table 13.2  *Comparisons of effective protection rates, 1979 and 1985*

|   |   | Absolute rates[a] | | Indexed differentials[b] | |
|---|---|---|---|---|---|
|   |   | *1979* | *1985* | *1979* | *1985* |
| 1 | All sectors | 124 | 112 | 100 | 100 |
|   | 1.1  Exportables | 97 | 97 | 78 | 87 |
|   | 1.2  Importables | 144 | 125 | 116 | 112 |
| 2 | Processing and agriculture | 101 | 99 | 100 | 100 |
| 3 | Manufacturing | 140 | 123 | 139 | 124 |
|   | 3.1  Exportable manufactures | 101 | 101 | 100 | 100 |
|   | 3.2  Importable manufactures | 158 | 133 | 156 | 132 |

*Sources:*
[a] Medalla 1986.
[b] Power and Medalla 1986.

Table 13.3   *Comparisons of relative effective protection rates, 1985-88 (agriculture = 100)*

|   |   | Book rates | | | Price comparisons | | |
|---|---|---|---|---|---|---|---|
|   |   | *1985* | *1986* | *1988* | *1985* | *1986* | *1988* |
| 1 | All sectors | 110 | 115 | 114 | 123 | 121 | 119 |
|   | 1.1  Exportables | 81 | 90 | 90 | 77 | 83 | 83 |
|   | 1.2  Importables | 134 | 135 | 134 | 167 | 157 | 152 |
| 2 | Processing and agriculture | 92 | 95 | 95 | 90 | 91 | 91 |
| 3 | Manufacturing | 119 | 125 | 124 | 144 | 139 | 135 |
|   | 3.1  Exportable manufactures | 84 | 93 | 93 | 79 | 86 | 86 |
|   | 3.2  Importable manufactures | 133 | 137 | 136 | 172 | 162 | 157 |

*Source:* Medalla 1990.

Currently the government is considering further reforms which include the reduction of the minimum tariff from 10 to 5 per cent and the raising of the maximum rate above 50 per cent. At the same time pressures are mounting for the restoration of import restrictions and the imposition of 60 per cent tariffs on certain liberalized items, as envisaged by the Senate opposition. The maintenance and further development of the liberalization process is therefore highly uncertain, as the import replacement industry lobby intensifies its attempts to retain or restore protection rents. In addition the government is again being forced to consider imposing *ad valorem* taxes on imports as an emergency revenue-raising measure, given an expected widening of the public sector deficit in 1990. Renewed efforts will therefore have to be made to safeguard and build upon the existing policy reforms in the coming decade.

## Industrial policy

The industrial policy initiatives of the new government can be considered under two broad headings: (i) investment and export incentives, and (ii) privatisation and deregulation measures. As discussed above, the period 1970 to 1980 saw the development of a wide range of investment and export incentives, though these were applied on an increasingly *ad hoc* basis as the decade progressed. The Aquino administration placed high priority in revising these measures under the 1987 Omnibus Investment Code. However, comparisons between the new code and its predecessors do not confirm that it marks a renewed commitment to export-led industrialization. For example, the new code grants domestic and export producers exemptions from taxes and duties on imported capital equipment and provides the credits to both groups for purchases of domestic capital equipment. This contrasts with the previous code which reserved these incentives for export producers. It would therefore appear that the new policies reflect a bias towards the interests of import-substituting industry groups. At the same time, the incentives have tended to favour capital rather than labour-intensive development, with the average capital to labour ratio for new and expansion projects rising from P120,000 to P224,000 between 1987 and 1988 (Medalla 1990, p. 47).

Turning to export incentive measures, it appears that the overall package has changed little in the last decade. The measures attempt to provide free-trade or neutral status to selective exporters, by granting tax and duty exemptions on imported inputs for manufacturing units that are either located in an export processing zone, or that utilize bonded manufacturing warehouse facilities. As discussed by Ali (1988), the new administration has not addressed the problems which surround the existing incentives. These relate to the exclusion of small-scale and indirect exporters, the lack of consideration of value-adding and employment generating effects, and the complex and tedious nature of the procedures. At the same time the government continues to promote the development of enclave manufacturing within export processing zones, despite evidence of the low social return of public investment in these facilities (Warr 1984). Such trends add further evidence of a lack of commitment by the new administration to either providing a 'level playing-field' for exporters through a process of comprehensive policy reform, or to systematically redressing existing biases by providing easy and automatic access to export credit and duty and tax exemptions.

In contrast to the case of investment and export incentives, the current emphasis on the privatisation of state manufacturing interests represents a new policy departure. It stems in part from a revulsion against the excesses of the previous administration, in part from the need to reduce the level of public debt and moderate the public sector deficit, and in part from the ideological consensus that has developed during the 1980s in the advanced industrial countries and the multilateral financing institutions. The privatisation programme envisages the eventual sale of 122 public sector enterprises and 399 of the non-performing assets formerly held by the Philippine National Bank and the Development Bank of the Philippines.

At the end of 1989, the Committee on Privatisation had approved the sale of 39 enterprises (representing about 28 per cent of the book value of all the public sector enterprises under consideration), of which 30 had been fully or partly disposed of, for a total sale value of P6.2 billion. Some 182 of the 399 non-performing assets had also been divested, realising a sale value of over P10.0 billion. Despite the measurable progress that has been made in the privatisation programme, much remains to be done. Indeed, the programme appears to be stalling as legal and bureaucratic feuds proliferate, involving ex-owners, nominees linked to the old government, and the 'temporary' public sector managers installed since 1986. At the same time public concern is being expressed about the transfer of assets to foreigners and the Filipino and Filipino-Chinese elites (Intal and Pante 1989, p. 6). There is thus a risk that the efficiency objectives of the privatisation programme will be subsumed in a new round of rent-seeking.

In the area of deregulation the new government moved rapidly to dismantle the sugar and coconut export monopolies and the meat, wheat and soybean import monopsonies. Competition was also introduced in the fertiliser trade and price controls were lifted on a number of food products. However, an interventionist mentality still prevails with price controls being imposed, for example, on nine basic items over the 1989 Christmas season. These controls are still in place for rice, cooking gas and cement. Similarly, in the area of financial liberalization, it is proving difficult to maintain the momentum of reform. While interest rates on both loans and deposits have been fully market-determined since late 1985, the repression of the financial market is being perpetuated by high reserve requirements, taxes on loans and interest income, and the compulsory allocation of 25 per cent of the loanable funds of commercial banks to agriculture and agrarian reform projects (Tolentino 1989). As is true elsewhere in the economy, the process of policy reform is hesitant and uncertain as the government reaches for the old levers of power to meet short-term objectives and placate powerful special interest groups.

## Conclusion

As has been illustrated by the Philippine experience, a wide range of factors may influence the timing, speed, and structure of events during policy reform episodes. It appears that in life, it is rare to find strong and decisive action that leads to a once-and-for-all improvement in the policy framework. All too often the best intentions of the protagonists are overwhelmed by external pressures, short-run expediencies, and poor timing. In these circumstances, admonitions to developing countries to emphasize rapid and fundamental policy changes may be of little practical relevance. While countries may appear to respond to this advice during periods of crisis, the resulting reforms are difficult to sustain. Contrary to the simplifications of technocrats, economic and political stability cannot be assumed. It is, therefore, important to select, time and phase individual policy reform measures with care, as steps towards the realization of broader long-term objectives. Demonstrable but limited successes may therefore be preferable to grand gestures, as the social consensus and implementing institutions are developed for more thoroughgoing policy adjustments.

## Notes

1   The views expressed in the paper are those of the author and do not necessarily reflect the views and policies of the Asian Development Bank. The author wishes to acknowledge the research assistance of Ms. Josie Balane and the secretarial services of Ms. Lori Macatiag.

2   The real exchange rate in Figure 13.1 has been calculated with respect to the US dollar, by dividing an index of relative exchange rates by an index of relative wholesale price changes. The results have been presented as deviations from parity (1975 = 100), with relative overvaluations being given a positive sign.

3   IMF Survey, November 17 1986, quoted by Hodgkinson (1988, p. 31).

## References

Aghevli, B.B. and Marquez-Ruarte, J. (1985), 'A Case of Successful Adjustment: Korea's Experience During 1980-84', IMF *Occasional Paper*, Washington, DC.

Alburo, F. and Shepherd, G. (1985), 'Trade Liberalization Experience in the Philippines, 1960-84', *Philippine Institute for Development Studies Working Paper*, no. 86-01, Manila.

Ali, I. (1988), 'Manufactured Exports from the Philippines: A Sector Profile and an Agenda for Reform', *Asian Development Bank Economic Staff Paper*, no. 42, Manila.

Asian Development Bank (1989), *Asian Development Outlook*, Manila.

Asian Development Bank (1990), *Asian Development Outlook*, Manila.

Baldwin, R.E. (1975), *Foreign Trade Regimes and Economic Development: The Philippines*, Columbia University Press, New York.

Bautista, R.M. and Power, J.H. and Associates (1979), *Industrial Promotion Policies in the Philippines*, Philippine Institute for Development Studies, Manila.

Broad, R. (1988), *Unequal Alliance 1979-86: The World Bank, the International Monetary Fund and the Philippines*, Ateneo de Manila University Press, Manila.

Dornbusch, R. and Helmers, F.L.C. (1988), *The Open Economy*, Economic Development Institute, World Bank, Washington, DC.

Hodgkinson, E. (1988), 'The Philippines to 1993: Making up Lost Ground', *Economist Intelligence Unit Special Report*, no. 1145, London.

Intal, P.S. (1987), 'Government Interventions and Rent Seeking', Department of Economics Discussion Paper 87-04, University of the Philippines, Los Banos.

Intal, P.S. and Pante, F. (1989), 'Can the Philippines Grow out of Debt?', paper presented at the Asian and Pacific Development Centre Conference on the Future of the Asia-Pacific Economies, Bangkok, November 8-10.

Medalla, E.M. (1986), 'Assessment of the Tariff Reform Program and Trade Liberalization', *Tariff Commission – Philippine Institute of Development Studies Joint Research Project*, Staff Paper Series no. 86-03, Manila.

Medalla, E.M. (1990), 'An Assessment of Trade and Industrial Policy, 1986-1988', Philippine Institute for Development Studies, Working Paper Series no. 90-07, Manila.

Montes, M.F. (1987), *Stabilization and Adjustment Policies and Programmes: Country Study 2, the Philippines*, World Institute for Development Economics Research, Helsinki.

Power, J. and Medalla, E. (1986), 'Trade Liberalization in the Philippines: Assessment of Progress and Agenda for Future Reform', Tariff Commission – Philippine Institute for Development Studies Joint Research Project, Staff Paper Series, no. 86-01, Manila, 1986.

Roemer, M. and Stern, J.J. (1981), *Cases in Economic Development: Projects, Policies and Strategies*, Butterworth, London.

Sicat, G.P. (1986), 'A Historical and Current Perspective of Philippine Economic Problems', Philippine Institute of Development Studies Monograph Series no. 11, Manila.

Snow, R.T. (1983), 'The Bourgeois Opposition to Export-Oriented Industrialization in the Philippines', Third World Studies Center, Paper Series no. 39, University of the Philippines, Manila.

Tolentino, V.B.J. (1989), 'The Political Economy of Credit Availability and Financial Liberalization: Notes on the Philippine Experience', *Savings and Development*, XIII-4, pp. 321-34.

UNIDO (1988), 'The Philippines: Sustaining Industrial Recovery through Privatization and Foreign Investment', Industrial Development Review Series, Vienna.

Warr, P. (1984), 'Export Promotion via Industrial Enclave: The Philippines Bataan Export Processing Zone', University of the Philippines School of Economics Occasional Paper.

World Bank (1985), 'Lending for Adjustment: An Update', *World Bank News*, Special Report, Washington.

World Bank (1987), *World Development Report 1987*, Oxford University Press for the World Bank, Washington, DC.

# Policy reform and export performance in Sri Lanka: some observations

## Introduction

In recent years a major policy prescription to achieve export-led economic growth for developing countries has been to move towards outward-orientation, making the economies more open to market forces and external influences. However, the extent of implementation of this policy prescription has varied substantially across countries. Policy reform in many cases has been partial, focusing mainly on the reduction in the extent of over valuation of the exchange rate and the opening up of imports to stimulate export growth. The experience of, among others, Bangladesh, China, Sri Lanka, Turkey and Mauritius, shows that export growth is possible under a partial policy reform but it does not necessarily promote long-term economic growth. Under a partially reformed policy environment the export sector is seldom integrated with the rest of the economy, and resources are misallocated, as limited reliance on market forces and an uneven structure of incentives for investment persist. In this chapter we consider Sri Lanka's trade policy reform and the resulting performance of its non-traditional export sector. Sri Lanka, which had a relatively open economy in the 1940s and early 1950s has gone through various attempts at liberalizing trade and introducing a more market-based mechanism.

## Policy reform

Prior to the 1977 economic reforms, the Sri Lankan economy was characterised by a slow growth of national income averaging annually at 2.8 per cent, unemployment at around 20 per cent of the labour force, and inflation ranging between 15–20 per cent. Manufacturing activities were mostly publicly owned and engaged in import substitute production, whose growth was stagnant. There were stringent government controls on foreign exchange, imports, prices, and credits, and the export sector was heavily taxed.

The 1977 economic liberalization, with greater emphasis on outward-orientation, focused on the foreign exchange rate and its allocation, the removal of quantitative restrictions on imports, the removal of price controls, tariff reform, foreign investment promotion, and financial sector liberalization.

The currency (SL Rs) was devalued by 46.2 per cent against the US dollar and the exchange rate was unified to the higher unofficial rate that was prevalent under the previous regime. Stringent controls on foreign exchange allocation were abolished. Subsequently, a floating exchange rate system was adopted in which the US dollar was the intervening currency. This enhanced the international competitiveness of Sri Lankan exports.

The pervasive quantitative restrictions (QRs) on imports were replaced by tariffs. Six bands of import tariff rates were introduced which ranged from zero per cent on essential consumer goods like rice, flour, and medicines, to a 500 per cent prohibitive rate on luxury goods. The rate on raw materials, capital goods and spare parts averaged 5-25 per cent. Although the new tariff rates were higher than before, they eliminated the premia attached to QRs. Many of the earlier tariffs had been made redundant by the quantitative restrictions. However, a subsequent reduction in the high level of tariffs, initially required to incorporate the effect of the removal of QRs, did not take place.

Price controls were removed except for a few essential consumer goods, and producer's prices were raised. The procurement price of rice was raised by 21 per cent. The system of global food subsidies was replaced by a food stamp programme aimed at the low-income groups of the population.

In order to attract private foreign investment and promote export growth a 'free trade zone' concept was adopted. Goods manufactured for export in or outside the export processing zones by foreign investors or jointly by foreign and local investors were allowed a duty- and tax-free import of inputs and export of outputs, and repatriation of profit, dividend, and capital. This has attracted a substantial foreign investment, provided employment to local labour, and earned foreign exchange.

In the financial sector interest rates were revised upwards to maintain a positive real rate and foreign banks were allowed to operate. The financial sector has widened and is less distorted than before. However, the interest rate structure is discriminatory and does not reflect the market-based rate (Jayamaha 1990).

The liberalization effort of 1977 in Sri Lanka indicated a drive towards an opening up of the economy to external influences, and an attempt to make it internationally competitive. However, the traditional exports like tea, coconut and rubber did not get much incentive from the devaluation as it was accompanied by an increase in export duties. Until recently the rate of export duties was significantly high (see Table 14.1).

The average import duty rate (realised tariffs plus business turnover tax on imports) as been increasing since the 1977 liberalization effort. It has risen almost three-fold over the last decade, from 13 per cent in 1980 to 38 per cent in 1989 (Table 14.1). In contrast, the average export duty rate has been gradually lowered, from 21 per cent in 1980 to 2 per cent in 1989. The implicit over-valuation of the exchange rate shows an upward trend. In recent years it has gone up to 19 per cent (Table 14.1).

Table 14.1   *Sri Lanka: implicit overvaluation of exchange rate and the degree of openness*

| Year | Average import tax (%) | Average export tax (%) | Implicit over-valuation of exchange rate (%) | Degree of openness (%) |
|------|------------------------|------------------------|------------------------------------------------|------------------------|
| 1980 | 13 | 21 | 2  | 83 |
| 1981 | 17 | 17 | 4  | 74 |
| 1982 | 18 | 12 | 8  | 66 |
| 1983 | 24 | 10 | 11 | 62 |
| 1084 | 33 | 9  | 14 | 62 |
| 1985 | 33 | 5  | 16 | 62 |
| 1986 | 36 | 5  | 19 | 54 |
| 1987 | 36 | 4  | 18 | 58 |
| 1988 | 34 | 3  | 18 | 58 |
| 1989 | 38 | 2  | 19 | 60 |

*Notes*

[a] Average import tax includes realised tariffs, and business turnover tax.

[b] Implicit overvaluation of foreign exchange was measured as weighted average tariff (tax) rate on imports and exports.

[c] The degree of openness was measured as the ratio of the foreign trade to GDP.

[d] Trade, tariff and GDP data taken from the Annual Reports, Central Bank of Sri Lanka.

The degree of openness in foreign trade, measured as the ratio of total trade to GDP has fallen steadily since 1980.

The overall structure and the level of protection in the manufacturing sector has not been substantially altered during the post-liberalization years. The effective protection rates in 1979 ranged from between 77 and 79 per cent with wide variation across the sectors and products and with an overall bias against exports (Cuthperston and Khan 1989). The level of effective protection shows an upward trend in the later years (Table 14.2). The weighted average effective protection rate for 1985 was estimated to be 64 per cent for the sample industries and 97 per cent for the whole sector; for 1987 the estimated level was 76 per cent for the sample industries and 107 per cent for the whole sector (Table 14.2). Furthermore, import substitutes were heavily protected (110 per cent for 1985 and 126 per cent for 1987) and exports were provided with much less protection (25 per cent for 1985 and 23 per cent for 1987).[1] This indicates an anti-export bias ranging between 0.60 in 1985 and 0.54 in 1987.[2]

There are controls on the entry of manufacturing firms, on prices in selected goods, and on minimum wage rates. As most incentives are government-regulated, the procedures involve substantial costs to both the government and private sector. In addition, there exists a large, mostly inefficient public enterprise manufacturing sector. While the initial liberalization effort was impressive, subsequent efforts to complete the process did not take place. The trade liberalization and related policy reforms, therefore, remained as an unfinished agenda. Sri Lanka has tended to rely

Table 14.2   *Sri Lanka: estimates of effective protection rates (%)*

| Manufacturing sectors | Sectors | | Sample firms | |
|---|---|---|---|---|
| | *1985* | *1987* | *1985* | *1987* |
| Food, beverages, tobacco | 198 | 197 | 135 | 134 |
| Textiles, clothing, footwear | 69 | 109 | 74 | 122 |
| Wood and wood products | 25 | 23 | 22 | 20 |
| Paper, printing and publishing | 578 | 327 | 1371 | 713 |
| Chemicals, petrol, rubber | 31 | 49 | 19 | 41 |
| Non-metallic minerals | 20 | 22 | 21 | 23 |
| Basic metals | 12 | 10 | 13 | 10 |
| Fabricated metals | 71 | 70 | 71 | 69 |
| Manufacturing nec | − 11 | − 10 | − 10 | − 10 |
| Manufacturing sector | 97 | 107 | 64 | 76 |
| Import substitutes | | | 110 | 126 |
| Exports | | | 25 | 23 |

*Source:* Walton (1988), Ministry of Finance.

on a piecemeal approach: development of export industries under 'free trade zone', and development of import competing industries under high protection.

## Non-traditional export performance

Non-traditional exports are promoted through a 'free trade zone' concept and managed by the Greater Colombo Economic Commission (GCEC) and Foreign Investment Advisor Committee (FIAC).[3] The non-traditional manufactured exports grew rapidly over the last decade (Table 14.3). Most originated from the foreign-owned or controlled manufacturing enterprises developed under the 'free trade zone' concept. The contribution of manufactured exports to total exports was 14 per cent in 1978, but had grown to 51 per cent in 1989, overtaking the traditional exports. In recent years the most rapidly growing export industry has been textiles and garments. The traditional exports like tea, rubber and coconut declined, partly due to the policy environment and partly as a result of the decline in international prices.

  The main objectives of promoting exports were employment creation, foreign exchange earning and improvement of balance of payments, transfer of technology, and increasing investment and growth (Budget Speech 1979).

  Over the 1978-89 period the investment in foreign investment projects grew very rapidly. The total investment in the GCEC enterprises reached Rs16,074 million (US$401 million), of which 46 per cent was private foreign investment. Likewise, the total investment in the FIAC enterprises reached Rs21,423 million (US$536 million), in which the private foreign investment share was 55 per cent. The majority of the enterprises are export-oriented and tourism-based.

Table 14.3   *Sri Lanka: value of exports, 1978-1989 (SDR million)*

|                          | 1978 | 1984 | 1985 | 1986 | 1987 | 1988 | 1989 |
|--------------------------|------|------|------|------|------|------|------|
| *Agricultural products:* | 525  | 866  | 689  | 480  | 458  | 471  | 477  |
| Tea                      | 327  | 605  | 425  | 281  | 280  | 288  | 296  |
| Rubber                   | 103  | 127  | 93   | 80   | 77   | 87   | 67   |
| Coconuts                 | 50   | 59   | 86   | 49   | 37   | 21   | 62   |
| Minor agri products      | 45   | 75   | 75   | 70   | 64   | 75   | 52   |
| *Manufactured goods:*    | 97   | 495  | 517  | 481  | 525  | 530  | 616  |
| Textiles and garments    | 97   | 290  | 288  | 291  | 339  | 333  | 382  |
| Petroleum products       |      | 126  | 140  | 72   | 68   | 53   | 48   |
| Other                    |      | 79   | 89   | 118  | 118  | 144  | 186  |
| *Other:*                 | 44   | 71   | 104  | 74   | 97   | 97   | 122  |
| Gems                     | 27   | 24   | 20   | 23   | 38   | 48   | 48   |
| Miscellaneous            | 17   | 47   | 84   | 51   | 59   | 49   | 74   |
| *Total*                  | 666  | 1432 | 1310 | 1035 | 1080 | 1098 | 1216 |

*Source:* Central Bank, *Annual Reports*, 1988, 1989.

The total capital expenditure up to 1989 incurred by GCEC in developing infrastructures amounted to Rs422 million (US$10.6 million), and other government agencies spent about Rs276 million (US$6.9 million). This represents the direct infrastructural costs of promoting exports through export processing zones.

Employment has been increasing steadily over the last decade in both GCEC and FIAC enterprises. In the GCEC enterprises the total number of workers reached 56,758 in 1989. The textiles and garment industry has employed mainly unskilled, uneducated, female labour.

The value of exports of the GCEC enterprises was about 20 per cent of total exports in 1989. The average net foreign exchange earnings have been about 30 per cent of the export value (Table 14.4). The weighted import (raw materials and capital goods) intensity of the GCEC enterprises averaged 72 per cent for the 1982-88 period, ranging between 61 per cent in 1983 to 78 per cent in 1982 (Table 14.5). There was considerable variation between sectors, from as low as 23 per cent for wood and wood products to as high as 98 per cent in services (Table 14.5).

Linkages of the GCEC enterprises with the productive sectors of the economy have been minimal as a result of their heavy dependence on imported raw materials and capital goods. The share of domestic raw materials in total raw materials use has been increasing slowly, from 0 per cent in 1979 to 6 per cent in 1989. As the textiles and garment industry consumes more than 80 per cent of the total imported raw materials, there appears very little chance for substitution of the imported raw materials. As has happened in most developing countries which have adopted free trade zones, the GCEC export enterprises source few of the local inputs, apart from wood, rubber and tea, labour, basic utilities and services.[4] There are two possible reasons for a very low backward linkage (i.e. local input content) – many of the

Table 14.4   *Performance of the GCEC industries*

| Year | Number of projects in operation cumulative | Total investment Rs.million | Foreign investment Rs.million | Foreign investment (%) | Number and employment cumulative | Total exports Rs.million | Net foreign exchange earnings Rs.million | Net foreign exchange earnings as % of exports |
|------|------|------|------|------|------|------|------|------|
| 1979 | 13 | 47 | 32.7 | 70 | 5876 | 152 | 30 | 20 |
| 1980 | 25 | 421 | 121.5 | 29 | 10581 | 529 | 120 | 23 |
| 1981 | 42 | 1675 | 1269 | 76 | 19727 | 1167 | 291 | 25 |
| 1982 | 52 | 2504 | 2050 | 82 | 24926 | 1653 | 437 | 26 |
| 1983 | 67 | 6273 | 5132 | 82 | 28705 | 2419 | 771 | 32 |
| 1084 | 81 | 8329 | 6098 | 73 | 32725 | 3553 | 1072 | 30 |
| 1085 | 77 | 10796 | 7298 | 68 | 35786 | 3802 | 1213 | 32 |
| 1986 | 91 | 13261 | 8577 | 65 | 45047 | 5396 | 1447 | 27 |
| 1987 | 96 | 15965 | 5450 | 53 | 50744 | 7534 | 2346 | 31 |
| 1988 | 101 | 16074 | 7420 | 46 | 54626 | 9594 | 3000 | 31 |
| 1989 | 109 | | | | 56758 | | | |

Average (1979-88) 30%.
*Source:* Greater Colombo Economic Commission.

Table 14.5   *Import intensity of manufactured exports of GCEC enterprises*

| Sectors | 1982 | 1983 | 1984 | 1985 | 1986 | 1987 | Average 1982-87 |
|------|------|------|------|------|------|------|------|
| Food, beverage, tobacco | 0.32 | 0 | 0.21 | 2.0 | 1.79 | 1.21 | 0.75 |
| Textiles, garments, leather | 0.76 | 0.79 | 0.71 | 0.70 | 0.76 | 0.72 | 0.74 |
| Wood, wood products | 0.29 | 0 | 0 | 0.05 | 0.45 | 0.22 | 0.23 |
| Paper, paper products | 0 | 0 | 0 | 0 | 0 | 0 | 0 |
| Chemicals, petroleum, coal, rubber, plastics | 0.52 | 0.12 | 0.49 | 0.38 | 0.53 | 0.38 | 0.41 |
| Non-metallic minerals | 2.20 | 0.28 | 0.83 | 0.6 | 0.69 | 0.90 | 0.80 |
| Fabricated metal | 4.36 | 0 | 0.65 | 0.69 | 1.04 | 1.01 | 0.90 |
| Manufactured nec | 1.44 | 0.31 | 0.77 | 0.52 | 0.66 | 0.78 | 0.70 |
| Services | 0.46 | 1.43 | 1.04 | 1.0 | 0.66 | 1.20 | 0.98 |
| Average | 0.78 | 0.61 | 0.71 | 0.69 | 0.75 | 0.75 | 0.72 |

*Note*
The averages shown vertically are the average import intensity of sectors for the period 1982-87. The averages shown horizontally denote the average import intensity of all the sectors per annum.
*Source:* Computed from GCEC data.

enterprises are peripheral within a global network often linked to buy-back arrangements, and the local suppliers are unable to satisfy quality standards, regularity of supply, supply volume and prices of the local inputs. Moreover, the policy regime has been focusing on employment creation and foreign exchange earning, giving little attention to other important aspects, such as linkages with the productive sectors of the economy and longer term growth and sustainability.

Transfer of technology is another area where the success of the GCEC enterprises has been minimal. As the majority of the GCEC enterprises are garment manufacturing and light assembling, involving simple technology, the transfer of technology seems to have been limited to the low technology in garments and simple assembly and manufacturing of components.

The efficiency gains from the foreign investment in general and export enterprises in particular emanate from the utilization of surplus (i.e. underemployed and unemployed) labour. The ratio of previous income to current income of the sample workers in the Katunayake Investment Promotion Zone ranged between 0.19 and 0.92 (Ramanayake 1982). The net economic benefit of GCEC enterprises is overwhelmingly the foreign exchange value of the payments to local labour and services, as returns to capital would be repatriated. This seems to be less than 10 per cent in most cases.

## Macroeconomic and sectoral performance

In recent years the GDP growth rate has fallen substantially (Table 14.6). During the 1978-82 period GDP grew at 6.2 per cent annually which was double than that of the pre-liberalization period (1970-77). The growth rate dropped to an average of 3.6 per cent during the 1983-88 period. The decline in agricultural output due to civil disturbances (Table 14.7), unfavourable weather conditions and inefficient management in the public sector contributed to the slower rate of GDP growth in recent years. In the manufacturing sector, the rapid growth of private sector output has been accompanied by sluggishness in the public sector. During 1983-88, the growth in the public sector manufacturing GDP has been negative. The partial liberalization has not improved the performance of this sector, which remains large but economically inefficient. A performance evaluation of 15 selected manufacturing public enterprises estimated rates of return ranging from 4 and 12 per cent over 1978-86 (Ministry of Finance 1989). These rates are far below the comparable opportunity cost of capital in the economy. The financial services sector has emerged as a dynamic sector in the economy as a result of the deregulation of the financial sector, and growth accounted for about one-tenth of the GDP growth between 1982 and 1988. The transport sector also benefited from the deregulation and has experienced a significant growth.

Large fiscal deficits averaging well over 10 per cent of the GDP have been the primary reason for Sri Lanka's macro-economic imbalances in the last decade (Table 14.8). The removal of the global food subsidies and introduction of a food stamps programme in 1979 helped to cut down fiscal deficits. In 1977 the food subsidies accounted for about 24 per cent of the government revenues and 4.6 per cent of the GDP; in 1981 it was reduced to 10.5 per cent of government revenues and 0.5 per cent of GDP. The improvements in the fiscal balance through the cut in the food subsidies were counter-balanced by the massive increases in public expenditure to

Table 14.6   *Growth performance, 1970-88*

|  | 1970-77 | 1978-82 | 1983-88 | 1986 | 1987 | 1988 | Sectoral contribution to growth | Share in GDP, 1988 |
|---|---|---|---|---|---|---|---|---|
|  | | *Annual averages* | | | | | | |
| *Agriculture* | 2.3 | 4.0 | 2.0 | 2.6 | −5.8 | 2.1 | 13.5 | 23.5 |
| Paddy | 2.1 | 5.3 | 2.4 | −2.5 | −18.0 | 16.4 | 3.4 | 5.3 |
| Tea | −0.1 | −1.8 | 3.1 | −1.3 | 1.0 | 6.4 | 2.1 | 2.5 |
| Rubber | −0.7 | −2.9 | −1.4 | 0.6 | −10.6 | 0.6 | 0.0 | 0.6 |
| Coconut | −2.4 | 4.7 | −4.9 | 2.8 | −24.6 | −15.7 | −3.1 | 2.1 |
| Forestry and fishing | −0.5[a] | 8.2 | 0.4 | 5.4 | 8.3 | −4.2 | 0.1 | 3.5 |
| Others | 6.2[a] | 4.1 | 3.8 | 6.1 | 1.7 | 1.4 | 11.1 | 9.5 |
| *Manufacturing* | 1.7 | 4.6 | 6.4 | 8.4 | 6.8 | 4.7 | 25.8 | 19.3[b] |
| Public sector | n.a. | 4.6 | −1.1 | 9.5 | −0.4 | −1.5 | n.a. | n.a. |
| Private sector[c] | n.a. | 4.6 | 13.9 | 7.3 | 14.0 | 10.9 | n.a. | n.a. |
| *Construction* | −0.3 | 11.0 | 1.1 | 1.5 | 1.8 | 1.5 | 2.2 | 7.1 |
| *Services* | 3.6 | 7.4 | 4.2 | 4.3 | 2.7 | 2.2 | 58.5 | 50.1 |
| *GDP* | 3.1 | 6.2 | 3.6 | 4.3 | 1.5 | 2.7 | 100.0 | 100.0 |

*Notes*

[a] For the period 1973-77.

[b] Includes mining.

[c] Estimated assuming that half the value-added in manufacturing is produced in the public sector.

[d] Defined as the increase in the sector's value-added between 1982 and 1988, divided by the increase in GDP in the same period.

*Source:* Central Bank of Sri Lanka and World Bank (1989b).

Table 14.7   *Impact of civil disturbances on economic performance, selected indicators, 1982-88*

|  | 1981 | 1982 | 1983 | 1984 | 1985 | 1986 | 1987 | 1988 |
|---|---|---|---|---|---|---|---|---|
| Total paddy production (million bushels) | 53 | 65 | 85 | 65 | 84 | 81 | 67 | 73 |
| Foreign investment (1980 US$) | 47 | 61 | 37 | 33 | 25 | 24 | 45 | 31 |
| Exports of garments (million pieces) | 53 | 76 | 81 | 124 | 159 | 167 | 185 | 186 |
| Exports of gems and diamonds (1980 US$) | 32 | 32 | 40 | 25 | 31 | 55 | 69 | 83 |
| *Tourist arrivals ('000)* | 371 | 407 | 338 | 318 | 257 | 230 | 183 | 183 |

*Source:* Central bank of Sri Lanka and World Bank (1989b).

finance the 'lead' projects. Moreover, the transfers to households (subsidies and pensions) and public enterprises (meeting their deficits) account for a substantial part of the government expenditure. Increases in defence expenditure as a consequence of the civil disturbances further aggravated the fiscal imbalances. On the revenue side, the collection of revenues was hampered by the civil disturbances resulting in a decline in revenue. The subsequent revisions in the import tax rates were related to the growing fiscal deficits .

Table 14.8  *Summary of central government operations, 1984-89 (Rupees million)*

| | 1984 | 1985 | 1986 | 1987 | 1988 Budget | 1988 Actual | 1989 Budget | 1989 Revised [a] |
|---|---|---|---|---|---|---|---|---|
| *Total revenue* | *34,061* | *36,249* | *37,238* | *42,697* | *46,223* | *41,749* | *58,119* | *53,156* |
| Tax | 29,939 | 30,442 | 31,272 | 35,119 | 39,738 | 35,945 | 49,334 | 44,723 |
| Non-tax | 4,122 | 5,807 | 5,966 | 7,578 | 6,485 | 5,803 | 8,785 | 8,434 |
| *Total expenditure and net lending* | *47,837* | *55,234* | *59,190* | *64,444* | *72,535* | *76,531* | *92,322* | *84,408* |
| *Overall deficit* | *−13,776* | *−18,985* | *−21,958* | *−21,747* | *−26,312* | *−34,784* | *−34,203* | *−31,251* |
| Grants | 3,293 | 3,306 | 3,753 | 4,677 | 5,000 | 6,588 | 5,600 | 6,989 |
| Foreign | 6,492 | 7,110 | 9,061 | 5,716 | 12,520 | 7,085 | 12,004 | 8,273 |
| Domestic | 3,991 | 8,569 | 9,143 | 11,356 | 8,787 | 21,111 | 16,599 | 15,989 |
| | | | (% of GDP) | | | | | |
| *Total revenue* | *22.2* | *22.3* | *20.8* | *21.7* | *20.7* | *18.7* | *23.2* | *21.3* |
| Tax | 19.5 | 18.7 | 17.4 | 17.9 | 17.8 | 16.1 | 19.7 | 17.9 |
| Non-tax | 2.7 | 3.6 | 3.3 | 3.9 | 2.9 | 2.6 | 3.5 | 3.4 |
| *Total expenditure and net lending* | *31.1* | *34.0* | *33.0* | *32.8* | *32.5* | *34.3* | *36.9* | *33.8* |
| *Overall deficit* | *−9.0* | *−11.7* | *−12.2* | *−11.1* | *−11.8* | *−15.6* | *−13.7* | *−12.5* |
| Grants | 2.1 | 2.0 | 2.1 | 2.4 | 2.2 | 3.0 | 2.2 | 2.8 |
| Foreign | 4.2 | 4.4 | 5.0 | 2.9 | 5.6 | 3.1 | 4.8 | 3.3 |
| Domestic | 2.6 | 5.3 | 5.1 | 5.8 | 4.0 | 9.5 | 6.6 | 6.4 |
| Defence & public order | 1.4 | 2.8 | 3.4 | 4.8 | 3.2 | 4.5 | 3.6 | 3.6 |

*Note*
[a] After policy measures.
*Source:* Central Bank of Sri Lanka and World Bank (1989b).

Not surprisingly, the foreign debt has grown rapidly over the last decade (Table 14.9). The total foreign debt was US$1.4 billion in 1978; in 1988 it reached US$5 billion. The debt service to export ratio reached about 30 per cent in 1988. The current account deficit has been reduced to around 9 per cent of the GDP in 1988, as against 20 per cent in 1980 (Table 14.10). The temporary boom in tea prices in 1984, more restrictive demand management policies and a more rapid devaluation of the exchange rate have helped to maintain a lower level of current account deficit in recent years.

## Conclusions

The post-1977 economic liberalization, although partial, seems to have helped the development of manufactured exports. The non-traditional export sector, particularly textiles and garments, has emerged as the leading employer of local labour and foreign exchange earner. However, the linkages with the domestic economy and the transfer of technology have so far been minimal.

The partial economic policy reform has made little contribution to improvement in resource allocation and longer term growth in the economy. A large part of the

Table 14.9 *Debt indicators, 1978-86*

|  | 1978 | 1980 | 1982 | 1983 | 1984 | 1985 | 1986 | 1987 | 1988[a] |
|---|---|---|---|---|---|---|---|---|---|
| *Total External Debt* | | | | | | | | | |
| As a % of exports | 144 | 148 | 220 | 223 | 177 | 227 | 260 | 266 | 266 |
| As a % of GDP | 50 | 48 | 60 | 59 | 51 | 60 | 62 | 67 | 71 |
| *Debt Service Ratios (%)* | | | | | | | | | |
| As a share of exports of goods and services | 13.5 | 17.0 | 21.9 | 24.2 | 17.1 | 22.5 | 26.0 | 27.5 | 29.6 |
| As a share of current account receipts | 12.9 | 15.7 | 17.7 | 18.2 | 14.7 | 17.9 | 21.7 | 23.1 | 24.9 |

*Note*
[a] Preliminary estimates.
*Source:* Central Bank of Sri Lanka and World Bank (1989b).

Table 14.10 *Balance of payments summary, 1980-86 ($US million)*

|  | 1980 | 1982 | 1984 | 1985 | 1986 | 1987 | 1988[c] |
|---|---|---|---|---|---|---|---|
| Exports (G + NFS) | 1,297 | 1,305 | 1,741 | 1,560 | 1,520 | 1,722 | 1,806 |
| (Merchandise f.o.b.) | (1,065) | (1,014) | (1,462) | (1,316) | (1,209) | )1,393) | (1,471) |
| Imports (G + NFS) | 2,205 | 2,205 | 2,140 | 2,290 | 2,273 | 2,398 | 2,563 |
| (Merchandise c.i.f.) | (2,051) | (1,990) | (1,928) | (2,038) | (1,970) | (2,073) | (2,241) |
| Net Factor income | −26 | −94 | −133 | −127 | −138 | −160 | −172 |
| (M&LT Interest Payments) | (−33) | (−69) | (−103) | (−111) | (−114) | (−120) | (−123) |
| Net current transfers[a] | 136 | 264 | 277 | 267 | 284 | 313 | 319 |
| *Gross foreign exchange reserves*[b] | | | | | | | |
| in US$ million | 246 | 351 | 546 | 427 | 348 | 263 | 260 |
| in months of imports | 1.4 | 2.1 | 3.4 | 2.5 | 2.1 | 1.5 | 1.4 |

*Notes*
[a] Mainly private remittances.
[b] As of end of year.
[c] Estimates for 1988.
*Source:* Central Bank of Sri Lanka and World Bank (1989b).

manufacturing sector remains heavily protected and inefficient and the anti-export bias is significant. The traditional exports have experienced a substantial decline since the mid-1980s partly because of the fall in international prices and partly because of the inefficient management of their production. The extent and the trend of subsequent changes in policy implies a reversal rather than further liberalization of the trade policy regime.

The new industrial policy, approved by the Cabinet in December 1989 is intended to:

(a)   transform the import substituting industries to export-oriented;
(b)   provide greater employment and income opportunities;
(c)   diversify the economy and strengthen the balance of payments; and
(d)   ensure a more equitable distribution of income and wealth.

The government's new policy measures also include mobilisation of resources for investment and exports, encouragement to foreign and local investments, reform of public enterprises, promotion of a competitive environment, establishment of large and small industries, promotion of research, training and marketing, and removal of administrative obstacles to investment, production and exports.

To sustain the growth and stability of the economy a more thorough implementation of trade policy reform seems necessary. In Sri Lanka, the macro-economic imbalances, and continued reliance on controls rather than market forces, seem to have been major impediments to further economic liberalization. Related to this is the problem of stabilization, as the economy was partly liberalized but not stabilized (Lal and Rajapatirana 1989). Another impediment to liberalization is the recent civil disturbances which have diverted the attention as well as the resources of the government. However, the GCEC exports do not seem to have been affected much by the civil disturbances; the most affected sector has been paddy, where there has been a significant fall in production. As in the case of many developing countries, a less than complete government commitment, administrative and institutional constraints in implementing reform programmes, inadequate understanding and belief regarding the potential advantages arising from trade policy reform, and vested interests in both government and the private sector, appear to be major impediments to the full implementation of policy reforms in Sri Lanka.

## Notes

1   This excludes the effects of excise duty in the calculation of effective protection. Edwards (1988) suggests that the effective protection for the manufacturing sector would decline to 30 – 35 per cent with the inclusion of excise duties in the calculation.

2   Anti-export bias was measured as the ratio of net effective protection to exports to net effective protection to import substitutes. A value of 1 indicates neutrality and a value of less than 1 implies anti-export bias.

3   GCEC is responsible for the establishment and operation of export processing zones, mainly with foreign ownership. GCEC projects are not given access to the domestic credit market. FIAC is responsible for the promotion of joint venture foreign investment projects outside export processing zones. In terms of tax incentives, FIAC projects are less favourably treated, however, they are given access to domestic credit market.

4   Exceptions to this have been wood, rubber and coir products, which largely use local raw materials.

# References

Bautista, R.M. (1988), *Impediments to Trade Liberalisation in the Philippines*, Thames Essays series, Gower, Aldershot.

Bevan, D. *et. al.* (1987), *East African Lessons on Economic Liberalisation*, Thames Essays series, *Gower, Aldershot.*

Cable, V. and Persaud, B. (eds.) (1987), *Developing with Foreign Investment*, Croom Helm, London.

Central Bank of Sri Lanka (1981), *Annual Report.*

Cuthpertson, A.C. and Khan, M..Z. (1991), 'Effective Protection to Manufacturing in Sri Lanka', mimeo, Colombo, Sri Lanka.

Department of National Planning, Ministry of Policy Planning and Implementation (1989), *Public Investment 1989-93*, Colombo, Sri Lanka.

Edwards, C. (1980), 'Lessons from South Korea for Industrial Policy in Sri Lanka: Some Observations', *Upanathi*, vol.3, no.2, July 1988.

Foreign Investment Advisory Committee (1988), *Annual Report*, Colombo, Sri Lanka.

Jayamaha, R. (1990), 'Policy Reform and Export Performance in Sri Lanka (1977-89)', mimeo, Central Bank of Sri Lanka, Colombo.

Greater Colombo Economic Commission (1988), *Annual Report*, Colombo, Sri Lanka.

Lal, D. and Rajapatirana, S. (1989), *Impediments to Trade Liberalisation in Sri Lanka*, Thames Essays series, Gower.

Ramanayake, D. (1982), *The Katunayake Investment Promotion Zone: A Case Study*, ILO/ARTEP, New Delhi.

Walton, G.N. (1988), 'Effective Protection and Comparative Advantage in the Manufacturing Sector of Sri Lanka', Ministry of Finance and Planning, Colombo, Sri Lanka.

Wanigatunga, R.C. (1987), 'Direct Private Overseas Investment in Export-Oriented Ventures: Recent Developments in Sri Lanka', in Cable and Persaud (eds.).

World Bank (1987), *Issues in Macro-Economic and Industrial Development Policy*, South Asia Programmes Department, Washington, DC.

World Bank (1988), *Sri Lanka: A Break with the Past: the 1989-90 Programme of Economic Reforms and Adjustment*, vols. I & II, Washington, DC.

World Bank (1989a), *Strengthening Trade Policy Reform*, vol. II, full Report, Washington, DC.

World Bank (1989b), *Sri Lanka: Recent Macro-Economic Developments and Adjustment Policies*, Washington, DC.

# Special economic zones and industrialisation in China

## Background

### *Self-reliance: the closed door*

For almost thirty years after coming to power, the Chinese Communist Party (CCP) maintained a foreign economic policy which it described as a 'Closed Door', partly in response to the US-led embargo. Apart from the aid received from the USSR in the early years, and the aid China itself provided to some sub-Saharan African countries later, this meant a more or less total prohibition of inflows or outflows of factors of production, including embodied and disembodied technology. It also meant that trade was limited to 'gap filling'. Imports were restricted to essential foodstuffs, raw materials and intermediate goods. Exports were limited to what was necessary to pay for them. The door was kept closed by the small number of central government agencies which controlled all international transactions. Under Mao, the policy of extreme self-reliance was encouraged at the provincial and municipal levels as well as on the national scale. In the industrial sector this resulted in widespread duplication of production facilities, with each province trying to be self-sufficient in heavy and light industry. As the manager of each factory controls the allocation of its output, the self-sufficiency policy sometimes leads to hopelessly uneconomic production.[1] In the town of Huanshi, for example, there are four steel mills. Daye Iron and Steel Mill belongs to the central government and the Xialu Steel Works was established by the provincial government. In view of the overall shortage of steel, the municipality had its own Second Haunshi Steel Works; and, in the face of an overall shortage of steel and prevented from having access to the output of any of these factories, the county government established its own Daye County Steel Works.

Such an uneconomic industrial structure could only be sustained by the total protection a completely controlled economy can provide. This protection, combined with a Marxist-Leninist style of planning, also meant that there was no effective quality control. The lack of concern for economic efficiency and the absence of quality control in turn meant that Chinese industry needed to be totally divorced from world markets in order to survive. As the Chinese currency was overvalued throughout this period, export sales of industrial products could only be made below cost,[2] or more or less given away through the aid programme. Inevitably, except in a few priority areas such as rocketry and nuclear weapons, relative levels of management and worker skills, technology and commercial know-how declined to well below best practice standards.

Even during the Cultural Revolution there were leaders who were concerned at the loss of development potential that the Closed Door policy engendered. Most notably Deng Xiao Ping, in a document published in 1975, 'Certain Questions on Accelerating the Development of Industry' (known as the 'Twenty Points'), drew attention to the problems and indicated possible ways to overcome them. One of them was to move away from self-reliance and to seek links with the world economy. He argued that 'the external market is very important and must not be neglected' and that 'Every industrial department must study the requirements of the international market and energetically increase the output of products which can be exported and have a high exchange value'. This position was attacked as a 'poisonous weed' by the supporters of the Gang of Four, because it involved reaching an accommodation with capitalism.

### Economic reforms: the open door

It was not until after the death of Mao and the replacement of the Gang of Four, and the relaxation of relations with the West, especially the USA, that conditions were such as to allow the translation of proposals for a more open economy into policy. Mao's successor as chairman of the CCP, Hua Guofeng, criticised the Closed Door policy and in the autumn of 1976 discussed the need to open up the economy, import advanced technology and develop an export base.[3] It took a while for those in favour of a more open economy to gain the political ascendancy, however, and it was not until the end of the landmark Third Plenum of the Eleventh Central Committee of the CPP, in late 1978, that the commitment to opening up was made public. Soon after the meeting it was announced that the prohibition of direct foreign investment in China, which had been in force since 1949, was being lifted.

It is important to note that throughout this debate on the role of trade, exports are only seen as a method of raising finance to pay for imports of advanced technology. In some cases the use of countertrade rather than market-based trade was advocated. Trade was not seen as a method of improving industrial efficiency. Nor did 'opening up' mean the sudden substitution of market forces for planning.

The policy reforms were piecemeal. There was no grand commission which produced a fully worked out new international economic policy. On the whole, apart from the fundamental shift on private foreign investment, the adoption of the Open Door Policy simply involved the amending of administrative practices which had constrained international economic activity. For example, the monopoly over trade of the Foreign Trade Corporations was broken and their branch offices, line ministries and provincial governments were allowed to trade on their own account. Second, a system of foreign exchange retention was introduced in 1979 according to which provincial governments and individual enterprises were, in principle, allowed to retain some part of their export earnings for their own use. Third, regulations on the movement of people, into and out of China, were liberalized – leading most notably to a boom in tourism in China. Finally, prohibition of overseas borrowing by government agencies and provincial governments was lifted.

### The emergence and evolution of the special economic zones

The initiation and evolution of the Special Economic Zones (SEZs) policy were also more or less *ad hoc* processes.[4] Chinese economists had studied the phenomenon of export processing zones, which had been mushrooming in developing countries. However, the initial impetus came, as with other features of the Open Door Policy, from Hong Kong. The Chinese Merchant's Steam Navigation Company (CMSN), owned by the Chinese government and based on Hong Kong, wished to expand.[5] It asked the mainland authorities for permission to develop an industrial park at Shekou, just over the border in Baoan County in Guandong province. Although controlled by the Chinese Ministry of Transport, the CMSN is run as a fully fledged major multinational corporation along classic capitalist lines. It seemed an excellent, politically acceptable vehicle for introducing experiments with market forces into China proper. Following the Third Plenum, the proposal was accepted and permission was given in January 1979 by the State Council and Party Central Committee to establish the Shekou Industrial District. There were no official announcements outlining the nature and functions of the Industrial District. Staff of CMSN simply let it be known in Hong Kong that they would be investing in the district and were open to proposals for joint ventures with non-Chinese, including Hong Kong, investors.

The Shekou seed sprouted quickly in a climate conducive to the development of ideas on economic reforms. The spatial restriction in the formation of a special district proved politically acceptable. It allowed the development of the concept of 'experiments with market forces,' contained within limited zones. The concept was extended beyond Shekou to include the whole of Baoan County and the sleepy border town of Shenzhen was raised to the same status as Guangzhou (Canton), the provincial capital. In September 1979 the Beijing Review reported a speech by Vice-Premier Gu Mu to the effect that two 'special districts' were being opened in Shenzhen and Zhuhai (adjacent to Macao in the same way as Shenzhen is to Hong Kong). In December the Guandong Provincial People's Congress introduced the phrase 'Special Economic Zones'. It announced the establishment of three such zones, in Shenzhen, Zhuhai and Shantou (a town further north along the Guangdong coast with a large diaspora).

Planning and political difficulties delayed the establishment of the fourth zone, at Xiamen in neighbouring Fujian Province, until October 1980. The choice of Xiamen was dictated by its position as the natural point for an economic bridge to Taiwan, – parallelling the role of Shenzhen for Hong Kong and Zhuhai for Macao.

The next development was not until 1988, when the economically backward Hainan Island off the Guangdong coast was raised to the status of a province, with the remit to adopt a SEZs style policy and develop five specialised zones on the island.

## Special economic zones: role and regulations

While the debate over the objectives and regulations for the zones continued, the zones just grew, in particular Shenzhen. To some extent policy began to be formulated in response to the developments, rather than to initiate them. After the initial opening up, investors, mainly from Hong Kong, poured money into Shenzhen for the development of housing, luxury hotels, theme parks, golf courses, massage parlours and farms, as well as processing and assembly industries. The investment was mostly on a joint venture basis. And as there was no private sector in China, the Chinese partner was always an official partner, a central ministry, provincial or municipal government, or state or collective enterprise. In other words, much of the development of the zones was being undertaken by an unusual collaboration between communists and capitalists. This was to have an important effect on their development. In many cases the investment in the zones was entirely Chinese, being established by the domestic entity to take advantage of the more liberal economic environment in the zones.

The absence of any clearly identified objectives for the zones, with well-defined rules and regulations to ensure that their operation was consistent with those objectives, has been the source of many problems. There is no central government document setting out the objective of the zones. Reading through official documents and speeches of political leaders on the issue it is clear that the zones were expected to help achieve a variety of objectives. It was hoped that they would:

- encourage the inflow of advanced technology and associated skills from the West;
- stimulate the increase in exports needed to help finance the imports of technology;
- introduce Western standards of management; generate an increase in employment; and
- act as growth poles to help develop the economy.

This is a lot to expect from one policy instrument, and the objectives are not necessarily complementary. In the view of one political analyst 'Operational goals were kept vague so as to attract and maintain political support'.[6] If this is correct, then the attempt to generate political support had its cost in terms of economic efficiency. The vagueness spread from the definition of the objectives through to the regulations for administering them, and on to the loose way in which those regulations were implemented.

The regulations which were established have some similar characteristics and content to those used to operate export processing zones in market economy countries, although in other ways they are markedly different. What the two systems have in common is that the regulations define ways in which economic policies applying elsewhere in the economy are applied in different ways in the zone. Where they differ is that in market economies the difference between the application of policies inside and outside of the zones is set in terms of the degree of liberalization. In China the difference is between the totally controlled domestic command economy and some positive degree of liberalization in the zones. The key regulations govern:

- the movement of goods and factors of production into and out of the zones from the rest of China and from abroad;
- taxes on incomes and sales;
- rights of and processes for the establishment (entry), operation and dis-establishment (exit) of enterprises;
- access to foreign exchange, and financial capital, domestic and foreign;
- the hiring and firing of labour;
- the use of land;
- access to bureaucratic support; and
- the provision of infrastructure.

Initially, the zones had a monopoly of liberalization along these lines. But growing acceptance of the need for economic reforms and lobbying from other provinces and cities, which resented the preferential treatment of the SEZs, combined to lead to the expansion of the areas covered by zone-like liberalization policies. In 1984, fourteen of the larger coastal cities, from Dalian in the north, to Beihai in the south and including the centrally controlled Tainjin and Shanghai, were allowed to adopt economic policies similar to those operating in the SEZs. In 1986 this permission was extended to the Pearl River and Yangzi River deltas and part of southern Fujian Province.

Despite the occasional set-back the Open Door policy has continued to develop. Since 4 June 1989 Chinese leaders have made a series of speeches giving prominence to the Open Door policy in general and to the five SEZs in particular. They have stressed that although the zones will be constrained within the overall planning framework of the national economy, market forces will be allowed to affect development in the zones and other areas covered by the policy. In June 1990, the government announced that a new zone, the Pudong Special Economic and Industrial Zone would be established in Shanghai, with regulations even more liberal than those applied to the existing SEZs.[7]

Is the emphasis the government is putting on the Open Door Policy justified? It has now been operating for ten years; what has it achieved? The rest of this paper addresses these questions. In the next section such available data are presented to indicate the achievement of the zones in the first ten years, with an account of some qualifications which have to be imposed on the data interpretation. It is suggested that the achievements are not as impressive as the available gross data suggest. The following section argues that many of the constraints limitingd the SEZs' achievement arise from their failure to establish a market-based mechanism. The system of distribution of resources through favoured connections, or *guanxi* effect as it is called in China, is identified as a major limitation.

## Special economic zones: achievements and limitations

It is difficult to say how far China has gone towards achieving the goals it set for its SEZs. This is because the relevant data do not always exist, or exist in various contradictory forms, which are not easy to interpret. On technology imports, the only data available are of actual foreign investment flows, which do not identify the nature, quality or quantity of technology involved. On import capacity, the only data are gross export earnings, which are not netted out for legal and illegal import 'content'. No data on imports and exports of inputs and outputs between the zones and the domestic economy are available, so it is not possible to assess the size of the 'economic bridge' between the two. Data on employment growth do exist, but there are problems with their interpretations. The following sub-sections should be read with these provisos in mind.[8]

*Investment and technology transfer*

From 1979, when the first foreign investment was allowed, until the end of 1989 the Chinese government reports that there have been 120,000 joint ventures established in China. These involved pledges of $12.5 billion worth of investment, of which $7.3 billion had been invested by the end of 1989.[9] For comparison, by the end of 1987 $1.9 billion had been invested in the five SEZs (and host cities). (The State Council Office for SEZs reports[10] that by the end of 1989 this had increased to roughly $3 billion, representing approximately one quarter of all foreign investment in China). Total domestic involvement in the zones over the same period was $10.6 billion. These investment figures include infrastructural and social investments, largely in the domestic figures, but some foreign investment was channelled into infrastructure.

Focusing on individual zones, the share of direct foreign investment going into industry in Xiamen Zone and city rose from 14 per cent over the period 1980/83 to 63 per cent in 1988. The share of domestic investment (by state owned enterprises, which accounts for the lion's share) going into industry in Xiamen also rose, from 13 per cent in 1981 to 38 per cent in 1988, although this included 14 per cent points in the paper and water industries. An increasing share of industrial investment was accounted for by foreign firms, the proportion increasing from 36 per cent in 1985 to 90 per cent in 1987. The share of state owned units' investment going into industry also rose, from 21 per cent in 1985 to 46 per cent in 1987. In 1987, industry was the main focus of foreign investors in Shantou (77 per cent) and Hainan (70 per cent). In Zhuhai, it was agriculture (66 per cent) and real estate (34 per cent) which took the largest share of foreign investment, in contrast to the disposition of domestic investment of just over half (51 per cent) went into industry.

There are no hard figures on the source of foreign investment by country of origin, although in conversations with officials the figures of two-thirds coming from Hong Kong are often quoted. Some of this is indirect investment from Taiwan and South Korea and other countries using intermediaries in Hong Kong. Some is from the mainland, being invested by Chinese companies through foreign subsidiaries, to take advantage of incentives for foreign investors. Almost all investment is through the medium of joint ventures in one form or another. Only twenty-six wholly foreign owned enterprises were established in the whole of China in 1984,[11] bringing the total to 74 at that time.

Data giving a detailed breakdown of types of industry invested in by foreigners are not available. Most ventures are small; the global figures quoted earlier suggest an average of around $100,000 for the whole of China in 1989, which is about the same as the $90,000 quoted for 1983 for Shenzhen (Crane 1990). Numerically, they are mostly export-oriented small-scale garment and plastics factories processing and assembling imported intermediate goods from Hong Kong, and to some extent from Taiwan, Singapore and South Korea. The technology involved in these industries is low level and suited to China's comparative advantage. Factories aimed at the domestic Chinese market, for example, producing colour televisions, tend to be larger scale and use more sophisticated technology than is consistent with China's comparative advantage. They survive by not having to compete on international markets or by having losses incurred from exporting absorbed by the state.[12]

Bearing in mind that one objective of SEZs was to increase the flow of modern and advanced technology, experience so far suggests that only a limited amount has been achieved. However, it is probable that there is no economic basis at the present time for a faster rate of transfer.

*Export growth*

Garments dominate exports from the zones, followed by simple (especially plastic), products such as umbrellas, toys and video cassettes, and foodstuffs in the case of Shenzhen (for Hong Kong) and Zhuhai (for Macao). Detailed figures are not available. The Office of the Leading Group for Foreign Investment and Special Economic Zones of the State Council reports[13] that in 1989 exports from the zones totalled $3.56 billion, or almost 9 per cent of China's total exports. Their contribution to net export earnings, however, will be much lower, as the import content of garment and plastics exports is very high. Allowance should also be made for outflows for equipment and debt and equity servicing, and smuggling. Of the total, $2.17 billion, or 61 per cent, came from Shenzhen, which is where Hong Kong investors dominate. Again, the evidence is very limited, but it does not appear that the SEZs' contribution to the growth of import capacity has been very impressive.

*Management techniques*

Not much progress has been made towards the achievement of the goal of attracting and learning from modern management techniques. Trans-national corporation-(TNC)-type, world-market-oriented companies have not been attracted to invest much in China, even by the incentives available in the SEZs. In the main, the foreign managers who have moved to work in China are only experienced in running relatively small companies with relatively short-run objectives. Their aim is to seek a fast payback period, and as we have already argued, they do so within the traditional

Chinese system. The skills which matter while operating in China are their skills in using their connections to keep operations running. They use Western-style skills outside China to organise finance for their operations and to market the output of their operations in China.

The new non-overseas-Chinese companies which have invested have been primarily focused on the domestic market, which gives limited scope for the application of Western management techniques. The failure of the zones to create market economy bases means that the managers do not spend their time responding to market forces, but mostly in dealing with the bureaucrats who control the levers of the command economy. And since the events of June 1989 they have had to spend increasing amounts of time managing relations with Party cadres, whose role and power in economic policy implementation has been enhanced. These are not the management skills the Chinese government was seeking to import.

### Employment growth

The total employment in Shenzhen in 1987 was 262,700, of which 220,400 was in state-run units and 42,300 in ventures involving foreign investors.[14] Of the totals, 33 per cent of those in state run units were in the industrial sector and 68 per cent of those in Enterprises with Foreign Investment (EFIs). Approximately 10 per cent of the labour force is employed directly by the Central, Provincial and Municipal governments, to manage the zones and surrounding areas.

### The growth pole objective

In terms of their role as growth poles, the gross industrial output of the four SEZs and host cities, plus Hainan was US$3.587 billion in 1987 (constant 1980 prices). Of this total, 38 per cent was accounted for by EFIs – (including joint ventures and wholly owned enterprises). Shenzhen accounted for 37 per cent of the total and 67 per cent of that of EFIs. Remember that much of this gross output represents imports of intermediate goods for processing and assembly industry. In Shenzhen, of total industrial output, 81 and 86 per cent of the output of EFIs is classified as being from light industry. The net domestic value-added of such industry is probably less than 10 per cent. In an umbrella factory in Xiamen, for example, of all the inputs only the thread used to sew the frame to the cloth is sourced in China.

### The limitations

While there are limited data on the 'benefit' side of the zones, and much of that is of poor quality, there are even less on the 'cost' side. As we have seen, the data on infrastructure, and direct investment by the local and central government in the zones, are of limited value. There are no data on the current costs of the bureaucracy involved in running the zones (although as noted above around 10 per cent of the labour force in the zones and host cities is directly employed by the government). Nor is data available on finance made available to enterprises by the banking system, or on the leakages into increases in illegal activities.

The raw, gross statistics on the zones are often quoted by the Government to support the claims that the reforms are working. Attention is usually drawn to the gross investment figures and export figures, and photographs of extensive high-rise real estate and infrastructural development. However, it is not surprising that if incentives are sufficient to draw major flows of resources into small areas then the impact will be noticeable. What matters is whether or not it represents an efficient use of resources.

It has already been suggested that the net effect of the developments in the zone are not as impressive as the gross figures imply, and that the resource costs of achieving those developments are high. In terms of foreign exchange they may well be a net drain on the economy; they certainly were in the early years. They have also failed to attract much of the advanced technology it was hoped that new investors would bring. The technology that most of the investors have brought in has been appropriate to conditions in China, that is, highly labour intensive and necessarily using competitively-produced, imported intermediate goods. Such modern technology as has been drawn in has been attracted by the domestic market. Finally, the costs of doing business in and of running the zones, is raised by huge bureaucratic overheads, by poor supplies of some services and infrastructural facilities, and by excessive supplies of others.

How can these limitations of the zones development be explained? Many factors can be put forward, in particular the confusion over policy objectives, which leads to inconsistencies in policy implementation off-putting to foreign investors. In addition, imperfections remain in the capital and labour markets and in the allocation of resources between the manufacturing and government sectors. One factor which goes a long way towards an explanation of the nature of these imperfections is what can be called the '*guanxi* effect'. This effect, found in Eastern Europe and the USSR too, is probably an inevitable consequence of introducing market forces into a communist society.

## The *guanxi* effect

The communist system does not encourage the cultivation of personal and firm level productivity, but the cultivation of connections with those people who control the distribution of resources: the *guanxi* effect. In a communist system the controllers are, for the most part, members of the Communist Party, so maximising behaviour leads individuals to seek membership of the Party, or the development of alliances with members. At the firm level, management will use access to their firm's products or services, the offer of employment opportunities in the firm, or presents in various forms – such as banquets – in order to ensure access to whatever inputs are needed to ensure its objectives are attained.

The *guanxi* effect is the fundamental dynamic of the communist system. No aspect of the communist economic system can be understood without reference to it. This includes the SEZs and their failure to achieve more than they have.

## *The* guanxi *effect and Special Economic Zones*

The *guanxi* effect goes a long way towards explaining the limited success of the SEZs and the very high cost to the Chinese economy of that limited success. There are other factors which help explain the inefficiency, in Western terms, of the Chinese economy in general and the SEZs in particular. The *guanxi* effect is the original factor of the Chinese situation.

In the context of the SEZs, the *guanxi* effect, on its own or in combination with other factors, reduces the effectiveness of the policy innovations as it:

- reduces the flow of foreign investment, the quality of associated technology transfer, its domestic value added and its net foreign exchange earnings;
- results in the waste of capital;
- raises labour costs and compromises China's comparative advantage; and
- raises bureaucratic costs.

### *Restrictions on the flow and quality of foreign investment*

Most trans-national corporations of the sort China would like to attract are not willing to invest directly in China. Worries about political stability are no greater than in many other developing countries, but the absence of a reliable legal framework is a critical bottle-neck. Most firms are unwilling or unable to use the *guanxi* system to substitute for the rule of law and the certainty of contracts. Some are prepared to operate in China on a limited risk basis by accepting management contracts or joint ventures with limited direct investment. Equity participation is frequently limited to access to technology, the supply of second-hand machinery and/or management fees. This is especially true of companies which own advanced technology, which they are reluctant to apply in China until they are confident that they will get an adequate and reliable economic return.

The group of entrepreneurs who do know how to use the *guanxi* system are the overseas Chinese, who are linked into it by family and culture. The result is that one or more of the objectives of the SEZs has to be compromised. The relatively low technology appropriate to Chinese conditions and owned by the overseas Chinese willing to invest in China has to be accepted to generate exports. Or foreign firms with access to higher level technology have to be given access to the Chinese market; therefore the foreign exchange cost of whatever technology they do supply is increased. The net foreign exchange receipts of the zones are also much lower than the gross figures advertised by the Chinese government, as the technology owned by the Hong Kong and other overseas Chinese investors willing to invest in China involves a low value-added content, using imported intermediate goods, with only simple processing and assembly activities being carried out in China.

### *Waste of capital*

Capital is not always made available to firms which have the highest marginal productivity of capital. It mostly goes to those with the best connections. Most firms in the zones are either directly owned and managed by Party or government entities or by these entities in collaboration with overseas firms,[15] some of which, as already noted, have been set up by the Chinese side specifically for this purpose. The *guanxi* effect determines which firms have access to capital for setting up and running firms. It also determines their ability to run losses.

The concept of exit in industry is unacceptable in China. Bankruptcy would involve too much loss of face for those who proposed and accepted the establishment of the enterprise. The officials involved in loss-making companies will use their *guanxi* to ensure either a direct flow of capital to cover the losses, or an indirect flow through other companies into which they can arrange for the loss making firms to be merged. This is the so-called 'soft budget constraint' of communist societies.[16] Wholly-owned Chinese firms, which exist to process Chinese raw materials supplied by the parent entity may have those raw materials and other inputs made available at subsidised prices, the losses being shifted to the parent. They are willing to do this to take advantage of the benefits of the more liberal policy environment in the zones, in particular, freer access to foreign exchange through higher retention rates and to imports.[17]

Apart from the capital wasted directly in the enterprises, capital is also wasted in the zones through excessive construction and excessive infrastructural development. One of the easiest ways of establishing a presence in the zones has been via construction. The early growth of Shenzhen in particular, starting from a more-or-less green-field site, was that of a construction boom. As already noted, a presence in the zones gave access to otherwise unobtainable privileges. Investing domestic capital in the construction of hotels and in housing for the new workers and for sale to expatriates, involves less economic, entrepreneurial and technical skill than establishing manufacturing industries. Agencies of the central and provincial governments used their connections to obtain the inputs and permissions to build in the zones, particularly Shenzhen. With no budget constraint to hold them back, the agencies invested in building beyond the point where the expected rate of return from the properties themselves could justify the investment.

Even at times of national restraint on capital investment, construction in the zones continued apace. With the right connections, there was no capital constraint and permission to build could be easily obtained. Even allowing for problems of statistical interpretation, spending on construction and infrastructure in Shenzhen has been running at a multiple of the foreign investment it is supposed to attract.[18] In the other zones it is high by Western standards, approximately two-thirds of total investment in Xiamen for example. Just as hopelessly uneconomic firms do not go bankrupt, nothing happens to officials and Party members who allocate capital for buildings which stay empty or infrastructure which rusts away.

*Increased labour costs*

Life in the zones is attractive by Chinese standards. Wages are higher[19] and there is a wider range of goods to spend them on, including imported goods. Facilities intended for tourists and foreign businessmen – hotels, international standard telecommunications, restaurants, discos, and golf courses, for example, can be taken advantage of. And in Shenzhen and Zhuhai residents can tune into Hong Kong and Macao radio and television. In a market economy such attractions would mean that employers could pick and choose between applicants for work and ensure that the best people got the jobs. If mistakes were made they could be easily rectified by firing the inadequate workers and replacing them from the queue of applicants. This is not possible in China, however, where there is no freedom of movement, residence and work permits being strictly controlled by the Party.

Employers, in addition to paying the higher wages, also have to recruit via the official labour bureau. The firms advise the bureau of their needs and are then sent workers. Even where, in theory, firms could operate independently, they are ill advised to do so, as they lose their *guanxi* and they may then have problems in running their business. It is more or less impossible to fire anyone, so firms often maintain an excessive work force, including some people who are unsuited to the work involved.[20] Individuals all over China use their *guanxi* to get jobs in the zones, at all levels. Connections and not qualifications, determine the composition of people moving into the zones.[21]

The higher wages and lower productivity of the work forces in the zones increase the labour costs of firms operating there and compromise their ability to take advantage of China's comparative advantage. It is another factor making potentiall export-oriented, internationally mobile firms less likely to invest in China. Hong Kong companies are increasingly investing in locations out of the zones. Only companies which can use their own *guanxi*, or that of their joint venture partners, to lower other input prices (including capital) or to pass on losses to offset the higher labour costs, will be willing to invest in the zones. For the most part, these are domestic Chinese firms and overseas Chinese firms with good connections. Other firms which can offer 'technology for markets' and exploit the domestic Chinese market behind protection, will also be willing to invest as they can pass on as higher prices those of the higher costs that they cannot cover with *guanxi*.

The overall impact of the *guanxi* effect in the labour market in the zones is to lower the level of foreign investment, to distort the composition of the investment which does take place, and to reduce international competitiveness.

*High costs of bureaucracy*

One of the most frequent complaints of investors in China concerns the deadening effect of bureaucracy. In a controlled economy the guardians of the resource flows, the bureaucrats, have to be dealt with at every turn. The *guanxi* system derives from this. In its extreme Chinese form it approaches a barter economy: telephone connections for plane tickets; housing for passports; or televisions for a blind eye. The arrangement can become multi-stage and complex. Anyone who holds a place in the system is unlikely to give up its privileges without a fight.

The regulations designed to implement the SEZs policy threaten the *guanxi* system by the proposal to introduce the 'one stop shop' approach of export processing zones in market economies. In fact, in the SEZs the system has not worked because of the tenacity with which the vested interests of those operating the existing *guanxi* network have protected those interests. The 'one stop shop' has simply become one more layer in the bureaucracy. When the SEZs administration cannot move the controllers' access to raw materials, infrastructure, services, labour and capital and licences, then the firms are forced to deal with the latter directly and the *guanxi* effect comes back into operation. Because the privileges available to firms operating in the zones are relatively so great, the rewards to office holders who control inflows of resources of all forms into and out of the zones are commensurably higher. A lot of *guanxi* capital is spent on seeking appointment to those offices and so there is a lot of pressure to seek an adequate return. They will, therefore, do everything they can to ensure that they extract the maximum return from everyone who is dependent on them.

The true *guanxi* system does not involve bribery based on cash payments. It involves an exchange of commodities or services, part of which may be delayed and even traded. Sometimes, however, officials may want items which those seeking their favour may not be able to supply quickly or at all, in which case they may be tempted to request payments in cash. Similarly, where the process of supplying their requirement involves an illegal activity, such as smuggling or forging, they may be tempted by the higher rewards of such activities to become directly involved. The higher rewards bring higher risks, however, and such officials are liable to be caught in the crack-down on corruption among cadres which the Party instigates from time to time.[22] Outright corruption of this type is probably no worse than in many other countries, although the greater extent of controls in the Chinese economy means that there is greater scope for its exploitation. The extensiveness of the *guanxi* system, made possible by the extensiveness of controls, is however unique to China and adds to the cost of doing business there, directly as well as by tying up capital and management time.

### Conclusion

Superficially, the SEZs established in China have had an impact on the economy, as measured by gross investment flows, gross export earnings, numbers of foreign managers operating in China, gross output and employment generation. However, closer examination suggests that the contribution is much less than it appears. The investment flows involve limited modern technology which generates limited net value added in China and imparts little in the way of modern skills. It also has dovetailed itself into the traditional Chinese way of doing things so that there has been little or no transfer of Western management techniques. The gross exports and production figures hide the fact that the import content is very high. After allowance is made for depreciation, transfer pricing at other than arm's length, profit repatriation and debt servicing and for illegal activities, it may well be that such net output growth as there has been, was bought with a net outflow of foreign exchange.

The major limitation on the success of the zones has been their failure to develop the market-style economy they were intended to encourage. The package of incentives available in the zones does not add up to a market economy. Those very incentives have attracted the attention of the controllers of resource flows in China and they have exploited them for their own ends. The system which allows them to do this is the *guanxi* system. The distortions imposed by the *guanxi* effect send out the wrong signals to managers and add to the cost of doing business in China. The objectives of the government are, in consequence, compromised. In Chinese terminology, it is the 'hard will/soft will' dichotomy. It is easy for politicians in Beijing to set up objectives and policies to help achieve them. It is something different to ensure that the cadres implement those policies in ways which ensure that the system moves towards the achievement of the policy objectives as efficiently as possible, or even at all.

## Notes

\* This paper is an output of a research project on Manufactured Exports from China being carried out at the National Centre for Development Studies (NCDS) of the Australian National University in collaboration with the Institute of Economics of the Chinese Academy of Social Sciences and Xiamen Municipality. Thanks are due to Wang Xiao Liu for help with the preparation of the data from NCDS project files and with the identification of relevant Chinese documents. Thanks are also due to Helen Hughes and Geng Su Ning for helpful comments on an earlier draft and to Ms. Geng for library research in Sussex.

1 The duplication of industrial production units was to some extent due to the policy of being ready for a war with Russia; when the primary concern is with war, considerations of efficiency are usually left in the background.

2 With losses being absorbed by the state.

3 Comparisons were being made both outside and inside China of the relative economic performances of Hong Kong and Taiwan with that of China.

4 For a full history of the evolution of Special Economic Zones see Crane (1990).

5 Established by the Quing government in the nineteenth century and later taken over by the Kuomintang government. The management revolted in 1949 and turned the company over to the Communist government, after which it became a state owned company.

6 Crane (1990), p. 36.

7 People's Daily, Overseas Chinese Language Edition, 29.5.90 and 31.5.90.

8 Unless otherwise specified, all data in this and the following sections are taken from NCDS project files.

9 People's Daily, Overseas Chinese Language Edition, 8.4.90.

10 In an interview with the author in April 1990.

11 See Nai-Ruenn Chen (1986), 'Foreign Investment in China: Current trends'.

12 Source of opinion: visits to Tianjin in 1987, Xiamen in 1987 and 1990 and Shenzhen in 1988 and 1990.

13 In an interview with the author.

14 Employment data for 1987 does not take into account the tens of thousands of construction workers, and workers without residence permits, who had been sent home after the recession of 1986.

15 By 1989, there were 2,585 joint ventures in Shenzhen along with 3900 firms run by Chinese entities from outside of the Zone, and 2077 by residents of the Zone. *People's Daily*, Overseas Edition, report on 'Shenzhen in 1989'.

16 See Kornai (1980).

**17**   Access to foreign exchange for Chinese firms in the zones was restricted early in 1990.

**18**   Crane, op. cit.

**19**   Wages are maintained at higher levels than obtain outside the zones as a matter of policy. This is partly a reflection of an attitude of not wanting foreigners to exploit Chinese labour, and partly intended to encourage foreign investors to use more capital intensive techniques.

**20**   In some cases firms will appoint relatives of high-ranking officials to sinecures, in order to bolster their *guanxi*.

**21**   Crane, (1990), p. 127, quotes the *Hong Kong Standard* as estimating that in the 1986 recession 'forty thousand people who had moved to Shenzhen by means of personal connections (*guanxi*), not technical expertise, were reported to be repatriated'.

**22**   The *People's Daily* report on Shenzhen in 1989 reported that during the anti-corruption campaign of that year, 122 Party members were penalised on the grounds of corruption, including the taking of bribes.

### References

Chen, Nai-Ruenn (1986), *Foreign investment in China: current trends*, US Department of Commerce, 1986, mimeo.

Crane, G.T.(1990), The Political Economy of China's Special Economic Zones, M.E. Sharpe Inc., Armonk, New York and London, p.33.

Kornai, J. (1986), 'The Soft Budget Constraint', *Kyklos*, vol. 390, Facs. 1.

*People's Daily*, Overseas Chinese Language Edition.

# Foreign investment and economic liberalization in China – a study of Guangdong province

The attracting of foreign investment by the People's Republic of China has been a key element of the Open Policy, introduced under the post-1978 reforms.[1] The Open Policy has been accompanied by fundamental changes in agriculture, and somewhat less far-reaching changes in industry and pricing policy. Guangdong province in the south, adjacent to Hong Kong, was chosen from the very beginning to be in the forefront of economic experimentation,[2] and has attracted far more foreign investment than any other region in China.[3] Some two-thirds of foreign investment in China has come from Hong Kong.[4] Although the Special Economic Zones (SEZs), three of which are in Guangdong, are the best known aspect of the Open Policy, more investment has gone to areas in China outside them. This appears to be true even within Guangdong in recent years,[5] and the province, with a population larger than that of Britain, in the 1980s was one of the fastest growing regions in the world.

This paper draws on material from interviews with over fifty companies from Hong Kong operating in the Pearl River Delta,[6] the economic core of the province and the area nearest to Hong Kong. It argues that the Hong Kong companies have brought substantial benefits to the region, even though their investment is 'low-tech', and that their relations with rural collective enterprises have allowed them to circumvent many of the rigidities of the Chinese system. Foreign investment has both been affected by the operation of the economic reforms, and by their partial nature; and foreign investment also casts light on how those reforms work in practice.

## Guangdong province and the Open Policy

Guangdong deserves attention not only as the region which has attracted more foreign investment than Beijing and Shanghai, but also as an area of remarkable economic performance. Elsewhere in this conference volume, Helen Hughes has described success in development in terms of countries' being able to double their gross domestic product each decade. Hong Kong, for example, succeeded in doing this during the first decade of the Chinese reforms (i.e. 1978-87), an average annual GDP growth rate of some 7 per cent.[7] During the same period, Guangdong's combined agricultural and industrial output (a common Chinese measure) grew at an average of 14 per cent, a quadrupling (Vogel 1989, p. 442).The original area of the Pearl River Delta[8] was able to quadruple its agricultural and industrial output from 1979 to 1986, and its industrial output alone over this period rose fivefold.

Guangdong (together with Fujian province immediately to the north) was given a special policy to help it spearhead the reforms, of which the Open Policy was a part. Tax payments were to be made for five years in the form of a fixed annual sum, with the province retaining revenue in excess of this. This in itself was a major departure from the Maoist era when, for a mixture of political and military reasons, large budgetary sums were transferred from provinces on the southern and eastern seaboard, to the less-developed interior, starving the coastal areas of new investment.[9] Banks were given more freedom to lend locally in Guangdong, and the province was given more leeway in setting prices and wages, and in allocating resources. Major political figures were sent to the province to mobilize support, including Yang Shangkun, now president of China, whose military contacts were important in getting the backing of the army (Vogel 1989, pp. 85-8).

The Open Policy involved a considerable decentralization of foreign trade decisions, previously tightly controlled by twelve nationally-run foreign trade corporations, with more freedom for Guangdong and Fujian than for other areas. Its most visible feature, however, was the setting up of SEZs (three in Guangdong, and one in Fujian, and discussed in more detail in David Wall's paper in this volume), conceived under the influence of export processing zones in other Asian countries, though much larger and more ambitious. They were intended as areas where new labour practices (such as a system of contract labour) and management techniques could be tried out, geographically contained from the rest of China and away from the main industrial areas in the east and north. Above all, they were designed to capitalize on the links with ethnic Chinese overseas. Hong Kong, in particular, was seen as a source not only of capital but of access to technology and marketing skills, following its rapid expansion of manufactured exports in the 1960s and 1970s. Smoothing the reintegration of Hong Kong into the People's Republic of China in 1997 clearly was a factor too, and the first and largest SEZ, Shenzhen, was set up in 1979 immediately over the border with Hong Kong's New Territories.

Guangdong also was heavily involved in the more general agricultural reforms, which were to affect significantly, the whole of China, and in industrial reform too. In agriculture, under the household responsibility system, commune land effectively was decollectivised and leased to peasant families, who could sell their produce privately once they had met required deliveries to the state. Many agricultural prices were decontrolled, and the expansion of food exports to Hong Kong also made farming in the province very profitable. Traditional patterns of local trade and specialisation in Guangdong, suppressed for several decades, reasserted themselves. Rising agricultural incomes increased the demand for consumer goods, and the considerable surplus rural labour released by the agricultural reforms found employment in rural collective enterprises run by townships and villages, the successors to the commune and brigade industries of the Maoist period. These enterprises operated largely outside the state planning system. Since local authorities frequently were heavily dependent on them for revenue, they tended to be run in a highly profit-orientated fashion, and proved receptive when Hong Kong companies sought local partners. State enterprises proved more difficult to reform. Workers were used to jobs for life, managers had little authority. Reforms designed to allow state enterprises to retain some of their profits (initially as a residual after profits targets had been met, and later as retained profits after taxation) faced the problem that decisions were made on the basis of administered prices for outputs and inputs, often far out of line with those on the free markets. Attempts to reform prices partially, by allowing firms to sell above-plan output on the free market, and buy some inputs at plan prices and additional supplies at free market prices led to opportunities for rent-seeking, as firms attempted to divert supplies to free markets whenever higher prices could be obtained there. State enterprises, when involved in partnerships with foreign companies, have proved far less flexible than local authority collectives.

## Guangdong and Hong Kong

During the first decade of the Chinese Open Door Policy, Hong Kong too was undergoing a major transformation. From 1979 to 1988 Hong Kong achieved a 2.2-fold expansion of its domestic exports, which were almost all manufactures, with a manufacturing workforce no higher at the end of the period than at the beginning. The workforce in textiles and apparel, generating over a third of domestic exports, remained constant, as did that of electrical appliances, and that of plastics dropped somewhat.[10] Underlying this was a massive relocation of production (and especially of the *expansion* of production) to China, particularly to Guangdong, in the face of rising land and labour costs in Hong Kong. By the late 1980s, prior to the autumn 1988 austerity measures (introduced to deal with extreme overheating in the Chinese economy), it was estimated that between 1.5 and 2 million workers in Guangdong were employed by companies working directly or indirectly for Hong Kong firms (Thoburn *et al.* 1990, Ch.1), compared to a manufacturing workforce in Hong Kong of 837,000 in 1988.[11]

Foreign investment by Hong Kong firms in China, and the differences between location in the SEZs and elsewhere, is influenced by the wide range of choice of contractual arrangements for foreign investors offered by the Chinese. There are five types:

    (i) processing and assembly arrangements, under which a fee is paid in foreign exchange to the Chinese side for labour and other services, and materials and machinery are supplied by the foreign investor (PA);

    (ii) compensation trade, where the foreign side supplies machinery and is repaid with instalments of the product (CT);

    (iii) cooperative (or 'contractual') joint ventures, where the Chinese contribution is mainly in kind, such as buildings and a factory site (CJVs);

(iv) equity joint ventures, where profits are split according to each side's equity contribution (EJVs); and

(v) wholly foreign-owned ventures (FVs).

Various features special to the Chinese situation complicate these arrangements and mean that contractual choice is still wider in practice.[12][13]

Through processing and assembly arrangements, Hong Kong firms were involved in areas in Guangdong outside the SEZs as soon as China started to 'open' to the outside world. Indeed, the earliest recorded foreign investment in China – a processing and assembly garment factory in Shunde county in the Pearl Delta – is claimed to have been in 1978, before the Shenzhen SEZ was opened. Local authorities, sometimes cities or towns, sometimes even villages, were involved in foreign co-operation in Guangdong. PA operations, set up using personal contacts from Hong Kong initially, and then local reputations passed on in Hong Kong by existing investors, were an easy and rapid means of providing employment for surplus agricultural labour and of earning revenue. The local authority would allocate land for factory sites, and sometimes provide buildings, and the Hong Kong side would design the factory, bring in the machinery, supply the raw materials, and market the produce. Local officials would smooth the path and help recruit labour, and the Hong Kong side would train the labour force. The lack of expertise required by the Chinese side was a distinct advantage to them, as was their lack of risk. Since these PA operations usually were newly established, with the Hong Kong side taking a substantial interest in their setting up and initial running, we would contend (against the view, for example of the World Bank, see World Bank 1988, p. 249) that PA has been a genuine form of foreign investment in China.

Hong Kong firms also have been involved in CJVs and EJVs. CT has most often been used along with PA arrangements, so the Chinese side could acquire ownership of the machinery. FVs have been very rare.[14] CJVs allow access to the domestic market, which PA does not. Operating PA arrangements, and CJVs too to some extent, require considerable familiarity with dealing with local officials, and this gives Hong Kong companies a considerable advantage over Western companies. Any Western involvement tends to be via a Hong Kong partner, for this reason. EJVs are the normal vehicle for Western involvement. This appears, to some extent, to be the result of greater familiarity of Western investors with EJVs as an investment vehicle, and that they had a much clearer legal framework than other contracts. EJVs have greater freedom of action with regard to import controls and exporting than do CJVs, which also makes them attractive both to Hong Kong investors and to prospective Chinese partners, if they have the official contacts to get approval.

### The locational choice of foreign investors in China

Why has Guangdong attracted the largest share of foreign investment in China, and why has much of this gone outside the SEZs? In part, the answer to Guangdong's success lies in the failure of China to attract Western investment, if China had attracted more Western investment it might well have gone to the industrial areas further north. At the cost of some over simplification,[15] Hong Kong investment in China can be described as export-orientated, seeking to lower costs by tapping the lower wages and factory-site costs of China, whereas Western investors have been interested in import-substituting projects to tap the large Chinese domestic market. For Hong Kong investors, Guangdong offers a culturally familiar environment, with Cantonese as a common language. It also offers close proximity, so that investors can remain living in Hong Kong but travel regularly to visit their factories. This is a particular advantage of Shenzhen SEZ, but many locations in the Pearl Delta too are well connected by road or hydrofoil to Hong Kong. It gives Guangdong an advantage over other parts of China; and also over other locations in South-east Asia, which also suffer from having higher wages than China and varying degrees of perceived hostility to ethnic Chinese investors.[16]

Western firms, although attracted by the Chinese market, have been discouraged by difficulties in converting Chinese currency earned by internal sales into foreign exchange, especially in the early years before some semi-free foreign currency exchange was allowed. They also have been discouraged by the bureaucracy and corruption in the SEZs, especially Shenzhen, and have preferred to go to well-established industrial areas such as Shanghai. In our interviews, we also found several Western companies in the Pearl Delta, attracted by its better investment climate. Investment bringing in genuine high technology was discouraged also by the difficulty, at least until after 1988, of getting approval for FVs, without which the technology might have to be shared with a Chinese joint venture partner.

Of course, the location of Hong Kong investment outside the SEZs is also due, to some extent, to official discouragement of it in the SEZs. In the mid-1980s, China experienced a foreign exchange crisis, due in part to speculative activities centred on the SEZs' special import privileges and the failure to export of the companies (including many domestic companies) set up there. Such exports as there were tended to come from Hong Kong export-processing investment. In 1984 Beijing instructed Shenzhen to make a more determined effort to attract investment which was both high-tech and export-orientated (although to some extent these were mutually exclusive categories), in order to justify its very heavy infrastructural costs. In 1984 fourteen major coastal cities, including the Guangdong provincial capital, Guangzhou (Canton), were designated as Open Cities, with the intention of attracting foreign investors. They were allowed to offer similar, though less generous, incentives to those of the SEZs (tax holidays, lower rates of profits tax than elsewhere in China, and the right to retain some foreign exchange earnings). However, by this time, much of Hong Kong investment anyway had been directed to locations within Guangdong outside the Zones, especially the Pearl River Delta. In 1985 the Pearl River (or 'Zhujiang') Delta was designated an Open Zone, along with the Minnan Delta region in Fujian province, and the Yangtse Delta further north, and was allowed to offer similar foreign investment incentives to those of the Open Cities. Since then, more and more areas have been declared 'open', and Hainan Island off the south coast of Guangdong has been designated a new SEZ.

The attractions of the Pearl River Delta, our interviews have shown, vary markedly from location to location. This is in part due to the fact that locations away from

Shenzhen have progressively lower wage levels the further one goes into Guangdong, but transport costs are another important element and locations with their own ports, such as Zhong Shan, or still nearer to Hong Kong, such as Dongguan, may be chosen. Vogel (1989, pp. 192-5) has distinguished three tiers of development in the Pearl Delta:

(i)    areas near Hong Kong and mainly involved in processing and assembly (Dongguan, Baoan, Panyu);
(ii)   more industrialized areas nearer to Guangzhou (such as Foshan and Shunde), and Guangzhou itself; and
(iii)  more remote areas (such as Taishan).[17]

Clearly, the attractivess of an area will vary in terms of these distinctions, but a more important factor has been the investors' perceptions of how helpful, free from corruption, and unbureaucratic are the officials in a particular place. Dongguan, for instance, has attracted large amounts of processing and assembly investment by its 'one-stop' office. Although investors in such an area will have to use their personal connections (*guanxi*) to get things done, the layers of officialdom will be less. Most important is the fact that the local authorities have a direct stake in a foreign investment's profitability, through either processing fees or direct participation, which makes for some mutuality of interest. Areas seen as incompetent or rapacious do not attract investment.

## The benefits of Hong Kong investment to the Chinese

It is necessary to distinguish benefits to the Chinese partners in foreign investments from those to the Chinese nation; for example, if the partner is a state company engaging in rent-seeking by using a joint venture to evade controls. Some genuine benefits, though, do seem to have been produced by the Hong Kong investors.

*Market access.*    Foreign investors in major Hong Kong export industries such as garments, plastics and toys often have close links to Western buying groups. Information about styling and quality, and the quality control brought by foreign investors, are vital ingredients for China to break into Western markets. The net foreign exchange contribution may be small in relation to gross export sales, because raw materials are imported, and because the Hong Kong side may cream off export revenue thorough transfer payments and commissions from buyers. However, the use of imported inputs has allowed such operations to expand rapidly, and to avoid many supply constraints of the Chinese economy, so the lack of 'backward linkage' is not necessarily to be deplored. Also, in the many processing and assembly ventures started with local authorities, after an initial period, the day-to-day running tends to be left more and more to the Chinese side, with visits from the investor. After the initial PA contract (usually lasting 3-5 years) has expired, renegotiation can take place or a looser form of subcontracting can occur when the Chinese side has gained the necessary experience.

*Technology transfer.* A clear finding of our interviews has been that the transfer of even mature, labour-intensive technology to China is not a trivial achievement. Companies in the Pearl Delta in the footwear industry, for example, using equipment from Taiwan, typically found they were getting in the early stages only a quarter of the output that the same equipment and size of labour force would have produced in Taiwan.[18] This problem was especially marked when the Chinese side was a state company using its own permanent workers in a CJV or EJV. To bring productivity up to international levels required substantial reform of the labour process, often in the teeth of opposition from the Chinese side, and also the longer term development of local input supply sources.

*Employment.* By the late 1980s the province had not only absorbed its surplus agricultural labour but was importing workers from other provinces. The employment of 1.5 to 2 million workers employed in factories with Hong Kong connections, already mentioned, contributed substantially.

However, tax payments made by foreign investors probably have been very low up to now, although figures are hard to obtain. Tax holidays of various lengths are offered by SEZs, Open Zones and Cities. These cut across the confusing differences in tax rates faced by foreign enterprises in different locations and activities. Competition between localities on the tax front further reduces tax receipts (for example, encouraging companies to change their name and take a new contract and tax holiday when an existing contract expires is a common practice in smaller localities). On the side of Government expenditure, attracting foreign investment into already developed areas may save on the Government-financed infrastructural costs which Shenzhen incurred. However, the latest (mid-1990) thrust of Government foreign investment policy to attract investment into the large, new Pudong area at Shanghai will have heavy infrastructural costs.

## The future

The Chinese reforms were running into serious problems well before the events of 4 June 1989 (see note 16), and the autumn 1988 macro-economic restrictions were made necessary, in part, by the explosive growth of investment by local authorities and provinces outside central government control.[19] Guangdong remains an attractive place for export-orientated Hong Kong investors, in spite of the restrictions placed on rural industries after 1988, and there are now indications that the strategy of concentrating development explicitly on the coastal areas of China (Wang Jun, 1989) has not been abandoned, as it first seemed after the recent upheavals. However, investors geared towards the domestic consumer goods industry have seen drastic falls in demand, and the lack of Western investment in China is likely to remain a disappointment to the Chinese for some time to come.

Notes

1  For a convenient discussion of the Chinese reforms see Feuchtwang *et al.* (1988).

2  For an excellent account of Guangdong province under reform see Vogel (1989).

3  From 1979 to 1988 Guangdong attracted 49.9 per cent of the contracted direct foreign investment (including compensation trade and processing and assembly of China, and 36.4 per cent of the actually utilized amount (Thoburn *et al.* 1990, Table 1.1).

4  The share of Hong Kong investment is complicated by the fact that some Taiwanese companies invest via Hong Kong, as do some Chinese mainland companies! Also, Western companies operating through Hong Kong offices are counted as being from Hong Kong. For further discussion see Pomfret (1989). Hong Kong also has invested in a number of South-east Asian countries (see Chen, 1983).

5  From 1979 to 1988 the SEZs attracted 24.6 per cent of the flow of actual (as opposed to merely contracted) direct foreign investment into China (*Beijing Review*, 1989). These figures exclude processing and assembly and compensation trade, and including these probably would lower the SEZ share further. In 1987, 43.9 per cent of the actual inflow of foreign capital (of which 60 per cent was direct foreign investment, including processing and assembly and compensation trade) into Guangdong went to the province's three SEZ cities (Guangdong Province,1988). (The different bases of these statistics illustrate the common problem of unclear statistical information on China).

6  In 1986 the Pearl River Delta Open Zone, with 16.2 per cent of Guangdong's population, produced 33.9 per cent of the province's industrial output. After the Zone was expanded, the respective 1987 figures were 27.1 per cent and 40.1 per cent (Guangdong Province, 1987 and 1988). The sample consisted of companies in a variety of locations and industries, and spread over the various types of contracts. The interviews were conducted jointly with economists from Zhong Shan University, Guangzhon. For a comprehensive write-up of the project's interview material, see Thoburn *et al.* (1990), and for a Zhong Shan contribution, see Lei Qiang (1988). We are very grateful to the Sir Run Run Shaw Foundation, Hong Kong, for financial support.

7  This average rate, though, conceals considerable variation from year to year. Unless otherwise stated, statistical data on Hong Kong and Guangdong come, respectively, from various issues of the *Hong Kong Annual Digest of Statistics* and the *Guangdong Statistical Yearbook*.

8  See note 6 above for a definition.

9  However, the productivity of capital investment in the interior seems to have been much lower than in the coastal areas, which included the traditional industrial centres such as Shanghai, and which had better developed infrastructure and a more highly skilled labour force. In 1983 the coastal provinces of China were producing 60 per cent of the gross value of China's industrial output, with only 43 per cent of the country's fixed assets (Yang 1990, pp. 237-8).

10  In 1988, 74 per cent of Hong Kong's domestic exports and 69 per cent of its industrial employment came from the textiles, clothing, electronics, plastic products, electrical appliances, and watches and clocks industries (Hong Kong Government 1989b, p. 76).

11  Such relocations have been documented for other countries too, for example, the West German textile and garment industry (Fröbel, Heinrichs, and Kreye 1980) and for various Japanese industries facing declining competitive positions (Ozawa 1979). However, it is the sheer scale of the Hong Kong relocation relative to the size of the Hong Kong economy, which is striking.

12  For example, different contracts require different levels of official approval. Until 1988,

for instance, FVs required approval from Beijing, and some firms in our sample had set up de facto FVs in the form of long-term CJVs, which required only county-level approval. On the other hand, some CJVs were short term (5-8 years), and were somewhat more like compensation trade, with the Hong Kong partners being repaid their investment as a prior claim on profits and the equipment belonging to China at the end of the contract. Indeed, the CJV was the most flexible of all the contracts. Even the sharing of profits does not have to be in proportion to the partners' capital contributions, and may vary over the life of the contract. For a discussion of the principles of contract choice in China, see Leung *et al.* (1991).

13 For China as a whole for 1979-88, the shares of actual foreign direct investment inflows were EJVs 40.9 per cent, CJVs 33.8 per cent, FVs 2.5 per cent, CT and PA 22.9 per cent (*Beijing Review*, 1989).

14 After 1988, however, the Chinese Government tried to encourage FVs. This was because the autumn 1988 austerity measures had made it difficult for prospective Chinese joint venture partners to raise bank finance to cover their equity contribution; and it was also in an attempt to attract more 'high-tech' investment by giving the foreign side total control.

15 Most of the Hong Kong CJVs and EJVs in our sample had some domestic sales, often because these were more profitable for the Chinese partners than were export sales (Thoburn *et al.* 1990, pp. 151-2). EJVs (and CJVs) in China as a whole tend to be distributed in a bipolar fashion (Pomfret, 1989, p.44), with a few large projects usually orientated towards the domestic market (such as Volkswagen in Shanghai) and a greater number of small, export-orientated ventures. Our interviews in Guangdong have dealt mainly with the latter type. They included some Western multinationals working through Hong Kong offices.

16 After the events of 4 June 1989, when the Chinese government used the army to put down mass student demonstrations in Beijing, many Western buyers of Hong Kong companies' exports put pressure on them to diversify out of China. Investigation of South-east Asian investment environments by several companies subsequently interviewed suggested Guangdong was still preferred.

17 A detailed map of Guangdong, showing these locations, can be found in Thoburn *et al.* (1990, p.xii).

18 See Pack (1987) for a discussion of the problem of different total factor productivities with the same technology.

19 It is worth noting, in passing, that the degree of centralised control over the economy in Maoist times often has been overstated (Lyons 1990). Auty (1990) makes the point that much of the independence intended by the reformers for enterprises actually passed into the hands of the local authorities controlling them.

## References

Auty, R.M. (1990), 'Heavy and Chemical Industry and Spatial Dispersion in a Large, Low-income Command Economy: China', University of Lancaster, mimeo.

*Beijing Review* (1989), 'The Utilization of Foreign Capital, 1979-88', 6-12 March.

Chen, E.K.Y. (1983), 'Multinationals from Hong Kong', in Lall (1983).

Feuchtwang, S., Hussain, A. and Pairault, T. (eds.) (1988), *Transforming China's Economy in the Eighties*, 2 vols., Zed Books, London.

Fröbel, F., Heinrichs, J. and Kreye, O. (1980), *The New International Division of Labour: Structural Unemployment in Industrialized Countries and Industrialization in Developing Countries*, Cambridge University Press, Cambridge (originally published in German by Rowohlt, Hamburg, 1977).

Guangdong Province (various years), *Guangdong Statistical Yearbook*, Guangzhou (in Chinese).

Hong Kong Government (1989a), *Hong Kong Annual Digest of Statistics*, Hong Kong.

Hong Kong Government (1989b), *Hong Kong 1989: A Review of 1988*, Hong Kong.

Lall, S. (ed.) (1983), *The New Multinationals: The Spread of Third World Enterprises*, Wiley, London.

Lei Qiang (1988), 'New Progress in Hong Kong and Pearl River Delta Industrial Cooperation', *Hong Kong and Macau Research*, Zhong Shan University, Guangzhou (in Chinese).

Leung, H.M., Thoburn, J.T., Chau, E. and Tang, S.H. (1991), 'Contractual Relations, Foreign Direct Investment and Technology Transfer. The Case of China', *Journal of International Development*, June.

Lyons, T.P. (1990), 'Planning and Interprovincial Coordination in Maoist China', *China Quarterly*, March.

Ozawa, T. (1979), 'International Investment and Industrial Structure: New Theoretical Implications from the Japanese Experience', *Oxford Economic Papers*, March.

Pack, H. (1987), *Productivity, Technology, and Industrial Development: A Case Study of Textiles*, Oxford University Press for the World Bank, New York.

Pomfret, R. (1989), 'Ten Years of Direct Investment in China', *Asian Perspective*, Fall/Winter.

Thoburn, J.T., Leung, H.M. Chau, E. and Tang, S.H. (1990), *Foreign Investment in China under the Open Policy. The Experience of Hong Kong Companies*, Gower/Avebury, Aldershot.

Vogel, E.F. (1989), *One Step Ahead in China. Guangdong under Reform*, Harvard University Press, Cambridge, Mass.

Wang Jun (1989), 'The Export-Orientated Strategy of China's Coastal Areas: Emulation and Prospects', University of Leicester, Economics Department Discussion Paper no. 116, September.

World Bank (1988), *China. External Trade and Capital*, Washington, DC.

Yang Dali (1990), 'Patterns of China's Regional Development Strategy', *China Quarterly*, June.

# Economic reform in Myanmar

The chapter examines recent policy changes in Myanmar. At least three aspects are of current interest, both in the context of economies undergoing some form of economic liberalization, and for socialist developing countries in the process of changing their political and economic regimes. First, is to understand what underlies the decision to revert from state-led socialist planning to a more market-oriented system. Second, is to evaluate the economic reforms to determine both their sustainability and direction. Third, is to determine to what extent the military government intend to continue their initial moves towards a broader process of democratisation. Since these factors are evidently interrelated, the chapter will seek to evaluate the argument that economic reform is a hostage to political reform (Vokes 1990), a view implicit in the approach adopted principally by the bilateral aid agencies, who have suspended assistance activities pending political reform and cessation of human rights abuses.

In order to explore these issues, the chapter will begin by comparing past economic trends with the current situation, including a brief survey of the recently introduced policy changes. The second section of the chapter seeks to assess policy initiatives (or the lack of them) by attempting to identify the main elements that determine and influence policy. Next, we attempt to show that the argument that economic change is a hostage to political reform represents a too simplistic analysis, and provide a more complex and historically-rooted analysis of Myanmar's political economy. The conclusion examines the lessons from the Myanmar case and considers their relevance, both to economies under repressive political regimes and to economies in the process of transforming from socialist to market-orientation.

## Economic conditions: past and present

Economic indicators have generally worsened during the 1980s. As Table 17.1 shows, real GDP has declined to a consistent pattern of negative growth rates. Investment as a proportion of GDP has continued to decline. Domestic inflation has risen from 5.7 per cent in the early 1980s to reach over 20 per cent by the end of the decade. The balance of trade has worsened with exports consistently falling since 1984. Imports have fallen more slowly. Both major exports, teak and rice, experienced drops in volume as well as value as the terms of trade became unfavourable (Catling and Dunning 1989). Prices for these commodities dropped 30 per cent between 1981 and 1987. Valuable foreign exchanges earnings have been soaked up by the debt service obligations from past borrowing and although debt levels are not high in comparison to neighbouring countries, the low export figures reveal a dramatic situation as far as the debt service ratio is concerned. Debt service obligations expressed in terms of current receipts amounted to nearly 90 per cent in 1987-88. Most loans are on a concessional basis so are not acutely affected by changes in world interest rates. Approximately 62 per cent are with bilateral agencies, 28 per cent with multinational agencies and only 10 per cent are commercial. The denominated currency is, however, more important, since 45 per cent of lending is denominated in Japanese yen and a further 9 per cent in German currency, both of which have appreciated against the US dollar.

Table 17.1 *Economic indicators, 1984-89*

|  | 1984 | 1985 | 1986 | 1987 | 1988 | 1989 |
|---|---|---|---|---|---|---|
|  | | | million $US | | | |
| Exports | 409 | 359 | 333 | 310 | 257 | 228 |
| Imports | −608 | −566 | −586 | −534 | −526 | −540 |
| Trade balance | −199 | −207 | −253 | −224 | −269 | −311 |
| Current acc balance | −232 | −226 | −298 | −257 | −305 | −351 |
|  | % change | | | | | |
| Real GDP | 4.7 | 4.9 | 2.9 | −1.1 | −4.2 | −8.3 |
| Industry | 4.2 | 8.5 | 2.5 | −4.4 | −3.9 | −9.8 |
| Agriculture | 4.9 | 2.7 | 2.2 | 0.4 | −6.4 | −13.2 |
| Consumer prices | 5.7 | 5.3 | 6.3 | 14.7 | 22.0 | 22.6 |

*Source*: IMF 1989.

The deteriorating economic conditions in the 1980s had a major impact on the government's financial position. Contributions from state-owned enterprises in the form of taxes and profits declined. Revenue from import duties also fell as the government attempted to reduce the level of imports in response to external imbalance. The overall budget deficit was kept to around 8 per cent of GDP because the government also cut capital expenditure of the state enterprises. Financing the public sector deficit has also been the main cause of monetary growth, which has proceeded in excess of real GDP growth and therefore fuelled inflationary pressures in the 1980s.

Prior to the change to a more market-oriented policy in 1988, Myanmar had been run by a centrally planned system of economic management for nearly thirty years. Almost all activities, including large-scale manufacturing, mining, communications, services and banking, were in state sector. The state also controlled foreign trade and maintained extensive interventions into the private sector. Economic policies were formed in the framework of fixed plans which set targets for production, investment, trade, inputs, foreign exchange and domestic credit. Wages in the public sector were held constant form the 1970s until the late 1980s. The exchange rate has remained unchanged. Prices were controlled and as a consequence, parallel markets existed in foreign exchange, lending and consumer goods.

Myanmar (then Burma) gained independence from British colonial rule in 1948, although initially foreign participation and control in the economy remained extensive. It was difficult to increase indigenous involvement in the economy in the post-independence years. Industrial expansion, which was set back by civil war and insurrection, did not reach pre-1940 levels until the mid-1950s. This was then followed by rapid growth of both state and private enterprises into the early 1960s. Throughout the latter part of the 1950s, the state gradually intervened in domestic and foreign private sectors in favour of indigenous involvement. Despite this, the period 1948-62 witnessed only limited nationalisation and a mixed economy emerged with an element of socialist influence. In March 1962, after a military coup by General Ne Win, the Revolutionary Council government came to power, introducing the 'Burmese Way to Socialism'. This declaration, described as 'sufficiently vague not to tie the government to an explicit set of policies, But sufficiently emotive to appeal to public sentiment' (Taylor 1987, p. 296), rested on three ideals: the elimination of alien influence; the promotion of state ownership; and the promotion of Burmanisation. In 1963, the government introduced the Enterprise Nationalisation Law, forbidding new private sector activities. Those that existed were to be taken over or run by supervising committees. The spate of nationalisation was complete by the late 1960s. Government also had control of the small-scale private sector.

The economy grew in the 1970s, assisted by the Burmese version of the Green Revolution through the 'Whole Township Programme', initiated in 1977 and subsequently reshaped as the 'High-Yielding Programme'. The high rates of investment in the public enterprise sector also contributed to growth during this period (IMF 1988). This was made possible by the high prices prevailing for the economy's principle commodity, rice. Public sector investment grew as marketing boards provided revenue through effectively siphoning-off surpluses. This also enabled the government to offer subsidised credit to the agricultural sector and strengthen industrial policies, which promoted import substitution. Throughout the 1970s the Revolutionary Council continued to emphasize industrialisation, particularly through state ownership, and industry's share of total capital expenditure rose from 3.5 per cent in 1962-3 to nearly 35 per cent by 1972-3 (Hill 1984). The private sector contracted with the exit of foreign investors. The small-scale sector remained significant, accounting for around 50 per cent of output concentrated in foods, beverages and textiles. Attempts were made to liberalize parts of the economy in the 1970s, partly as a result of pressure from multilateral lending institutions. Reforms attempted to counter the effect of government restrictions imposed on state-run enterprises by giving then greater autonomy and less budgetary support. In 1975 the government passed the 'Guidelines for Operating on Commercial Lines', which appeared to result in improved financial performance of the firms in state ownership, in the short term (Hill 1984).

The private sector during these centrally planned years was provided limited encouragement with the passing of the 1977 'Right of Private Enterprise Law', which defined more clearly the role of the private sector, and for those that registered, provided guarantee against nationalisation until 1994. Nevertheless, uncertainty remained and the private sector was reluctant to invest. The Chamber of Commerce became dormant with members only continuing to meet in a social context. Many of the important entrepreneurs turned to managing public enterprises under restrictive conditions imposed by the government.

The first major step towards liberalization in the 1980s came in September 1987, when the government removed restrictions on trade in major crops. The intention of these measures was to allow farmers to sell their output at market-determined prices, as well as make decisions on the type of crops they should grow. Marketing is still not fully free and the government has reintroduced official procurement in some cases. Myanmar was also classified as a Least Developed Country by the UN in 1987, in a move to alleviate the debt situation. More substantial reforms were announced when the military State Law and Order Restoration Council (SLORC) took over in September 1988 as a self-declared caretaker government following substantial civil unrest.

The government declared that it would depart from central planning and move towards a more open-door policy. In November 1988 government enacted the Foreign Investment Law and made official border trade with its neighbouring countries, although some exports were excluded from border trade arrangements. The Foreign Investment Law permitted foreign investors to form wholly-owned enterprises or joint ventures, especially those engaged in exporting activities. Foreign investment was also to be induced by a number of incentives, including tax holidays and tax exemptions, particularly for businesses that re-invest their profits. In March 1989, the SLORC introduced the State-Owned Economic Enterprise Law, which essentially opened the door for the private sector to compete in activities previously the exclusive domain of the public sector.

Further measures to increase the competitiveness among financial institutions and to strengthen their capacity to facilitate investment finance were enacted in 1990 through the Central Bank of Myanmar Law, the Finance Institutions of Myanmar Law and the Myanmar Agricultural and Rural Development Bank Law. These provided the framework for a more conventional role for a central bank in the use of monetary instruments, and opened further channels for investment finance for the private sector.

## Policy stance

In this section we examine the policy stance of the main agents that have influenced policy reform in Myanmar. In general, the impetus for reform has been internal and reflects, as we shall argue, a survival response to mounting internal political and social unrest. This is not to deny that external agencies have been unable to influence economic reforms, even though their bargaining positions have been relatively weak and the degree of conditionality, therefore, correspondingly low.

The government of Myanmar, throughout the period of relative isolation, preferred aid to foreign investment. Indeed, with the lack of contact with technological development and declining exports, aid levels, mainly from bilateral sources, rose substantially after 1972. In 1970-71 aid flows stood at 21.7 million dollars, rising to 460 million by 1977-78 and 505 million dollars in 1980-81. Bilateral aid was suspended in September 1988 following social unrest and the government-led repression of demonstrations for political reform. The bilateral donors have withdrawn support on the basis that it will not be resumed until the interim government introduces political changes. The elections held in May 1990 to provide the basis for a constituent assembly which would draw up a new constitution, gave victory to opposition parities, an overwhelming majority of seats going to the National League for Democracy (NLD) led by Aung San Suu Kyi, charismatic daughter of Burma's first independence leader, Aung San. The lack of progress in this area, and what appears to be a carefully orchestrated campaign to destabilise opposition parties and weaken their ability to influence further potential development, has involved serious human rights abuses (confirmed by the UN Commissioner for Human Rights) which, in turn, has led to a hardening of attitudes among donors. Underlying the decision to withdraw aid assistance is the argument that economic conditions, already deteriorating, will worsen and eventually culminate in greater social unrest, and result in an untenable position for the SLORC government. This view presupposes that external aid flows, in the form of physical investment and technical assistance, are required to support economic development, and the economic progress is dependent on 'open door' and liberalization strategies.

An allied stance can be seen in the role played by the IMF in Myanmar, which is perhaps unique in comparison to their role in other developing countries. Although Myanmar had previous loans of 27 millions dollars in 1981, and special facilities of 55 million dollars in 1982/83, there is no IMF lending at the present time. Standby arrangements are being negotiated but the only formal role played in Myanmar by the IMF is through technical assistance to support institutional strengthening rather than policy.

The IMF have negotiated with the government on the following premises (IMF 1989). First, although the earlier attempts in the mid-1970s to reform met with some success in strengthening import substitution and were extensively financed by foreign loans, the impact of those policies eventually worsened as the government extended its sphere of intervention in the economy. Second, the reforms were never comprehensive enough. Third, recent indications are that there will be adverse effects on inflation and the balance of payments as the government over-runs its expenditure, both by giving pay awards (to avoid social unrest) and by increasing non-wage expenditure (defence and beautification measures prior to the elections).[1] These will adversely affect inflation and the balance of payments. Fourth, the failure to reform the exchange rate. The official rate has appreciated while the parallel rate, which determines a large share of domestic unofficial prices, has depreciated rapidly in recent months.

In negotiation, the IMF adopts two policy strands to its approach. It advocates first, through stabilization policy, a reduction in demand pressures and second, via structural adjustment measures, a realignment of domestic prices from their distorted position. Initially, then, the government would be required to cut current expenditure as a prerequisite for further reform. The IMF would in time make further assistance conditional on a radical reform of the civil service.

Several stages are envisaged for the short to medium term:(i) establish financial stability and reduce inflationary pressures by lowering the domestic rate of monetary growth via cuts in government (current) expenditure; (ii) increase revenue via increase in public enterprise efficiency; and (iii) reform of the exchange rate with trade liberalization.

The IMF's recent mission rationalises the above approach by claiming:

The experience of several countries (both middle income and developing ones) with liberalisation and progressive reliance on market mechanisms shows that the payoffs in terms of growth and development of the economy can be substantial, as the elimination of distortions in goods markets, foreign trade, and financial markets promotes the disappearance of parallel markets, the widening of the tax base, the strengthening of confidence of domestic and foreign investors and the eventual emergence of new productive activities and employment opportunities. (IMF Mission Report 1990)

The IMF's analysis is conducted on the basis of two scenarios; one portrays an unchanged policy situation in which the government continues along its present path. Of course, the interpretation of this path involves assessing the strength of commitment to undertake and carry through existing policies. Under this scenario, growth is expected to be constrained by a shortage of foreign exchange as traditional exports decline. Present policy aims are not pointed toward debt rescheduling. Debt service arrears will increase. Such a scenario implies that imports will decline further and with low public investment, capital formation will decline. Under present policy, GDP growth is expected to be less than 2 per cent with increases in prices, the balance of payments deficits, of debt, and the budget deficit.

The other scenario assumes the adoption of a comprehensive structural adjustment programme which is supported by international aid and debt relief. Under this GDP target is 5 per cent, with inflation reduced to 6 per cent over five years. The balance of payment deficit as a ratio to GDP will also be reduced. Delivering support of this kind has conditions, which include reforms to the tax, money and exchange rate regimes.

The UNDP stands alone among the multilateral and bilateral agencies in continuing to provide direct external assistance to the government of Myanmar. Even the IMF programmes are channelled through the UNDP in a twinning arrangement. This is in contrast to the World Bank, who have not approved lending since 1987 and have not dispersed all outstanding credits in earlier lending programmes. UNDP reports emphasize structural adjustment similar in concept to the World Bank variety, in particular stressing the role of the private sector. Country priorities identified for IPF (Internal Programme Funding) include supporting projects linked to agricultural development, widening the tax base and curbing public expenditure, privatisation of public enterprises, realigning agricultural prices to world prices and institutional strengthening. In broad terms, the UN departs from the bilaterals' and international financial institutions' stance in continuing to maintain 'a presence', in spite of the internal difficulties. Most support is in the form of technical assistance, which through gradualism and continued dialogue with the government attempts to influence policy and strengthen the government's capacity to implement reforms.

The government itself has been the main instigator of reform. This appears to have been partly in response to pressure from bilateral agencies, most notably from Japan, and to deteriorating economic conditions, which in turn engendered political and social pressure for reform. As Table 17. 2 shows, the government has enacted a range of laws and indicated its intention to reform parts of the fiscal system, the public enterprise and banking sector. It has also repeatedly indicated that it will revise the constitution over the next two years.

## Interpreting the policy stance

In this section we explore the consequences of each policy position and argue that implementing economic changes is not entirely dependent on political reform. Such a view assumes that capital inflows and technical assistance are required to achieve sustainable development, and these in turn will not emerge from external sources until there is evidence of political change in the direction of a greater degree of democratisation, and a reduction of human rights abuses.

Undoubtedly, the present situation is characterised by a relatively low degree of economic efficiency and utilisation of human resource capability, and the question remains to what extent these deficiencies can be overcome without external assistance.

Again, Table 17.2 outlines some possible consequences for each policy stance. The bilateral model relies on a number of tentative assumptions. First, it assumes that economic conditions will continue to deteriorate, because the government will fail or lacks the will to implement economic reforms. Second, like all systems of sanctions, it relies on no external party breaking ranks. Finally, it assumes that all participants to the embargo on aid are in agreement concerning the degree of political reform that would be necessary to ensure that aid flows are resumed. All three assumptions are open to debate. Furthermore, individual participants to the aid boycott may themselves be applying inconsistent rules to the Myanmar case, relative to other cases (i.e. the failure of some countries, notably USA and UK, to impose aid embargoes

Table 17.2 *Policy stances and possible consequences*

| | Government | IMF | UN | World Bank | Bilateral |
|---|---|---|---|---|---|
| *Policy concern* | Failing socialism/ central planning<br><br>Debt relief<br><br>Maintenance of Burmanisation | Inflation<br><br>Debt<br><br>Balance of Payments<br><br>Budgetary Burden | Bias towards industrialisation to neglect of rural/ agricultural sectors<br><br>Lack of institutional support to implement reforms<br><br>Debt issue<br><br>Budgetary burden of public enterprises | | Aid suspended on human rights issue<br><br>Democratisation |
| *Policies* | Closed door policy replaced by open door policy<br><br>replaced by market oriented policy<br><br>Fiscal changes<br><br>Competition for the public sector<br><br>Joint ventures<br><br>Competition in the banking sector<br><br>Relief for public enterprises (debt for equity swops) | Reduce government (current) expenditure<br><br>Fiscal reforms<br><br>Strengthen monetary management<br><br>Adjust exchange rate prerequisites<br><br>Civil service reform | Private sector development<br><br>Strengthen policy analysis<br><br>Institutional development | Cut aggregate demand<br><br>Devaluation<br><br>Liberalisation internal and external sectors | Project based technical assistance/ training<br><br>Infrastructure |

Table 17.2  (*contd*)

| | | | | | |
|---|---|---|---|---|---|
| *Consequences* | Partial reforms | Low growth/high growth scenarios | Strengthen institutional capacity | Inappropriate package for economy | Bottlenecks in training and institutional development |
| | Unclear signals to private sector | Lack of institutional structure for implementation | | | |
| | Public enterprise difficulties | Centralisation of economic power | | | |
| *Gainers/ Losers* | State-owned corporations | Ministry of Planning and Finance | Prime Ministers' Office | | |
| | Existing regime (gradualism) | Customs and Revenue Department | Private entrepreneurs | | |
| | Overseas investors | | | | |

on China following the 1989 Tianeman Square incidents and their aftermath, or on the USSR following its interventions in the Baltic states) which may weaken the credibility of the aid embargo stance. Britain had already signalled its intention to maintain good relations with China through the recent (early 1991) visit by the Foreign Secretary, effectively consigning earlier positions over human rights and demonstrations in China to the dustbin of history, and doubtless an example which will have been noted by the Myanmar leadership. The hostage to political reform view may, anyway, be too simplistic because it fails to interpret correctly the direction of domestic policy being pursued by the Myanmar government. The 'Hostage' scenario assumes that some form of structural adjustment, externally supported, is required for medium-term development. Again, the theoretical justification for this strategy is not water-tight and has been shown to be inappropriate when applied to economies in decline (for example, Guyana) (Mosley, Harrigan and Toye 1991). Moreover, it takes insufficient account of the comparative advantage, especially in labour costs, enjoyed by Myanmar in the Asean and Pacific regions (Vokes 1990).

The above argument applies with equal weight to the IMF policy stance. Further, this policy stance begs the question as to what degree of political change will release external assistance to support a structural adjustment programme. Views about the required degree of political compromise vary among donors, and some may be willing to resume activities with smaller degrees of democratisation. This would inevitably weaken the bilateral coalition but may also obviate the need for a comprehensive adjustment package if one significant donor resumed lending activities (i.e. Japan).

The IMF policy stance also has both interim and longer-term costs to consider. In the IMF approach imports are likely to rise with foreign investment in the transition period. The current account deficit is expected to improve later. The gap in the interim period, however, is expected to be filled by external assistance. The IMF approach, therefore, has a political connotation by assuming a favourable outcome for the resumption of aid. Inconsistently, the IMF currently provides technical assistance to Myanmar without requiring any political change. The external assistance estimates embodied in IMF proposals for the future are not insignificant, exceeding total World Bank lending between 1973-87. The IMF estimates that external assistance of 0.6 billion dollars in year one is required to take care of debt arrears and 0.36 billion dollars for each year of the structural adjustment programme.

Further, the anticipated cuts in government expenditure and corresponding employment presuppose growth in the private sector, which in turn may be contingent on reforms to the financial sector and exchange rates regimes. Both have proved sticky negotiating points in the current dialogue between the IMF and government.

The hostage model, then, seriously oversimplifies the government's position and role regarding economic reform. It assumes a coherent body half-heartedly pursuing reforms for self-interest. However, the policy formulating process and capacity to implement policy are clearly more complex than is portrayed in this model.

First, the political and administrative system is by no means monolithic: decision-making, and procedures of implementation, operate in different ways at different levels; and also may differ in specific policy arenas, some being less politically sensitive than others, for example, health. Although all major policies must be approved by SLORC, action and interpretation of policy within the bureaucracy may differ. Examples also exist of decisions made in the bureaucracy being reversed by the SLORC-dominated cabinet. Second, decision-making is highly unpredictable; before his retirement in 1987, Chairman Ne Win would make arbitrary decisions whose theoretical rationale was obscure. For example, unannounced decisions to demonetise in an attempt to break up parallel money markets took place twice in the 1980s, but were not made by either the Central Bank or the Ministry of Planning and Finance. Third, the current wave of reforms, despite the centrality of decision-making, emanate from different levels of government and stem from different agenda. Overall reform can be described as piecemeal and the significance of each reform measure varies in economic and political terms. Reform measures with significant political connotations are initiated and sanctioned by the SLORC, while reforms which may be less politically sensitive, yet have wide-spread economic consequences, can be initiated through the bureaucracy and only require SLORC endorsement. In some cases, (e.g. energy, health), special interdepartmental committees (akin to British cabinet committees) act as a link between SLORC and the bureaucracy. The hostage argument also assumes that economic recovery is not possible without external capital injections. This is based on the premise that the present military-based government lacks the will and ability to implement market-oriented reforms. In turn, the government's policy stance is conceivably based on exploiting the economy's considerable mineral resources; reviving exports from a very low level; and defusing opposition. It is significant that in the open door policy introduced after 1988 but dropped in 1990, the major forms of foreign investment have been in risk-taking oil and gas exploration. Substantial rents were extracted from the foreign investors, which assisted with immediate balance of payments deficits. It is also conceivable that exports, at a historical low, could with internal policy changes revive and increase the economy's' ability to purchase imports (also at a relatively low level).

The argument about opposition is germane to the economic reform process in the sense that a reforming government which lacks legitimacy and authority will find it difficult to secure the co-operation and energies required to ensure the success of innovative policies. Since 1987, the Myanmar government has faced considerable and widespread opposition, given dramatic shape in the May 1990 elections, which produced an overwhelming victory for political groups antagonistic to the military government. Since then, however, opposition has been substantially weakened, partly through legal and political attacks upon opposition representatives, and partly through increased military pressure on ethnic rebels in the region.

Clearly, at the same time, economic reforms are working slowly so that the government's 'stick and carrot' strategy is somewhat one-sided, with rather more stick than carrot. In terms of investment, particularly in the private sector, domestic investors and foreign entrepreneurs have, to some extent, opted for a cautious approach, preferring to act only when the administrative machinery of government has absorbed and made implementable policy outlined in the legislative changes already enacted and when greater political stability is ensured. Although investment, principally in the form of joint ventures with state-owned enterprises, has taken place, it as yet has not been on a large scale. Domestic investors appear to have been reluctant to take over large overmanned public enterprises, though the extent to which there are real opportunities to do so remains unclear.

## Conclusion

The decision to revert from centrally-planned socialism to a more market-oriented system can be explained at one level by arguing that the Myanmar state was never socialist but only centrally planned. Certainly, the Burma Socialist Programme Party was the only authorised political party in Burma after 1962, but as the Asian Survey stated in that year 'a more plausible explanation for the Council's 'Marxist' sympathies (in the 1960s) is... to win over the rank and file of the communists and fellow-travellers, thus terminating the fifteen year insurrection. Once (this was done) the Council would proceed with a non-ideological development programme' (cited in Nyun 1989). This has not prevented others including it in the category of socialist developing countries (see Morawetz 1980, UNIDO 1989). The economy was also well placed to change because as a result of the relative isolation the economy was no longer in danger of being dominated by foreign interests. The paradox then was that although socialism was central to the anti-colonial struggle and independence period, it was never embraced by the population as a whole. Indeed, deeply ideologically committed groups were believed to be destabilising elements in the 1970s for the ruling government. It has been suggested that Burmese socialism could be 'described as a middle path between the social democracy of the bourgeois right and the communism of the bourgeois left' (Taylor 1987; p. 297). It could be claimed, therefore, that it is not socialism that is being relinquished but central planning and a degree of self-reliance. Present policy can be viewed as a survival strategy in response to deteriorating economic conditions. In part these have been attributable to mismanagement, but also to unfavourable movements in the terms of trade, particularly in the 1980s. The survival strategy is based on the notion that benefits can be achieved in the relative short term. These benefits will largely accrue to a middle income urban business class that is emerging on the basis of trade and business activities stimulated by some liberalization measures, and partly explains why there has been an emphasis on joint venture arrangements. In the longer term, substantial investment in oil and gas exploration are key elements which the government hopes will assist economic transformation as well as minimising external dependency. However, measures to reallocate resources and widen the export base have been side-stepped. The exchange rate realignment, in particular, has represented a sticking point as far as negotiations with the IMF have been concerned.

Similarly, scenarios about Myanmar's future cannot be viewed without taking into account its political history. The evolution of the present political situation has to be placed in the context of a long-standing authoritarian regime and therefore, can be represented as a process that is adapting to a long tradition in politics. War, violence and crises have been endemic in Burmese political history, and the stability of the 'nation' of Burma has been under constant threat in the post-independence period, both from external sources (China) and internal sources (communists, ethnic insurgents). These features attract little understanding or sympathy from bilateral agencies, particularly those demanding complete democratisation. Other donors, such as Japan, would probably resume aid and investment with a lesser degree of political change, or even on the basis of a stability founded on military power.

The survival strategy is also more likely to work in view of the fact that although the economy was in relative isolation for thirty years, it never became completely outdated. Under the political regime intellectual exchange and innovation was to a large extent discouraged and there was an exodus of some of the country's talent, but contact with other countries did remain. Aid-assisted programmes were quite significant in the 1970s and the early part of the 1980s. The present government is, in principle, committed to take opportunities to break its relative isolation, although, as has been shown, without large-scale international support. This is not to deny that present policy is short-sighted in terms of the loss of investment in human capital as a result of the closure of schools and higher educational institutions in an attempt to eliminate sources of political opposition. Policymakers at the highest level in Myanmar still seem to be uncertain about the best economic strategies to pursue. Although privatisation is a stated policy objective, it is only being implemented through the joint venture arrangements, and the desire to hold on to the power and resources vested in large state corporations perhaps accounts for the lack of enthusiasm. In contrast to Vietnam, Mongolia, Angola and Mozambique, political reform is lagging behind economic reform in Myanmar,[2] a strategy which may be tenable from the government's point of view, so long as technology can be acquired through joint venture arrangements, there is no significant external interference, ownership of public assets is retained (although selling some to pay off immediate debts and acquire funding for military defence is accepted) and the government can halt and stabilize the short-term economic decline.

To argue that economic reform is a hostage to political reform is a simplification of the development alternatives available to Myanmar, and also rests on a misconception of Burmese political traditions. Although investment in infrastructure is likely to be a key element in rehabilitating the economy, and the demand for external finance is considerable, this view minimises the options available to the government. On the one hand, external capital inflows can occur with varying degrees of acceptable political change and, therefore, contribute to economic recovery, and on the other hand, this narrow interpretation ignores alternative possibilities involving solutions being found to the mismatch between resource endowments and resource potential. Above all, it rests on the assumption that all external agencies will put political morality and preference before economic self-interest, an assumption which must be highly questionable except in the short term.

## Notes

1   It is not clear, for example, what resources will be used to pay for the recent (early 1991) huge arms deal with China, estimated to be worth up to $1.1 billion.

2   See discussion in Lenschow (1991).

## References

Catling, J. and Dunning, A. (1989), *Myanmar ITC Sectoral Review Mission*, International Trade Centre, UNCTAD/GATT (August-September).

Hill, H. (1984), 'Industrialisation in Burma in historical perspective', *Journal of Southeast Asian Studies*, vol. XV, no. 1 (March), pp. 134-49.

IMF (1988), *Burma: Recent Economic Development*, Washington DC (June), pp.1-85.

IMF (1989), *Myanmar: Staff Report*, Washington DC (December).

Lenschow, A. (1991), 'Political and economic liberalisation in socialist developing countries', Report for Management Development Programme, UNDP (January).

Morawetz, D. (1980), 'Economic lessons from some small socialist developing countries', *World Development*, vol. pp. 337-69.

Mosley, P., Harrigan, J. and Toye, J. (1991), *Aid and Power: the World Bank and Policy-based Lending in the 1980s*, Routledge, London.

Nyun, T. (1989), 'Country in-depth study: Myanmar', Institute of Economics, Yangon, Myanmar (September), pp. 1-57.

Taylor, R. (1987), *The State in Burma*, Charles Hurst.

UNIDO (1989), *Industry Sector Review Mission to Myanmar*, Vienna (June), pp. 1-61.

Vokes, R (1990), 'Burma and Asia – Pacific Dynamism: Problems and prospects of export-oriented growth in the 1990s' in M. Than and J. Tan (eds.), *Myanmar Dilemmas and Options: The Challenge of Economic Transition in the 1990s*, Asean Economic Research Unit, Institute of Southeast Asian Studies, pp. 19-247.

# Economic reform and industrialisation in the Socialist Republic of Vietnam

## Introduction

The Socialist Republic of Vietnam (hereafter Vietnam) is one of the poorest countries in the world. Accurate estimates of per capita Gross Domestic Product (GDP) are not available, in part because Vietnam uses the net material product system (NMP), used in CMEA countries, rather than the UN System of National Accounts (SNA). Preliminary estimates by the 1989 UNDP Mission to Vietnam (UNDP 1990), however, put per capita GDP at anywhere between US$ 100-200.

Although extremely poor, it is generally accepted that Vietnam has considerable achievements to its credit with respect to socio-economic development. It has developed an effective and comprehensive health service which covers both urban and rural areas. The literacy rate, especially of women, is high and there is, at least on the surface, a low degree of inequality in income distribution. Educational and health facilities are under strain at the present time, however, and past achievements may well be undermined by economic reforms that do not have adequate safeguards built into them. In addition, malnutrition remains a serious public health problem and there is a housing crisis (the result of rapid population growth, urbanisation and war), which can only be described as critical.

As of April 1989, the population was 64.4 million, reflecting a growth rate over the previous decade of 2.1 per cent per annum. Approximately 20 per cent of the population lives in urban areas (with Hanoi and Ho Chi Minh City – previously Saigon – accounting for one-half of the urban total) and 39 per cent of the population is below the age of 15 (UNDP 1990, Table 3.5, p. 36). The recorded labour force in all sectors of the economy was estimated at 28.75 million in 1989 (UNDP 1990, Table 3.6, p. 38), representing 77 per cent of the economically active population (15 years and over). Unemployment was officially estimated at 5.2 per cent but it would be generally accepted that this is a gross underestimate. Demobilisation, following the withdrawal from Cambodia in September 1989, the return of Vietnamese workers from the former CMEA countries and the Middle East and perhaps most importantly, the rationalisation of state enterprises (it was reported in 1990, for example, that state-run companies had laid off nearly a million workers in the previous year – *International Herald Tribune*, 30 November 1990) have together raised the unemployment rate to perhaps 20 per cent (*The Guardian*, 14 December 1989) and a figure of 5 million persons unemployed was widely quoted in 1989.

### Crisis and reform

The post-1945 development of the Vietnamese economy, the problems that the chosen 'model' of development have given rise to and the more recent reform process, cannot be properly understood unless placed within their appropriate historical context. Indeed, the recent development of Vietnam must be seen against a background of approximately 35 years of armed conflict, against the Japanese, the French and the United States. In brief, in 1858 the French seized Da Nang and in 1884, all Vietnam came under French colonial rule. In 1945, following the defeat of Japan, Ho Chi Minh declared Independence in Hanoi. The attempt by France to re-establish its colonial position was finally defeated in 1954, followed by the division of the country into two at the Geneva Conference of that year. 1975 marked the defeat of American intervention and the reunification of the country, with the Socialist Republic of Vietnam established in 1976. (For a brief overview of Vietnam's recent history, and the evolution of pre-1980s economic policy, see White 1983).

In addition to the massive destruction and disruption of this extended period of military conflict (and in particular, the damage inflicted on the population and the environment by American military involvement), Vietnam has been effectively isolated internationally since its 1978 'invasion' of Cambodia to remove the notorious Pol Pot regime. It can truly be said that Vietnam won the war (for independence and unification) but lost the subsequent peace. Only the USSR, the GDR, Sweden, Finland and a number of international agencies (the UNDP, UNICEF, the WFP, etc.) have provided significant aid to Vietnam in the post-1978 period. The legacy of war, international isolation and the cost of maintaining a huge army have all played a key role in the events leading to reform and economic reconstruction.

Historical and external factors which have conditioned the Vietnamese development 'model' must be considered in conjunction with the attempt to implement what Post and Wright (1989, p. 4) refer to as the 'received ideas' of socialism.[1] Initial industrialisation efforts were strongly influenced by the Soviet experience, with its emphasis on centrally planned industrialisation aimed at the domestic production of capital goods and other heavy industrial activities. The state supplied the input and capital requirements of enterprises and set quantitative output targets.

Vietnam's First Five Year Plan (1961-65) emphasised rapid industrialisation and the creation of a heavy industrial base. High rates of growth were initially achieved but at the expense of growing tensions and inefficiencies, which became increasingly apparent during the 1970s (de Vylder and Fford 1988, p. 28). In particular, state enterprises lacked access to modern technologies and their costs of production were high and the quality of their products was low by international standards. There were imbalances between consumer demands and domestic suppliers and the scarcity of foreign exchange led to shortages of imported inputs, raw materials and spare parts, resulting in significant under-utilisation of installed capacity. de Vylder and Fford (1988, pp. 28-29) argue that, in effect, Vietnam was faced by a set of constraints, both structural and policy-induced, common to many other less developed countries pursuing 'inward-looking' development strategies – a neglected agricultural sector unable to produce an adequate supply of basic foodstuffs; a neglected foreign trade sector unable to generate sufficient foreign exchange and a deteriorating budget situation because of the inability of tax revenues to cover expenditure requirements.

During the war years (1964-75), industrial output grew at an estimated annual rate of 5.9 per cent. With the reunification of the country in 1975 and the creation of the Socialist Republic in 1976, a Second Five Year Plan (1976-80) was launched. The target rate of growth for industrial production was 16-18 per cent per annum but the actual rate achieved was only an estimated 0.6 per cent per annum. The years 1979 and 1980 were characterised by economic crisis with food and basic consumer goods shortages, as well as shortages of inputs to the agricultural and industrial sectors.

As a consequence of the failure to realise plan targets, the Fifth Party Congress in 1982 adopted a set of 'new economic orientations'. These included, *inter alia*, a transfer of resources to the agricultural sector, a shift in emphasis from heavy to light industries and the recognition of the need to promote exports. There was also a partial deregulation of production activities by the granting of greater autonomy to individual enterprises, especially with respect to the procurement of imported raw materials and the development of export markets.

The Third Five Year Plan period (1981-85) was characterised by what de Vylder and Fford (1988, p. 72) aptly describe as the 'ebb and flow' of economic reform. Although output targets for the industrial sector were exceeded, 'the authorities failed to address the fundamental problems of the Vietnamese economy' (de Vylder and Fford 1988, p. 67) and the government itself provided a remarkably frank evaluation of the problems facing the industrial sector:

- investment had been scattered over too many projects without priority or complementarity; construction periods were over-run and many projects remained unfinished;
- limitations in capital resources, raw material supplies and energy supplies were not fully anticipated by planners;
- insufficient attention was given to the creation of export-oriented activities;
- there was insufficient specialisation and co-operation between enterprises;
- science and technology for industry remained weak and there was only limited technological progress;
- excessive bureaucratic centralisation restricted initiative and creativity in production enterprises (UNDP 1990, p. 125).

A re-assessment of economic policies was carried out in 1986 and a framework of economic reforms was approved by the Sixth Party Congress in December 1986. With the exception of 35 key Enterprise Unions (including coal, electricity, steel, chemicals and fertilisers and a number of light consumer goods), the basic mechanisms and apparatus of control were abolished. Enterprises were given the freedom to determine wage rates and employment; they became increasingly responsible for obtaining their own capital and to determine their financial affairs. Loss-making units were to be closed down or shifted to an alternative form of ownership.

The processes of commercialisation and liberalisation were further formalised by the Council of Ministers Decree 217 of December 1987. The restrictions placed on the 35 key items referred to above were abolished and the state was no longer to be directly involved in the management of production and distribution. Controls were relaxed and the holding of foreign exchange by enterprises and direct access to foreign markets was made possible. A new law on Foreign Investment was also enacted (see below) (UNDP 1990, p. 126)

The remainder of the 1980s witnessed the continued transformation of Vietnamese economic policy. Fford (1989) argues that by mid-1989, the allocation of resources was no longer based upon the direct administrative mechanisms of a 'Soviet-style' centrally planned model of development. Vietnam was far in advance of many other socialist economies in terms of the reform of its traditional economic management system, and the transformation of the economy had been rapid and profound.

This was achieved, in part, he argues because the actual operation of the 'traditional' Soviet model in both the pre-1976 Democratic Republic of Vietnam and the post-1976 Socialist Republic was neither 'normal' not 'expected' (Fford 1989, p. 7). In particular, there was the development of 'outside relations', which gave economic agents the experience of managing economic activities in a commercial manner and which permitted them to adapt rapidly to the changing economic environment. Fford argues that Vietnam is not yet a market economy, as neither capital nor labour markets are yet fully developed, and that a number of necessary reforms (see below) have yet to be introduced. Nevertheless, the 'successes in reforming the Vietnamese economy are considerable' (Fford 1989, p. 5). In part, this is due to the apparent success of a number of macro-economic reforms which require a brief mention. The anti-inflation policy appears to have been successful in bringing the inflation rate down from perhaps over 700 per cent in early 1987 to below 250 per cent in early 1988, to perhaps an annualised rate of about 1 per cent between April to September 1989 (Fford 1989; Wood 1989), through extremely tight monetary and fiscal policies. The severe fiscal squeeze was largely achieved by cuts in government expenditure, especially the elimination of subsides both producers and consumers. Interest rates, negative in real terms prior to March 1989, were over 6 per cent per month in real terms in April 1989, although they fell in subsequent months (UNDP 1990, Table 4.5, p. 54).

Most remarkable of all, however, was the approximately five-fold devaluation of the Dong against the US dollar in 1989, and the maintenance of the official rate within 10 per cent of the informal market rate. That Vietnam has simultaneously pursued price reform/liberalization, devaluation and an effective anti-inflationary policy is not in doubt. How it has managed to do so relatively successfully, however, still remains an open question (Wood 1989, is not wholly convincing as to *how* this was achieved).

The Vietnamese economic reform and liberalization process (*Doi Moi*) is in many ways unique in the socialist developing world. The rapidity of economic reform has not, as yet (July 1991) been matched by equally rapid political reform,[2] and there is no indication that Vietnam is moving in the direction of a multi-party political democracy (as has happened in Mongolia, for example). The Vietnamese have not formally abandoned their socialist development objectives (as has occurred, for example, in a number of Eastern European economies), although it was not obvious (in mid-1989) that they had any idea of the nature of the 'model' of development that would emerge as a result of economic liberalization. In addition, there are a number of economic problems, at the macro, regional and enterprises level (to which we will briefly return in the subsequent sections of this paper), which do not as yet appear to have been fully appreciated and confronted.

## The industrial sector: performance, problems and prospects

Table 18.1 presents an overview of the growth of industrial output. Relatively rapid growth was experienced over the period 1980-88, with the consumer goods sector growing significantly faster than the heavy industry (producer goods) sector. Provincial and local state industry in general grew faster than centrally-managed industry. The fall in industrial output of 4 per cent in 1989 is attributable to the macro-economic adjustment measures taken.

Table 18.1  *Industrial output growth (gross at 1982 prices)*

| Annual rate of growth | 1976-80 | 1980-85 | 1986 | 1987 | 1988 | 1989 |
|---|---|---|---|---|---|---|
| State | −2.7 | 7.8 | 6.2 | 8.6 | 13.4 | −4.1 |
| *Central | −4.2 | 7.5 | 5.9 | 6.4 | 10.6 | −1.8 |
| *Provincial and local | 3.8 | 9.9 | 6.2 | 11.1 | 13.6 | −5.0 |
| Small-scale industry | 6.5 | 10.8 | 6.0 | 10.7 | 11.7 | −3.8 |
| Means of production (Group A) | 6.4 | 6.2 | 4.5 | 4.0 | 3.8 | −6.3 |
| Consumer goods (Group B) | −2.4 | 10.7 | 8.0 | 9.6 | 16.8 | −3.0 |
| *Total* · | 0.6 | 9.1 | 6.1 | 9.5 | 12.6 | −4.0 |

*Source:* Statistics, 1976-89, General Statistical Office. UNDP 1990, Table 9.1, p. 119.

Different growth rates have resulted in changes in the composition of industrial output (see Table 18.2). In 1980, the light industry sector accounted for just over 62 per cent of total gross industrial production and by 1989, it had risen to 71 per cent.[3] In part, the more rapid growth of the light industry sector was a result in changes on the allocation of investment.

Table 18.2   *Composition of gross industrial production, 1980–88 (%)*

|                | 1980 | 1982 | 1983 | 1984 | 1985 | 1986 | 1987 | 1988 | 1989 |
|----------------|------|------|------|------|------|------|------|------|------|
| Heavy industry | 37.8 | 34.4 | 34.1 | 32.9 | 32.7 | 32.2 | 32.2 | 29.7 | 28.9 |
| Light industry | 62.2 | 65.6 | 65.9 | 67.1 | 67.3 | 67.8 | 67.8 | 70.3 | 71.1 |

*Source:* Statistics, 1976–89, General Statistical Office. UNDP 1990, Table 9.2, p. 121.

Employment (Table 18.3) grew faster in the light in the light industry/consumer goods sector as compared to the heavy industry/producer goods sector. Indeed, there was a fall in employment in the means of production sector (Group A) of approximately 10 per cent between 1987 and 1988, as compared to a growth of just under 10 per cent in consumer goods (Group B) over the same period. Productivity growth (Table 18.4) has been higher in the light industry sector and higher in local rather than centrally-managed enterprises. Of the approximately three million people employed in the industrial sector in 1988, just over 2 million were employed in the co-operative, handicraft and private sub-sector (Table 18.3).

Table 18.3   *Employment in industry ('000)*

|                          | 1980 | 1986 | 1987 | 1988 |
|--------------------------|------|------|------|------|
| Group A                  | 370  | 439  | 459  | 410  |
| Group B                  | 274  | 371  | 401  | 434  |
| Central                  | 343  | 417  | 435  | 433  |
| Local                    | 300  | 394  | 425  | 411  |
| Co-operative and private | 1605 | 2184 | 3013 | 2102 |
| *Total*                  | 2248 | 2653 | 2873 | 2946 |

*Source:* Statistics, 1976–89, General Statistical Office. UNDP 1990, Table 9.4, p. 123.

There are important regional variations in industrial structure. Heavy industry, which includes iron and steel, chemicals, cement, fertilisers and machinery and equipment, tends to be concentrated in the north. Light industries, on the other hand, although throughout the country, tend to be concentrated in the south. Industrial output from the non-state sector also tends to be concentrated in the south and the regional implications of development in general, and economic reform and liberalization in particular, will require greater attention in the future as compared to their (apparent) relative neglect in the past.

The post-reform period has been characterised by buoyant growth in both consumer goods and producer goods production (estimated at 11 per cent and 10 per cent per annum respectively) (Fford 1989, p. 30). Fford (1989, p. 32) argues that there is evidence of resource re-allocation occurring, favouring those sectors most sensitive

Table 18.4   *Productivity: gross industrial production per employee, 1984-87*
*(% annual productivity growth)*

|  | 1984 | 1985 | 1986 | 1987 (est) |
|---|---|---|---|---|
| Gross industrial production | | | | |
| – per employee | 9.2 | 1.7 | 2.7 | 4.1 |
| by sector | | | | |
| – heavy industry | 7.6 | 1.7 | 0.7 | 1.0 |
| – light industry | 8.9 | 1.4 | 3.6 | 5.0 |
| by management system | | | | |
| – central management | 6.9 | 3.1 | 6.0 | – 4.2 |
| – provinicial and local | | | | |
| management | 10.3 | 2.2 | 3.6 | 5.0 |

*Source:* UNIDO 1989, *Vietnam's Industrial Development – An assessment*, Table 2.7. UNDP 1990, Table 9.5, p. 123.

to market conditions and most able to adapt to the rapidly changing economic environment. Especially high rates of growth were recorded for electricity, water pumps, glass, electric light bulbs, tinned goods, frozen fruit and vegetables and a number of other light durable and non–durable consumer goods (Fford 1989, p. 33). There were falls in the output of coal, insecticides and small tractors.

Fford (1989, p. 32) concludes:

Vietnamese industry appears increasingly healthy in purely economic terms, with greater competition and sensitivity to market demand. Methods of capital mobilisation and utilisation are developing rather fast and conditions are becoming ripe for the evolution of financial and credit markets to support profitable units. This sector is becoming more adapted to international markets and is clearly capitalising on the valuable experiences of the past few years.[4]

### The export of manufactured goods

The government of Vietnam has placed great emphasis on the export of processed and manufactured goods. Vietnam's geographical location makes it well-placed to serve the rapidly growing markets of the so-called Pacific Rim; its rich and varied raw material base is as yet not fully exploited, and its well-educated, literate and disciplined low-cost labour force gives it a comparative advantage in a wide range of labour-intensive processing and assembly activities which the more advanced Newly Industrialising Countries (NICs) in the region no longer engage in.

Already in 1989, Vietnam was exporting an increasingly wide range of manufactured goods. These included processed marine products (to Singapore, Japan, Hong Kong and Canada); glass products; garments (both contract work for the USSR and exports to Japan, Taiwan, Australia and Canada); cotton yarn and silk; processed forestry products and bicycle tyres and tubes and other rubber products. Plans have been announced for the creation of a number of export processing zones (EPZs), which together with Law on Foreign Investment (see the next section) are expected to attract export-oriented direct foreign investment (DFI). As an additional incentive to export promotion, enterprises are allowed to export directly and keep for their own use a substantial proportion of the foreign exchange earned. Although effective as an export promotion device, however, this policy raises serious questions concerning the use to which available foreign exchange is put (discussed further below).

The problems faced by exporters are in part a sub-set of the problems faced by all enterprises in general in Vietnam. The quality of manufactured goods is often low; there is a lack of information on marketing, insurance, shipping, international banking, etc., especially in the north of the country; enterprises that do not have direct access to foreign exchange will find it difficult to re-equip and modernise their plants, acquire necessary inputs, etc., and telecommunications in particular are poorly developed, making contact with trading partners difficult and hampering data collection, analysis and dissemination, especially with respect to international prices and market conditions. Macro-economic stability is also a necessary condition for successful export promotion and we will return to these wider issues in the final section of the paper.

## The role of direct foreign investment

In its Law on Foreign Investment in Vietnam (promulgated in January 1988), the government designated a number of sectors of the national economy as having a high priority with respect to foreign capital. They include: high technology industries using skilled labour; foreign exchange earning service sector activities (for example, tourism, ship repair); labour-intensive industries using local natural resources and raw materials, and the construction of infrastructure facilities.

DFI may take various forms (business co-operation ventures, joint ventures, fully-owned foreign subsidiaries) and the law offers a fairly standardised package of financial incentives and guarantees (against expropriation and nationalisation).

The government established in early 1989 the State Committee for Co-operation and Investment (SCCI), with responsibility for the management and administration of DFI in Vietnam. Its functions are to provide guidance to foreign investors concerning laws and regulations, to examine and evaluate proposals, to determine investment priorities, to monitor and supervise the operations of enterprises and to analyse the consequences of DFI. The SCCI is, in effect, the final decision-making body on all foreign investment proposals

As of mid-1990, the SCCI has issued 173 investment licenses involving a total investment of US$ 1.1 billion (UNDP 1990, p. 133). Data for a slightly earlier period are given in Table 18.5 and clearly indicate that the largest amount of DFI is directed at the oil and gas sector. The agriculture and forestry sectors are also of significance, as is the development of processed marine products, especially shrimps, for export, The manufacturing sector has so far attracted less and this might well be a cause for concern in the future, given that the government sees DFI as essential for the re-equipment and modernisation of production enterprises in the manufacturing sector to raise productivity, improve quality and hence competitiveness.

Table 18.5    *Foreign investment projects approved as of June 1989*

| Sector | No. of projects | Amount ($US mil) | Percentage |
|---|---|---|---|
| Agri. forestry, and agri. processing projects | 7 | 122.5 | 19.1 |
| Shrimp farming for export | 4 | 104.2 | 16.3 |
| Oil exploration | 6 | 288.0 | 45.0 |
| Other mining exploration | 3 | 2.5 | 0.4 |
| Electronics assembly plants | 5 | 2.6 | 0.4 |
| Mechanics (production, repair) | 3 | 8.2 | 1.3 |
| Light industry | 14 | 20.9 | 3.3 |
| Transport and communication | 5 | 39.7 | 6.2 |
| Tourism | 14 | 49.6 | 7.7 |
| Other | 2 | 2.2 | 0.3 |
| *Total* | 63 | 640.4 | 100.0 |

*Source :* State Planning Committee. UNDP, 1990, Table 3.4, p. 35.

The majority of the investment proposals relate to the south of the country, where infrastructural facilities are more developed and the 'market economy' better understood. As of 1989, there were some ambiguities and omissions in the foreign investment code, relating to labour regulations in particular. UN technical assistance was anticipated to train Vietnamese personnel in project evaluation techniques and in the monitoring and regulation of foreign investment projects.

Again, to anticipate some of the issues raised in the final section of this paper, the Vietnamese have a perhaps somewhat unrealistic view as to the potential benefits and costs of DFI. The potential benefits arising form the transfer of technology (both embodied and disembodied) and the gaining of access to overseas markets, in particular, are not in doubt. Of importance, too, is the self-confidence that the Vietnamese display in their ability to bargain effectively with, and get a good deal from, foreign capital. Such self-confidence is not always justified, however. An ill-defined and lax investment code, with inexperienced and perhaps untrained personnel manning the regulatory apparatus, together with a less than full appreciation of the costs that DFI can impose, may well mean that foreign investment will have largely negative consequences for the Vietnamese economy, which may ultimately lessen the economic benefits of liberalization and reform.

### The development of the private sector

The emergence (or in some cases, the re-emergence) of private sector enterprises is one of the most striking features of the Vietnamese reform process. The Resolution on New Regulations for the Non-State Economic Sector (Resolution No. 16 of July 1988) asserts a determination to 'fully tap the potentials of the non-state economic units ... and turn them into important components of the national economy in the period of transition to socialism' (it is not clear if the ambiguity of the final phrase is deliberate or not).

A number of principles are outlined regarding 'non-state production units':

- They will operate outside the state planning process;
- they will not be discriminated against by monopoly state organs that supply raw materials and spare parts;
- they may procure their own supplies of raw materials and spare parts;
- they may procure, on an equal footing, supplies of machinery and equipment from state units;
- those producing for export may use foreign exchange earnings as they wish;
- exporting enterprises may negotiate their own foreign sales contracts;
- they may secure technology and technical training from state enterprises on making appropriate payment; and,
- they may enjoy patent and copyright protection on their own inventions

The private sector requires a stable environment for its development and the government is committed to its creation, in part through the establishment of the Council for Non-State Enterprises in early 1990 to promote the interests of the private sector (UNDP 1990, p. 130). It is also recognised that the development of this sector needs to be complemented by the establishment of legislation relating to domestic investment, commerce and company laws (including bankruptcy laws); changes in credit, banking and financial institutions and eventually, the creation of a Stock Exchange.

The development of the small-scale industry sector is both important in its own right and as an integral part of the emerging private sector. It has always played an important role in the Vietnamese economy, and it accounts for a significant proportion of industrial production and exports. It is estimated that between 1.5-1.8 million people are employed in the small industry/handicraft sector (UNDP 1990 p. 128).

The government hopes to create 2 million additional jobs in the small industry/handicraft sector over the period 1991-95, but at an estimated cost per job created of US$500 (implying a total investment of over US$ 1 billion), this target is unlikely to be achieved without substantial foreign financial and technical assistance, which appears unlikely to be forthcoming in the near future.

## Outstanding policy issues

As has been indicated at several points throughout this paper, the reform and liberalization process is creating problems for which there are no easy or straightforward answers. This is not surprising, as economies such as Vietnam which have embarked on reform are moving into uncharted waters, in which the textbook model of the 'market economy' is of only very limited relevance. Reform processes create their own dynamics, creating new problems at the same time as they provide solutions to existing problems. The depth and the rapidity of the reform process in Vietnam, coupled with its unique historical, political and geo-strategic characteristics, all add to the complexity of the process of change and the intractability of the problems faced.

The focus of this paper has been the industrialisation process in Vietnam and the impact of reforms on the industrial sectors' future development. Essentially, there are four dimensions to the reform process – macro, regional, sectoral and enterprise level – and we will consider each briefly in turn, although in reality, of course, they are not neatly separated from one another.

We have already argued that the macro-economic environment, and the maintenance of macro-economic stability, are of prime importance for successful and sustained industrialisation. The major macro-economic issues relate to the management of the balance of payments and the maintenance of an exchange rate that is not too far from a market-determined equilibrium rate. The need to promote exports has been given explicit recognition by the government, but as we have argued above, the earning of additional foreign exchange by individual enterprises should not be at the expense of a rational allocation and utilization of that foreign exchange. Certainly, as of mid-1989, there was much casual evidence to suggest that foreign exchange was being wasted by enterprises importing vast quantities of durable consumer goods.

The further development of the commercial banking sector, with the technical capacity to play a more active role in the provision of finance to productive enterprises, is essential. This in turn has implications for the role that the Central Bank (the State Bank of Vietnam) will perform in the future, and for the design and implementation of monetary, credit and interest rate policies. Banking reforms in 1988 and interest rate reforms in 1989 were followed by decrees in 1990 which increased the independence of the banking system and allowed the Central Bank to perform the functions required of it in a market-oriented system (UNDP 1990, p. 55). There are still considerable limitations in the banking system, however, and a continuing need for technical and financial assistance to support the restructuring process.

The development of the financial sector and monetary policy must be complemented by fiscal reform and the implementation of appropriate fiscal policies. At the macro-level, this relates to government expenditure policies which have undergone considerable reform in recent years (Spoor 1988; UNDP 1990, pp. 46-9), price stability and the development of a tax base to generate sufficient revenues. State enterprise reform, plus the emergence of private sector enterprises make the institution of an effective and equitable direct tax system imperative.

Finally, at the macro-level, we return to the question of development objectives. As noted above, the Vietnamese government has not abandoned its socialist objectives, but equally, it has perhaps not yet been able to think through the relationship between the process of reform and liberalization on the one hand, and the achievement of socialism, on the other hand. Question of equity versus efficiency need to be confronted and the impact of reforms on the labour market, the labour process and their impact on women in particular, need to be investigated.

With respect to the regional dimension of the reform and industrialisation process, little can be added to that already noted above. The geography of Vietnam, its poorly developed transport and communications networks, the differing economic, political and institutional development of the north and the south and the implied differences in abilities to respond to, and cope with, the demands of the 'market economy', will together generate problems that will require active regional development programmes to overcome. In addition, we have already suggested above that DFI will tend to concentrate in the south, adding to the problems of regional imbalance.

At the sectoral level, a number of problems of industrial strategy require brief mention. The balance between import substituting industries on the one hand, and export-oriented activities on the other, is a complex issue that requires a pragmatic response. Inter-sectoral balances (between industry and agriculture) and intra-sectoral balances (both between different industrial sub-sectors and different enterprises), have perhaps been somewhat neglected in the past (notwithstanding official development rhetoric) and will need to be given priority in the future. The acquisition of foreign technology and the development of indigenous technological capabilities, in part related to the role of DFI in the industrial sector, are issues that will demand greater attention than they have so far been accorded.

Finally, at the level of the individual enterprises, the reform and liberalization process continues to generate a whole range of problems which we can no more than briefly mention here. The issues relate, *inter alia*, to: ownership rights and new forms of ownership through perhaps the limited sale of equity in selected state enterprises; the separation of the ownership functions of the state from the management functions of the enterprise (Dellmo *et al.* 1990); possible conflicts between development priorities, on the one hand, and commercial considerations on the other; and the move away from grant to loan finance of investment.

Many enterprises in the manufacturing sector are characterised by obsolete equipment, lack of spare parts, poor organisational structures, lack of maintenance and repair, lack of cost and quality consciousness and too little effort to increase the technical levels of both products and productive processes (UNDP 1990, p. 135). The rehabilitation of existing enterprises (re-equipment and modernisation) should, in many cases, take precedence over the creation of new productive capacity. Managerial weakness need to be overcome and there is an urgent need for more and better training in a wide range of business-related skills, such as general management, cost accounting, marketing, etc.

The government of Vietnam is, of course, aware of these problems and is committed to the implementation of policies to overcome them – the more effective mobilisation of domestic capital, the encouragement of the private sector, an expanded role for foreign capital, more effective technology transfer, etc. The recognition of the existence of a problem is an important first step in its solution, and to focus on problems is not to deny what has been achieved in the past (both in the pre- and post-reform periods), nor is it to understate the development potential of the country. What this paper has tried to emphasize, however, is how little economists actually know (compared with what they assert or think that they know) about the transition from a centrally planned to a market-oriented economy, and to urge perhaps some degree of caution on policy markers so that past achievements are not sacrificed to more hypothetical future benefits.

## Notes

*The author was a member of the UNDP Economic Mission to Vietnam in 1989. The views expressed in the paper are those of the author only, however.

1 It has been usual (for example, Post and Wright 1989; Fford and de Vylder 1988) to describe Vietnam in the light of the perceived 'failure' of the centrally planned, heavy industry 'model', as a typical, resource-constrained economy, characterised by the continuous reproduction of shortages, that is, continuous underproduction. Although there is some truth in that assertion at the general, descriptive level, intuition and casual empiricism have convinced the present author that this characterisation does not take us very far in our understanding of the development process in Vietnam. Equally, the assertion by Fford and de Vylder (1988, p. 13) that Vietnam is 'currently the victim of an economic crisis largely the result of in appropriate development policies that the authorities are now trying to correct' so ignores the historical context and political economy (of which those authors are both well aware) as to be largely meaningless. A comparative study of Vietnam and the Democratic Peoples' Republic of Korea (North Korea), with respect to their historical development, political economy, development objectives and policies, etc., would be most instructive.

2 Some changes occurred at the Seventh Congress of the Vietnamese Communist Party (June 1991) with the appointment and/or promotion of a number of economic reformers. It is still the concern of the party leadership, however, that Vietnam should not be allowed to slip into 'east European-style turmoil' (*The Guardian*, 21 June 1991). See also report in *The Economist*, 6 July 1991).

3 It is of interest to note that as per capita incomes rise, it is more usual to observe an increase in the share in total output (or value added) of the heavy industry sector. For a critical review of the literature, see Nixson 1990.

4 Given the state of much of Vietnamese industry, this is a remarkably sanguine conclusion. It is true that certain durable and non-durable consumer goods industries, especially those that have managed to break into export markets, largely located in the south of the country, are able to respond positively and rapidly to the reformed economic environment. But in the north, much of the industrial sector is so ill-equipped, with management not familiar with a market economy, and with very undeveloped infrastructural facilities, that it is difficult to find grounds for optimism. We refer to these problems in the concluding section.

## References

Dellmo, H., Granlund, J. and Gustafsson, A. (1990), *Vietnam's Economic Reforms and their Effects on State Enterprises*, Department of Economics, University of Lund, Sweden, Minor Field Study Series, no. 13.

Fford, A. (1989), 'The Socialist Republic of Vietnam since mid-1988 – Major policy changes and socio-economic developments', Report for SIDA, mimeo, Hanoi (December)

Fford, A. and de Vylder, S. (1988), *Vietnam – An Economy in Transition*, Swedish International Development Authority, Stockholm.

Nixson, F. (1990), 'Industrialisation and structural change in developing countries', *Journal of International Development*, vol.2, no. 3 (July).

Post, K. and Wright, P. (1989), *Socialism and Underdevelopment*, Routledge, London and New York.

Spoor, M. (1988), 'Reforming state finance in post-1975 Vietnam', *Journal of Development Studies*, vol. 24, no. 4, (July).

UNDP (1990), *Report on the Economy of Vietnam*, report prepared for the Socialist Republic of Vietnam, State Planning Committee, Hanoi (December).

White, C. (1983), 'Recent debates in Vietnamese development policy' in White, G., Murray, R. and White, C. (eds.), *Revolutionary Socialist Development in the Third World*, Wheatsheaf, Brighton.

Wood, A. (1989), 'Deceleration of inflation with acceleration of price reform: Vietnam's remarkable recent experience', *Cambridge Journal of Economics*, vol. 13.

# Bibliography

Agarwala, R. (1983), 'Price Distortions and Growth in Developing Countries', World Bank Staff Working Paper no. 575, Washington, DC.

Aghevli, B.B. and Marquez-Ruarte, J. (1985), 'A Case of Successful Adjustment: Korea's Experience During 1980-84', IMF *Occasional Paper*, Washington, DC.

Alavi, R. (1987), The Three Phases of Industrialisation in Malaysia, 1957-1980s, MA dissertation, UEA, Norwich, UK.

Alburo, F. and Shepherd, G. (1985), 'Trade Liberalization Experience in the Philippines, 1960-84', *Philippine Institute for Development Studies Working Paper, no. 86-01*, Manila.

Ali, I. (1988), 'Manufactured Exports from the Philippines: A Sector Profile and an Agenda for Reform', *Asian Development Bank Economic Staff Paper no. 42*, Manila.

Amsden, A. (1989), *Asia's Next Giant: South Korea and Late Industrialisation*, Oxford University Press, New York.

Asian Development Bank (1989), *Asian Development Outlook*, Manila.

Asian Development Bank (1990), *Asian Development Outlook*, Manila.

Auty, R.M. (1990), 'Heavy and Chemical Industry and Spatial Dispersion in a Large, Low-income Command Economy: China', University of Lancaster, mimeo.

Auty, R.M. (1990) 'The Korean heavy industry drive re-evaluated', Paper presented at the conference 'The Impact of Policy Reform on Trade and Industrial Performance in Developing Countries', 21-22 June 1990, University of Bradford (mimeo).

Balassa, B. and Hughes, H. (1969), 'Statistical indicators of industrial development', Economics Department Working Paper no. 45, May 1969, World Bank, Washington, DC.

Balassa B. (1980), 'The process of industrial development and alternative development strategies', *World Bank Staff Working Paper 438*, World Bank, Washington. DC.

Balassa, B. (1982), 'Development Strategies and Economic Performance' in *Development Strategies in Semi-Industrialized Countries*, Oxford University Press, London.

Balassa, B. (1986), 'Economic Incentives and Agricultural Exports in Developing Countries', Paper presented at the Eighth Congress of the International Economic Association, New Delhi, India.

Balassa, B. (1988), 'Inventive Policies and Agricultural Performance in Sub- Saharan Africa' World Bank PPR Working Paper no. 77, Washington, DC.

Balassa, B. (1990), 'Incentive Policies and Export Performance in Sub-Saharan Africa, *World Development*, vol. 18, no. 3.

Baldwin, R.E. (1975), *Foreign Trade Regimes and Economic Development: The Philippines*, Columbia University Press, New York.

Baldwin, R.E. (1989), 'The Political Economy of Trade Policy', *Journal of Economic Perspective* (Fall).

Baldwin, R.E. (forthcoming) 'High Technology Exports and Strategic Trade Policy in Developing Countries: The Case of Brazilian Aircraft' in G. K. Helleiner (ed.), *New Trade Theory and Industrialisation in Developing Countries*, Oxford University Press, New York and London.

Barbier, J.P. (1988), 'Nouvelles politiques industrielles en Afrique Subsaharienne ou les écueils de la course au large', *Notes et études*, CCCE, no. 15, Paris.

Barbier, J.P. (1989), 'Réflexion sur la competitivité. Comparaison Afrique – Asie', *Notes et études*, CCCE, no. 26, Paris.

Barichello, R.R. (1988) 'Indonesia Trade Reforms in the mid-1980s: Policies, processes and political economy', mimeo.

Bautista, R.M. and Power, J.H. and Associates (1979), *Industrial Promotion Policies in the Philippines*, Philippine Institute for Development Studies, Manila.

Bautista, R.M. (1988), *Impediments to Trade Liberalization in the Philippines*, Thames Essays series, Gower.

Behrman, J.R. and Deolalikar, A.B. (1988), 'Health and Nutrition' in H. Chenery and T. N. Srinivasan, *Handbook of Development Economics*, vol. 1, North Holland, Elsevier Science Publishers, The Netherlands, pp. 631-712.

*Beijing Review* (1989), 'The Utilization of Foreign Capital, 1979 – 88', 6-12 March.

Bergsman, J. (1974), 'Commercial Policy, Allocative Efficiency, and X- Efficiency', *Quarterly Journal of Economics*, 88 (August), pp. 409-33.

Bertola, G. and Faini, R. (1991), 'Import demand and non-tariff barriers: the impact of trade liberalization', *Journal of Development Economics*, vol. 34, pp. 269-86.

Bevan, D. *et al.* (1987), *East African Lessons on Economic Liberalization*, Thames Essays series, Gower.

Bevan, D.L., Collier, P. and Gunning, J.W. (1987), 'Consequences of a commodity-boom in a controlled economy: accumulation and redistribution in Kenya 1975-1983', *The World Bank Economic Review*, vol. 1, no. 3.

Bhagwati, J. and Srinivasan, T.N. (1973), 'The general equilibrium theory of effective protection and resource allocation', *Journal of International Economics*, 3, pp. 259-81.

Bhagwati, J. (1978), *Foreign Trade Regimes and Economic Development: Anatomy and Consequences of Exchange Control Regimes*, Ballinger, Cambridge, Mass.

Bhagwati, J. (1981), *The Theory of Commercial Policy*, vol. 1., MIT Press, Cambridge, Mass.

Bhagwati, J. (1988), 'Export-promoting trade strategy: issues and evidence', *The World Bank Research Observer*, vol. 3 (January).

Bhagwati, J. (1989) 'Is free trade passé after all?' *Weltwirtshaftliches Archiv*, Band 125, Heft 1.

Binswanger, H. (1989), 'How agricultural producers respond to prices and governments', Paper presented at First Annual World Bank Conference on Development Economics, Washington, DC, April 27-28.

Bourgignon, F. and Morrisson, C. (1989), *External Trade and Income Distribution*. Development Centre Studies, OECD, Paris.

Broad, R. (1988), *Unequal Alliance 1979-1986: The World Bank, the International Monetary Fund and the Philippines*, Ateneo de Manila University Press, Manila.

Caballero, R. J. and Corbo, V. (1989), 'How does uncertainty about the real exchange rate affect exports?', World Bank PPR Working Paper no. 221, Washington, DC.

Cable, V. and Persaud, B. (eds.) (1987), *Developing with Foreign Investment*, Croom Helm,

London.

Catling, J. and Dunning, A. (1989), *Myanmar ITC Sectoral Review Mission*, International Trade Centre, UNCTAD/GATT (August-September).

Caves, R.E. (1980), 'International trade and industrial organization: Introduction', *Journal of Industrial Economics*, 29 (December), pp. 113-18.

Central Bank of Sri Lanka (1981) *Annual Report*.

Central Statistical Office (Harare), *Quarterly Digest of Statistics*.

Chambas, G. (1989), 'Aide française et ajustement au Sénégal', Rapport rédige à la demande de Elliot Berg Associates, CERDI.

Chambas, G. (1990a), 'La reforme fiscale au Sénégal (1986-90)', *Etudes et documents provisoires*, CERDI.

Chambas, G. (1990b), *Note sur la fraude douanière en Côte d'Ivoire et au Sénégal*, CERDI.

Chambers, R. (1989), 'Tariff reform and the uniform tariff', CECTP, World Bank, Washington, DC.

Charmes, J. (1989), *Economie enregistrée secteur informel et comptabilité nationale au Sénégal 1977-88*, Direction de la Statistique, PAGD, Dakar.

Chee Peng Lim (1987), *Industrial Development: An Introduction to the Malaysian Industrial Master Plan*, Pelanduk Publications, Malaysia.

Chen, E.K.Y. (1983), 'Multinationals from Hong Kong', in Lall (1983).

Chen, E.K.Y. (1989), 'Trade policy in Asia' in S. Naya, M. Urrutia, M. Shelley and A. Fuyentes (eds.), *Lessons in Development: A Comparative Study of Asia and Latin America*, International Center for Economic Growth, San Francisco, pp. 55-76.

Chen, Nai-Ruenn (1986), Foreign investment in China: current trends, US Department of Commerce, mimeo.

Chenery, H.B. and Syrquin, M. (1975), *Patterns of Development, 1950-1970*, Oxford University Press, London.

Chenery, H., Robinson, S. and Syrquin, M. (1986), *Industrialization and Growth: A Comparative Study*, Oxford University Press, New York.

Christian Michelsen Institute (1987), *Kenya: Country Study and Norwegian Aid Review*.

Cody J., Kitchen, R. and Weiss, J. (1990), *Policy Design and Price Reform in Developing Countries*, Wheatsheaf, Brighton.

Condon, R. and de Melo, J. (1986), 'Industrial organization implication of QR trade regimes: evidence and welfare costs', Paper prepared for meetings of Applied Econometric Association, Istanbul (December 10-12), World Bank, Washington, DC.

Cooper, R.N. (1971), 'Currency Devaluation in Developing Countries', *Essay in International Finance Series*, no. 86, Princeton University, (June).

Corbo, V. and de Melo, J. (1987), 'Lessons from southern cone policy reforms', *World Bank Research Observer 2*, no. 2.

Corden, W.M. (1974), *Trade Policy and Economic Welfare*, Oxford University Press, London.

Corden, M. (1987), *Protection and Liberalization: A Review of Analytical Issues Issues*, IMF, Washington DC.

Corden, W.M. (1989) in G.M. Meier and W.F. Steel (eds.), *Industrial Adjustment in Sub-Saharan Africa*, Oxford University Press for the World Bank, Oxford.

Courcel, M. (1987), 'Possibilité et conditions d'une intervention plus dynamique du secteur privé au Sénégal', Club du Sahel, Paris.

Crane, G.T. (1990), *The Political Economy of China's Special Economic Zones*, M.E. Sharpe Inc., Armonk, New York and London, p. 33.

Cuthpertson, A.C. and Khan, M.Z. (1991), 'Effective Protection to Manufacturing in Sri Lanka', mimeo, Colombo, Sri Lanka.

DANIDA (1989), *Cooling, Coldstorage and Distribution of Fish, Sector Evaluation, Synthesis Report,* (May).

Dellmo, H., Granlund, J. and Gustafsson, A. (1990), *Vietnam's Economic Reforms and their Effects on State Enterprises,* Department of Economics, University of Lund, Sweden, Minor Field Study Series, no. 13.

Department of National Planning, Ministry of Policy Planning and Implementation (1989), *Public Investment 1989-93.*

Devarajan, S. and Rodrik, D. (1989), 'Trade liberalization in developing countries: do imperfect competition and scale economies matter?', *American Economic Review, Papers and Proceedings,* (May).

Deyo, F. (ed.), (1987), *The Political Economy of the New Asian Industrialism,* Cornell University Press, Ithaca and London.

Diaz Alejandro, C.F. (1965), *Exchange Rate Devaluation in a Semi-industrialized Country,* MIT Press, Cambridge, Mass.

Diaz-Alejandro, C.F. (1975), 'Trade policies and economic development' in P. Kenen (ed.) *International Trade and Finance: Frontiers for Research,* Cambridge University Press, Cambridge.

Dornbusch, R. and Yung Chul Park (1987), 'Korean Growth Policy', *Brookings Papers on Economic Activity,* no. 2, Washington, DC, pp. 389-454.

Dornbusch, R. and Helmers, F.L.C. (1988), *The Open Economy,* Economic Development Institute, World Bank, Washington, DC.

Easterly, W.R. and Wetzel, D.L. (1989), 'Determinants of growth: survey of theory and evidence,' World Bank PPR Working Paper no. 343 (December), Washington, DC.

Economist Intelligence Unit, *Country Profile Zimbabwe* (annually), London.

Economist Intelligence Unit, *Country Report: Zimbabwe, Malawi (quarterly),* London.

Edwards, C.B. (1975), *Protection, Profits and Policy: An Analysis of Industrialisation in Malaysia,* PhD thesis, UEA, Norwich, UK.

Edwards, C. (1980), 'Lessons from South Korea for Industrial Policy in Sri Lanka: Some Observations', *Upanathi,* vol. 3, no. 2, July 1988.

Edwards, S. (1987), 'Comment programmer les mesures de libéralisation économique dans les PVD?', *Finances et développement,* vol. 24, no. 1.

Edwards, S. (1989), 'Exchange Rate Misalignment in Developing Countries', *Research Observer,* vol. 4, no. 1, (January), pp. 3-21.

Edwards, S. (1989a), 'Openness, outward orientation, trade liberalization and economic performance in developing countries', World Bank PPR Working Paper no. 191, Washington, DC.

Edwards, S. (1989b), *Real Exchange Rates, Devaluation and Adjustment: Exchange Rate Policy in Developing Countries,* MIT Press, Cambridge, Mass.

Elliot Berg and Associates (1990), *Adjustment Postponed: Economic Policy Reform in Senegal in the Eighties.* Report prepared for USAID, Dakar, Alexandria.

Enos, J. and Park, W. (1988), *The Adoption and Diffusion of Imported Technology: The Case of Korea,* Croom Helm, London.

Erzan, R., Kuwahara, H., Marchese, S. and Vossenaar, R. (1988), *The Profile of Protection in Developing Countries.* UNCTAD Discussion Paper no. 21, New York.

Erzan, R. (1989), 'Would general trade liberalization in developing countries expand south-south trade?', World Bank PPR Working Paper no. 319 (December), Washington, DC.

Evans, D. (1989), 'Visible and invisible hands in trade policy reform', mimeo, Institute of Development Studies, (July).

Feuchtwang, S., Hussain, A. and Pairault, T. (eds.) (1988), *Transforming China's Economy in the Eighties*, 2 vols. Zed Books, London.

Fford, A. and de Vylder, S. (1988), *Vietnam – An Economy in Transition*, Swedish International Development Authority, Stockholm.

Fford, A. (1989), 'The Socialist Republic of Vietnam since mid-1988 – Major policy changes and socio-economic developments', Report for SIDA, mimeo, Hanoi, (December).

Fields, G.S. (1989), 'Changes in poverty and inequality in developing Countries', *The World Bank Observer*, 4(2) pp. 167-85.

Findlay, R. (1984), 'Growth and development in trade models' in R. Jones and P. Kenen, (eds.), *Handbook of International Economics*, vol.I, North-Holland, Amsterdam.

Finger, J.M. and Lair, S. (1987), 'Protection in developed and developing countries – an overview', *Journal of World Trade Law 2*, no. 6.

Fisher, I. (1933), 'The debt-deflation theory of great depressions', *Econometrica*.

Fischer, S. (1984), *Real Balances, the Exchange Rate, and Indexation: Real Variables in Disinflation*. NBER Working Paper no. 1497, Cambridge, Mass.

Fischer, S. (1989), 'The economics of government budget constraint', World Bank PPR Working Paper no. 224, Washington, DC.

Fitzgerald, B. and Monson, T. (1989), 'Preferential credit and insurance as means to promote exports', *World Bank Research Observer*, (January), 4 pp. 89-114.

Fontaine, J.M. and Georgopoulos, M. (1991), 'Protection tarifaire et instabilite des prix internationaux: une note' in J.M. Fontaine (ed.) *Contrôle du Commerce Extérieur et stratégies de Développement Economique*, Presses Universitaires de France, Paris.

Fontaine, J.M. (1992), 'Import Liberalisation in Kenya' in J. M. Fontaine (ed.), *Foreign-Trade Reform and Development Strategies*, Routledge, London, (forthcoming).

Foreign Investment Advisory Committee (1988), *Annual Report*.

Fransman, M. (1982), *Industry and Accumulation in Africa*, Heinemann, London.

Fröbel, F., Heinrichs, J. and Kreye, O. (1980), *The New International Division of Labour. Structural Unemployment in Industrialized Countries and Industrialization in Developing Countries*, Cambridge University Press, Cambridge (originally published in German by Rowohlt, Hamburg, 1977).

GATT (1980), *The Tokyo Round of Multilateral Trade Negotiations - II Supplementary Report*, Geneva.

Geourjon, A.M. (1988), 'La protection commerciale' in P. and S. Guillaumont (eds.), *Stratégies de Développement comparées zone franc et hors zone franc*, Economica, Paris.

Geourjon, A.M. (1990), 'Evaluation de l'expérience du Sénégal en matière d'adjustement structurel; la politique commerciale et industrielle', Rapport rédigé à la demande de Elliot Berg Associates, CERDI, Clermont-Ferrand.

Geourjon, A.M. (1991), 'La libéralisation des eim dans le cadre de la Nouvelle Politique Industrielle au Sénégal', a paraître dans un ou rage collectif sous la direction de J. M. Fontaine, PUF, Paris.

German Development Institute (1985), *Evaluation of the Co-operation between the European Community and the Caribbean ACP States, V. Final Report*, (November).

Goldstein, M. (1986), *The Global Effects of Fund-Supported Adjustment Programmes*, Occasional Paper 42, IMF, Washington, DC.

Goldstein, M. and Montiel, P. (1986), 'Evaluating Fund stabilization programs with multi-country data: Some methodological pitfalls', *IMF Staff Papers*, vol. 33, no. 2.

Grais, W., de Melo, J. and Urata, S. (1986), 'A general equilibrium estimation of the effects of reductions in tariffs and quantitative restrictions in Turkey in 1978' in T. N.Srinivasan and J. Whalley, (eds.), *General Equilibrium Trade Policy Modeling*, MIT Press, Boston.

Greater Colombo Economic Commission (1988), *Annual Report*.

Green, R.H. (1987), *Ghana: Stabilisation and Structural Shifts'*, Wider, Helsinki.

Greenaway, D. and Read, G. (1990), 'Empirical evidence on trade orientation and economic performance in developing countries' in C. Milner (ed.) *Export Promotion Strategies.* Harvester Wheatsheaf, Hemel Hempstead.

Grossman, G.M. and Helpman, E. (1989), *Comparative Advantage and Long-run Growth*, National Bureau of Economic Research Working Paper no. 2809, Cambridge, Mass.

Guangdong Province (various years), *Guangdong Statistical Yearbook*, Guangzhou (in Chinese).

Gunasekera, D. and Tyers, R. (1991), 'Imperfect competition and returns to scale in a newly industrialising economy', *Journal of Development Economics*, vol. 34, pp. 223-247.

Hachetts, D. (1988), 'Chile: trade liberalization since 1974', paper prepared for a Conference in São Paulo, April 1988, World Bank, Washington, DC.

Haggard, S. (1988), 'The politics of industrialization in the Republic of Korea and Taiwan', in H. Hughes (ed.), *Achieving Industrialization in East Asia*, Cambridge University Press, Sydney, pp. 260-82.

Halevi, N. (1989), 'Trade liberalization in adjustment lending' background paper for *Strengthening Trade Policy Reform*, Sec. M89-1454/1 CECTP, World Bank, Washington, DC.

Hamilton, C. (1986), *Capitalist Industrialization in Korea*, Westview Press, Boulder, Colorado.

Hanlon, J. (1984), *Mozambique: the Revolution under Fire*. Zed Books, London.

Harberger, A.C. (1959), 'The fundamentals of economic progress in developing countries – using the resources at hand more effectively', *American Economic Review*, vol. 49, p. 134ff.

Harberger, A. (1964), 'Some notes on inflation' in W. Baer and I. Kertenctzky (eds.), *Inflation and Growth in Latin America*, C.D.Irwin, Homewood, Ill.

Harberger, A.C. (1974), 'Notes on the dynamics of trade liberalization', prepared for a conference on trade liberalization, Santiago, Chile (October).

Harberger, A.C. (1988), 'Issues in the design of tariff reform', CECTP, World Bank, Washington, DC.

Harberger, A.C. (1989), 'Applications of Real Exchange Rate Analysis', *Contemporary Policy Issues 7* (April) pp. 1-25.

Harris, L. (1988), 'Financial reform and economic growth: a new interpretation of South Korea's experience', in Harris *et al. New Perspectives on the Financial System*, Croom Helm, London.

Havrylyshyn, O. (1989), *Poland: Policies for Trade Promotion*, UNDP/World Bank Trade Expansion Program, Washington, DC.

Havrylyshyn, O. (1990), 'Trade policy and productivity gains in developing countries: a survey of the literature', *World Bank Research Observer*, vol. 5, no. 1.

Havrylyshyn, O. (1990), *The Timing and Sequencing of Liberalization: Yugoslavia*, Basil Blackwell, London.

Haynes, J. (1989) in T.W. Parfitt and S.P. Riley, (eds.), *The African Debt Crisis*, Routledge, London.

Helleiner, G. (1990), 'The macroeconomic effects of Fund-supported adjustment programs', *IMF Staff Papers*, vol. 37, no. 2.

Herderschee, J. (1990), *Incentives for Exports: a case study of Taiwan and Thailand*, unpublished PhD thesis, National Centre for Development Studies, Canberra (mimeo).

Hill, H (1984), 'Industrialisation in Burma in historical perspective', *Journal of Southeast Asian Studies*, vol. XV, no. 1, (March), pp. 134-149.

Hodgkinson, E. (1988),'The Philippines to 1993: Making up Lost Ground' *Economist Intelligence Unit Special Report*, no. 1145, London.

Hong, W. (1979), *Trade, Distortions and Employment Growth in Korea*, Korea Development Institute, Seoul.

Hong Kong Government (1989a), *Hong Kong Annual Digest of Statistics*, Hong Kong.

Hong Kong Government (1989b), *Hong Kong 1989. A Review of 1988*, Hong Kong.

Huc, M.M. (1989), *The Economy of Ghana: The First Twenty-Five Years since Independence.* Macmillan, London.

Hughes, H. (1974), 'Assessment of policies towards direct foreign investment in the Asian-Pacific area' in P. Drysdale (ed.), *Direct Foreign Investment in Asia and the Pacific*, Australian National University Press, Canberra, pp. 313-43.

IDA (1982), *IDA in Retrospect*, Oxford University Press, Oxford.

IDS (1984), 'Development States in East Asia', *IDS Bulletin*, April, vol. 15, no. 2, Sussex, UK.

IDS (1989), *Discussion Paper 270*, (November).

IMF (1988), *Ghana: Statistical Annex*, Document SM/88/242 mimeo, Washington, DC.

IMF (1988), *Burma: Recent Economic Development*, Washington DC, (June), pp. 1-85.

IMF (1989), *Myanmar: Staff Report*, Washington DC, (December).

IMP (1985), *Medium and Long Term Industrial Master Plan, Malaysia 1986-1995*, UNIDO, August 1985, Vienna.

Intal, P.S. (1987), 'Government Interventions and Rent Seeking', Department of Economics Discussion Paper 87-04, University of the Philippines, Los Banos.

Intal, P.S. and Pante, F. (1989), 'Can the Philippines Grow out of Debt?', Paper presented at the Asian and Pacific Development Centre Conference on the Future of the Asia-Pacific Economies, Bangkok, November 8-10.

Isaacman, A. and Isaacman, B. (1983), *Mozambique: from Colonialism to Revolution.* Westview, Boulder, Colorado.

Jacquemin, A. (1982),'Imperfect market structure and international trade: some recent research', *Kyklos*, 35, (Fasc.1), pp. 75-93.

Jaeger, W. (1989), 'The impact of policy on African agriculture: an empirical investigation', (December 14), mimeo, World Bank AFTTF, Washington, DC.

Jayamaha, R. (1990), 'Policy Reform and Export Performance in Sri Lanka (1977-89)', mimeo.

Jomo, K. S. (ed.) (1985), *The Sun Also Sets*, Insan, Kuala Lumpur.

Judet, P. (1989), 'La Nouvelle Politique Industrielle au Sénégal: évaluation, ouvertures', *Notes et études*, CCCE, no. 32, Paris.

Jung, W. and Marshall, P. (1985), 'Exports, Growth and Causality in Developing Countries', *Journal of Development Economics*, 18 pp. 1-12.

Kaldor, N. (1978), 'The effects of devaluations on trade in manufactures' in *Further Essays on Applied Economics*, Duckworth, London.

Kaplinsky, R. (ed.) (1984), *Third World Industrialisation in the 1980s*, Cass, London (see also the *Journal of Development Studies*, (1984), vol. 21, no. 1).

Katseli, L. T. (1986), 'Discrete devaluation as a signal to price setters: suggested evidence from Greece' in S. Edwards, S. and A. Liaquat (eds.), *Economic Adjustment and Exchange Rate in Developing Countries*, University of Chicago Press, Chicago.

Kavoussi, R. (1984), 'Export Expansion and Economic Growth: Further Empirical Evidence' *Journal of Development Economics*, 14 pp. 241-50.

Keesing, D. and Singer, A. (1989), 'How to provide high-impact assistance to manufactured exports from developing countries', CECTP, World Bank, Washington, DC.

Keynes, J. M. (1936), 'The German Transfer Problem', *Economic Journal*, vol. 39.

Khan, M. (1990), 'The macro-economic effects of fund-supported adjustment programs', *IMF Staff Papers*, vol. 37, no. 2.

Kierzkowski (ed.) (1984), *Monopolistic Competition and International Trade*, Clarendon Press, Oxford.

Kiguel, M. and Liviatan, N. (1988), 'Inflationary rigidities and orthodox stabilization policies: Lessons from Latin America', *World Bank Economic Review*, 2 (September), pp. 273-298.

Killick, T. (1990), *The Adaptive Economy: Adjustment Policies in Low- income Countries*, Overseas Development Institute, London.

Kim, M. (1987), 'Korea's adjustment policies and their implications for other countries' in V. Corbo, M. Goldstein and M. Khan, (eds.), *Growth Oriented Adjustment Programs*, IMF and World Bank, Washington, DC.

Kim, Y.C. and Kwon, J.K. (1977), 'The utilization of capital and the growth of output in a developing economy', *Journal of Development Economics*, 4 pp. 205-78.

Kirkpatrick, C. and Maharaj, J. (1991), 'The effects of trade liberalization on industrial sector productivity performance in developing countries' in J. M. Fontaine (ed.), *Libéralisation due Commerce Extérieur et Strategies de Développement Economique*, Presses Universitaires de France, Paris.

Knox, J., Robinson, P. and Stoneman, C. (1988), 'Zimod: A Simple Computer Model of the Zimbabwe Economy', *Social Science Computer Review*, vol. 6, no. 1.

Knudsen, O and Nash, J. (1990), 'Domestic price stabilization schemes in developing countries, *Economic Development and Cultural Change*, (January).

Koester, U, Schafer, H. and Valdes, A. (1989), 'External demand constraints for agricultural exports – an impediment to structural adjustment policies in sub-Saharan African countries', *Food Policy* 14 (February), no. 3.

Kornai, J. (1986), 'The Soft Budget Constraint', *Kyklos*, vol. 390, Facs. 1.

Kravis, I.B. (1986), 'The three faces of the International Comparison Project', *The World Bank Research Observer*, 1(1), (January), pp. 3-26.

Krueger, A.O. (1974), 'The political economy of the rent seeking society', *The American Economic Review*, 64(3), (June), pp. 291-303.

Krueger, A.O. (1978), *Foreign Trade Regimes and Economic Development: Liberalisation, Attempt and Consequences*, Ballinger, Cambridge, Mass.

Krueger, A.O. (1981), 'Interactions between inflation and trade objectives in stabilization programs' in W. Cline and S. Weintraub (eds.), *Economic Stabilization in Developing Countries*, Brookings Institution, Washington, DC.

Krueger, A.O. and Tuncer, B. (1982), 'An empirical test of the infant industry argument', *American Economic Review*, 72(5), pp. 1142-52.

Krueger, A. (1984), 'Trade policies in developing countries' in R. W. Jones and P. B. Kenen (eds.), *Handbook of International Economics*, vol. 1, Elsevier, New York.

Krueger, A.O. (1985), 'Import Substitution versus Export Promotion', *Finance and Development*, vol. 22, no. 2.

Krugman, P.R. (1987), 'Is free trade passé?', *Economic Perspectives*, 1(2), pp. 131-44.

Kulatunga, S. (1990), *Export development prospects and problems*, UNDP/ITC project GHA/87/004, (June).

L'Heriteau, M.F. (1990), 'Réforme du secteur bancaire et perspectives de crédit au secteur privée', Caisse Centrale de Coopération Economique, (Rapport interne), Paris.

Lal, D. and Rajapatirana, S. (1989), *Impediments to Trade Liberalisation in Sri Lanka*, Thames Essays series, Gower, 1989.

Lall, S. (ed.) (1983), *The New Multinationals: The Spread of Third World Enterprises*, Wiley, London.

Landau, D. (1983), 'Government expenditure and economic growth: a cross-section study', *Southern Economic Journal*, 49, pp. 783-92.

Lanzarotti, M. (1992b), *La Corée du Sud: le développement d'un pays sous-développé*, Presses Universitaires de France, Paris, (forthcoming).

Lanzarotti, M. (1992a), 'Exchange rates and subsidies in an export-promotion policy: the case of South Korea' in J. M. Fontaine (ed.), *Foreign-Trade Reform and Development Strategies*, Routledge, London, (forthcoming).

Lee, E. (1979), 'Egalitarian peasant farming and rural development: the case of South Korea', *World Development*, vol. 7, pp. 493-517.

Leenhardt B. and L'Heriteau, M.F. (1989), 'Situation Macro-économique et Montaire du Ghana', Caisse Centrale de Coopération Economique (Document de Travail), Paris.

Lei Qiang (1988), 'New Progress in Hong Kong and Pearl River Delta Industrial Cooperation', *Hong Kong and Macau Research*, Zhong Shan University, Guangzhou (in Chinese).

Lenschow, A. (1991), 'Political and economic liberalisation in socialist developing countries', Report for Management Development Programme, UNDP (January).

Leung, H.M., Thoburn, J.T. Chau, E. and Tang, S.H. (1991), 'Contractual Relations, Foreign Direct Investment and Technology Transfer. The Case of China', *Journal of International Development*, forthcoming.

Lim Youngil (1981), 'Government policy and private enterprise: Korean experience in industrialisation', *Korean Research Monograph 6*, Institute of East Asian Studies, University of California, Berkeley.

Linn, J.F. and Wetzel, D.L. (1990), 'Public finance, trade and development: what have we learned?' in V. Tanzi (ed.), *Fiscal Policy in Open Developing Economies*, IMF, Washington DC.

Little, I.M.D., Scitovsky, T. and Scott, M.F. (1970), *Industry and Trade in Some Developing Countries: A Comparative Study*, Oxford University Press, New York and Oxford.

Little, I. (1982), *Economic Development*, Basic Books, New York.

Logeay, D. (1990), 'L'industrie sénégalaise: ses perspectives après la Nouvelle Politique Industrielle', Note de travail, CCCE, Paris.

Lopez, R. (1989), 'Trade policy, growth and investment' background paper for *Strengthening Trade Policy Reform* Sec M89-1454/1, CECTP, World Bank, Washington, DC.

Lowenthal, J., Chambas, G., Lewis, J., and Smith, J.T. (1990), *Tax Reform in Senegal 1986-1990*, Project Impact Evaluation Report, Dakar.

Luedde-Neurath, R. (1986), *Import Controls and Export-Oriented Development: A Reassessment of the South Korean Case*, Westview, Boulder, Colorado.

Lyons, T.P. (1990), 'Planning and Interprovincial Co-ordination in Maoist China', *China Quarterly*, (March).

Mackie, J.A.C. (1988), 'Economic growth in the ASEAN region: the political underpinnings' in H. Hughes (ed.), *Achieving Industrialization in East Asia*, Cambridge University Press, Sydney, pp. 286-326.

Mackintosh, M. (1985), 'Economic Tactics: Commercial Policy and Socialization of African Agriculture', *World Development*, vol. 13, no. 1.

Maddison, A. (1982), *Phases of Capitalist Development*, Oxford University Press, New York.

Marsden, K. (1983), 'Links between taxes and economic growth: some empirical evidence', World Bank Staff Working Paper no. 605, Washington, DC.

Marsden, K. and Belot, T. (1987), 'Private enterprise in Africa: creating a better environment', *World Bank Discussion Paper No. 17*, World Bank, Washington, DC.

Matin, K. (1989), 'Macroeconomic environment and trade policy' in *Strengthening Trade Policy Reform*, Sec M89-1454/1, CECTP, World Bank, Washington, DC.

Medalla, E.M. (1986), 'Assessment of the tariff reform program and trade liberalization', Tariff Commission – Philippine Institute of Development Studies Joint Research Project, Staff Paper Series no. 86-03, Manila.

Medalla, E.M. (1990), 'An Assessment of Trade and Industrial Policy, 1986- 1988', Philippine Institute for Development Studies, Working Paper Series no. 90-07, Manila.

Meier, G. and Steel W. (1989), *Industrial Adjustment in Sub-Saharan Africa*, Oxford University Press, EDI series in Economic Development, Oxford.

Michaely, M. (1986), 'The Timing and Sequencing of a Trade Liberalization Policy' in Choksi, A. and Papageorgiou D. (eds.), *Economic Liberalization in Developing Countries, Basil Blackwell, Oxford.*

Michaely, M (1986) *Guidelines for Country Economists for the Review and Evaluation of Trade Policies*, World Bank CPD Discussion Paper 1986-87 Washington DC.

Michaely, M, Papageorgiou, D. and Choksi, A. (1991), *Liberalizing Foreign Trade: Lessons of Experience in the Developing World*, Basil Blackwell, Oxford.

Michalopoulos, M. (1987), 'World Bank programs for adjustment and growth' in V. Corbo, M. Goldstein and M. Khan (eds.), *Growth-Oriented Adjustment Programs*, IMF and World Bank, Washington, DC.

Michell, T. (1988), *From a Developing to a Newly Industrialised Country: The Republic of Korea, 1961-82*, ILO, Geneva.

Ministry of Finance, *Economic Reports*, various years, Kuala Lumpur.

MIPS (1984), *Final Report of the Malaysian Industrial Policies Studies (MIPS) Project*, IMG Consultants Pty Ltd, Sydney, Australia.

MMR (1989), *Malaysian Management Review*, journal of the Malaysian Institute of Management, August 1989, vol. 24, no. 2, (a special issue on the New Economic Policy), Kuala Lumpur.

Mohammad, S and Whalley, J. (1984), 'Rent-seeking in India: its costs and policy significance', *Kyklos*, 37, pp. 387-413.

Montes, M.F. (1987), *Stabilization and Adjustment Policies and Programmes: Country Study 2, the Philippines*, World Institute for Development Economics Research, Helsinki.

Morawetz, D. (1980), 'Economic lessons from some small socialist developing countries', *World Development*, vol 8, pp. 337-369.

Mosley, P. (1990), 'Structural Adjustment : a general overview, 1980-89', IDPM Discussion Paper no. 21, University of Manchester.

Mosley, P., Harrigan, J. and Toye, J. (1991), *Aid and Power: the World Bank and Policy-based lending in the 1980s*, Routledge, London.

MTR (1989), *Mid-Term Review of the Fifth Malaysia Plan, 1986-1990*, Government of Malaysia.

Nam, Chong-Hyun (1986), *Export Promoting Policies Under Countervailing Threats: GATT Rules and Practices*, World Bank Discussion Paper no. VPER59, Development Policy Issues Series, Washington, DC.

Nau, H.R. (1989), *Domestic Politics and the Uruguay Round*, Colombia University Press, New York.

Nellis, J. (1986), 'Public Enterprise in Sub-Saharan Africa', *World Bank Discussion Paper no. 1*, World Bank, Washington, DC.

Nelson, N.M. (1989), 'The politics of long-haul economic reform' in J. M. Nelson *et. al.* (eds.), *The Politics of Economic Adjustment*, Washington, DC.

Nishimizu, M. and Page, J.M. Jr. (1982), 'Total factor productivity growth, technological progress and technical efficiency change: Yugoslavia, 1965-78' *Economic Journal*, pp. 920-36.

Nixson, F. (1990), 'Industrialisation and structural change in developing countries', *Journal of International Development*, vol. 2, no. 3, (July).

Nogues, J. (1987), 'The timing and sequencing of trade liberalization – Peru', mimeo, World Bank, Washington, DC.

Nogues, J. (1989), 'Latin America's experience with export subsidies', World Bank PPR Working Paper no. 182, Washington, DC.

Nyun, T. (1989), 'Country in-depth study: Myanmar', Institute of Economics, Yangon,

Myanmar, (September), pp. 1-57.

O'Connell, S.A. (1989), 'Uniform trade taxes, devaluation and the real exchange rate', World Bank PPR Working Paper Series no. 185, (April), Washington, DC.

Ocampo, J.A. (1987), 'The macro-economic effect of import controls: a Keynesian analysis', *Journal of Development Economics*, no. 27.

Ottoway, M. (1988), 'Mozambique: from Symbolic Socialism to Symbolic Reform', *Journal of Modern African Studies*, vol. 26, no. 2.

Oyejide, A. (1991), 'Impact of price-based and quantity-based import control measures in Nigeria' in J. M. Fontaine (ed.), *Foreign-Trade Reform and Development Strategies*, Routledge, London, (forthcoming).

Ozawa, T. (1979), 'International Investment and Industrial Structure: New Theoretical Implications from the Japanese Experience', *Oxford Economic Papers*.

Pack, H. and Westphal, L. (1986), 'Industrial Strategy and Technological Change', *Journal of Development Economics*, vol. 22, pp. 87-128.

Pack, H. (1987), *Productivity, Technology, and Industrial Development: a Case Study of Textiles*, Oxford University Press for the World Bank, New York.

Pack, H. (1988), 'Industrialisation and trade' in H. Chenery and T. N. Srinivasan (eds.), *Handbook of Development Economics*, vols. 1 and 2, Elsevier, New York.

Panagariya, A. (1989), 'On the theory of tariff reforms', (August 20, revised October 25) mimeo, CECTP, World Bank, Washington, DC.

Panoutsopoulos, V.D. (1990), *The Supply Determinants of the Developing Countries – Penetration of the United States Market for Manufactures*, unpublished PhD thesis, National Centre for Development Studies, Canberra.

*People's Daily*, Overseas Chinese Language Edition.

Pomfret, R. (1989), 'Ten years of direct investment in China', *Asian Perspective*, Fall/Winter.

Post, K. and Wright, P. (1989), *Socialism and Underdevelopment*, Routledge, London and New York.

Power, J. and Medalla, E. (1986), 'Trade liberalization in the Philippines: assessment of progress and agenda for future reform', Tariff Commission – Philippine Institute for Development Studies Joint Research Project, Staff Paper Series, no. 86-01, Manila.

Pursell, G. (1989), 'Issues in import policy reforms' in *Strengthening Trade Policy Reform*, Sec M89-1454/1, CECTP, World Bank, Washington, DC.

Rajaram, A. (1989), 'Tariff and tax reforms: do Bank recommendations adequately integrate revenue and protection objectives?', CECPE, World Bank, Washington, DC.

Ram, R. (1985), 'Exports and economic growth: some additional evidence', *Economic Development and Cultural Change*, 33, pp. 415-25.

Ramanayake, D. (1982), *The Katunayake Investment Promotion Zone: A Case Study*, ILO/ARTEP, New Delhi.

Richardson, J.D. (1989), 'Empirical research on trade liberalisation with imperfect competition: a survey', *OECD Economic Studies*, no.12, (Spring).

Ridell R.C. (ed.) (1990), *Manufacturing Africa: Performance and Prospects of Seven Countries in Sub-Saharan Africa*, James Currey and Heinemann, London.

Riedel, J.R. (1988), 'Economic development in East Asia. Doing what comes naturally?' in H. Hughes (ed.), *Achieving Industrialization in East Asia*, Cambridge University Press, Sydney, pp. 1-38.

Rodrik, D. (1988), 'Imperfect competition, scale economies, and trade policy in developing countries' in R. E. Baldwin (ed.), *Trade Policy Issues and Empirical Analysis*, University of Chicago Press, Chicago.

Rodrik, D. (1988), 'Liberalization, sustainability and the design of structural adjustment programs', CECTP, World Bank, Washington, DC.

Roemer, M. and Stern, J.J. (1981), *Cases in Economic Development: Projects, Policies and Strategies*, Butterworth, London.

Romer, P.M. (1989), 'What determines the rate of growth and technological change?', World Bank PPR Working Paper Series no. 279, Washington, DC.

Sachs, J. (1987), 'Trade and exchange rate policies in growth-oriented adjustment programs', Department of Economics, Harvard University, Cambridge, Mass.

Sarkar, P. and Singer, H.W. (1989), 'Manufactured exports and terms of trade movements of less developed countries in recent years (1980-87)', *IDS Discussion Paper*, no. 270, (November).

Scalapino, A. *et. al.* (eds.) (1985), *Asian Economic Development – Present and Future*, Institute of East Asian Studies, University of California, Berkeley.

Schiller, C. (1988), *The Fiscal Role of Price Stabilization Funds: The Case of Côte d'Ivoire*, IMF Working Paper, Washington, DC.

Schydlowsky, D. (1982), 'Alternative approaches to short-term economic management in developing countries', in T. Killick (ed.) *Adjustment and Financing in the Developing World*, IMF, Washington, DC.

Scully, G.W. (1988), 'The political economy of free trade and protectionism', Paper prepared for Conference on the Political Economy of Neo- mercantilism and Free Trade, Big Sky, Montana, June 9-11.

Shafaeddin, M. (1988), 'Agricultural price policies and the oil boom, wheat and meat in Iran', *Food Policy*, (May), pp. 185-98.

Shafaeddin, M. (1990), 'Investment, imports and economic performance of developing countries' in H. W. Singer, N. Hatte and R. Tondon (eds.), *Adjustment and Liberalization in the Third World*, New World Order Series, vol. VII, Ashish Publishing House, New Delhi.

Shafaeddin, M. (1991a), 'The impact of devaluation on cost, profitability and competitiveness of manufacturing exports of developing countries', (forthcoming).

Shafaeddin, M. (1991b), 'The role of imports and direct contribution of devaluation to inflation in effectiveness of nominal devaluation', (forthcoming).

Shalizi, Z. and Squire, L. (1986), 'Tax policy for sub-Saharan Africa Country Policy Department', Resource Mobilization Division, World Bank, Washington, DC.

Sicat, G.P. (1986), 'A historical and current perspective of Philippine economic problems', Philippine Institute of Development Studies Monograph Series no. 11, Manila.

SIDA (1986a), *Manufacturing Fishing Vessels: an Evaluation of SIDA- Supported Industrial Rehabilitation in Somalia, Evaluation Report*, (written by S. Larsson, J. Valdelin).

SIDA (1986b), *Developing Entrepreneurs: An Evaluation of Small Scale Industry Development in Botswana, 1974-84, Evaluation Report*, (written by J. O. Agrell, B. D. Bergman, P. Hallerby, K. Ring).

SIDA (1988a), *Sisterhood on Trial: An Evaluation of the Performance and Linkages of the Sister Industries in Tanzania, Evaluation Report*, (written by S. Carlsson, S. Alange, K. Forss, S. Malai, S. Scheinberg).

SIDA (1988b), *Improve your Business: An Evaluation of an ILO-SIDA Regional Small-Scale Business Promotion Project in Africa*,(written by C. Lindahl and R. Dainow).

Singer, H.W. (1989), 'The relationship between debt pressures, adjustment policies and deterioration of terms of trade for developing countries (with special reference to Latin America)', Institute of Social Studies, The Hague, Working Paper Series no. 59, (July).

Singh, A. (1982), 'Industrialisation in Africa: A structuralist view' in M. Fransman (1982).

Snow, R.T. (1983), 'The bourgeois opposition to export-oriented industrialization in the Philippines', Third World Studies Center, Paper Series no. 39, University of the Philippines,

Manila.

Spoor, M. (1988), 'Reforming state finance in post-1975 Vietnam', *Journal of Development Studies*, vol. 24, no. 4, (July).

Steel, W.F. (1988), 'Adjusting Industrial Policy in Sub-Saharan Africa', *Finance and Development*, vol. 25, no. 1.

Stoneman, C. (1990), 'Zimbabwe opens up to the market', *Africa Recovery*, vol. 4, no. 3-4, (October-December) pp. 18-23.

Sturzenneger, A. (forthcoming), 'The political economy of price discrimination in the Argentine Pampas' in A. O. Krueger, M. Schiff and A. Valdez (eds.), *The Political Economy of Agricultural Pricing Policy in Selected Latin American Countries*, World Bank, Washington, DC.

Syrquin, M. (1988), 'Patterns of structural change' in H. Chenery and T. N. Srinivasan (eds.), *Handbook of Development Economics*, vol. I, North Holland, Elsevier Science Publishers, Amsterdam, pp. 203-27.

Tawney, R.H. (1926), *Religion and the Rise of Capitalism: A Historical Study*, John Murray, London.

Taylor, L. (1978), 'Contractionary effects of devaluation', *Journal of International Economics*, (August), pp. 445-57.

Taylor, L. (1981), *Structuralist macro-economies*, Basic Books, New York.

Taylor, R. (1987), *The State in Burma*, Charles Hurst.

Taylor, L. (1988), *Economic Openness: Problems to the Century's End*, World Institute for Development Economics Research, Helsinki.

Taylor, L. (1988), *Varieties of Stabilization Experiences*, Clarendon Press, Oxford.

Thoburn, J.T., Leung, H.M., Chau, E. and Tang, S.H. (1990), *Foreign Investment in China under the Open Policy. The Experience of Hong Kong Companies*, Gower/Avebury, Aldershot.

Thomas, C. (1974), *Dependence and Transformation*, Monthly Review, New York.

Thomas, V. (1989), 'Developing country experience in trade reform', World Bank PPR Working Paper no. 295, Washington, DC.

Thomas, V. and Nash, J. (forthcoming), *Best Practices: Lessons in Trade Policy Reform*, Oxford University Press, New York and Washington, DC.

Tolentino, V.B.J. (1989), 'The political economy of credit availability and financial liberalization: notes on the Philippine experience', *Savings and Development*, XIII-4, pp. 321-34.

UNCTAD (1986), *Protectionism and Structural Adjustment, Introduction and Part I*, TD/B/1081, Geneva.

UNDP (1988) with Government of Netherlands, ILO, UNIDO, *Development of Rural Small Industrial Enterprise: Lessons from Experience*.

UNDP (1990), *Report on the Economy of Vietnam*, report prepared for the Socialist Republic of Vietnam, State Planning Committee, Hanoi, (December).

UNIDO (1984), *Handbook of Industrial Statistics*, UN, New York.

UNIDO (1988), 'The Philippines: sustaining industrial recovery through privatization and foreign investment', Industrial Development Review Series, Vienna.

UNIDO (1989), *Industry Sector Review Mission to Myanmar*, Vienna, (June), pp. 1-61.

Valdes, A. and Zietz, J. (1980), *Agricultural Protection in OECD Countries: Its Costs to Less Developed Countries*, International Food Policy Institute, Washington, DC.

Van Dijk, M.P. (1986), *Sénégal: Le secteur informel de Dakar*, L'Harmattan.

van Liemt, G. (1988), *Bridging the Gap: 4 NICs and the Changing International Divisions of Labour*, ILO, Geneva.

Vogel, E.F. (1989), *One Step Ahead in China. Guangdong under Reform*, Harvard University Press, Cambridge, Mass.

Vokes, R (1990), 'Burma and Asia–Pacific Dynamism: Problems and prospects of export-oriented growth in the 1990s' in M. Than and J. Tan (eds.), *Myanmar Dilemmas and Options: The Challenge of Economic Transition in the 1990s*, Asean Economic Research Unit, Institute of Southeast Asian Studies, pp. 219-47.

Wade, R. (1988), 'Taiwan, China's duty rebate system', CECTP, World Bank, Washington, DC.

Wade, R. (1989), 'The role of government in overcoming market failure: Taiwan, Republic of Korea and Japan' in H. Hughes (ed.), *Achieving Industrialization in East Asia*, Cambridge University Press, Sydney, pp. 129-63.

Walton, G.N. (1988), 'Effective Protection and Comparative Advantage in the Manufacturing Sector of Sri Lanka', Ministry of Finance and Planning, Colombo, Sri Lanka.

Wang Jun (1989), 'The Export-Orientated Strategy of China's Coastal Areas: Emulation and Prospects', University of Leicester, Economics Department Discussion Paper no.116, (September).

Wanigatunga, R.C. (1987), 'Direct private overseas investment in export-oriented ventures: recent developments in Sri Lanka' in Cable and Persaud (eds.).

Warr, P. (1984), 'Export promotion via industrial enclave: the Philippines Bataan Export Processing Zone', University of the Philippines School of Economics Occasional Paper.

Warr, P.G. (1987), 'Malaysia's industrial enclaves: benefits and costs', *The Developing Economies*, vol. XXV, no. 1.

Weber, M. (1922), *Sociology of Religion*, Methuen, London.

Weiss, J. (1984), 'Manufacturing as an engine of growth: revisited' *Industry and Development*, no. 13, pp. 39-62.

Weiss, J. (1988), *Industry in Developing Countries*, Croom Helm, London.

White, C. (1983), 'Recent debates in Vietnamese development policy' in White, G., Murray, R. and White, C. (eds.), *Revolutionary Socialist Development in the Third World*, Wheatsheaf.

White, G. (ed.) (1988), *Development States in East Asia*, Macmillan, London.

White, G. and Wade, R. (1988), 'Developmental States and Markets in East Asia: an Introduction', in G. White (ed.), *Developmental States in East Asia*, Macmillan, London.

Wood, A. (1989), 'Deceleration of inflation with acceleration of price reform: Vietnam's remarkable recent experience', *Cambridge Journal of Economics*, vol. 13.

World Bank (1980), *World Development Report*, World Bank, Washington, DC.

World Bank (1981), *Accelerated Development in Sub-Saharan Africa: An Agenda for Action*, Washington DC.

World Bank (1982), *World Development Report, Washington,* World Bank, Washington, DC.

World Bank (1983), *World Development Report*, Oxford University Press for the World Bank, London.

World Bank (1985), 'Lending for adjustment: an update', *World Bank News*, Special Report, Washington, DC.

World Bank (1986), *Structural Adjustment Lending: A First Review of Experience*, Report no. 6409, World Bank Operations Evaluation Department, Washington, DC.

World Bank (1986a), *Korea: Managing the Industrial Transition*, Report No. 6138- KO, Washington, DC.

World Bank (1986b), *World Development Report 1986*, Washington, D.C., pp. 106-9.

World Bank (1987), *La Banque Mondiale et le Senegal 1960-1987*, Report no. 8041, Washington, DC.

World Bank (1987), *Issues in Macro-Economic and Industrial Development Policy*, South Asia Programmes Department.

World Bank (1987), *World Development Report 1987*, Oxford University Press for the World

Bank, Washington, DC.

World Bank (1987a), *Trade and Industrial Policies in the Developing Countries of East Asia*, Report No. 6952, Washington, DC.

World Bank (1987b), *World Development Report 1987*, Washington, DC.

World Bank (1988), *China: External Trade and Capital*, Washington, DC.

World Bank (1988), *Sri Lanka: A Break with the Past: the 1989-90 Programme of Economic Reforms and Adjustment*, vols. I & II.

World Bank (1988), *Adjustment Lending: An Evaluation of Ten Years of Experience*, Policy and Research Series, no. 1, World Bank, Washington, DC.

World Bank (1988a), *Adjustment Lending: An Evaluation of Ten Years of Experience*, Policy and Research Series, no. 1, Washington, DC.

World Bank (1988b), 'Chile – agricultural sector brief', LA4AG (May 25), Washington, DC.

World Bank (1988c), 'Mexico: trade policy reform and economic adjustment', (August 23), Report 7314-ME, LATTF, Washington, DC.

World Bank (1988d), *World Development Report 1988*, Washington, DC.

World Bank (1989a), *Strengthening Trade Policy Reform*, vol. II, Full Report, Washington, DC.

World Bank (1989b), *Sri Lanka: Recent Macro-Economic Developments and Adjustment Policies*, Washington, DC.

World Bank (1989), *Malaysia: Matching Risks and Rewards in a Mixed Economy*, World Bank, Washington, DC.

World Bank (1989), *Strengthening Trade Policy Report*, vol. II, (November), Country Economics Department, Washington, DC.

World Bank and UNDP (1989), *Africa's Adjustment and Growth in the 1980s*, World Bank, Washington, DC.

World Bank (1989), *Sub-Saharan Africa: From Crisis to Sustainable Growth*, Washington, DC.

World Bank (1989a), 'The long-term perspective for sub-Saharan Africa: a strategy for recovery and growth', Washington, DC.

World Bank (1989a), *Sub-Saharan Africa: From Crisis to Sustainable Growth*, World Bank, Washington, DC.

World Bank (1989b), 'The role of foreign direct investment in financing developing countries', Board Memorandum (July 11), Washington, DC.

World Bank (1989b), *Ghana: Public Expenditure Review 1989-91*, mimeo, Washington, DC.

World Bank (1990), *Report on Adjustment Lending II* (March), Country Economics Department, Washington, DC.

World Bank (1990), *World Development Report*, Oxford University Press for the World Bank, Washington, DC.

Yang Dali (1990), 'Patterns of China's regional development strategy', *China Quarterly* (June).

Young, K., Bussink, W. and Hasan, P. (1980), *Malaysia: Growth and Equity in a Multiracial Society*, World Bank/Johns Hopkins University Press, Baltimore.

Yusuf, S. and Peters, R. (1985), 'Capital accumulation and economic growth: the Korean Paradigm', *World Bank Staff Working Paper*, no 712, Washington, DC.

Zarour, C. (1989), *Etude du secteur informel de Dakar et de ses environs*, Phases I, II et III, USAID, Dakar.

# Index